MW00718770

Understanding NATO in the 21st Century

Understanding NATO in the 21st Century enhances existing strategic debates and clarifies thinking as to the direction and scope of NATO's potential evolution in the 21st century.

The book seeks to identify the possible contours and trade-offs embedded within a potential third "Transatlantic Bargain" in the context of a U.S. strategic pivot in a "Pacific Century". To that end, it explores the internal adaptation of the Alliance, evaluates the assimilation of NATO's erstwhile adversaries, and provides a focus on NATO's operational future and insights into the new threats NATO faces and its responses.

Each contribution follows a similar broad tripartite structure: an examination of the historical context in which the given issue or topic has evolved; an identification and characterization of key contemporary policy debates and drivers that shape current thinking; and, on that basis, a presentation of possible future strategic pathways or scenarios relating to the topic area.

This book will appeal to students of NATO, international security, and international relations in general.

Graeme P. Herd is Senior Programme Adviser and Senior Fellow of the Leadership and Conflict Management Programme at the Geneva Centre for Security Policy (GCSP). At the GCSP he is Co-Director of its International Training Course in Security Policy and Co-Director of its Master of Advanced Studies in International and European Security (MAS) Programme, accredited by the University of Geneva.

John Kriendler is Professor of NATO and European Security Issues at the College of International Security Studies, George C. Marshall European Center for Security Studies, Germany. He has served as a U.S. foreign service officer and held the following NATO positions: Deputy Assistant Secretary General for Political Affairs and, subsequently, Head of Council Operations in the Crisis Management and Operations Directorate.

Contemporary Security Studies

Series Editors:
James Gow
and
Rachel Kerr
King's College London

This series focuses on new research across the spectrum of international peace and security, in an era where each year throws up multiple examples of conflicts that present new security challenges in the world around them.

Understanding NATO in the 21st Century
Alliance strategies, security and global governance
Edited by Graeme P. Herd and John Kriendler

Understanding NATO in the 21st Century

Alliance strategies, security and global governance

Edited by Graeme P. Herd and John Kriendler

Routledge
Taylor & Francis Group

LONDON AND NEW YORK

First published 2013
by Routledge
2 Park Square, Milton Park, Abingdon, Oxon, OX14 4RN

Simultaneously published in the USA and Canada
by Routledge
711 Third Avenue, New York, NY 10017

Routledge is an imprint of the Taylor & Francis Group, an informa business

British Library Cataloguing in Publication Data
A catalogue record for this book is available from the British Library

Library of Congress Cataloging in Publication Data
Understanding NATO in the 21st century: alliance strategies, security and global governance/edited by Graeme P. Herd and John Kriendler.
　　p. cm. – (Contemporary security studies)
　　Includes bibliographical references and index.
　　1. North Atlantic Treaty Organization–History. 2. North Atlantic Treaty Organization–Foreign relations. 3. North Atlantic Treaty Organization–Military policy. 4. Security, International. 5. World politics–21st century. I. Herd, Graeme P. II. Kriendler, John.
　　UA646.3.U33 2013
　　355'.031091821–dc23　　　　　　　　　　　　　　　　2012025036

ISBN: 978-0-415-43633-5 (hbk)
ISBN: 978-0-203-07600-2 (ebk)

Typeset in Baskerville
by Wearset Ltd, Boldon, Tyne and Wear

Printed and bound in the United States of America by Publishers Graphics, LLC on sustainably sourced paper.

For Sara and Philip with love

Contents

Contributors

Phillip Cornell is Special Advisor to the Executive Director of the International Energy Agency.

Pál Dunay is Director of the International Training Course in Security Policy at the Geneva Centre for Security Policy (GCSP), and was formerly Director of the Hungarian Institute of International Affairs, as well as Head of the Security Policy Department of the Hungarian Ministry of Foreign Affairs (1991).

Graeme P. Herd is Senior Programme Adviser and Senior Fellow of the Leadership and Conflict Management Programme at the Geneva Centre for Security Policy (GCSP). At the GCSP he is Co-Director of its International Training Course in Security Policy and Co-Director of its Master of Advanced Studies in International and European Security (MAS) Programme, accredited by the University of Geneva.

Jeffrey Hunker was Senior Director for Critical Infrastructure at the U.S. National Security Council under the Clinton Administration.

John Kriendler is Professor of NATO and European Security Issues at the College of International Security Studies, George C. Marshall European Center for Security Studies, Germany. He has served as a U.S. foreign service officer and in NATO as Deputy Assistant Secretary General for Political Affairs and Head of Council Operations in the Crisis Management and Operations Directorate.

Gustav Lindstrom is Head of the Emerging Security Challenges Program at the GCSP.

Julian Lindley-French is Eisenhower Professor of Defence Strategy at the Netherlands Defence Academy, Special Professor of Strategic Studies at the University of Leiden and Senior Associate Fellow of the Defence Academy of the United Kingdom.

Matthew Rhodes is Professor of National Security Studies at the George C. Marshall Center (GCMC) in Garmisch-Partenkirchen, Germany.

Michael Rühle is Head of the Energy Security Section in the Emerging Security Challenges Division at NATO Headquarters; he was previously Head of Speechwriting in the NATO Secretary General's Policy Planning Unit.

Thierry Tardy is Senior Fellow at the GCSP; he has conducted research at the Foundation for Strategic Research in Paris and taught at the Graduate Institute of International and Development Studies in Geneva and the Institute of Political Studies and the War College in Paris.

Klaus Wittmann is Senior Fellow at the Aspin Institute Germany. He served for 42 years in the German Bundeswehr and was formerly Director Academic Planning and Policy at the NATO Defense College, Rome.

Acknowledgments

The editors could not have brought this volume to fruition without the support of others and as a result the sum of this book is more than its parts. First and foremost, the contributors were unfailingly timely and responsive to the demands of the editing process. The anonymous reviewers provided excellent insights which helped us to create a more coherent narrative and analysis of policy debates and possible future developments within the various chapters. We thank two interns at the Geneva Centre for Security Policy – Charles Simpson and Stainslas Phanorod, BA students at Northeastern University in Boston – for help with references, the bibliography, style and copy-editing of the text. We would also like to thank Andrew Humphrys, Senior Editor, Military, Strategic and Security Studies at Routledge for championing this project from its inception and Allie Hargreaves from Wearset for so conscientiously seeing it through to its completion. Lastly, we would formally like to acknowledge participants and academic and policy-practitioner experts at the Geneva Centre for Security Policy and the George C. Marshall European Center for Security Studies who have, over the years, through discussions and debates provided the inspiration for a volume of this nature.

Abbreviations

3-Cs	Coherent, Coordinated, and Complimentary
ABIR	Airborne Infrared
ABM	Anti-Ballistic Missile
ACE	Allied Command, Europe
ACG	Azeri-Chirag-Guneshli pipeline
ACT	Allied Command Transformation
AFPAK	Afghanistan-Pakistan
ALTBMD	Active Layered Theatre Ballistic Missile Defence System
ANA	Afghan National Army
ANSF	Afghan National Security Forces
ANTPY	Army Navy Transportable Radar System
ARRC	Allied Rapid Reaction Corps
ASEAN	Association of South-East Asian Nations
BCM	Billion Cubic Meters
B/D	Barrels per Day
BMD	Ballistic Missile Defense
BRIC(S)	Brazil, Russia, India, China (South Africa)
BTC	Baku-Tblisi-Ceyhan pipeline
BTU	British Thermal Unit
C2BMC	Command, Control, Battle Management, and Communications
CA	Comprehensive Approach
CBO	Congressional Budget Office (U.S.)
CCDDOE	Cooperative Cyber Defense Center of Excellence
CDMB	Cyber Defense Management Board
CEIP	Critical Energy Infrastructure Protection
CEP	Civil Emergency Planning
CERT	Computer Emergency Response Teams
CFE	Conventional Forces in Europe
CIA	Central Intelligence Agency
CIP	Critical Infrastructure Protection
CoE	Center of Excellence
COIN	Counter-Insurgency

CPE	Civilian Planning Element
CSCE	Commission on Security and Cooperation in Europe
CSTO	Collective Security Treaty Organization
DCA	Duel-Capable Aircraft
DDoS	Distributed Denial of Service
DDPR	Deterrence and Defense Posture Review
DNI	Director of National Intelligence
DoD	Department of Defense (U.S.)
DoS	Department of State (U.S.)
DSACEUR	Deputy Supreme Allied Commander, Europe
EADRCC	Euro-Atlantic Disaster Response Coordination Center
EAPC	Euro-Atlantic Partnership Council
EBAO	Effects-Based Approach to Operations
EBO	Effects-Based Operations
EBRD	European Bank for Reconstruction and Development
EPAA	European Phased Adaptive Approach
ESCD	Emerging Security Challenges Division
ESDI	European Security and Defense Identity
EU	European Union
EU(POL)	European Union (Police Mission)
FOC	Full Operational Capability
FOFA	Follow On Forces Attack
FRG	Republic of Germany
FYROM	Former Yugoslav Republic of Macedonia
G6 (G7, G8, G20)	Group of Six (may also be a broader Group of Seven, Eight, or Twenty)
GAO	General Accounting Office (U.S.)
GAS	Golden Age of Gas Scenario
GCC	Gulf Cooperation Council
GDP	Gross Domestic Product
GDR	German Democratic Republic
GHMA	Global Humanitarian Mine Action
GIROA	Government of the Islamic Republic of Afghanistan
HRF(L)	High Readiness Force (Land)
IASC	Inter-Agency Standing Committee
ICBM	Inter-Continental Ballistic Missile
ICI	Istanbul Cooperative Initiative
ID	Identity
IEA	International Energy Agency
IED	Improvised Explosive Device
IFC	International Financial Corporation
IJC	Integrated Joint Command
IO	International Organization
IOC	International Oil Company
IMF	International Monetary Fund

INF	Intermediate-range Nuclear Forces
IPAP	Individual Partnership Action Plan
IR	International Relations
IRBM	Intermediate Range Ballistic Missile
ISAF	International Security Assistance Force
ISI	Inter-Services Intelligence
KFOR	Kosovo Force
LNG	Liquefied Natural Gas
MAP	Membership Action Plan
MBTU	Million British Thermal Units
MC	Military Committee
MD(WP), (MP)	Mediterranean Dialogue (Work Program), (Military Program)
MEADS	Medium Extended Air Defense System
MENA	Middle East and North Africa
MLF	Multilateral Nuclear Force
MRBM	Medium Range Ballistic Missile
N-11	Next Eleven
NAC	North Atlantic Council
NACC	North Atlantic Cooperation Council
NATO	North Atlantic Treaty Organization
NCIRC	NATO Computer Incident Response Capability
NDPP	NATO Defense Planning Process
NGO	Non-Governmental Organization
NGV	Natural Gas Vehicle
NOC	Nationalized Oil Company
NPG	Nuclear Planning Group
NPR	Nuclear Posture Review
NPS	New Policy Scenario
NPT	Non-Proliferation Treaty
NRC	NATO–Russia Council
NSC	National Security Council
NSWP	Non-Soviet Warsaw Pact
NTM-A	NATO Training Mission-Afghanistan
NWFZ	Nuclear-Weapons-Free-Zones
NWS	Nuclear Weapons State
OAE	Operation Active Endeavour
OCHA	Office for the Coordination of Humanitarian Affairs
OECD	Organization for Economic Cooperation and Development
OEF	Operation Enduring Freedom
OPEC	Organization of Petroleum Exporting Countries
OSCE	Organization for Security and Cooperation in Europe
PAA	Phased Adaptive Approach
PAPDI	Partnership Action Plan on Defense Institution Building

PAP-T	Partnership Action Plan against Terrorism
PAROS	Prevention of an Arms Race in Outer Space
PARP	Planning and Review Process
PCM	Partnership Cooperation Menu
PfP	Partnership for Peace
PJC	Permanent Joint Council
PPM	Parts per Million
PPWT	Prevention of the Placement of Weapons in Outer Space and the Threat of Use of Force Against Outer Space Objects
PRT	Provincial Reconstruction Teams
R&D	Research and Development
SACEUR	Supreme Allied Commander, Europe
SACT	Supreme Allied Commander Transformation
SALW	Small Arms and Light Weapons
SCADA	Supervisory Control and Data Acquisition
SCEPC	Senior Civil Emergency Planning Committee
SCO	Shanghai Cooperation Organization
SEA	Science and Environment
SHAPE	Supreme Headquarters, Allied Powers, Europe
SIPRNet	Secret Internet Protocol Router Network
SLV	Space-Launched Vehicle
SM-3	Standard Missile Three
SME	Subject Matter Expert
SOP	Standard Operating Procedure
SRBM	Short Range Ballistic Missile
START	Strategic Arms Reduction Treaty
TCM	Trillion Cubic Meters
TCN	Troop Contributing Nations
TCP	Trans-Caspian Pipeline
THAAD	Terminal High Altitude Area Defense
TMD	Theater Missile Defense
TNW	Tactical Nuclear Weapons
TWH	Tera-Watt Hours
UN	United Nations
UNAMA	UN Assistance Mission to Afghanistan
UNDP	UN Development Program
UNHCR	UN High Commissioner for Refugees
UNSC	UN Security Council
UNSCO	UN Special Commission
UK	United Kingdom
US(DOS)	United States (Department of State)
USSR	United Soviet States of Russia
WGA	Whole of Government Approach
WMD	Weapons of Mass Destruction
WW2	World War Two

1 NATO in an age of uncertainty
Structural shifts and transatlantic bargains?

Graeme P. Herd and John Kriendler

Introduction

The future of NATO, for so long the cornerstone of the transatlantic partnership, has profound implications for the cooperative or competitive nature of transatlantic relations and thus for regional and global security. On the eve of NATO's Chicago "Implementation Summit" (20–21 May 2012) a range of influential policymakers and commentators argued for the need for NATO to undertake internal reform and adapt to a changing strategic context. Jamie Shea, NATO's deputy assistant secretary general for Emerging Security Challenges, contended that "By adding 'smart planning and smart thinking' to 'smart defense,' NATO can best survive the age of austerity intact and be ready for the world that awaits beyond it."[1] Charles A. Kupchan, in testimony before the Senate Committee on Foreign Relations, noted that Ivo H. Daalder, the U.S. permanent representative to NATO, has argued that the Alliance is more needed than ever, reminding us that NATO heads of state declared that NATO "remains an essential source of stability in an unpredictable world."[2] NATO's Operation Unified Protector in Libya has been declared a "victory", and NATO moves towards "transition" in Afghanistan by the end of 2014.

Alliances are defined as "an association to further the common interests of the members; *specifically*: a confederation of nations by treaty" and "a league or compact for mutual support or common action."[3] Mutual support or common action can cover a lot of ground, most often focused on security. States that face common threats or challenges have a shared interest in responding through a common effort, supported by collective organizational structures and procedures. There are of course costs of membership in international organizations, including alliances, in terms of constraint on freedom of action and also political and financial costs. But rational states will join together in an alliance when the benefits appear to outweigh the costs. For NATO to survive and flourish it must advance the interests of its members. It will survive only as long as it accomplishes things allies wish at an acceptable cost.[4]

For allies to use NATO effectively to accomplish things they wish, they need first to have compatible (not identical) interests. At a fundamental level: "Alliances are made by states that have some but not all of their interests in common. The common interest is ordinarily a negative one: fear of other states."[5] Interests can change and evolve, as they have in the case of NATO, but if they are no longer compatible, the Alliance will lose its importance.[6] It is thus necessary for the Alliance to have the ability to be able to forge compatible views on the nature and importance of threats as well as their management. It needs appropriate capabilities to effectively combat such threats, the political will to deploy capabilities for this purpose and the mechanisms for timely collective decision-making. This study will interrogate the likelihood that NATO, given its past, can measure up to the challenges of defining shared political objectives relevant for the evolving security environment; can marshal military capabilities to support those objectives; and can provide for the evolutionary development of ends and means responsive to the "new war" model dominated by insurgency and terrorism, notwithstanding NATO's legacy obligations to deter any threat or use of force against all allies and respond effectively if any allies were attacked.

is this new?

NATO policy debates: budget cuts and increased heterogeneity

When we examine current NATO policy debates, NATO official documents and pronouncements argue that NATO is adapting to a changing strategic context, though consensus in the academic community is harder to find.[7] However, it is clear that some analysts and commentators share the view, for a range of reasons, that NATO allies are increasingly uninterested in NATO's future. As NATO moves into the second decade of the 21st century, its role, purpose, utility and very existence as the core transatlantic security alliance is increasingly questioned. On the eve of his retirement, U.S. Defense Secretary Robert Gates warned that NATO could face "a dim if not dismal" future if military spending shortages, national caveats, and the political will to contribute to NATO missions were not addressed, given, among other things, that his generation's "emotional and historical attachment to NATO" is "aging out."[8] NATO Secretary General Rasmussen's "Annual Report 2011" confirmed these fears: 18 allies had lower defense expenditures than 2008, with further reductions announced or anticipated; the U.S.'s share of the NATO defense budget had grown while European contributions had decreased; while three allies were at or above the agreed recommended defense spending levels of 2 percent of GDP, 15 allies spent less than 1.5 percent; and only eight allies met the agreed recommended 20 percent or more of defense budgets on major equipment, while six spent less than 10 percent. As Rasmussen noted, "The majority of Allies are facing difficulty in maintaining the proper balance between short-term operation and longer-term investment expenditures in light of decreasing defence budgets and increased expenditures rising from the cost of contributions to current operations."[9] Although burden sharing disputes have been a constant feature of NATO's evolution, the impact of the financial debt crisis cuts deeper – the U.S., UK, France, and Germany, as well as other, smaller allies, are all slashing defense budgets – and is likely to be longer lasting than any similar downturn in Alliance history.

Another significant factor which challenges the implied terms and conditions of the post-Cold War "Transatlantic Bargain" is growing heterogeneity within NATO. This can be seen in divergent strategic orientations and different perceptions of NATO's utility. General Martin Dempsey, Chairman of the U.S. Joint Chiefs of Staff, noted in January 2012: "All trends are shifting to the Pacific. Our strategic challenges will largely emanate out of the Pacific region."[10] Secretary of State Hillary Clinton had already announced in November 2011 that this was a "U.S. Pacific Century," with President Obama in 2009 accepting the mantle of America's first "Pacific President."[11] This "pivot"[12] from Europe to the Asia Pacific and Middle East regions highlights the declining strategic importance of Europe in U.S. strategic thinking, a decline confirmed by recent U.S. Department of Defense Strategic Guidance and the planned reduction of ground troops stationed in Europe.[13] Related to this is damage done to the perception of U.S. competence and credibility in the aftermath of the Iraq intervention and continuing serious difficulties in Afghanistan.

In addition, rather than emphasizing collective security and crisis management, NATO European allies – particularly the small states – emphasize a regionally anchored deterrence and defense posture, with Russia seen as the primary threat. As Julian Lindley-French (Chapter 8) notes: "The simple fact is that the Afghanistan campaign never crossed the threshold between peace and war in many NATO capitals to justify the investment of forces and resources in order to succeed." Considering Operation Unified Protector in Libya, Germany could not reach a consensus with France and the UK, few allies took part (due to lack of finance, military capability restrictions, or political support), and it was clear that European allies are incapable of conducting major military operations without substantial U.S. enabling support. Secretary of Defense Robert Gates commented:

> However, while every alliance member voted for Libya mission, less than half have participated at all, and fewer than a third have been willing to participate in the strike mission. Frankly, many of those allies sitting on the sidelines do so not because they do not want to participate, but simply because they can't. The military capabilities simply aren't there.[14]

Lastly, heterogeneity is not only apparent in NATO allies' approaches to the new threats identified at the Lisbon summit – from cyber to energy to terrorism – which impact allies differently and render reaching a consensus on collective action difficult, but also to the evolving nature of the Alliance. Phillip Cornell (Chapter 12) examining energy security contends that: "the blurred lines between traditional security and economic interchange (especially energy flows) caused by globalization present new challenges." Moreover, Jeffrey Hunker (Chapter 10) who focuses on cyber security begins with the admonition: "National and alliance security topics prefaced with cyber – war, security, defense, deterrence, attack, power, doctrine, operations – are all evolving, so to say inchoate, fields."

How to explain heterogeneity: structural power shifts and realist theory

It is frequently argued that policymakers find contemporary international relations (IR) academic scholarship irrelevant and inaccessible, of limited value, even counterproductive as a guide to the conduct of "real-world" policy. General academic IR theories address the "why?" questions, and favor universal abstraction and long-term explanatory-predictive utility. Practitioners need immediate but approximate understandings of context-specific problems – they focus on "how to?" questions necessary to design and implement effective security policies. A theorist-practitioner dichotomy emerges: academics have a written culture replete with academic jargon, where individual creativity, accuracy, and elegance are primary concerns and plagiarism a hanging offence; practitioners inhabit an oral plain-language culture in which ideas are understood to be a public good and a premium is placed on group work, precision, concision, and the generation of real-time answers. While it is true that academics argue to conclusions and policymakers argue to decisions, it is also apparent that policymakers need sound conclusions to reach informed decisions. Can IR theory bridge this gap and so aid policy? Is theory an essential tool of statecraft?

Theories and concepts are an abstract set of ideas that are coherent and internally consistent, providing a simplified picture of how the world works and so rendering it comprehensible. They are intensely practical and useful. Without theory we exchange diagnostic tools for information overload – we have no means to organize, prioritize, and filter information, to discern patterns, establish salience, and explain causes. Theory is founded upon description, analysis and ultimately can be prescriptively rich, generating useful policy recommendations. By equipping practitioners with both a common vocabulary and a framework that locates a specific situation, issue, or event in a broader context, IR theories facilitate the design and implementation of effective strategic responses. As important policy debates rest on competing theoretical visions, effective policymakers identify and question whether embedded theoretical assumptions hold in any given context, conscious that a reliance on flawed theory can lead to foreign policy disasters.[15]

NATO has existed for over 60 years. The long-term viability of the organization is dependent on three interconnected factors. First, changes to the global distribution of power. Second, the U.S.'s ability to adapt its grand strategy to maintain primacy as changed power distribution creates new international orders. Third, the ability of allies to re-forge a workable "Transatlantic Bargain" that provides reciprocal benefits for all allies.

The structural or neo-realist approach to international relations focuses on the international system. It contends that how and where power is configured within a unipolar, bipolar, or multipolar world determines state behavior. Systemic pressures are understood to either underpin a status quo through balance of power responses, according to "defensive realists," or a continual struggle for predominance, primacy, and hegemony, according to "offensive realists." "Defensive realists" such as Kenneth Waltz and Robert Jervis argue that the logic of the international system tends towards maintaining the *status quo* and equilibrium via the balance of power, rather than primacy: the opportunity costs of predominance and primacy outweigh the benefits, and cooperation among states reduces the risks of international anarchy and minimizes the effects of the security dilemma: "Wars would be much more frequent – even if the first choice of all states was the status quo – if they were less risky and costly, and if peaceful intercourse did not provide rich benefits."[16] "Offensive realists," including most notably John Mearsheimer, argue states must either struggle for supremacy, for hegemony – maximize power through expansionist/foreign interventionist behavior – or fail to survive: "Great Powers … are always searching for opportunities to gain power over their rivals, with hegemony as their final goal."[17] For most states regional hegemony is the goal, as global hegemony is hard to establish. Robert Keohane notes that hegemons are able and willing to create and enforce international norms and enjoy decisive economic, technological, and military dominance:

> If discord is to be limited, and secure conflict avoided, governments' policies must be adjusted to one another. That is, cooperation is necessary. One way of achieving such mutual policy adjustment is through the activities of a hegemonic power, either through ad hoc measures or by establishing and maintaining international regimes that serve its own interests while managing to be sufficiently compatible with the interests of others to be widely accepted.[18]

"Offensive realists" argue that the "balance" approach proposed by "defensive realists" does not work because there is no way of knowing what constitutes a safe margin over neighbors, the future intentions and capabilities of potential rival states cannot be predicted, and states that cheat the system to gain more power cannot be stopped.

NATO itself was created and evolved during a period of rapid structural change. The international system shifted from being multipolar to bipolar in 1948–49. In response, the U.S. adopted a grand strategy that, in the words of G. John Ikenberry, aimed to secure Euro-Atlantic stability and lead a liberal internationalist order

> embodied in the Atlantic Charter, the Bretton Woods agreements, the Marshall Plan, and the United Nations. It was a project aimed at putting the major industrial states on a stable and cooperative footing. It was a project organised around ideas about trade, democracy, social advancement and multilateral frameworks to manage and stabilize a modern international order.[19]

In return for an Article 5 commitment by the U.S. to guarantee through its nuclear umbrella European territorial integrity, the European allies supported U.S. leadership of a liberal internationalist global order. This bargain gave a direction and purpose to NATO's role within an unwritten and largely implied and assumed compact or contract.[20]

What were the fundamental key characteristics of the Cold War paradigm? This stable bipolar Cold War system was characterized by institutionalized politico-ideological competition and military-nuclear rivalry managed, regulated, and ritualized by agreed rules of the game. As Kenneth Waltz has argued,

> States are less likely to misjudge their relative strengths than they are to misjudge the strength and reliability of opposing coalitions. Rather than making states properly cautious and forwarding the chances of peace, uncertainty and miscalculation cause wars. In a bipolar world uncertainty lessons and calculations are easier to make.[21]

A liberalist approach to international relations contends that the transformational power of ideas, values, culture, and civilization matter in international relations. The U.S. and U.S.S.R. held a preconceived image of their own modernity paradigm as defining a distinct path of human progress that was logical, rational, and interest driven while the other's was "ideological." In effect, and at an ideological level, a battle between two opposing post-enlightenment models of socio-economic development and political systems was in progress during the Cold War. Superpowers were able and willing to create and enforce international norms and strove to gain decisive economic, technological, and military hegemony. These models were post-enlightenment in the sense that each stressed the role of the individual, standardization, and engineering and planning. They were opposing in that state socialism in the U.S.S.R. placed an emphasis on social justice and role of the industrial proletariat, while liberal capitalism in the U.S. focused on individuality and role of the stakeholding middle class.[22] Such was the conviction, the strength of the ideal each side promoted, that a type of universalism in each bloc's foreign policy was apparent. This fed indigenous exceptionalist and hegemonic political cultures, so creating a self-sustaining dynamic. Non-aligned states in the "Third World" can be construed either as victims of a Cold War extended to their territories or, equally, as independent actors, able to adopt and instrumentalize Cold War ideologies for the purposes of domestic development and mobilization.[23] Third World Cold War civil wars can be understood as symptomatic of a deeper struggle between "First" (U.S.) or "Second" (U.S.S.R.) World post-enlightenment modernity models and traditional values and customs.

According to realist international relations theory, two coherent blocs under Great Power tutelage balanced each other's imperialist aspirations. A cold hard assessment of the facts of power politics led to deterrence ("balance of terror") and containment strategies being enacted by the U.S.S.R. and the U.S. and their respective allies in NATO and the Warsaw Treaty Organization, in an effort to prevent the hegemony of either side over the course and content of international politics. The Cold War in East Asia created a series of bilateral alliance structures known as the San Francisco system between the U.S. and Japan, U.S. and Republic of Korea (ROK), and U.S. and Australia, and "the basic framework of US policy towards China was created during the peak of the Cold War."[24] In contrast to the European experience, the Cold War in East Asia was hot and manifested itself in warfare:

> First in the Chinese civil war and then in Korea, Indonesia, Malaysia, and Indochina – particularly Vietnam – the Cold War raged not as an ideological-propaganda battle between rival superpowers, but in dogged, often fratricidal combat that costs millions of lives and retarded economic development as well as political democratization.[25]

U.S. Secretary of State Henry Kissinger's secrete negotiations in Beijing in 1971 resulted in President Nixon's official visit in 1972 and the construction of the Shanghai Communiqué, a masterful demonstration of strategic ambiguity, to create a deterrent mechanism against the use of force in the Taiwan Straits. This rapprochement strengthened Sino-U.S. relations and allowed for triangulation politics between the U.S., China, and U.S.S.R.: the "normalization of Sino-U.S. relations tilted the balance of power in the Cold War against an apparently invincible Soviet Union."[26]

The international system changed once more in 1989–90, from bipolar to unipolar, as the Soviet glue that had held the Alliance together came unstuck and the U.S.S.R. and its alliance system imploded: "The Soviet Union's collapse vaulted the United States into a position of seemingly unchallengeable dominance in the international system."[27] The end of the Cold War raised the question of NATO's future raison d'être and relevance after its main mission appeared to be fulfilled. As former NATO Secretary General Lord Robertson pointed out, differences have always existed but tended to be kept under tight wraps during the Cold War to avoid "the spectre of Soviet troops pouring through the Fulda Gap."[28] This structural change encouraged reflection and a re-examination of interests and self-images, and resulted in a U.S. grand strategy based around the notion of engagement of former strategic adversaries and enlargement of market-democratic systems. The "Transatlantic Bargain" this time was based on continued U.S. engagement ("the American pacifier"[29]) in European defense while the Europeans allies agreed to accept a wider collective security and crisis management role for NATO, as well as enlargement of the Alliance. As Karl-Heinz Kamp and Kurt Volker have noted:

> Washington accepted the free riding of many European allies because NATO, as a whole, still served U.S. interests, some Europeans at least still made serious efforts to meet military requirements, and Europe accepted U.S. political leadership most of the time.[30]

Unipolarity is being gradually being superseded – but by what? The transition from Cold War bipolarity to a unipolar moment in the post-Cold War era has been crowned, according to Richard Haass, by an era of nonpolarity, where power is diffuse – "a world dominated not by one or two or even several states but rather by dozens of actors possessing and exercising various kinds of power."[31] Highlighting the emergence of what he terms an "interpolar" world – defined as "multipolarity in an age of interdependence" – Grevi suggests that managing existential interdependence in an unstable multipolar world is the key.[32] Zbigniev Brzezinski argues that American hegemony is declining and the resultant global structure requires effective governance institutions put in place before the U.S. loses influence: "Because the new global political realities are pointing to a decline in traditional Western domination, the Atlantic community must become open to as much participation by successful non-Western states as is feasible."[33] Ian Bremmer suggests that we are moving into a G-Zero world in which no global leadership is in evidence: "there is no single country or bloc with the political or economic leverage to drive a truly international agenda. The result is uncertainty and conflict over international economic co-ordination, financial regulatory reform, trade policy and climate change."[34] This global power vacuum reflects and is caused by lack of self-confidence amongst European states and strategic clarity in the U.S., by the increased size of the G-20 and the lack of shared values of its members, and the unwillingness of China, India, and Brazil to bare the financial and political costs of new international responsibilities. This power vacuum, he argues, will benefit some governments, institutions and companies that can adapt to a leaderless world. "Winners" include pivotal states such as Brazil and Turkey and "rogues with powerful friends" – this category includes North Korea, Iran and Myanmar – who have support from allies with vested commercial and geopolitical interests. "Losers" include the "referees" of the international system, that is, the regional and global architecture that once served to secure and further U.S. primacy following the end of World War II – NATO, the United Nations (UN), the World Bank and International Monetary Fund – as well as "exposed states," such as Japan and Israel, which are over-reliant on U.S. military strength.

The global financial crisis is widely perceived to accelerate a centrifugal shift in the relative balance of financial, economic, and moral power from the U.S. and Europe to Brazil, Russia, India, and China (the BRIC states) – fast growing developing countries, which were predicted in 2003 (when together they constituted less than 15 percent of the entire GDP of the world's largest six economies combined (G6)) to form a powerful economic grouping that would surpass the share of global GDP of the G6 by 2050, if not sooner.[35] Goldman Sachs also highlighted the potential of the next echelon of states to become this century's largest economies, coining the acronym Next-Eleven (or N-11 states).[36] The status of "emerging power" represents an acknowledgement and recognition that high economic growth and large and growing populations are central to such an identity.[37] Indeed, in 2010 China – "the world's factory" – passed the U.S. as the world's largest energy consumer and world's number one automobile manufacturer, and possesses the world's fastest super-computer. In that year it surpassed Japan as the world's second largest economy, having become the world's largest exporter, with an average 10.5 percent growth over the last 10 years, and holding the world's largest foreign reserves – $3.2 trillion.[38] Even in the military sphere where U.S. primacy is overwhelming – in 2009 the U.S. accounted for a 46.5 percent share of global military spending, with France (4.2 percent), UK (3.8 percent), and Russia (3.5 percent) in the top five global spenders – China moved to second spot (6.6 percent).[39]

This evident redistribution of power is especially visible in the context of the global financial crisis and the relative decline of the U.S. and Europe:

> Although the Great Recession is not the cause of America's hegemonic decline, it has had three important effects. First, by propelling China's rise it accelerated the relative decline of the United States. Second, it exacerbated America's economic problems and worsened the (already poor) U.S. fiscal outlook. Third, the Great Recession has had a major perceptual impact.[40]

From Brussels, Javier Solana has observed: "the crisis is accelerating the power shift from the West to the East. This is true both in terms of material resources (military and economic) and ideological pull."[41] From Moscow, Fyodor Lukyanov, influential editor of the journal *Russia in Global Affairs*, supports this contention, noting that

> shifts in the global economic balance have weakened the West's monopoly on the world's modernization reservoir. For the first time ever, the theme of modernization is not tied exclusively to Europe, but includes the Chinese, South Korean, and Singaporean models of development.[42]

From Washington D.C., a U.S. National Intelligence Council report, aptly entitled *Mapping Global Trends 2025 – A Transformed World*, predicts a revolutionized global multipolar international system, as new players gain seats at the international high table to which they will bring new stakes and rules of the game.[43]

As the strategic effects of current and ongoing structural change have not yet resulted in a consensus about what they mean, perceptions and misperceptions can play a heightened role in shaping our understanding. The current economic crisis and financial constraints confronting NATO member states – not least the Eurozone crisis – have weakened the Alliance and created a perception that debtor democracies may become more dependent on creditor autocracies. The economic crisis raises the question: are democracies dysfunctional (relative to state capitalist and other authoritarian political systems)? Charles Kupchan notes that an unstable multipolar order has emerged after a U.S. withdrawal from a bi- then unipolar order, and argues that transitional multipolar orders, especially, are volatile:

> The end of the American era is not just about the end of American primacy and the return of a world of multiple centers of power. It is also about the end of the era that America has played such a large role in shaping – the era of industrial capitalism, republican democracy, and the nation-state.[44]

The accelerated power shift to East Asia, as well as regime instability in Tunisia, Egypt, Libya, Syria, and the other implications of the Arab Spring all provide an immediate strategic context within which NATO will need to adapt or fail. In this dramatically changed strategic context, is the post-Cold War "Transatlantic Bargain" fit for purpose?

Future scenarios

The process of thinking about the future is more important than any specific forecast. The identification of current policy debates and potential trends offered by each chapter encourages dialogue among strategic thinkers and students of international relations and provides us with points of reflection and reference as we draw conclusions. The process of identifying potential trends within policy areas – whether NATO's nuclear policy, enlargement, or relations with Russia – is very much hostage to underlying structural trends though not dictated by them. Uncertainty renders forward projections of what *could* be redundant, though an awareness of uncertainty has a value in itself as it allows us to challenge sacred cows, received wisdom, and cherished ideas and assumptions; the process of alternative future projection generates fresh perspectives and new frameworks.

This first introductory chapter has provided an explanation of the evolution of the Alliance that is linked to realist thinking in international relations. In each of the subsequent chapters we have asked the contributors to follow a similar broad tripartite structure: an examination of the historical context in which the given issue or topic has evolved; an identification and characterization of key contemporary policy debates and drivers that shape current thinking; and, on that basis, a presentation of possible future strategic pathways or scenarios relating to the topic area. We have not prescribed a scenario-straightjacket – supposing a competitive bipolar or cooperative multipolar system and instructed contributors to reflect on what this might mean in different issue areas. Rather, we have encouraged the contributors to draw their own conclusions from the perspective of the topic area they address, in order to optimize insights and facilitate reflection in the conclusions.[45]

The chapters are ordered around an intuitive logic which lends itself to greater coherence. The internal adaptation of the Alliance is explored in Chapters 2 and 3. Chapter 2 outlines the history and evolution of NATO, stressing European perspectives. It is written by both editors who are joined by Brigadier General (ret.) Dr. Klaus Wittmann, who after serving for 42 years in the German Bundeswehr was in his last assignment, Director Academic Planning and Policy at the NATO Defense College, Rome. In Chapter 3 Dr. Matthew Rhodes, a Professor of National Security Studies at the George C. Marshall Center (GCMC) in Garmisch-Partenkirchen, Germany, provides a U.S. perspective on NATO. We then move to a series of three chapters examining the assimilation of NATO's erstwhile adversaries. Chapter 4, by Dr Pál Dunay, highlights NATO enlargement and brings with it insight gleaned from being Director of the International Training Course in Security Policy at the Geneva Centre for Security Policy (GCSP), Director of the Hungarian Institute of International Affairs, as well as Head of the Security Policy Department of the Hungarian Ministry of Foreign Affairs (1991). In Chapter 5 Dr. Graeme P. Herd, a Senior Fellow at the GCSP addresses the issue of NATO partnerships. In Chapter 6, John Kriendler, currently Professor of NATO and European Security Issues at the GCMC, then examines NATO–Russia relations. In a long career as a U.S. Foreign Service officer, he served as

NATO Deputy Assistant Secretary General for Political Affairs and subsequently, Head, Council Operations in the Crisis Management and Operations Directorate.

Having addressed NATO's institutional evolution and NATO's outreach to former adversaries, through Chapters 7–9 we now turn our focus to NATO's operational future. Dr. Thierry Tardy, Senior Fellow at the GCSP, begins in Chapter 7 by highlighting NATO's Comprehensive Approach, and bringing insights gained from a research background (Foundation for Strategic Research in Paris) and teaching experience (Graduate Institute of International and Development Studies in Geneva and Institute of Political Studies and the War College in Paris). In Chapter 8 Professor Julian Lindley-French, Eisenhower Professor of Defence Strategy at the Netherlands Defence Academy, Special Professor of Strategic Studies at the University of Leiden and Senior Associate Fellow of the Defence Academy of the United Kingdom, turns our focus to NATO operations in Afghanistan. In Chapter 9, Michael Rühle, Head of the Energy Security Section in the Emerging Security Challenges Division at NATO Headquarters, turns our attention to NATO's nuclear policy. He was previously Head of Speechwriting in the NATO Secretary General's Policy Planning Unit.

The last section before the conclusions focuses on new threats and responses. As Senior Director for Critical Infrastructure at the U.S. National Security Council, Jeffrey Hunker led the development and implementation, under the Clinton Administration, of the first national strategy for cyber security and brings this expertise to NATO and cyber security in Chapter 10. NATO and Missile Defense in Chapter 11, which is addressed by Dr. Gustav Lindstrom, Head of the Emerging Security Challenges Program of the GCSP. We then turn to NATO and Missile Defense in Chapter 11, which is addressed by Dr. Gustav Lindstrom, Head of the Emerging Security Challenges Program of the GCSP. Here Phillip Cornell, Special Advisor to the Executive Director of the International Energy, responsible for policy advice and speechwriting to the head of the organization, examines NATO and energy security. In our penultimate Chapter 12, Phillip Cornell, Special Advisor to the Executive Director of the International Energy, responsible for policy advice and speech writing to the head of the organization, examines NATO and energy security.

As it is our hope that this volume will enhance existing strategic debates and clarify thinking as to the direction and scope of NATO's potential evolution, in the final chapter the editors seek to synthesize and reflect upon the findings within each of the core chapters in this book and on that basis identify the possible contours and trade-offs embedded within a potential third "Transatlantic Bargain."

Notes

1 J. Shea, *Keeping NATO Relevant*, Carnegie Endowment, Policy Outlook, April 2012, p. 17. Online. Available: http://carnegieendowment.org/2012/04/19/keeping-nato-relevant/acl9 (accessed 30 May 2011).

2 Prepared statement by C.A. Kupchan before the Senate Committee on Foreign Relations, *United States Senate*, 2nd Session, 112th Congress. Hearing on "NATO: Chicago and Beyond," 10 May 2012. Online. Available: www.cfr.org/nato/nato-chicago-beyond/p28204 (accessed 11 May 2011).

3 Merriam Webster Online Dictionary. Online. Available: www.merriam-webster.com/dictionary/alliance (accessed 11 May 2011).

4 K.W. Abbott and D. Snidal, "Why States Act Through Formal International Organizations," Chapter 1 in P.F. Diehl and B. Frederking (eds), *The Politics of Global Governance: International Organizations in an Interdependent World*, 2nd edn, Boulder CO: Lynne Rienner, 2001, pp. 9–43.

5 K. Waltz, *Theory of International Politics*, Reading: Addison-Wesley, 1979, p. 166.

6 H.A. Kissinger, L.H. Summers, and C.A. Kupchan, "Renewing the Transatlantic Partnership," New York: Council on Foreign Relations, 2004, p. 4.

7 J. Sperling and S.V. Papacosma (eds), *NATO at 60: In a Stable Crisis*, Kent, Ohio: Kent State University Press, 2012; F. Heisbourg *et al.*, *All Alone? What US Retrenchment Means for Europe and NATO*, London: Centre for Europe Reform, March 2012; G. Aybet, and R.R. Moore (eds), *NATO In Search of a Vision*, Washington D.C.: Georgetown University Press, 2010.

8 R. Burns and D. Butler, "Gates: NATO Alliance Future could be 'Dim, Dismal'," *Associated Press*, 10 June 2011. Online. Available: http://news.yahoo.com/s/ap/20110610/ap_on_re_eu/eu_gates_nato_doomed (accessed 12 June 2011).

9 NATO, "Secretary General's Annual Report 2011," 26 January 2012. Online. Available: www.nato.int/cps/en/SID-68267CB2-C8C6573E/natolive/opinions_82646.htm.

10 E. Pilkington, "Barack Obama Sets out Plans for Leaner Military in Historic Strategy Shift: President says armed forces will move away from large-scale ground warfare and focus more on China in wake of budget cuts," *The Guardian*, 5 January 2012. Online. Available: www.guardian.co.uk/world/2012/jan/05/barack-obama-plans-leaner-military.

11 H. Clinton, "America's Pacific Century," *Foreign Policy*, Vol. 189, November 2011, pp. 57–63.

12 "Rebalancing" is the current term of choice.

13 U.S. Department of Defense, "Defense Budget Priorities and Choices," January 2012. Online. Available: www.defense.gov/news/Defense_Budget_Priorities.pdf; Secretary L. Panetta, "Balance Military Budget and Security Needs," Senate Armed Services Committee (Budget Request) in Georgia, 14 February 2012. Online. Available: www.defense.gov/speeches/speech.aspx?speechid=1650. See also B. Giergerich, "NATO's Smart Defence: Who's Buying?" *Survival*, Vol. 54, No. 3, June–July 2012, pp. 169–177.

14 "Transcript of Defense Secretary Gates's Speech on NATO's Future," *Wall Street Journal*, 10 June 2012.

15 For discussions and debates on how policy and theory relate, see: S.M. Walt, "International Relations: One World, Many Theories," *Foreign Policy*, No. 110, Spring 1998, pp. 29–46; J. Lepgold, "Is Anyone Listening? International Relations Theory and the Problem of Policy Relevance," *Political Science Quarterly*, Vol. 113, No. 1, 1998, pp. 43–62; B.W. Jentleson, "The Need for Praxis: Bringing Policy Relevance Back in," *International Security*, Vol. 26, No. 4, 2002, pp. 169–183; S.M. Walt, "The Relationship between Theory and Policy in International Relations," *Annual Review of Political Science*, Vol. 8, 2005, pp. 23–48; F. Chernhoff, *The Power of International*

Theory: Reforging the Link to Foreign Policy-Making Through Scientific Enquiry, London: Routledge, 2005; S.D. Krasner, J.G. Stein, and R.O. Keohane, "Autobiographical Reflections on Bridging the Policy-Academy Divide," *Cambridge Review of International Affairs*, Vol. 22, No. 1, 2009, pp. 111–128; J. Nye, "Bridging the Gap between Theory and Policy," *Political Psychology*, Vol. 29, No. 4, 2008, pp. 593–603.

16 R. Jervis, "Cooperation Under the Security Dilemma," *World Politics*, Vol. 30, No. 2, 1977–78, p. 176.

17 J.J. Mearsheimer, *The Tragedy of Great Power Politics*, New York, Norton, 2001, p. 29.

18 R.O. Keohane, *After Hegemony: Cooperation and Discord in the World Political Economy*, Princeton, NJ: Princeton University Press, 1984, p. 243.

19 G. John Ikenberry, "Question Two: What Would a New Transatlantic Bargain Look Like?," in Mark D. Ducasse (ed.), *The Transatlantic Bargain*, NDC Forum Paper 20, January 2012, p. 83.

20 K-H. Kamp and K. Volker, "Towards a New Transatlantic Bargain," Carnegie Endowment for International Peace, Policy Outlook, 1 February 2012. Online. Available: http://carnegieendowment.org/files/transatlantic_bargain.pdf.

21 Waltz, *Theory of International Politics*, p. 168.

22 O. Arne Westad, "The New International History of the Cold War: Three (Possible) Paradigms," Berath Lecture, *Diplomatic History*, Vol. 24, No. 4, Fall 2000, p. 556.

23 S. Krasner, *Structural Conflict: The Third World against Global Liberalism*, Berkeley: University of California Press, 1985, p. 294: "Conflict between the North and the South is endemic. It is a product of deep asymmetries of power that leave almost all developing countries exposed to shocks from the international environment."

24 "Sino-U.S. ties in multipolar era," *Chinadaily.com.cn*, 21 January 2011.

25 Y. Koike, "Cold War with China not inevitable," *The Australian*, 10 January 2011, p. 10. Yuriko Koike is a former minister of defense and national security advisor of Japan and chairwoman of the executive council of the Liberal Democratic Party. In addition, the breakdown of relations between Hanoi and Beijing in 1978–79 has been characterized as a "new cold war." G. Porter, "Asia's New Cold War," *The Nation*, 9 September 1978, pp. 209–212.

26 "Peace Under the Heavens," Editorial, *The Straits Times Singapore*, 2 July 2011.

27 C. Layne, "Conclusion" in K.P. Williams, S.E. Lobell, and N.G. Jesse, *Beyond Great Powers and Hegemons: Why Secondary States Support, Follow or Challenge*, Stanford, California: Stanford University Press, 2012, p. 223.

28 D.S. Hamilton (ed.), "Transatlantic Transformations: Equipping the Alliance for the 21st Century," Washington, D.C.: Centre for Transatlantic Relations, 2004, p. 25; J. Sireci and D. Coletta, "Enduring without an Enemy: NATO's Realist Foundation," *Perspectives: Central European Review of International Affairs*, Vol. 17, No. 1, Summer 2009, pp. 57–81.

29 "Europe may not remain peaceful without the American pacifier. Indeed, there is likely to be intense security competition among the great powers with the ever-present possibility that they might fight among themselves, because upon American withdrawal Europe would go from benign bipolarity to unbalanced multi-polarity, the most dangerous kind of power structure." Mearsheimer, *The Tragedy of Great Power Politics*, p. 394.

30 Kamp and Volker, "Toward a New Transatlantic Bargain," p. 6.

31 R. Haass, "The Age of Nonpolarity: What Will Follow U.S. Dominance?" *Foreign Affairs*, Vol. 87, No. 3, 2008, pp. 44–56.

32 G. Grevi, *The Interpolar World: A New Scenario*, EU-ISS Occasional Paper No. 79, Paris, 2009.

33 Z. Brzezinski, *Second chance: Three Presidents and the Crisis of American Superpower*, New York: Basic Books, 2007, p. 212.

34 I. Bremmer, "Every Nation for Itself: Winners and Losers in a G-Zero World," *South China Morning Post*, 25 March 2012, p. 15.

35 Goldman Sachs, *Dreaming with BRICs: The Path to 2050*, Global Economics Paper No. 99, 2003.

36 Bangladesh, Egypt, Indonesia, Iran, Mexico, Nigeria, Pakistan, the Philippines, South Korea, Turkey, and Vietnam constitute the N-11. See Goldman Sachs, *The N-11: More than an Acronym*, Global Economic Paper No. 153, March 2007; Goldman Sachs, *The Long Term Outlook for the BRICs and N-11 Post-Crisis*, Global Economics Paper No. 192, December 2009.

37 Bruno Losch, "Fabrications and Illusions of Emergence," in C. Jaffrelot (ed.), *Emerging States: The Wellspring of a New World Order*, New York, Columbia University Press, 2009, p. 17.

38 The IMF predicts that China will overtake the US to be number 1 in total GDP by 2016. "China 'No. 1 economy by 2016': reports," *The Global Times*, 26 April 2011.

39 S. Perlo-Freeman *et al.*, "Military Expenditure," *SIPRI Yearbook: 2010*, Oxford, Oxford University Press, 2010, p. 203.

40 C. Layne, "Conclusion," pp. 226–227.

41 J. Solana, "Discours du Haut Représentant de l'Union européenne pour la Politique étrangère et de sécurité commune," Annual Conference of the EU Institute for Security Studies, 30 October 2008.

42 F. Lukyanov, "Tapping into West's Modernization Reservoir," *Moscow Times*, 16 December 2009, Online. Available: www.themoscowtimes.com/opinion/article/tapping-intowests-modernization-reservoir/396223.html (accessed 19 October 2010); R. Chan, "The West's Preaching to the East Must Stop," *Financial Times*, 4 January 2010, p. 11.

43 U.S. National Intelligence Council, *Global Trends 2025: A Transformed World*, November 2008. Online. Available: www.dni.gov/nic/NIC_2025_project.html. This report was all the more startling given its predecessor published in 2004 predicted that the U.S. would still control the levers of global power and discounted counter-balance. See U.S. National Intelligence Council, *Mapping the Global Future: Report of the National Intelligence Council's 2020 Project*, December 2004. Online. Available: www.foia.cia.gov/2020/2020.pdf.

44 C.A. Kupchan, *The End of the American Era: U.S. Foreign Policy and the Geopolitics of the Twenty-First Century*, Knopf, 29 October 2002, p. 303; C.A. Kupchan, "The Democratic Malaise," *Foreign Affairs*, 1 January 2011. Online. Available: www.foreignaffairs.com/articles/136783/charles-a-kupchan/the-democratic-malaise (accessed 4 June 2012).

45 See for example, NATO, "Multiple Futures Project – Navigating Towards 2030: Findings and Recommendations," Final Report, April 2009. Online. Available: www.act.nato.int/media/Multiple_Futures/20090503_MFP_finalrep.pdf.

2 NATO's Genesis and adaptation

From Washington to Chicago

*Graeme P. Herd, John Kriendler and
Klaus Wittmann*

Introduction: genesis

It is worth recalling the stark challenges that the Cold War posed.

> For those who came of age during the Cold War, its key features are
> etched in our memories. From the late 1940s until the demise of the
> Soviet Union, the Cold War defined the main contours of the interna-
> tional landscape. It was, at its core, an ideologically charged confron-
> tation between the United States and its Allies on one side, and the
> Soviet Union and its satellites on the other. Publics on both sides of
> the Atlantic understood that the stakes involved were nothing less
> than the preservation of their way of life – in addition to life itself.[1]

President Truman described NATO's creation as

> a neighborly act taken by countries deeply conscious of their shared
> heritage as democracies that had come together determined to
> defend their common values and interests from those who threatened
> them.... [The Washington Treaty's] goal was to establish a zone of
> peace in an area of the world that had been at the heart of ... two wars
> [in 1919 and 1939].[2]

As former Deputy Secretary of State Strobe Talbott wrote in *Foreign Affairs*:
"[E]ven at its inception, NATO was about more than just banding together
against a common enemy; it was about creating, consolidating, and
expanding a zone of safety within which common values and cooperative
institutions could prosper."[3]

From 1945 to 1949, Western European countries and the U.S. and Canada
viewed the expansionist policies of the Soviet Union with increasing concern
as it became clear that the Soviet Union was going to maintain its military
forces at full strength. In view of the declared ideological aims of the Communist Party of the Soviet Union, it was evident that appeals for respect for
the UN Charter and for the international settlements reached at the end of

World War II would not guarantee the national sovereignty or independence of democratic states faced with the threat of outside aggression or internal subversion.

By 1947, Europe was essentially divided into two blocs and Western European leaders moving towards a mutual assistance pact. France and the UK signed a mutual defense treaty in March 1947. On 17 March 1948, Belgium, France, Luxembourg, the Netherlands, and the United Kingdom signed the Brussels Treaty to build up "a common defense and to strengthen economic and cultural ties." Each member pledged to come to the aid of any other member who came under attack. This was the formation of the Western Union, which the U.S. and Canada attended as observers. (This later became the now defunct Western European Union). A month later, in April 1948, the Canadian Prime Minister, Louis St. Laurent, proposed a single mutual defense system linking Europe and North America to supersede the Western Union.

In June 1948 the Unites States Senate adopted the Vandenberg Resolution, which recommended that the U.S. associate with regional collective bodies for "mutual aid" and was ratified by the U.S. Senate by 64–4. This marked the end of a U.S. policy of no permanent alliances outside the Western Hemisphere which had lasted since George Washington's Farewell Address to Congress on 17 September 1796. Between July and September 1948, talks in Washington between the U.S., Canada, and Western Union powers prepared the ground for the North Atlantic Treaty (Washington Treaty) which was signed on 4 April 1949 by twelve nations (Belgium, Canada, Denmark, France, Iceland, Italy, Luxembourg, the Netherlands, Norway, Portugal, the United Kingdom, and the United States) despite the dispatch of a hostile memorandum from Stalin to each potential member.

What was NATO intended to do? In broad terms: unite North America and Western Europe in a community of nations with common interests and values; serve as a forum for consultation and decision-making; and provide for the collective defense of member nations. Although not stated explicitly in the Washington Treaty, it was clear that what the Alliance was designed to defend allies against was the threat posed by the Soviet Union. As the late Ronald D. Asmus, a senior Clinton administration official, who played a key role in NATO enlargement, wrote, "NATO's core purpose was to defend the freedom, territory and interests of its members from whatever threatened them."[4]

NATO was based on democratic principles and consensus decisions, and it developed only defensive plans. It stood in clear opposition to the Stalinization of East-Central Europe (1945–49) and the Warsaw Pact, established in 1955, which it correctly regarded as an instrument of Soviet hegemony and the means through which a doctrine of limited sovereignty was enforced upon its members (East Germany 1953, Hungary 1956, and Czechoslovakia 1968). In contrast to NATO, an alliance of sovereign nations, the Warsaw Pact was the extended arm of the Soviet general staff.

1949–54: containment

Containment and "forward strategy" were the keystones of U.S. and NATO policy towards the Soviet Union. Developed by George F. Kennan, a State Department expert on Soviet affairs, the idea was to contain the Soviet Union and stop any Soviet advance as far forward as possible. His famous "long telegram," signed anonymously by "Mr. X" and sent from the U.S. embassy in Moscow in February 1946, argued that the long-term expansion of the USSR was rooted in its history but fuelled by ideology, and that the threat was largely political and economic.[5] Containment had a defensive goal. It recognized that the Soviets were unlikely to be dislodged, but that measures could be taken to prevent the extension of Soviet influence westward. As former State Department Policy Planning Director Richard Haass noted, containment's second, subordinate goal was "regime change."[6] Kennan wrote:

> It is entirely possible for the United States to influence by its actions the internal developments both within Russia and throughout the international Communist movement … The United States has it in its power to increase enormously the strains under which Soviet Policy must operate, to force upon the Kremlin a far greater degree of moderation and circumspection than [the Kremlin] has had to observe in recent years, and in this way to promote tendencies which must eventually find their outlet in either the break-up of, or the gradual mellowing of Soviet power.[7]

He later called this "political-warfare initiative," which led to the development of CIA covert operations, his greatest mistake, and said the expansion of NATO to Russia's borders "would be the most fateful error of American policy in the entire post-cold war era."[8] It is useful to keep these views in mind in light of the impact of NATO enlargement on NATO–Russia relations.

Related to containment, there was also agreement that a "forward defense strategy" should be adopted in Europe, i.e., that any aggression should be resisted as far east as possible, in order to ensure the defense of all NATO European countries. Such thinking was influenced by the invasion of South Korea and the potential need to defend Europe against similar aggression. In 1956 the "Report of the Three Wise Men" facilitated the creation of NATO's political structures – the Korean War put the "O" (for organization) into NATO through the strengthening of the role of the NATO Secretary General, among other developments.[9]

While the North Atlantic Council agreed in September 1950 to implement a Forward Defense, the strategy demanded that forces be available to NATO. The Council instructed the defense committee to plan for an integrated force under the centralized command of a supreme commander adequate to deter Soviet forces. This implied that Europe would be defended largely on German territory, and the Council therefore considered the political and military participation of Germany. Decisions in Lisbon in February 1952 took into account a detailed analysis of each nation's defense capabilities. Ministers adopted firm force goals of 50 divisions, 4,000 combat aircraft and strong naval forces to be in place by end of 1952. However, these ambitious force goals were never achieved. In the absence of the necessary conventional forces, U.S. nuclear weapons remained essential for NATO's deterrence strategy. However, most strategists and military officers involved in these matters considered that the relatively few bombs and nuclear-capable bombers that the United States had on hand could not deal a decisive enough blow to the powerful Soviet military to prevent it from attaining its primary military and political objectives in the event of a general war in Europe. Nonetheless, early indications that firmness paid off included the Soviet withdrawal from Iran and its decision to reduce pressure on Turkey.

The Forward Defense Strategy came under eventual criticism by European military officers who expressed concern that there would not be time for U.S. and UK reinforcements to be deployed in the event of a massive surprise Soviet tank attack. This reflected a strategic dichotomy between the European focus on forces in place and the U.S. focus on deploying reenforcements after an attack.[10]

1954–60: massive retaliation

Between 1954 and 1960 NATO was guided by the strategy of "massive retaliation." This was a policy of deterrence based on the threat that NATO would respond with every means at its disposal, specifically including nuclear weapons, to aggression against any of its member countries. President Eisenhower recognized that America could not afford to re-arm its conventional forces to the extent that it could defeat a major Soviet attack in Europe. In 1954, National Security Council Memorandum (NSC) 162 ushered in a new U.S. strategic concept which became the cornerstone of the doctrine of massive retaliation. Thus, "Deterrence Theory was in part the creation of governments' in London and Washington intent to cut defense spending by substituting threats of nuclear retaliation for costly mass armies."[11]

Unlike his predecessor President Truman, President Eisenhower viewed nuclear weapons as weapons of "first resort." They would be used *en masse*, at the tactical and the strategic levels, from the very start of a general war between American and Soviet forces. NATO allies, under similar budgetary constraints as the U.S., eagerly accepted the proposal to deploy tactical nuclear weapons to front line units in Europe as the least painful solution to the problem of the inferiority of their conventional forces. Nuclear weapons, strategic and tactical, were, in a sense, "defense on the cheap," avoiding the costs of increased conventional forces, which appealed to the European allies.[12] Ministers decided in Bonn, in May 1957, to introduce tactical nuclear weapons into Europe to be able to fight an escalating nuclear and conventional battle with the Warsaw Pact ending in a strategic attack using nuclear weapons if required. This concept was the basis for Military Committee Document 70 (MC-70), a strategy that retained the concept of forward defense but with the addition of tactical nuclear weapons that would be used at an early stage to try to limit the war and avoid resort to a strategic exchange.

After the shock of the launching of the first Soviet Sputnik, NATO Ministers decided in late 1957 to deploy to Europe Intermediate Range Ballistic Missiles (IRBMs) under the command of Supreme Allied Commander Europe (SACEUR) and that nuclear warheads would be deployed to Europe. These developments led to a balance of conventional and nuclear forces. The Europeans always worried that the advent of the tactical nuclear and theatre nuclear weapons could "decouple" the U.S. from Europe in the event of a major Soviet invasion and that the two superpowers would fight a nuclear battle on European territory. Only the presence of a sizeable U.S. force stationed in Europe, as a sort of hostage in the eventuality of a Soviet invasion, soothed European fears.

1961–91: flexible response

By 1960, President Kennedy had explored more fully the notion of a limited Soviet offensive and realized that the strategy of massive retaliation was becoming less and less credible. The deteriorating situation in Berlin in 1961 led to the creation of the Allied Command Europe (ACE) Mobile Force, consisting of five air mobile battalions and four fighter squadrons. Furthermore, in 1962, the Athens Guidelines pledged that the U.S. and UK would consult with their allies before using nuclear weapons. In 1963, the forces available to SACEUR were strengthened by the assignment in war of the UK nuclear bomber force and three U.S. Polaris submarines to replace the IRBMs. The Nuclear Planning Group (NPG) was established to coordinate Alliance strategic and tactical nuclear policy and to institutionalize nuclear consultations within the Alliance. France's withdrawal from the integrated military command in 1966 was of historical significance, represented a major crisis in NATO's history, and reflected and reinforced a series of debates and controversies that took place at NATO headquarters on the role, missions and duties of the Alliance.

After a long debate, spanning several years, NATO ministers decided in 1967 to adopt a new strategy: "flexible response," a gradual strengthening of conventional forces deployed well forward, early escalation to the use of battlefield nuclear weapons, and up the scale. Flexible response provided NATO with the advantages of flexibility and of creating uncertainty in the minds of any potential aggressor about NATO's response in the case of a threat to the sovereignty or independence of any ally. The concept was designed to ensure that aggression of any kind would be perceived as involving unacceptable risks. This strategy was one main outcome of the Harmel Report (1967), whose purpose was to "study the future tasks which face the Alliance and its procedures for fulfilling them in order to strengthen the Alliance as a factor for durable peace."[13]

According to the Harmel Report, NATO's first function was to maintain adequate military strength and political solidarity to deter aggression and other forms of pressure and to defend the territory of member countries if aggression should occur. Its second function was to pursue the search for progress towards a more stable relationship in which the underlying political issues could be solved. Military security and a policy of détente were not seen as contradictory but complementary, with collective defense a stabilizing factor in world politics. In fact collective defense was seen as the necessary condition for effective policies directed towards a greater relaxation of tensions. The Harmel Report noted that the way to peace and stability in Europe rests in particular on the constructive use of the Alliance in the interest of détente with the participation of the USSR and the U.S. necessary to achieve a settlement of the political problems in Europe.[14]

Another historical development of the eighties was brought about by NATO's so-called "double-track decision" adopted in 1979 and following the stationing of Soviet SS-20 intermediate-range missiles. German Chancellor Helmut Schmidt had pointed to the danger of decoupling Europe from US security interests through weapons able to hit Europe but not the United States. The double-track decision followed the dual logic of the Harmel Report, this time through firmness in the stationing of Pershing II missiles and ground-launched cruise missiles (GLCM) in several Allied European states (amid fierce opposition from an ever growing "peace movement"), coupled with a disarmament offer. This combination led, between Presidents Reagan and Gorbachev, to the "zero solution", with the INF Treaty of 1987 eliminating an entire category of intermediate-range nuclear weapons. It was a NATO success that eventually contributed to overcoming the Cold War.

Flexible response, which remained NATO strategy to the end of Cold War in 1991, was elaborated in the "Strategic Concept for the Defense of the Atlantic Area" (MC 14/3). It is worth noting, as Ivo Daalder has pointed out, that allies were never able to "agree on a single, coherent interpretation of the strategic concept of Flexible Response," but that compromises, reflected in the deliberate ambiguity of the concept were made to maintain alliance cohesion.[15] Among the key factors accounting for the differences were the security dependence of Western Europe on the U.S. and its proximity to the Soviet Union and Warsaw Pact.

Important developments affected the concept. The October 1983 Montebello Agreement saw the withdrawal of 1,400 nuclear warheads from

Europe. NATO nuclear forces were then down to their lowest level for 20 years. In November 1984 NATO developed the "Follow on Forces Attack" (FOFA) concept, based on the development of new technology and less reliance on nuclear weapons.

The concept was to attack the second operational echelons and the administrative tails of the first echelons of the attacking Warsaw Pact forces from the air with precision-guided weapons, preferably in the defiles of the East German forests and hills well before they could become engaged. This would mean there would be no reinforcements or re-supply for the first echelons, which could then be destroyed by NATO forces along the Inner German Border. The FOFA concept was made possible by the introduction of precision-guided weapons into the U.S. arsenal.

For the first time since the very early days of the Alliance, the balance was shifting decisively toward primacy of conventional forces over nuclear forces in NATO's strategic thinking. Nuclear weapons were now becoming weapons of last resort. This was the direction in which NATO Strategy was evolving as the Cold War ended. In considering the evolution of NATO strategy, it is important to keep in mind that allies did not develop it in isolation but rather in response to the evolution of Soviet military strategy. The evolution of the Soviet and, once established, Warsaw Pact threat, was a key driver of NATO strategic evolution until the end of the Cold War.

To sum up, NATO had a slow start in the 1940s but was able to establish firm foundations in the early 1950s through the securing of the American commitment to Europe, the creation of an integrated command structure, re-armament of West Germany, the establishment of an enduring transatlantic bargain and the building of a nuclear deterrent. In the 1960s the conventional build-up and adaptation of a better balance between military and security strategy occurred. The concept of flexible response and the Harmel Doctrine provided ingredients for internal consensus and external coherence. The 1970s were characterized by partial success with détente, Soviet stagnation, and efforts to rally and restore partnership and stay competitive with the USSR. The 1980s witnessed the acceleration of defense in ways that ended the USSR's quest for military supremacy. Perseverance, U.S. leadership, UK and German support, influence distributed according to degree of national resource contribution, and planning mechanisms which helped instill technical analysis and effectiveness in fashioning political bargains characterized NATO's utility during the Cold War.[16]

1991–2010: post-Cold War adaptation

Since the end of the Cold War, allies, acting with other like-minded states in and around Europe, took several steps to remake the European state system by basing relationships with other countries, wherever possible, on cooperation and understanding rather than on reciprocal military preparations and insecurity. It allowed them to give greater weight to other components of security, especially its political aspects. This was based on the "broad concept of security" – the awareness that, in addition to the indispensable military dimension, security had political, diplomatic, economic, social, cultural, and ecological aspects. Key NATO developments can be summarized as in Table 2.1.

Strategic Concept 1991: a blueprint for change

After the Cold War, NATO needed a fundamental public document to reflect its defensive nature, changed orientation and continued relevance. In 1991 it moved beyond the Harmel Report's "defense and détente" to three mutually reinforcing elements: dialogue, cooperation, and the maintenance of a collective defense capability. The new post-Cold War Strategic Concept was agreed and published in November 1991 at the NATO Rome Summit. It was the authoritative statement of the Alliance's objectives and provided the highest level of guidance on the political and military means to be used in achieving them. It was a public document which bore little resemblance to previous classified concepts which had provided guidance for NATO during the Cold War. It emphasized the end of the Cold War threat but the emergence of new risks, a broader approach to security, and

Table 2.1 Key NATO developments

Year	Event	Outcome
1990	London Summit	Political will to change the military strategy and to extend a hand to former adversaries
1991	Rome Summit	Blueprint for change and a new Strategic Concept, expressing a "strategy without an adversary"
1992	Oslo Ministerial	Interlocking institutions
1994	Brussels Summit	New missions and Partnership for Peace
1996	Berlin Ministerial	European Security and Defense Identity (ESDI)
1997	Madrid Summit	Open Door (first round of NATO's Eastern enlargement)
1999	Washington Summit	New Strategic Concept
2002	Prague Summit	New members, new partners, new capabilities
2004	Istanbul Summit	Operations, Partnerships, Capabilities
2006	Riga Summit	Transformation, Comprehensive Approach
2008	Bucharest Summit	Commitments, Operations and Enlargement
2009	Strasbourg/Kehl	Declaration of Alliance Security, commissioning of a new Strategic Concept, Afghanistan
2010	Lisbon	New Strategic Concept, Afghanistan, Russia, Partnership
2012	Chicago Summit	Afghanistan, Defense Capabilities, Deterrence and Defence Posture Review, Partnerships

the necessity of cooperation with former adversaries as opposed to confrontation. An emphasis on crisis management was also apparent: "The success of the Alliance's policy of preserving peace and preventing war depends even more than in the past on the effectiveness of preventive diplomacy and successful management of crises affecting the security of its members."[17] It maintained the security of its member nations as NATO's fundamental purpose but combined this with the specific obligation to work toward improved and expanded security for Europe as a whole.

The 1991 Strategic Concept also provided guidance to military planners, elaborated in more detail by its companion document MC 400. The relevant military aspects reflected the changing security environment. Many of the changes that have taken place in the Alliance since 1991 can be traced to the 1991 Strategic Concept. Conventional forces were to be reduced in size and held at lower levels of readiness. Importance was attached to greater flexibility and mobility of conventional forces. The Strategic Concept concluded that the maintenance of a comprehensive in-place linear defensive posture was no longer necessary and called for an increased role for multinational forces so that all allies would more visibly share the risks and burdens of Alliance membership.

The 1991 Strategic Concept had far-reaching consequences, but the extraordinary pace of events in the first half of 1990s required that NATO's Strategic Concept be re-examined. The break-up of the Soviet Union, 1992 support of peacekeeping, subsequent involvement in peacekeeping and peace enforcement operations in Bosnia and Herzegovina, and the increasing interest in a European Security and Defense Identity (ESDI) were just some of the key changes to the strategic environment in this period that made this revision necessary.

Strategic Concept 1999: continuity and change

In Madrid in July 1997, allies decided the 1991 Strategic Concept should be updated by 1999. As Ronald Asmus wrote, the new Strategic Concept, which was agreed on at the Washington Summit in April 1999, "emphasized an enlarged NATO assuming new missions to project stability beyond its immediate boarders as one central pillar of a new Euro-Atlantic community."[18] The 1999 Strategic Concept defines the Alliance's fundamental security tasks, both in terms of collective defense and new activities in the fields of crisis management and partnership, to enhance security and stability of the Euro-Atlantic area.

The strategy notes that the strategic environment was marked by continuing and generally positive change. It reaffirmed that the threat of general war in Europe had virtually disappeared but that there were other risks and uncertainties, such as ethnic conflict, the abuse of human rights, political instability, economic fragility, and the spread of nuclear, biological, and chemical weapons and their means of delivery. It emphasized, again, the broad approach to security, encompassing complementary political and military means, and emphasizing cooperation with other states that share the Alliance's objectives remains a central feature.

Paragraph ten of the Strategic Concept lists the following fundamental security tasks for the Alliance, as guidance, especially for defense and operational planning:

1 "To provide one of the indispensable foundations for a stable Euro-Atlantic security environment, based on the growth of democratic institutions and commitment to the peaceful resolution of disputes;"
2 "To serve as an essential transatlantic forum for Allied consultations on any issues that affect their vital interests, including possible developments posing risks for members' security, and for appropriate co-ordination of their efforts in fields of common concern;"
3 "To deter and defend against any threat of aggression against any NATO member state as provided for in Articles Five and Six of the Washington Treaty" and to enhance security and stability of the Euro-Atlantic area through
4 crisis management and
5 partnership.

With regard to partnership, NATO had to enhance its "ability to promote wide-ranging Partnership, cooperation, and dialogue with other countries in the Euro-Atlantic area, with the aim of increasing transparency, mutual confidence and the capacity for joint action with the Alliance."[19]

The 1999 Strategic Concept encompassed a number of essential elements. These included the preservation of the transatlantic link, underlining the indivisibility of European and North American security, and the maintenance of military capabilities effective for the full range of foreseeable circumstances. It also included the development of the ESDI within the Alliance and enlargement. The Strategic Concept confirmed that the ESDI would continue to be developed within the Alliance on the basis of decisions take by Alliance Foreign Ministers in Berlin in 1996 and thereafter. It stated that this process required close cooperation between NATO, the Western European Union and, if and when appropriate, the European Union. The Concept confirmed the Alliance's openness to new members and that accession invitations were to be expected. Finally, the Concept supported arms control, disarmament, and non-proliferation.

The Strategic Concept also addressed the threat of terrorism, but in what appeared to be a peripheral way. Paragraph 20 stated that

> Any armed attack on the territory of the Allies, from whatever direction, would be covered by Articles 5 and 6 of the Washington Treaty.

However, Alliance security must also take account of the global context. Alliance security interests can be affected by other risks of a wider nature, including acts of terrorism, sabotage and organized crime, and by the disruption of the flow of vital resources.

The final part of the 1999 Strategic Concept established guidelines for the Alliance's forces, translating the purposes and tasks of the preceding sections into practical – albeit necessarily general – instructions for NATO force and operational planners.

In the 1999 Strategic Concept, significant changes in nuclear policy sections were neither needed nor wanted as allies wished to avoid public debate. With regard to nuclear forces, allies reiterated that with the radical changes in the security situation, NATO's ability to defuse a crisis through diplomatic means or, if necessary, to mount a conventional defense had greatly improved. It was therefore possible to significantly reduce sub-strategic nuclear forces. Allies emphasized that "The fundamental purpose of the nuclear forces of the allies is political: to preserve peace and prevent coercion and any kind of war." Allies noted that "The circumstances in which any use of nuclear weapons might have to be contemplated ... [are] extremely remote."[20]

Throughout most of the 1970s and 1980s, NATO maintained a broad mix of nuclear weapon systems. After the Cold War NATO took several unilateral steps to cancel planned modernization programs for its nuclear forces and make a significant reduction in the types of nuclear systems deployed. Now, the only land-based nuclear weapons available to NATO are U.S. nuclear bombs capable of being delivered by dual-capable aircraft of several allies. Also with the end of the Cold War, NATO terminated the practice of maintaining standing peacetime nuclear contingency plans and associated targets for its sub-strategic nuclear forces. As a result, NATO's nuclear forces no longer target any country. In another unilateral initiative, in December 1996, NATO foreign and defense ministers announced that NATO countries had "no intention, no plan, and no reason to deploy nuclear weapons on the territory of new member countries, nor any need to change any aspect of NATO's nuclear posture or nuclear policy, and that it does not foresee any future need to do so."[21]

When we compare the 1991 with the 1999 Strategic Concept, there are some obvious differences, but the continuities in the evolution of the post-Cold War security environment are also reflected. By 1999 more highly developed cooperative mechanisms had been created; greater weight was given to crisis management; there was more attention to proliferation and Weapons of Mass Destruction (WMD); there was greater focus on ESDI; and the implications of the new strategy for deployability, sustainability, and interoperability were clearer.

The strategy approved at the Washington Summit in April 1999 represented another important stage in the evolution of the Alliance's approach to security throughout the preceding decade, an evolution that started from the strategies developed in response to the Cold War. These strategies – like MC 14/3 – inevitably emphasized more the military elements of security to respond to the conditions of the prolonged and sometimes acute confrontation with the Soviet Union and the Warsaw Pact.

The relevance and topicality of the 1999 Strategic Concept were soon questioned by the terrorist attacks of September 2001, NATO's Afghanistan mission, the Iraq war, the Russo-Georgian conflict, as well as a growing awareness of globalized security challenges for which there are no military solutions. However, for several years there was great reluctance at NATO Headquarters and in member capitals to set about a revision of the 1999 document. A "very divisive process" was feared, while proponents of a new Strategic Concept countered this apprehension with the question whether allies were not so divided on several central issues that a uniting effort was urgently needed.[22] To document its continuing relevance in the diffuse security environment of the 21st century, a convincing new mission statement was indispensable.

To that end NATO heads of state and government commissioned a new Strategic Concept to be completed by NATO's next Summit scheduled to take place in Lisbon, November 2010. New Secretary General Anders Fogh Rasmussen chose a procedure drastically different from the way the last two Strategic Concepts had been developed – namely by year-long negotiations among the member nations over numerous revolving drafts, out of the attention of a broader public, resulting in texts fraught with diplomatic formulae, compromise language, and "constructive ambiguities."

NATO's 2010 Strategic Concept: a blueprint for the future?

Particular difficulties had to be taken into account in drafting the 2010 Strategic Concept: NATO's engagement in a problematic mission in Afghanistan; unwillingness of "post-heroic" societies, exacerbated by the financial and economic crisis, to sacrifice for security; lack of agreement among NATO members on fundamental issues regarding NATO's character, role, tasks, and policy; an impression of weakening solidarity among allies; divergent threat perceptions among more diverse allies resulting from enlargement; and finally, NATO's image, particularly in the Muslim World, as an instrument of often problematic U.S. policy, or for some among allied populations and the media, as a relic of the Cold War.

Since the question of NATO's continued relevance and its public support were so crucial, the Secretary General adopted an "inclusive and participatory approach" and "interactive dialogue with the broader public," undertaken by a group of twelve experts under the chairmanship of former U.S. Secretary of State Madeleine Albright. The Albright group effectively "loosened ground" as it were, in preparing consensus, fuelling public debate and interest in NATO, getting the strategic community involved, providing transparency as well as inducing member states to clarify their positions and "show the color of their cards."

The Strategic Concept which allies adopted papers over some persisting divisions, as is always the case in such documents, but is a solid achievement as it rallies allies to NATO's purpose and recommits them to it and to Alliance solidarity. The document identifies and focuses on three core tasks: (1) defense and deterrence, (2) security through crisis management, and (3) promoting international security through cooperation. These core tasks are introduced by enduring principles: NATO's purpose to safeguard the freedom and security of all its members, its character as a unique community of values, the affirmation of the primary responsibility of the United Nations, and the critical importance of the transatlantic link between Europe and North America.

With regard to collective defense, the commitment in Article 5 of the Washington Treaty (mutual assistance in the case of an armed attack) is restated unequivocally, and "remains firm and binding." This was necessary in light of concerns expressed, particularly by new allies who feared that this commitment could be diluted or taken less seriously by NATO members who, "surrounded by friends and Allies," might give priority to out-of-area operations and harmony with Russia. Reassurance came to be seen as the precondition for everything NATO does and for achieving agreement on other issues in the Strategic Concept.[23] As a reflection of that reassurance the Strategic Concept pledges NATO to "carry out the necessary training, exercises, contingency planning and information exchange for assuring our defense against the full range of conventional and emerging security challenges, and provide appropriate visible assurance and reinforcement for all Allies."

Noting, however, that "The Euro-Atlantic area is at peace and the threat of a conventional attack against NATO territory is low," the Strategic Concept addresses an array of present and future security challenges, including proliferation of nuclear and other weapons of mass destruction, ballistic missiles, cyber attacks, international terrorism, threats to critical energy infrastructure, and threats posed by emerging technologies. All are seen as areas of Alliance solidarity, without implying that they can be countered mainly with military means or necessarily fall under Article 5. The threat assessment is very broad, the security challenges are seen as diffuse, volatile, and unpredictable, and possible NATO action will have to be decided on a case-by-case basis. The reference to climate change, whose long-term consequences can have severe implications for global security, is, however, vague. Recognizing that crises and conflicts beyond NATO's borders can impact on the Alliance's security, the Strategic Concept declares prevention and management of crises as well as stabilization of post-conflict situations and support of reconstruction as necessary NATO engagements. Monitoring and analyzing the international environment are important contributions to prevention, which calls for broader and more intense political consultations among allies and with partners, about "dealing with all stages of a crisis."

The elaboration of the third core task, "Promoting international security through cooperation," starts with arms control, but its commitment to "create the conditions for a world without nuclear weapons" is limited to the goals of the Nuclear Non-Proliferation Treaty. Further reduction of nuclear weapons is linked to concomitant steps by Russia. On conventional arms control, the statement, "to strengthen the conventional arms control regime in Europe," does not present necessary novel ideas.

Partnerships (including cooperation with other institutions such as the UN and the European Union (EU)) are emphasized, building on the existing formats (Partnership for Peace, Mediterranean Dialogue, Istanbul Cooperation Initiative, Ukraine, Georgia) and seeking to enhance them.

Regarding other security-relevant institutions, only the United Nations (with the intent to give impetus to the 2008 UN-NATO Declaration) and the European Union are mentioned. Some space is devoted to the relationship with the latter, but as long as this cooperation is blocked for political reasons, the statements remain largely declaratory.

The Lisbon Summit was widely interpreted as a breakthrough in NATO's cooperation with Russia. NATO, which does not pose a threat to Russia, is seeking a "strategic partnership" with the expectation of reciprocity from Russia. Convinced that "the security of NATO and Russia is intertwined," NATO proposes enhancing political consultations and practical cooperation in the areas of shared interest, such as missile defense, counter-terrorism, counter-narcotics, counter-piracy, as well as using the full potential of the NATO–Russia Council for dialogue and joint action. Then President Medvedev's cautious agreement at Lisbon to explore missile defense cooperation was seen as an important advance.

Finally, on "Reform and Transformation," the Strategic Concept states intentions seen in previous documents: sufficient resources, deployability and sustainability of forces, coherent defense planning, interoperability, commonality of capabilities, standards, structures, and funding. A continual reform "to streamline structures, improve working methods and maximize efficiency" is pledged, once again.

The new Strategic Concept is an important document in a number of regards. First, in spite of the vision of a nuclear-weapon-free world, it emphasizes the need for nuclear deterrence as long as nuclear weapons exist; second, although many global security challenges are not of a predominantly military nature, NATO enlarges its ambition as a security provider; third, while NATO remains a regional organization, it avoids an insular, Eurocentric perspective but looks towards the global horizon; fourth, in spite of recent problems with the enlargement process and Russian indignation about it, the Alliance maintains its open door policy for European countries fit for accession and able to make their contribution to European security; and, finally, without antagonizing Russia, it takes seriously the concerns of Central and Eastern European allies.

The development of the new Strategic Concept was dissimilar to the general experience in the sense that normally such basic documents are not particularly visionary and forward-looking. They tend, rather, to be mainly the codification of previous decisions: theory follows events, concepts come after reality. This was the case with the 1999 Strategic Concept, whilst the 1991 document was an exception because of the revolutionary situation. It is to the credit of the expert group and the Secretary General that the Lisbon Strategic Concept is impressively programmatic and future-oriented.

The well crafted text conceals that there is a lack of solid agreement on a number of issues, such as the question whether NATO is a regional or a global organization, its political or military character, the balance between collective defense and its expeditionary orientation, the assessment of certain security challenges and their emphasis in the view of individual allies, the NATO-EU relationship and its political "blockage," whether there is a require-ment for a UN Security Council mandate, the approach to Russia, nuclear weapons policy among others. In some of these areas, the consensus reached may quickly collapse in light of concrete tasks, requirements, and challenges.

On NATO's reach and character, one can read from the Strategic Concept that NATO continues to regard itself as a regional organization, but one with a global perspective, which emphasizes consultation among allies, as envisaged in Article 4 of the Washington Treaty. And the peren-nial debate whether NATO is a military or a political organization should at last be put to rest: it is a political-military security organization that puts its unique capabilities at the service of international security. These capabil-ities are the military forces of allies and partners, the integrated command structure, common defense and force planning, NATO's experience in multinational military cooperation and its expertise in training. But regard-ing it as the hub of the international system would be counter-productive, and its place in that system appears to call for better definition.

In any event, the new Strategic Concept will be only as good as its implementation. This is recognized in the Lisbon Summit Declaration which contains many urgent taskings to foreign and defense ministers as well as to the Council at the level of ambassadors. The Strategic Concept must be read alongside the Summit Declaration and the NATO–Russia Council Joint Statement. The Alliance's new Strategic Concept makes a good case for NATO's relevance in the 21st century, and, after the amazing adaptation this Cold-War Alliance underwent after the end of East–West confrontation, it marks another significant transformational step. What is needed is for allies to demonstrate political will and provide the resources for implementing what they have proclaimed.

The European perspective

The NATO consensus decision-making process is a complex negotiation among allies, who frequently and not unexpectedly have different views.

Although European perspectives have been noted on a number of issues above, it is worth emphasizing that differences between the U.S. and European allies and among the European allies have characterized the history of the Alliance. In the current context, for instance, there are significant European concerns about the following, among other issues:

- Doubts about the continuing U.S. commitment to NATO in light of its pivot toward the Asia-Pacific region;
- concern whether Washington is willing to exercise the leadership role that it has in the past;[24]
- disagreements about how much of the Alliance burden European allies and Canada should carry;
- differences over Afghanistan, including the process of transition and speed of withdrawal and paying for maintaining the Afghan National Security Forces;
- disagreement about the prospect of further expeditionary operations;
- differences over emerging threats which affect allies differently;
- continuing differences among allies over relations with Russia;
- differences over the importance of missile defense, and how the burden of costs should be shared.

In the past, the existential threat posed by the Soviet Union and Warsaw Pact forced allies to compromise, but with that factor absent and in light of the complex new security environment, such compromises are more difficult to achieve. In addition the disappointing contributions of the Common Foreign and Security Policy and the increasing turbulence that is buffeting the European Union serve to undermine the focus of attention and sap resources from the European defense project.

Notes

1 R. Haass, *Charting a New Course in the Transatlantic Relationship*, Remarks to Centre for European Reform, London, 10 June 2002.
2 R.D. Asmus, *Opening NATO's Door: How the Alliance Remade Itself for a New Era*, Council on Foreign Relations Book, New York, Chichester, West Sussex: Columbia University Press, 2002, pp. 46–57.
3 S. Talbott, "From Prague to Baghdad: NATO at Risk," *Foreign Affairs*, Vol. 81, No. 6, November/December 2002, pp. 46–57.
4 Asmus, *Opening NATO's Door*, p. 12.
5 R.L. Kugler, *Commitment to Purpose: How Alliance Partnership Won the Cold War*, Santa Monica, CA: Rand, 1993, p. 26.
6 R. Haass, "Regime Change and its Limits," *Foreign Affairs*, Vol. 84, No. 4, July/August 2005, p. 68.
7 Haass, *Opening NATO's Door*, p. 68.
8 T. Weiner and B. Crossette, "George F. Kennan Dies at 101; Leading Strategist of Cold War," *New York Times*, 18 March 2006. Online. Available: www.nytimes.com/2005/03/18/politics/18kennan.html?pagewanted=1 (accessed 16 June 2011).

 9 R.S. Jordan and M.W. Bloome, *Political Leadership in NATO: A Study in Multinational Diplomacy*, Boulder, CO: Westview Press, 1979.

10 D. Middelton, "NATO 'Forward Defense' Draws Fire," *New York Times*, 11 January 1982.

11 C.J.V. Murphy, cited in W.J. Thies, *Friendly Rivals: Bargaining and Burden Shifting in NATO*, Armong, NY: M.E. Sharpe, 2003, p. 4.

12 See I.H. Daalder, "Introduction," in *The Nature and Practice of Flexible Response: NATO Strategy and Theater Nuclear Forces since 1967*, New York: Columbia University Press, 1991.

13 P. Harmel "The Future Tasks of the Alliance. Report of the Council," North Atlantic Council Ministerial Communiqué: Brussels, NISCA 4/10/1, C-R (66)68&69, 15 December 1967.

14 Stanley Sloan convincingly argues that NATO's 1967 Harmel Report not only injected a new sense of purpose into the Alliance after a series of crises, but that it also gave NATO the enhanced "political" personality that enabled the Alliance to play a crucial role in winding down the Cold War almost 25 years later. M. Rühle, "Re-examining the transatlantic bargain" (Review of Stanley Sloan, *NATO, the European Union and the Atlantic Community: The Transatlantic Bargain Reconsidered*, Boulder, CO: Rowman & Littlefield, 2002), *NATO Review*, 2003, pp. 23–25.

15 I.H. Daalder, *The Nature and Practice of Flexible Response*, p. xv.

16 The authors are grateful to Richard Cohen, former faculty member at the George C. Marshall Center European Center for Security Studies for information he provided while at the Marshall Center on the evolution of NATO strategy during the Cold War.

17 NATO, "The Alliance's Strategic Concept agreed by the Heads of State and Government participating in the meeting of the North Atlantic Council," Rome, 8 November 1991. On the development of the 1991 and subsequent 1999 Strategic Concepts, see K. Wittmann, "The Road to NATO's New Strategic Concept," in G. Schmidt (ed.), *A History of NATO: The First 50 Years*, Vol. 3, Basingstoke, New York, 2001, pp. 219–237.

18 Asmus, *Opening NATO's Door*, p. 13.

19 NATO, "The Alliance's Strategic Concept."

20 NATO, "The Alliance's Strategic Concept approved by the Heads of State and Government participating in the meeting of the North Atlantic Council," Washington D.C., 23–24 April 1999. Online. Available: www.nato.int/cps/en/nato-live/official_texts_27433.htm (accessed 31 August 2011).

21 Ibid.

22 K. Wittmann, "NATO's new Strategic Concept should be more than a 'Shopping List'," in *The European Security and Defense Union*, Vol. 4, 2009, pp. 35–37. See also K. Wittmann, "Towards a new Strategic Concept for NATO," Forum Paper 10, NATO Defense College, Rome, September 2009; K. Wittmann, "NATO's New Strategic Concept: An Illustrative Draft," Berlin, 2010; D.S. Yost, "NATO's evolving purposes and the next Strategic Concept," *International Affairs*, Vol. 86, No. 2, 2010, pp. 489–522.

23 R. Asmus, S. Czmur, C. Donnelly, A. Ronis, T. Valasek, and K. Wittmann, *NATO 2020: Assured Security; Dynamic Engagement*, Analysis and Recommendations of the Group of Experts on a New Strategic Concept for NATO, Policy Brief, London: Centre for European Reform, 17 May 2010.

24 See K-H. Kamp and K. Volker, "Toward a New Transatlantic Bargain," Carnegie Endowment for International Peace, Policy Outlook, 1 February 2012. Online. Available: http://carnegieendowment.org/files/transatlantic_bargain.pdf.

3   U.S. perspectives on NATO

Matthew Rhodes[1]

Introduction

On paper, 2010 marked a highpoint in the United States' valuation of
NATO. In May, the Obama administration's National Security Strategy
reaffirmed that the "relationship with our European allies remains the cornerstone for U.S. engagement with the world."[2] At Lisbon in November,
the Alliance as a whole adopted a Strategic Concept strongly reflective of
U.S. positions as well as a summit declaration endorsing the U.S.-crafted
counterinsurgency plan for Afghanistan to 2014. Nonetheless, Secretary of
Defense Robert Gates' mid-2011 warning of NATO's possibly "dim, if not
dismal future" laid bare the resurgence of American doubts. Richard
Haass, president of the country's most influential foreign policy think-
tank, added that Gates "may not have been pessimistic enough."[3] Such
currents of skepticism and frustration have existed since NATO's birth,
but international trends suggest they will intensify in the decades ahead.
Absent a fresh animating mission which is shared and meaningfully supported by the rest of NATO, U.S. views of alliance with Europe will likely
drift into 21st century variants of their pre-Cold War norm. Absent robust
commitment from its *primus inter pares*, NATO will likely drift toward
irrelevance.

Historical context

The ambivalence of America's historical relationship with Europe will be
familiar to many readers of this volume. Nevertheless, a brief review provides a useful reminder that close alliance has not been a given. Prior to
World War II, the United States' wary distance from future allies in Europe
"became more than a policy; it became an expression" of an exceptionalist
self-perception "which contrasted the simple virtues of [the American]
Republic with the subtle and complex qualities (some said corruptions) of
Europe."[4]

George Washington, the country's first President, famously set the tone
in his farewell address in 1796:

> The great rule of conduct for us, in regard to foreign nations, is in extending our commercial relations to have with them as little political connection as possible ... Europe has a set of primary interests which to us have none or a very remote relation ... [It is thus] our true policy to steer clear of permanent alliances with any portion of the foreign world.[5]

Through the 19th century, Washington's tenet gained expression in moves such as the formal end of the alliance with France which had been concluded during the American War for Independence, as well as declaring the Monroe Doctrine, which condemned further European colonization in the Western Hemisphere, as a unilateral statement rather than the joint one proposed by Great Britain.[6] The isolationist position was reinforced by two declared wars with European powers, the War of 1812 with Great Britain and the Spanish–American War of 1898, as well as periodic diplomatic crises in between that threatened to escalate into armed conflict.

The 20th century only slowly changed this outlook. The U.S. remained out of World War I until 1917 and then pointedly entered as an "associated" rather than allied power. After the war's conclusion, the U.S. Senate blocked entry into the League of Nations. During the 1930s, Congress passed a series of Neutrality Acts aimed at keeping the country out of the approaching World War II until the Japanese attack on Pearl Harbor. America embraced deeper alliance engagement during that conflict, with especially close military coordination with Great Britain through the Combined Chiefs of Staff. After the war, the Senate approved membership in the United Nations.

Still, the additional step to NATO and other peacetime alliances remained uncertain. U.S. forces underwent steep demobilization after the war's end. In 1947, Senator Robert Vandenberg advised President Harry Truman that congressional support for initiatives such U.S. aid to Greece and Turkey and the Marshall Plan would require dramatizing the Soviet threat in a way that would "scare the hell" out of the country. At the outset of 1948, the Truman administration still dismissed British proposals for U.S. participation in a European alliance, worrying this could jeopardize the fragile support for economic assistance and perpetuate a disproportionate American burden for the continent's defense.[7]

Moves such as the communist seizure of power in Czechoslovakia and the Soviet blockade of Berlin helped overcome this reluctance. Even so, the U.S. insisted that the Article V security guarantee in the 1949 Washington Treaty not apply to European colonial possessions and preserve each members discretion to respond to attacks on others through "such action as it deems necessary" in accordance with its own "constitutional processes." It took the outbreak of the Korean War in the following year for the U.S. to embrace the NSC-68 planning document's more militarily robust version of containment and solidify its commitment to the long-term forward presence and integrated military structures that defined NATO for the next four decades.

Post-Cold War policy debates and drivers

The Cold War's end resurrected arguments that U.S. interests would be better served by disbanding alliances and returning forward deployed forces to the U.S.[8] Successive Presidential administrations have instead pursued new objectives for NATO despite reduced troop levels in Europe. Nonetheless, a set of interacting factors have perpetuated debate on NATO's place in U.S. policy.

Geopolitics

The distribution of global power remains a baseline condition shaping U.S. approaches to security. Given NATO's origins in a bipolar order, shifts toward either uni- or multipolarity present particular challenges.

Now sometimes forgotten is that journalist Charles Krauthammer's declaration of a "unipolar moment" at the end of 1990[9] initially remained in dispute. Echoing Paul Kennedy's analysis of "imperial overstretch," prominent 1992 Presidential candidate Paul Tsongas quipped that the prevailing recession showed "the Cold War is over and Japan won." As late as 1993, realist scholar Kenneth Waltz assessed that nuclear weapon stockpiles left the old bipolar order still in place.[10]

By the end of the 1990s, however, American "hyperpower" went virtually unchallenged.[11] A typical survey of indicators circa year 2000 would have noted that U.S. military spending of $300 billion was five times greater than that of its nearest competitor's (Russia) and equal to the budgets of the next 15–20 countries combined. America's wide qualitative edge in global mobility and precision weaponry had proven decisive in conflicts from the Persian Gulf to the Balkans and underlay its capacity to "command the commons" of global air and sea lanes.[12] With an annual Gross Domestic Product (GDP) of $12 trillion, the American economy comprised more than a quarter of global output, enjoyed faster growth than Europe or Japan, and led in development and application of information technologies. Additional factors such as long-standing constitutional democracy, ubiquitous popular culture, and leading positions in key international institutions provided unmatched reserves of so-called "soft power."[13]

Under such conditions, NATO's added-value seemed limited. Indeed, by 2008, the United States had further extended its military predominance by doubling its defense budget after 9/11. William Wohlforth and Stephen Brooks, unipolarity's most systematic analysts, argued that America's historically unparalleled position rendered the usual external constraints on its security policy, including the need to cultivate cooperation and legitimacy, inoperable.[14]

Already in the late 1990s, Clinton administration Secretary of State Madeleine Albright's reference to the U.S. as "the world's indispensable nation" hinted at the spread of this view among policymakers. It grew more pronounced among officials and their so-called neo-conservative supporters[15] during the first term of the George W. Bush administration. It peaked with debates preceding the initial intervention in Iraq, which U.S. Ambassador Nicholas Burns would term a "near-death experience" for NATO. Open calls by leaders such as France's Jacques Chirac and Germany's Gerhard Schroeder for a "multipolar order" and attempts at "soft balancing" via institutions reinforced American views of NATO as an unwelcome constraint akin to the Lilliputians' binding of Gulliver.[16]

Some analysts remain confident of uni-polarity's durability. Since the middle of the last decade, however, conventional wisdom has been shifting toward the notion of a "post-American world."[17] The U.S. intelligence community itself forecast multipolarity to become a fact of life by 2025.[18] Such expectations assume at least relative decline for the U.S., possibly steeper decline for Europe, and ongoing rise for China, India, and other emerging powers.

The financial and economic crisis that began in the United States in spring 2007 greatly accelerated the spread of this outlook. From that time to fall 2008, the U.S. economy lost nearly half its stock market value, a quarter of household net worth, and more than five million jobs. The freeze-up of credit markets following the collapse of the Lehman Brothers investment firm in September 2008 pushed the U.S. government to extend hundreds of billions of dollars in emergency government funds to prevent the rapid dissolution of other financial institutions. Such measures helped avert a full-blown depression, but recovery has been halting. In early 2012 unemployment remained stuck above 8 percent while surging government debt (surpassing annual GDP) had become the nation's most contentious political issue.

Security resource repercussions have begun. On top of suggestions that America's formidable conventional capabilities represent outmoded "wasting assets,"[19] by spring 2011 Secretary Gates conceded the post 9/11 "gusher" in military spending had been turned off. President Obama called in April for cumulative savings in the defense budgets of the next dozen years of $400 billion, which military planners worry could double.[20] The 10 percent cut in the State Department's budget for that year set back prior plans for increased spending on diplomacy and development.

In regards to soft power, the financial crisis canceled out the rebound in foreign views of the United States that accompanied the transition from Bush to Obama. Beyond damaging America's "reputation for success,"[21] it undermined the general attractiveness of the liberal economic and political models the U.S. has espoused for decades. In the words of Chinese Vice Premier Wang Qishan, "The teachers now have some problems."[22]

Prognoses for Europe tend to be even more pessimistic, but its present geopolitical weight should not be overlooked. In 2010, the European

Union represented the world's largest economic unit with a collective GDP over $16 trillion. The EU and its members provide more than $50 billion, or 60 percent, of global development aid each year.[23] They account for 20 percent of U.S. trade and nearly $3 trillion in mutual investment. NATO Europe militaries count two million troops. Serious pre-crisis books envisioned the continent as a coequal pillar of a tri-polar order with America and China,[24] or even as the hegemonic model of post-sovereign multilateralism.[25]

Nonetheless, the continent's place in international affairs and the foreign policy calculus of the United States now seems poised instead for decline. A few major countries such as Germany and Poland have weathered the past years' financial crisis relatively well. However, debt-driven sovereign wealth crises for a growing number of Eurozone countries such as Portugal, Italy, Ireland, Greece, and Spain have raised the specter of prolonged weak growth and a possible breakup of monetary union. Blows to the prospect of a Common European Security and Defense Policy dealt by disunity on Libya and other issues, as well as growing support for strongly Euroskeptic parties, further threaten EU capacity for action and soft-power appeal.

Per Secretary Gates' "dismal future" remarks, the effects of the crisis are also exacerbating shortcomings in Europe's military capabilities and thus longstanding tensions over burden-sharing within NATO. In February 2011 the Alliance's Secretary General Anders Fogh Rasmussen noted European members' collective defense budgets had declined by $45 billion in the preceding two years, helping boost the U.S. share of spending from less than half of NATO's total a decade ago to roughly three-quarters now.[26]

Demographic trends will intensify these problems. According to the United Nations Population Division, by 2050 the world's population will increase by over two billion while that of Europe will decline by several tens of millions. Meanwhile, by 2025 the continent's average age will rise from 40 to 45 and the effective old-age dependency ratio (retirees over 65 relative to the working population 20–64) will increase from 37 percent to 48 percent. Foreseeable effects will include rising health care and pension costs, intensified pressure on other expenditures, a shrinking pool of youth available for military service, and increased wariness of military action.[27]

Projections for emerging economies in Asia and elsewhere present an opposite image. Based on their continued impressive growth through the financial crisis, in late 2009 the investment firm Goldman Sachs forecast the "BRIC" (Brazil, India, Russia, and China) economies would equal those of the G-7 in size by 2032, with China having claimed the top spot from the U.S. five years earlier.[28] In spring 2011 the IMF set China's ascension in 2016 under purchasing power parity.[29] Also in stark contrast to Europe, China's military spending tripled over the past decade while

India's increased by 60 percent.[30] These countries' rise need not present a threat per se, but their more traditional "zero-sum" view of international relations could both spark new conflict and weaken cooperative efforts to address global challenges.[31]

One potential consequence of these trends would be a general drop in American capacity and desire for international leadership. Nearly half the respondents in the most recent Pew Center opinion polls agree the U.S. should "mind its own business" internationally, up from 18 percent in 1964 and 30 percent in 2002.[32] Reflecting the previously noted budgetary pressures, President Obama's June 2011 address on force reductions in Afghanistan stressed "[i]t is time to focus on nation-building here at home."[33] Economic factors also played a role in the announced withdrawal in January 2012 of two additional U.S. combat brigades from Europe by 2014.[34] Prior to his retirement, Secretary Gates told West Point cadets that anyone advocating another land war in the Middle East or Asia "should have his head examined."[35] Meanwhile, Senator John McCain, Obama's opponent in the 2008 election, lamented isolationism's return "center stage" within the Republican Party.[36]

A second possibility would leave a strained United States still striving to exert leadership but finding its NATO allies unable or unwilling to serve as meaningful partners. As former French Foreign Minister Hubert Vedrine observed in late 2009, Americans may already be coming to view Europe as "not a priority, not a problem, and not a solution to [their] problems."[37] The logical next step would be to stop "overinvesting" in an "underperforming" NATO in favor of a more diversified "portfolio" of security partnerships.[38]

Some steps by the Obama administration have reinforced perceptions along these lines. Elevating the G-20 over the G-7 as the leading forum for discussions about the global economy diluted European voices on that issue. Scheduling moves such as Obama's skipping commemorations of the fall of the Berlin Wall in favor of a tour of Asia in November 2009 and, later, the decline of an invitation to meet EU leaders in Madrid in May 2010 were taken as signals of disinterest. The shift from retired Marine General Jim Jones to Tom Donilon in the key post of National Security Advisor at the end of 2010 replaced a former NATO Supreme Allied Commander with the administration's leading advocate of a "re-balancing of resources" toward Asia,[39] presaging the "pivot" toward that region rolled out in late 2011.

The future of collective defense

The 2010 Strategic Concept reaffirmed collective defense as a central task for NATO. The original concern of "keep the Russians out" remains the key focus for a few newer members, but the United States has placed higher priority on adapting collective defense to emerging issues such as terrorism, energy security, cyber threats, and missile defense.[40] The Concept's recognition of such threats as potential Article V triggers (despite some members' reservations) represented an American diplomatic success. In each case, however, practical achievements will require further decisions on sensitive issues and follow up commitment.

Al-Qaeda's attacks on the World Trade Center and Pentagon in September 2001 made terrorism the United States' top security concern. NATO's first-time invocation of Article V the following day signaled other members' shared concern and solidarity. The U.S. opted to execute its initial campaign against the Al-Qaeda-allied Taliban government in Afghanistan outside the NATO framework. However, the succeeding International Security Assistance Force (ISAF) in that country, as well as the maritime Operation Active Endeavor (OAE) in the Mediterranean, have been formal NATO operations.

In other respects NATO's counterterrorism role has been limited. One factor is the awkward fit between an inter-state military alliance and threats from non-state networks. Transatlantic intelligence and police cooperation has tended to be bilateral or via the European Union rather than through NATO. Other problematic factors include divergence between assessments of the threat and European critiques of U.S. detention, interrogation, and data screening practices, especially during the George W. Bush administration. These differences have narrowed but not disappeared under President Obama.

Proliferation of nuclear weapons and ballistic missile technology has been a related U.S. focus. Transatlantic cooperation on tactical missile defense for deployed military forces accelerated after the 1991 Gulf War. It culminated in 2005 with the agreement to develop an Active Layered Theater Ballistic Missile Defense System (ALTBMD), a network of national radars and interceptors linked by a NATO command and control system.

The prospects for strategic missile defense remained more controversial, largely due to Russian concern for its effects on strategic stability and deterrence. A lengthy, classified feasibility study of the issue authorized at the Prague Summit in 2002 concluded territorial missile defense for NATO was technically feasible, and the 2008 Bucharest Summit declaration called for incorporation of the Bush administration's planned European "third site" in a NATO-wide system. The Obama administration's shift to a "phased adaptive approach" that would cover all of NATO further boosted support. By fall 2011 allies including Poland, Romania, Spain, and Turkey had agreed to host land- or sea-based components.

Some areas of contention remain. One is the termination of the trilateral U.S.-Germany-Italy Medium Extended Air Defense System (MEADS) project, which will end the highest-profile example of transatlantic scientific-industrial collaboration in this field.[41] Another is the potential terms of Russian involvement.[42]

Attention to threats to government and civilian computer networks has soared in recent years along with increasing reliance on them. Suspected Russian-sponsored attacks on key websites in Estonia and Georgia erupted during conflicts with those countries in 2006 and 2008. An unnamed "foreign intelligence agency" (possibly Russian or Chinese) penetrated the U.S. military's Central Command network in 2008 as well.[43] Criminal groups and hackers have also stepped up attacks on defense contractors. With strong U.S. encouragement, NATO has taken a number of steps in response, including establishing a Cyber Defense Coordination Center at NATO headquarters, a NATO Computer Incident Response Capability at SHAPE, and a Cooperative Cyber Defense Center of Excellence in Tallinn. The new Strategic Concept envisions further sharing of information and possible means of support for targeted members in the future. In June 2011, the Alliance issued a revised Policy on Cyber Defense.

These initial measures point to this area as a promising avenue for further cooperation, though their effectiveness has yet to be fully tested. Moreover, as congressional comments on the Obama administration's May 2011 International Strategy for Cyberspace were reiterated, serious questions remain over means of ascertaining sources of attack as well as militaries' roles in potential countermeasures.

The parallel field of energy security encompasses strategies for assuring dependable supplies while minimizing potentially negative environmental effects. NATO's role in these areas has been a lower priority for the U.S., and transatlantic (as well as intra-European) unity regarding both sides of the equation has been strained. The German-backed Nordstream gas pipeline project highlighted differences over increased energy imports from Russia. One recent analysis laments NATO's failure to provide meaningful reassurance for other would-be exporters and predicts that diverging U.S. interests in sources of supply will further reduce its concern for Europe's energy security.[44] American and European delegations also failed to forge a common position at the 2009 U.N. climate summit in Copenhagen, where President Obama eventually negotiated a partial framework accord with four non-European leaders.

Wider NATO

Since the Cold War the United States has also pushed for NATO to broaden its geographic scope. In 1993 Senator Richard Lugar argued the Alliance would go either "out of area or out of business." The phrase connoted openness to additional members and partners as well as to military operations beyond member states' territory. In both cases, U.S. expansiveness has contrasted with the more limited regionalism of many European members.

Enlargement and partnerships

The most significant U.S.-backed outreach initiative has been the Partnership for Peace (PfP), launched in 1994 as a flexible framework for military-to-military cooperation, security consultations, and (where desired) membership preparation for former Warsaw Pact and other non-NATO countries in Europe. Subsequent formal fora have included the Mediterranean Dialogue (for North Africa and the Levant), the Istanbul Cooperation Initiative (for Persian Gulf states), individual programs for Russia, Ukraine, Georgia, and "global partners" who have worked closely with NATO in international missions such as Japan, South Korea, Australia, New Zealand, and Mongolia.

Although partners themselves have provided some of the impetus for these initiatives, the U.S. has encouraged them as a means of serving a number of goals. They build mutual confidence and interoperability with foreign militaries that are potential partners in overseas missions. Those prospectively leading to membership in particular may also promote democratization and regional stability, matters of special urgency in the wake of the violent breakup of the former Yugoslavia. Their successful culmination can then integrate reliably Atlanticist voices from what former Secretary of Defense Donald Rumsfeld termed "New Europe" into the Alliance. Accordingly, the U.S. played a driving role in all three rounds of enlargement that have brought a dozen new members to NATO since 1999.

While the enlargement policy remains seen as a success, its continued utility is uncertain. With few exceptions, new allies are small countries whose accession has "water[ed]-down [NATO's] military capabilities."[45] Criticism of post-accession "backsliding" among new entrants has been prominently voiced in Washington.[46] Their sometimes overestimated Atlanticism is moderating.[47] Moreover, potential future candidates are on the whole less clearly interested, prepared, and/or supported by existing allies.[48]

Expeditionary operations

Widening has also entailed NATO involvement in far-flung humanitarian and counterterror-linked military missions, the latter overlapping with new forms of collective defense. By serving as a "consensus engine," NATO offers to deliver both greater diplomatic legitimacy and material assistance for potentially risky deployments.[49] Participation in them has become a de facto expectation of countries seeking closer ties or membership.

To be sure, the potential benefits have not eliminated American ambivalence regarding NATO participation. Alliance decision making can impinge on military efficiency through lost time and compromises on targets and tactics. Critiques of this effect in the Balkans informed the

Bush administration's decision to decline a formal NATO role in its initial intervention in Afghanistan. Secretary of Defense Donald Rumsfeld expressed the preference for ad hoc coalitions of the willing by arguing "the mission should determine the coalition" rather than the reverse. NATO's most useful role from this perspective is to serve as a "toolbox" of familiar, interoperable partners with varied niche capabilities.

In addition, other members' operational contributions can be limited. Only a small fraction of European forces are deployable, and they are short of key capabilities such as airlift, smart weapons, and intelligence. U.S. planes accounted for two-thirds of the total sorties flown during the Allied Force air campaign against Serbia in 1999.[50] Restrictive national caveats for many allies' forces in Afghanistan produced the exaggerated quip that ISAF stands for "I Saw Americans Fight."

As a candidate for President, Barack Obama pledged to "strengthen NATO by asking more of our allies."[51] However, the tripling of American forces in Afghanistan to 100,000 in his first two years in office was met with an ultimately disappointing mix of smaller, often temporary deployments and announcements of withdrawal. Despite the administration's insistence on what one advisor described as "leading from behind" in the Libya operation,[52] the alliance remained reliant on U.S. for the initial strikes against Libyan air defenses, aerial refueling, and surveillance. Only six other allies carried out airstrikes.[53]

Frustration with these shortcomings could reinforce U.S. wariness of future overseas missions. It thus remains crucial for NATO to conclude its operations in Afghanistan in particular, in a way that at a minimum "preserves a sense of shared purpose."[54] Still, the Strategic Concept's recommitment to "crisis management" notwithstanding, a reduction in the scale, if not immediately the number, of shared expeditionary actions seems likely. Indeed, the January 2012 U.S. Defense Strategic Guidance emphasizes that "U.S. forces will no longer be sized to conduct large-scale, prolonged stability operations."[55]

A shift to smaller, more deliberately targeted deployments would not be bad in itself. However, it would lessen America's immediate incentive to invest in joint training and other forms of defense cooperation with its NATO allies. It would also reduce the positively unifying effects of shared operational service.

Transatlantic community

NATO's character as not only an instrumental alliance but also a "security community"[56] of shared identity and values has helped explain its durability. However, these too are challenged by sources of divergence. In terms of cultural heritage, in the late 1990s Stephen Walt highlighted the declining percentage of Americans of European descent (falling below half around 2040), the fading "affinity for the 'old country'" among European

Americans after multiple generations, and the shift of population from the Atlantic-oriented northeast to the south and west.[57] As a generalization, Americans' greater religiosity and national pride contrast with Europeans' post-modern secularism.[58] Perhaps relatedly, Americans are also more likely to believe in the efficacy of military force in international affairs. Finally, as Secretary Gates also pointed out in his farewell remarks at NATO, there is an accelerating generational transition on both sides of the Atlantic from leaders for whom the original Cold War context for NATO had been a defining experience to ones for whom it represents a historical abstraction.

President Obama embodies several of these changes. As a law student at Harvard, he wrote of being uninspired by travel in Europe, associating the continent more with colonialism in places such as his father's Kenya than high culture and freedom.[59] On his tour of Asia in November 2009 he recalled his childhood in Hawaii and Indonesia in presenting himself as "America's first Pacific President." The flipside is that his heritage may leave him the "first [modern] president who is not Atlanticist by default."[60]

Republican alternatives seem no less aloof. Contrary to the perceptions above, former Massachusetts governor Mitt Romney, the nominee facing Obama in the 2012 election, formally launched his campaign by accusing the president of taking direction "from the capitals of Europe."[61] The influential Tea Party movement within the Republican Party is largely split between neo-isolationists and "Jacksonian" unilateralists in foreign policy outlook.[62]

Commitment to freedom and democracy has also defined the community, as exemplified by the pre-NATO Atlantic Charter signed by Roosevelt and Churchill in 1941. However, despite its recent ebb, the dramatic spread of democracy on all continents the past few decades has reduced the extensive Cold War overlap of NATO with "the Free World."[63] More recently, as noted, the financial crisis has aggravated doubts about democracy's efficacy and health, even within NATO members.

Future scenarios

Per this volume's introduction, inertial extension of NATO's past presents the simplest image of its future. A "muddling through" scenario suggests that the United States will continue to act on the basis of global power and responsibilities. American officials will periodically complain about allies' lagging commitment and sometimes prefer to work outside NATO structures. Still, despite decades of warnings to the contrary, NATO will retain a marked place in U.S. policy as a uniquely robust framework for addressing security challenges, old and new. Even without a clear unifying vision, it will remain the worst form of international engagement, except for all the others. However, the driving forces reviewed here suggest escaping marginalization will become increasingly difficult. The alternative

Scenarios

potential futures presented below illustrate how those factors could lead to vastly diminished U.S. interest in NATO (if not a "reversion to aversion") as well as two paths by which NATO could remain a core American priority. Internal variations can be imagined for all three.

1.   Under the first scenario, the United States remains the world's most powerful state, but its influence is increasingly constrained by other states and non-state actors. A recent resurgence of technology-led growth has begun to lose momentum just as the Social Security pension program moves into deficit. After a short-lived respite, polarization and disengagement again dominate internal politics. Internationally, the country has scaled back the scope of its ambition from guarantor of a liberal global order to "off-shore balancer."[64] In that role, it provides selective support to other key states to prevent any regional power from dominating its neighborhood. Dynamic growth in Asia and more recently Africa has made the Indian Ocean rim that policy's central focus.[65]

Europe remains a significant but diminished economic partner. Differentiated effects of aging and uneven success in integrating immigrants have weakened the cohesion of the European Union. European states and corporations pursue independent relations with rising powers to their south and east, often at odds with American objectives. Under these circumstances several states have dissolved their armed forces or converted them into lightly armed gendarmerie, and the U.S. has withdrawn its last permanent units from the continent. NATO continues as a formal institution with additional members from the Balkans. However, outside some notable successes in cyber defense, its activities rarely go beyond holding conferences, issuing reports, and providing loose coordination of disaster relief. The last top-level summit took place in the late 2010s and the turn of the century prediction that America would someday ascribe no greater significance to European views or the workings of NATO than to "pronouncements of ASEAN or the Andean Pact"[66] would have come to pass. Now ASEAN is taken more seriously.

2.   Under a second scenario, China has emerged as a global peer economic competitor to the United States and, as noted in Chapter 2, it has steadily increased its military spending and modernized its armed forces. The process of Taiwan's peaceful reintegration further strengthened China's economy as well as its regional military position, as did the departure of U.S. forces from Korea after that country's unification as a neutral state. China's cyber espionage and mercantilist reach into much of Africa, the Middle East, and Latin America continue to frustrate both the United States and Europe, while its cautious internal political opening has encouraged a more assertively nationalist leadership.

Russia has proven a key factor in the balance. For years, critical observers viewed the country suspiciously as the source of a "new Cold War" of economic pressure and military intimidation in its immediate neighborhood.[67] In the context of more competitive Sino-US relations, Russia initially intensified its efforts to bandwagon with the rising China against the United States via the Shanghai Cooperation Organization (a quasi-"association of autocracies"[68]). However, bilateral disputes over energy contracts, military technology, and Chinese migration in Siberia gradually led to greater hedging and balancing between the two. Following the rise of a new generation of reformers into political office, Russia's application for NATO membership received strong support on both sides of the Atlantic. As also noted in Chapter 6, its membership resolved lingering disagreements over missile defense and unblocked the long impasse over other former Soviet states' accession. The extension of mutual collective defense to these new allies also opened the way for cooperative development in information technology as well as energy and mineral resources in the region.[69]

Finally, under a third scenario the Arab Spring of 2011 proved a turning point in world affairs and NATO's evolution. Eventual success for the Alliance's mission in Libya was followed by deployment of a small stability support force to Syria at the request of the post-Assad government, as well as lightly armed peacekeepers along Israeli–Palestinian borders after a surprise breakthrough for a two-state solution. Such unfolding developments energized cooperation with Mediterranean Dialogue and Istanbul Cooperation Initiative partners on energy security, missile defense, and both political and security sector reform, while also inspiring democracy movements elsewhere.

Afghanistan suffered through several more years of violence and instability. By the time most NATO forces withdrew in 2014, improved but still flawed Afghan governing structures and security forces were in place. Ironically, the prospect of deterioration catalyzed greater cooperative engagement by surrounding states with NATO in brokering an enduring political settlement. Chinese and Russian pressure promoted a constructive role from Iran, despite that country's deep differences with the U.S. and NATO on other issues. The experience improved mutual relations among all the countries involved.

The messy, protracted process of adjustment to the Great Recession finally produced a return of steady, widely shared economic growth after 2015. NATO-led countermeasures to "cyber shocks" were credited with averting another, more serious global downturn. Though traditional defense spending has remained below 2 percent of GDP for most European allies, successful steps toward "smart defense" and the shift to unified "international security budgets" (adding intelligence, diplomacy, and development assistance) have boosted comprehensive approaches to security.

An earlier establishment of a Transatlantic Free Trade Area further aided growth and economic ties, enhanced the international influence of the participants,[70] and helped lay the groundwork for a merger of NATO and the EU into the North Atlantic and European Union. This new conglomeration serves as the most active node of a growing network of regional organizations, states, and non-governmental organizations promoting "responsible sovereignty"[71] and democratic good governance around the world. Its "free world"[72] vision has provided a unifying focus and helped its members and partners better address transnational challenges such as epidemic disease, organized crime, and climate change.

Conclusion

U.S. Ambassador to NATO Ivo Daalder's effort to contextualize Secretary Gates' criticisms by reaffirming that "we all need NATO" was compelling. Our "world of complex and unpredictable challenges and threats" calls for a strong, effective Alliance.[73] Yet demand by itself does not guarantee supply. From the standpoint of U.S. commitment to NATO, the scenarios presented above appear in ascending order of desirability but descending order of probability. The first scenario assumes simple adaptation of the NATO "superstructure" to existing base-level trends. The second and third scenarios anticipate more creative leadership on both sides of the Atlantic amidst greater departures in underlying trajectories. For all the reasons discussed in this chapter, marginalization is becoming NATO's default future in American security policy. U.S. belief in NATO remains necessary but insufficient for the Alliance's viability. The future strength of that belief will be determined in large part by internal American developments. It will also crucially depend, however, on European allies' interest and ability to deal with their side of the sources of transatlantic drift and thereby "make the case" for NATO's continued added-value.[74] Absent deliberate effort and luck, cries of "wolf" regarding NATO's future seem finally poised to be right.

Notes

1 The views expressed in this chapter are solely those of the author and do not reflect the official policy or position of the George C. Marshall Center, the U.S. Department of Defense, or the U.S. government.
2 White House, *The National Security Strategy of the United States of America*, May 2010, p. 41.
3 R. Haass, "Continental Drift," *Washington Post*, 19 June 2011. Haass is President of the Council on Foreign Relations.
4 D. Fromkin, "Entangling Alliances," *Foreign Affairs*, Vol. 48, July 1970, p. 688.
5 Available: http://avalon.law.yale.edu/18th_century/washing.asp.
6 J.L. Gaddis, *Surprise, Security, and the American Experience*, Cambridge: Harvard University Press, 2004, pp. 23–24.
7 W. Thies, *Why NATO Endures*, Cambridge: Cambridge University Press, 2009, pp. 95–99.
8 See for example E. Gholz, D.G. Press, and H.M. Sapolsky, "Come Home America: A Strategy of Restraint in the Face of Temptation," *International Security*, Vol. 21, No. 4, Spring 1997, pp. 5–48.
9 C. Krauthammer, "The Unipolar Moment," *Foreign Affairs*, Vol. 70, No. 1, America and the World 1990/91 (1990/1991), pp. 23–33.

10 K. Waltz, "The Emerging Structure of International Politics," *International Security*, Vol. 18, No. 2, Autumn 1993, pp. 44–79.

11 The term hyperpower, or "hyperpuissance," was coined by then-French Foreign Minister Hubert Vedrine.

12 B. Posen, "Command of the Commons: The Military Foundations of U.S. Hegemony," *International Security*, Vol. 28, No. 1, Summer 2003, pp. 5–46.

13 J. Nye, *Soft Power: The Means to Success in World Politics*, New York: Public Affairs, 2004.

14 S. Brooks and W. Wohlforth, *World Out of Balance: International Relations and the Challenge of American Primacy*, Princeton: Princeton University Press, 2008.

15 See R. Kagan, "Power and Weakness," *Policy Review*, No. 113, June/July 2002. Online. Available www. policyreview.org/JUN02/kagan.html.

16 See for example T.V. Paul, "Soft Balancing in the Age of U.S. Primacy," *International Security*, Vol. 30, No. 1, 2005, pp. 46–71 and J. Joffe, *Überpower: The Imperial Temptation of America*, New York: Norton, 2006.

17 F. Zakaria, *The Post-American World*, New York: W.W. Norton, 2008.

18 U.S. National Intelligence Council, "Global Trends 2025: A Transformed World," 2008.

19 A. Krepinevich, "The Pentagon's Wasting Assets: The Eroding Foundations of U.S. Power," *Foreign Affairs*, Vol. 88, No. 4, July/August 2009, pp. 18–33.

20 C. Whitlock, "Pentagon Girds for Deeper Cuts," *Washington Post*, 21 July 2011. The sequestration provision of the Budget Control Act of August 2011 would impose another $500 billion in defense cuts over the coming decade unless alternative deficit reductions were agreed.

21 L.H. Gelb, *Power Rules: How Common Sense Can Rescue American Foreign Policy*, New York: Harper, 2009, p. 230.

22 R.C. Altman, "The Great Crash 2008: A Geopolitical Setback for the West," *Foreign Affairs*, Vol. 88, No. 1, 2009, p. 11.

23 Delegation of the European Union to the USA, "International Aid," 20 September 2010.

24 P. Khanna, *The Second World: Empires and Influence in the New World Order*, New York: Random House, 2008.

25 M. Leonard, *Why Europe Will Run the 21st Century*, New York: Public Affairs, 2005.

26 J. Blitz, "NATO Chief Warns Europe over Defence Budgets," *Financial Times*, 8 February 2011.

27 European Defence Agency, "An Initial Long-Term Vision for European Defence Capability and Capacity Needs," October 2006, pp. 10–12. Online. Available: www.eda.europa.eu/webutils/downloadfile.aspx?fileid=106. See also J. Simon, "The Future of the Alliance: Is Demography Destiny?" in G. Aybet and R. Moore (eds), *NATO in Search of a Vision*, Washington, D.C.: Georgetown University Press, 2010.

28 J. O'Neil and A. Stupnytska, *The Long-Term Outlook for the BRICS and N-11 Post-Crisis*, Global Economics Paper No. 192, Goldman Sachs, 4 December 2009.

29 World Economic Outlook, April 2011. Online. Available: www.imf.org/external/pubs/ft/weo/2011/01/index.htm.

30 A.F. Rasmussen, "NATO after Libya," *Foreign Affairs*, Vol. 90, No. 4, July/August 2011, p. 3. As calculated by the Stockholm International Peace Research Institute.

31 G. Rachman, *Zero-Sum Future: American Power in an Age of Anxiety*, New York: Simon and Schuster, 2011.

32 Pew Research Center for the People and the Press, "Views of Middle East Unchanged by Recent Events, Public Remains Wary of Global Engagement," 10 June 2011. Online. Available: http://pewresearch.org/pubs/2020/poll-american-attitudes-foreign-poilcy-middle-east-israel-palestine-obama.

33 B. Obama "Remarks by the President on the Way Forward in Afghanistan," 22 June 2011. Online. Available: www.whitehouse.gov/the-press-office/2011/06/22/remarks-president-way-forward-afghanistan.

34 The decision represented a return to previous Bush administration plans to withdraw two brigades after an announcement in April 2011 that only one brigade would be withdrawn by 2015. It fell short however of some bipartisan calls in Congress for greater reductions.

35 R. Gates, speech at the United States Military Academy, 25 February 2011. Online. Available: www.defense.gov/speeches/speech.aspx?speechid=1539.

36 R. McGregor, "Hawks Attack Republican Isolationism," *Financial Times*, 20 July 2010.

37 S. Erlanger, "Europe Still Loves Obama, but Doubts Creep In," *New York Times*, 1 November 2009.

38 K. Schake, "The Allies We Need," *The American Interest*, Vol. 6, No. 5, May/June 2011, p. 55.

39 J. Horowitz, "Is the Donilon Doctrine the New World Order?" *Washington Post*, 21 December 2010.

40 The latter three are discussed in more depth in separate chapters in this volume.

41 R. Tiron, "Italy Joins Germany in Fight for Lockheed Missile System," *Bloomberg News*, 19 July 2011.

42 The author benefited from information provided by John Kriendler on this topic.

43 See W. Lynn, "Defending a New Domain: The Pentagon's Cyberstrategy," *Foreign Affairs*, Vol. 89, No. 5, September/October 2010, pp. 97–108.

44 M. Hulbert, "Plea for a Bold Strategic Energy Shift: Brussels Should Bet on Beijing," *European Energy Review*, 11 July 2011. Online Available: www.europeanenergyreview.eu/site/pagina.php?id=3124.

45 A. Michta, *The Limits of Alliance: The United States, NATO, and the EU in North and Central Europe*, Lanham, MD: Rowman and Littlefield, 2006, p. 17.

46 See C. Gati, "Backsliding in Central and Eastern Europe," testimony prepared for the House Foreign Affairs Committee, 25 July 2007. Online. Available: http://foreignaffairs.house.gov/110/gat072507.htm and "The Putinization of Hungary," *Washington Post*, 26 December 2010. Online. Available: www.washington.post.com/wp-dyn/content/article/2010/12/26/AR2010122601791.html

47 See J. Cienski, "The Polish Tiger," *Foreign Policy Dispatch*, 27 May 2011. Online. Available: www.foreignpolicy.com/articles/2011/05/27/the_polish_tiger.

48 R. Asmus, "Europe's Eastern Promise: Rethinking NATO and EU Enlargement," *Foreign Affairs*, Vol. 87, No. 1, January/February 2008, pp. 95–106.

49 W. Clark, *Waging Modern War: Bosnia, Kosovo, and the Future of Conflict*, New York: Public Affairs, 2001, p. 14.

50 E. Larson *et al.*, *Interoperability of U.S. and NATO Allied Air Forces: Supporting Data and Case Studies*, Santa Monica, CA: RAND, 2003, pp. 19, 43–45.

51 B. Obama, Speech at the Ronald Reagan Building, 15 July 2008. Online. Available:www.americanrhetoric.com/speeches/barackobama/barackobamairaqwarreaganbuilding.htm.

52 R. Lizza, "The Consequentialist," *Atlantic Monthly*, 2011. Online. Available: www.newyorker.com/reporting/2011/05/02/110502fa_fact_lizza.

53 For a glass-half-full analysis, see T. Valasek, "What Libya Says about the Future of the Transatlantic Alliance," Center for European Reform, July 2011. Online. Available: www.cer.org.uk.

54 A. Michta, "NATO's Last Chance," *National Interest*, Vol. 6, No. 5, May/June 2011, p. 60.

55 U.S. Department of Defense, "Sustaining U.S. Global Leadership: Priorities for 21st Century Defense," January 2012, p. 6.

56 The term was first used by Karl Deutsch in *Political Community and the North Atlantic Area: International Organization in Light of Historical Experience*, Princeton: Princeton University Press, 1957.

57 S. Walt, "The Ties that Fray," *National Interest*, No. 54, Winter 1998/99, pp. 3–11.

58 See P. Norris and R. Inglehart, *Sacred and Secular: Religion and Politics Worldwide*, Cambridge: Cambridge University Press, 2004.

59 Noted by T. Garton Ash, "The US has Lost its Focus on Europe," *Guardian*, 7 October 2009.

60 T. Valasek, "Central Europe and Obama: Is the Special Relationship Over?" in A.W. Mitchell *et al.* (eds), *Building the New Normal: U.S.-Central European Relations 2010–2020*, Center for European Policy Analysis, May 2011, p. 26.

61 J. Keating, "Romney's Pitch: Obama is a 'European' Leader," the Passport blog of *Foreign Policy* magazine, 2 June 2011. Online. Available: http://blog.foreign-policy.com/posts/2011/06/02/romneys_pitch_obama_is_a_european_leader.

62 W.R. Mead, "The Tea Party and American Foreign Policy," *Foreign Affairs*, Vol. 90, No. 2, March/April 2011, pp. 28–44.

63 "In 1973, forty of the 150 countries (26.7 per cent) in the world were democracies. In 2007, 119 of 193 countries (61.7 per cent) were democracies." M. McFaul, *Advancing Democracy Abroad*, Lanham, MD: Rowman and Littlefield, 2010, p. 58.

64 C. Layne, "From Preponderance to Offshore Balancing: America's Future Grand Strategy, *International Security*, Vol. 22, No. 1, Summer 1997, pp. 86–124. See also Mearsheimer, *The Tragedy of Great Power Politics*.

65 See R. Kaplan, *Monsoon: The Indian Ocean and the Future of American Power*, New York: Random House, 2010.

66 Kagan, "Power and Weakness."

67 E. Lucas, *The New Cold War: Putin's Russia and the Threat to the West*, New York: Palgrave MacMillan, 2008.

68 R. Kagan, *The Return of History and the End of Dreams*, New York: Knopf, 2008.

69 Z. Brzezinski, *The Choice: Global Domination or Global Leadership*, New York: Basic Books, 2004, pp. 101–103.

70 G.J. Ikenberry, "The Rise of China and the Future of the West," *Foreign Affairs*, Vol. 87, No. 1, January/February 2008, pp. 23–37.

71 S. Krasner, "An Orienting Principle for Foreign Policy," *Policy Review*, No. 163, October 2010. Online. Available:: www.hoover.org/publications/policy-review/article/49786.

72 T. Garton Ash, *Free World: America, Europe, and the Surprising Future of the West*, New York: Random House, 2005.

73 I.H. Daalder, "Who Needs NATO? We All Do," *New York Times*, 18–19 June 2011. Online. Available: www.nytimes.com/2011/06/18/opinion/18iht-eddaalder.html (accessed 29 June 2011).

74 T. Valasek, "Central Europe and Obama: Is the Special Relationship Over?" pp. 28–29.

4 NATO enlargement

Close to the end?

Pál Dunay

When taking a look at more than 60 years of NATO history, it is clear that the Atlantic Alliance has been continually concerned with the matter of enlargement. Enlargement has not only been on the minds of the organization's leaders and member state politicians, but has also been a constant feature in political practice. During the last six decades, the number of member states has increased from 12 to 28, i.e., the founding members of NATO now represent the minority in the organization.

This chapter, after a brief presentation of the history of NATO enlargement, will address recent debates and then briefly analyze the prospects for further enlargement. It will deal with the question of whether it is well founded to assume that lessons drawn from the past can be useful for the future of enlargement. Last, but not least, it draws some conclusions for the future of the Alliance in the absence of the contribution that continuing enlargement can make to NATO's legitimacy.

A short history of enlargement

Enlargement, the addition of new members, is part of the external relations of every inter-governmental organization and equally applies to NATO. However, during the Cold War NATO did not have to establish a sophisticated set of relations with other countries. Beyond the member states were the adversaries and the rest of the world. And the rest of the world, with the Cold War focus on Europe, did not matter much. Still, the Alliance enlarged three times during the Cold War. Each enlargement absorbed the external perimeter of NATO, and twice with a clear geo-strategic objective: In 1952 Greece and Turkey joined NATO, both being neighbors of the "eastern bloc." Turkey's accession was of particular strategic importance due to its land and sea border with the Soviet Union and control of the Bosphorus. In 1955 the accession of the Federal Republic of Germany (FRG) demonstrated the irrevocable division of Europe between East and West that formally served as the pretext for the establishment of the Warsaw Treaty Organization in May 1955. The third Cold War enlargement in 1982 brought Spain into the Alliance. This was related more with the democratic transformation of that country than with geo-strategic considerations.

The end of the Cold War resulted in a "non-enlargement enlargement" of NATO. With the unification of the two Germanys, or more precisely with the absorption of the German Democratic Republic (GDR) by the FRG, the territory of NATO increased without an increase in the number of member states. Since then the debate has been continuing, as to whether the West promised Soviet leadership that NATO would not enlarge further East in return for its consent to German unification. The debate has remained inconclusive[1] and increasingly academic as the Alliance has increased its membership three times since the end of the Cold War and will most probably continue to grow modestly.

The external relations of the Alliance, similarly to those of other western institutions when the Cold War ended, started with relatively low-intensity exchanges, with the prime purpose of mutual familiarization. It was essential to be aware of the strategy of the East-Central European countries that were still members of the moribund Warsaw Treaty. Pertinent questions included how much they were committed to democracy, human rights, civilian control, and the democratization and modernization of their armed forces. Exchanges began bilaterally and then moved to multilateralism in late 1991 with the establishment of the North Atlantic Cooperation Council (NACC), a loose forum for exchange that focused on political matters and addressed the concerns of NATO's new partners. It did not contribute to military exchanges. Its multilateral format was a major disadvantage in that partner countries had to address their security concerns in front of other states, on some occasions those states which were the source of the perceived threat. Although the NACC served a useful purpose, allies wished to enhance NATO's increasingly dense and multifaceted relations with partners with a more operational partnership, and it was replaced by the Euro-Atlantic Partnership Council (EAPC) in 1997.

The moment that NATO enlargement became a real possibility, the framework of multilateral exchanges between the Alliance and the applicants became insufficient. In 1993 it was clear that NATO could not give answers to key questions about enlargement. As stated by the German Minister of Defense:

> I cannot see one good reason for denying future members of the European Union membership in NATO ... I am asking myself whether membership in the European Union should necessarily precede accession to NATO. In developing yardsticks for NATO membership, we should not apply rigid criteria. We need to make a clear analysis of common interests, values and political aims.[2]

Germany was supportive of enlargement for reasons of history, geography, and its significant influence in the prime candidate countries. German support was important whereas U.S. support was indispensable. In 1994 some speeches by the U.S. leadership gave early, though not entirely unambiguous, signals of movement in support of enlargement in Washington.[3] In doing so, the Clinton administration also demonstrated its awareness of its responsibility to foster an open debate. Namely, as the U.S. was the most influential player in NATO enlargement, it did not want to make early commitments and hence prejudge the outcome of the (first wave of the) enlargement process. In spite of this, Secretary of Defense William Cohen had reached the conclusion a few weeks before the Madrid NATO Summit that invitations to join the Alliance would be limited to three countries.

In 1993 the U.S. considered that more should be offered to the East-Central European countries that made the most convincing achievements during the transition process. Nevertheless, in the autumn of 1993, Washington was not yet ready for enlargement. Agreement was achieved within NATO to establish a new tailor-made mechanism that would focus heavily on military-to-military contacts, though not necessarily confined to such contacts. "Tailor-made" meant a multi-bilateral mechanism established between NATO, on the one hand, and individual East-Central European countries, on the other. Many in East-Central Europe regarded the offer to launch the Partnership for Peace program as a delaying tactic to postpone decisions about enlargement. The voicing of reservations went so far that the U.S. leadership had to send its then UN ambassador Madeleine Albright and NATO's former Supreme Allied Commander, John Shalikashvili, to tour some of the region's capitals to assuage their concerns.

On the one hand, NATO probably noticed the pressure of the East-Central Europeans (particularly the Czechs, the Hungarians, and the Poles) for membership while, on the other hand, Russian resistance to NATO enlargement remained insufficiently resolute. This allowed the situation to move quickly, and NATO published its enlargement study in 1995 which stressed two key organizing principles. First, NATO did not want to import conflicts and instability into the alliance. Therefore, countries with pending ethnic or external territorial disputes, including irredentist claims or internal jurisdictional disputes had to settle them by peaceful means in accordance with Organisation for Security and Co-operation in Europe (OSCE) principles. Second, enlargement would be decided on a case-by-case basis. The first point meant that the eventual territorial disputes did not have to be resolved by the time invitations to negotiate membership were extended, but the aspirant countries had to convince allies of the promise of a resolution. The second point avoided that the level of preparedness of one candidate would affect the accession prospects of others.

It took another two years before invitations to negotiate accession were extended to the Czech Republic, Hungary, and Poland. It was clear there would be no Eastern enlargement without Warsaw. The Czech Republic, after the separation from Slovakia and under the iconic leadership of President Vaclav Havel, had developed steadily. Although some doubts were raised about Hungary under the conservative government of 1990–94, it would have been difficult to exclude Hungary under the less nationalistic forces that came to power in 1994, particularly for Germany due to Budapest's special role in German unification.

The decision about enlarging NATO was almost exclusively political, with military considerations playing almost no role. However, they did appear at a late stage in the process. Although several estimates were prepared by the RAND Corporation and the Congressional Budget Office concerning the cost of enlargement, the Alliance considered a different set of factors. It estimated the costs and found them minimal for NATO. It focused on the minimum level of interoperability, particularly the ability to host reinforcement by air and on land. In that sense the three countries met the requirement although, as it turned out later, their military preparedness varied considerably and was even lower than had been estimated. NATO immediately drew some conclusions from the first wave of Eastern enlargement for the future. At the Washington Summit of April 1999, a month after the first Eastern enlargement, it adopted the Membership Action Plan (MAP). Its aim was to complement the military-operational aspects of Partnership for Peace for those countries with the prospect of joining the alliance. With the MAP, NATO provided a mechanism to ensure, in a more systematic way, that the aspirant countries had achieved the necessary level of interoperability as well as meeting the non-military requirements for membership. With this, the period of time needed to achieve interoperability could be extended. Part of the process of developing interoperability could take place within the MAP on the way to membership and less would then remain for the post-accession phase.

NATO's first eastern enlargement was a symbolic political act as it demonstrated that the change of political orientation of East-Central European countries was followed by their strategic realignment, in spite of opposition from the outside. This broke the ice. In fact, Russia was opposed to the process that was effectively pushed for by the candidates and actively supported by the Alliance, in particular some of its most influential members. Moscow's opposition remained confined to political stratagems related to its desire to maximize its own benefits for the "concession" it made when it "acquiesced" in Eastern enlargement.[4] Hence, a cost-benefit analysis has demonstrated that (the first wave of) Eastern enlargement was affordable.

With NATO's second eastern enlargement in 2004, its membership increased from 16 in 1989 to 26 in 2005. The major rearrangement of international security concerns, with terrorism taking center stage among threats, put enlargement in a different light. As it would be largely impossible to confine terrorism geographically, it was seen as necessary to build "inclusive" structures, including alliances, to address terrorism. The enlargement of NATO could thus serve this additional purpose, which certainly intensified the support of those allies whose main concern was the threat of terrorism.

Within 15 years, every former so-called Non-Soviet Warsaw Pact (NSWP) country had become a NATO member. This second round included Estonia, Latvia, and Lithuania, reflecting that enlargement could include the former republics of the Soviet Union. Even though Russia continued to dislike NATO enlargement, it was ready to accept a symbolic compensation in the transition from the Permanent Joint Council to the NATO–Russia Council, including the adjustment of the council to one in which Russia was included in equal status to allies.[5] John Kriendler is correct in Chapter 6 to stress that, for Moscow, the NATO accession of Estonia, Latvia, and Lithuania was particularly difficult to accept. Western cooperation in the post-9/11 environment, including recognition that Russia was also fighting terrorism on its own territory, first and foremost in the North Caucasus, softened Russian opposition. Furthermore, and this is regrettably less frequently mentioned, the ease with which President Putin's leadership "accepted" the largest ever enlargement of NATO, including the Baltic states, demonstrated that the power elite may more easily manipulate popular perception in international politics than in those fields where large population groups are directly engaged (like health, social services, or education). The leadership of a country like Russia may decide whether to attribute high political importance to a matter such as NATO enlargement and "play it up" through the media if it is interested in creating controversy or "play it down" if it seeks compromise on the matter. That said, the second round of post-Cold War NATO enlargement went smoothly overall.

The third wave of eastern enlargement addressed some states in the Western Balkans. It was not the first time though, as Slovenia's membership had already broken the mould in the former Yugoslav area. Three states of that region appeared on NATO's agenda: Albania, Croatia, and Macedonia. The accession of the three had been extensively debated and prepared at NATO HQ before it was put on the agenda of NATO's Bucharest summit in April 2008. Although it seemed a routine matter, it turned out to be far more complex. Namely, Greece continued to oppose Macedonia's accession at the summit due to a disagreement on the name of the state. The issue was whether the latter could carry the same name as one of the administrative entities of Greece or should retain the name "the Former Yugoslav Republic of Macedonia (FYROM)" or some other formulation other than "Macedonia." As the problem was not resolved, Greece continued its opposition and was soon supported by then French President Nicolas Sarkozy (who has Greek roots) and a number of other NATO member states. Therefore only two states (Albania and Croatia) were admitted, increasing the number of NATO members from 26 to 28. Macedonia had to be satisfied with the text of the Bucharest summit: "we agreed that an invitation to the Former Yugoslav Republic of Macedonia will be extended as soon as a mutually acceptable solution to the name issue has been reached."[6] Macedonia had no reason to be dissatisfied as the text made clear there was no other reason to deny Macedonia NATO membership than the pending name dispute. The matter, in response to Macedonia's raising the issue, was pending in front of the International Court of Justice.[7] The Court in its judgment concluded that "the Respondent [Greece – P.D.] failed to comply with its obligation ... by objecting to the Applicant's [Macedonia's/FYROM's] admission to NATO at the Bucharest Summit."[8] The inflexible attitude of both parties may disappoint policymakers and analysts who think Macedonian membership would enhance stability in the Western Balkans. At the May 2012 Chicago Summit, NATO reiterated that an invitation would be extended to FYROM "as soon as a mutually acceptable solution to the name issue has been reached within the framework of the UN, and strongly urge intensified efforts towards that end."[9]

The limited strategic importance of this pending matter indicates that the continuation of NATO enlargement in the Western Balkans is not deeply rooted in major strategic considerations. It is more important for a different set of reasons. First, to demonstrate that any state that meets the fairly loosely defined requirements of membership can expect an invitation and this will lead in due time to the completion of enlargement in the zone once identified as *Zwischeneuropa*. This means that NATO continues to live up to its long held promise of an open door policy and will gradually absorb the countries between the eastern borders of Germany and the western borders of the former Soviet Union. Second, the Alliance's policy also demonstrates the understanding that under the current conditions when certain phenomena (terrorism, the potential to gain access to weapons of mass destruction by non-state actors, cyber attacks, etc.) threaten international security far more concretely than some states, the potential advantages of an inclusive alliance are significant. For these reasons, the push to enlarge NATO to include states from the Western Balkans, not least FYROM, Montenegro and Bosnia and Herzegovina, is viewed positively by NATO allies.[10]

It would go beyond the purpose of this chapter to analyze the performance of the states that have joined the Alliance since the end of the Cold War. Nevertheless, a few preliminary conclusions can be drawn. First, politically, the new members have been at the forefront of commitment to the transatlantic nature of NATO, though not without some variation. Namely, new members which prioritized a "classical" (i.e. state-based) threat perception (e.g. Estonia, Latvia, Lithuania, and Poland), and hence relied more strongly upon NATO generally, and the U.S. in particular, to provide for their security, demonstrated a clearer commitment to the Alliance than some others. The overall commitment of new members was tested when they, as members of "new Europe," to use the term of then

U.S. Secretary of Defense Donald Rumsfeld, did not oppose the military operation in Iraq in 2002–03. Second, militarily they have all contributed to NATO's most important mission, in Afghanistan, and also to peace operations in the Western Balkans. As they are small and medium-sized countries, their contribution had to remain limited, similar to many "older" members whose contributions were also limited, as seen from the perspective of the United States. Third, the defense transformation of the new members of NATO has been uneven. This has been partly due to the slow intellectual transformation, dependent first and foremost on generational change within the defense establishment. Technical modernization was also slow partly due to limited available resources, many zigzags in domestic politics, and insistence of governments on prestige projects which have taken resources away from necessary elements of technical modernization.[11] It would be an exaggeration to conclude, however that some new members should either "shape up or ship out."[12] Taken together, the new members contributed to NATO both politically and operationally. Certainly, they understand that membership in the alliance has a "tit for tat" element. Namely, they should contribute to the common efforts even when they do not feel directly affected in order to maintain the necessary solidarity among their allies.[13] In sum, the commitment of new members to NATO exists although it is not backed by daily action in every respect.

Current debates on enlargement

While the attention of NATO decision-makers focused upon the Western Balkans at the 2008 Summit, in fact political interest had already turned to a region that was far more controversial in terms of enlargement, namely the post-Soviet space. A question emerged as to whether NATO should cross the Rubicon and first offer the MAP and then extend invitations to negotiate accession to states in that area.

The 12 newly independent successor states of the former Soviet Union represented a wide variation of governments from illiberal democracy to outright dictatorship. This changed with the so-called color revolutions, and the issue of membership for some of these countries later became a focus of NATO discussions. The issue appeared as two successor states of the former Soviet Union, Georgia and Ukraine, sought to fulfill their aspirations of membership. In the case of Georgia there was no hesitation, whereas Ukraine gave mixed signals. The appearance of Georgia and Ukraine on NATO's enlargement agenda presented some of the basic issues of NATO enlargement in a new light. According to the Washington Treaty the criteria for membership are both substantive and procedural. "The Parties may, by unanimous agreement, invite any other European state in a position to further the principles of this Treaty and to contribute to the security of the North Atlantic area to accede to this Treaty."[14]

As far as the substantive issues are concerned, it is clear that the membership of non-European states cannot be considered. This did not cause any problem in the Cold War decades, as Turkey is at least partly a European state. The question remains open, however, where the borders of Europe lie in the east. It is accepted that the states of the South Caucasus are European, and we live with the double identity of Central Asia (Asian in the UN, European in the OSCE), so it is probable that states which are adjacent to the European part of Russia are European, and those that neighbor it beyond the Urals mountains are not. This would not prevent the accession of Georgia (much less Ukraine) to NATO.

The meaning of "contributing to the security of the North Atlantic area" is also subject to interpretation. It raises three questions. First, is the candidate prepared and ready to contribute to the security of the North Atlantic area? Second, is the Alliance ready to recognize that the candidate would make a contribution to security? Third, is there any external (f)actor that would influence the situation? The candidate may well be able to contribute to security, but if NATO is not willing to recognize that, the candidate's attempt to gain membership will fail. There may be a special situation if both the candidate is ready and the Alliance recognizes its achievements but an external (f)actor influences the situation. Namely if an external power expresses the view that the granting of membership to a candidate would be against its interest to such an extent that it would do its utmost to prevent it. In other words it indicates that it would undermine the potential security enhancement which would derive from granting membership. What should NATO do in such a situation? Grant membership and bear the consequences for the security of the North Atlantic area or stop short of it and give in to the blackmail of the external player? The dilemma is real and far from philosophical. When the Russian Federation expressed its strong opposition to the expansion of NATO to the former Soviet area, the member states took this into consideration, while emphasizing that no external state has a veto on NATO's enlargement decisions.[15]

NATO members represented a span of different views. The Bush administration derived its response from the declarations of the alliance proper, to which it had, of course, made key contributions and with which the U.S. had agreed: the Alliance remained open for accession to every European democracy that wanted to join NATO and met the accession requirements. The views of other members were partly influenced by their relationship with the U.S. and the Russian Federation and much less by the true appreciation of the qualities of the candidates. This is where the third element appears: the need for unanimous agreement. There was clearly no consensus regarding an invitation to Georgia and Ukraine to negotiate NATO accession or even to offer them such a perspective through their admittance to the MAP. Two issues dominated the debate: whether Georgia's and Ukraine's admittance would contribute to security or undermine it; and whether admitting the two countries into the Alliance would send the right or the wrong signal to Moscow. These irreconcilable positions brought about the situation in which the Declaration of the Bucharest Summit stopped short of granting the two countries status, but also spoke unambiguously of the future membership. "We agreed today that these countries will become members of NATO … MAP is the next step for Ukraine and Georgia on their direct way to membership. Today we make clear that we support these countries' applications for MAP."[16]

When taking a closer look at the text, the following is clear: (1) NATO did not offer MAP to Georgia and Ukraine. The opposition of some NATO members effectively blocked the strong preferences of other members, primarily the U.S. and Poland.[17] A decision on MAP was then postponed until the December 2008 meeting of NATO foreign ministers. Bearing in mind that the meeting was scheduled for the period following the U.S. presidential election, it meant that unless it won the election the U.S. Republican administration would be in a comparatively weak position to ask for a favor from its allies. (2) The reference to MAP as if it were the direct path to membership was debatable. On the one hand, the title "Membership Action Plan" indicated that accession can stem from MAP. On the other hand, however, when MAP was introduced at the NATO summit in 1999 the Summit Declaration clearly declared: "Participation in the Membership Action Plan … does not imply any timeframe for any such decision [i.e. on membership – P.D.] nor any guarantee of eventual membership."[18] One can conclude that member states can ultimately decide whether membership is granted to applicants that have been through the MAP process, or not. (3) The delaying of the decision resulted in essence, in further delay: "Both countries have made progress, yet both have significant work left to do … we have decided to provide further assistance to both countries in implementing needed reforms as they progress towards NATO membership."[19] (4) In the time that passed between the Bucharest summit and the meeting of NATO foreign ministers, Georgia and Russia fought a war over South Ossetia and Abkhazia. This situation also demonstrated that Russia had the resolve to take extreme steps in order to prevent an unfavorable change of the status quo in the post-Soviet space. The decision not to move forward on Georgia's membership aspirations raises the issue of whether the "preventive" NATO integration of Georgia could have prevented the war.[20] Would Russia have been ready to fight a war against a NATO member state in its self-declared sphere of influence? Bear in mind, however, that Georgia initiated the hostilities in August 2008 by shelling Tsinvali, although contemplating this does not bring us closer to answering the above question.

Since the heated days of 2008, NATO member states including the most influential one, have behaved more responsibly and avoided raising expectations of membership for Georgia. Raising expectations are not necessarily a bad thing as they may contribute to preparing the international environment for an eventual decision. There is, however, a problem of raising expectations when there is no chance of satisfying them. Expectations generated by the George W. Bush administration on the prospect of Georgian NATO membership were unrealistic, since it was not possible for one ally to make a decision contrary to the carefully calculated interests of others. Since then, the two highly disputed proposed enlargements, those of Georgia and Ukraine, have followed different paths, although their outcomes may well be the same. Georgia continues to pursue NATO membership. In light of the mixed domestic political record of the Georgian government, as well as Tbilisi's continuing conflict with the Russian Federation, it is highly unlikely that the necessary support could be generated within NATO for Georgian membership any time soon. At the Chicago Summit of May 2012 the situation resulted in a very carefully crafted text on Georgia's membership prospect. It continued to emphasize Tbilisi's strategically important contribution, among others "as the second largest non-NATO troop contributing nation to ISAF." It also again reiterated respect for the "territorial integrity and sovereignty of Georgia within its internationally recognised borders." However, the NATO summit declaration also recognized the need for further reform progress and stated that allies "continue to encourage and actively support Georgia's ongoing implementation of all necessary reforms, including democratic, electoral and judicial reform, as well as security and defence reforms. We stress the importance of conducting free, fair, and inclusive elections in 2012 and 2013."[21] The Bucharest promise was repeated.

Ukraine has abandoned its membership aspirations, which were never supported by the majority of its population anyway. With the coming to power of President Yanukovych who (then as prime minister) initiated the suspension of the consideration of Ukrainian MAP status in September 2006, and in light of strong and continuing Russian opposition, it was not surprising that he curtailed Ukraine's NATO membership aspirations. For the time being, Ukraine has given up on this matter, which could not have been realized soon in any case (both due to the lack of support by the Ukrainian population and of NATO member states), and which would have been regarded by Russia as a provocation. Since July 2010 Ukraine has identified itself as "a European non-aligned state."[22] The U.S. Secretary of State commented on this decision:

> Ukraine ... has apparently decided that it is not going to pursue an application to NATO and is not going to join the CSTO either, that it is going to ... remain non-bloc or independent ... That's Ukraine's decision. The doors to NATO remain open, but our point regarding Ukraine was that it should be up to Ukrainians to decide and that no other country should have the right to veto the Ukrainian decision.[23]

Those who believed that the Presidency of Mr. Yanukovych would be characterized by unconditional meeting of Russian requests on a broad range of security issues were in for a surprise. As Zbigniew Brzezinski noted, "When he was in the opposition to Viktor Yushchenko, Yanukovych did everything to thwart NATO exercises in Ukraine. Now that he is president he authorizes them again and in the most provocative manner possible."[24] In sum, it seems that although Ukraine no longer aspires to NATO membership, Kyiv may be the first example of pragmatic cooperation with the Alliance without choosing between East and West.

Scenarios for the future

When analyzing the prospects of NATO and its enlargement our starting assumption is that NATO will continue to exist. This is based on the overwhelming interest of most European member states and the U.S. (despite burden-sharing dissatisfaction) to continue to link the U.S. to European security. Another assumption is that no so-called "black swan" events will affect international security and change the current posture fundamentally. The foundations of international security will not go through a paradigm shift equivalent to the end of the Cold War or 9/11. If these two assumptions hold, there are three options. First, enlargement will regain its centrality in the Alliance and will become (again) a major driving factor of NATO's legitimacy and agility. Second, enlargement will continue until the completion of the accession of the Western Balkan states and will then pause for some time. Third, enlargement will soon stop due to a lack of further credible European candidates and the reluctance of the Alliance to revise the Washington Treaty to make the accession of extra-European states possible. No analysis can claim credibility without identifying the likelihood of different scenarios.

If we extrapolate forward based on current trends, the rest of the Western Balkans become NATO members, but enlargement does not continue to include states from the former Soviet space. There are 54 OSCE states that do not face recognition problems, including the five former Soviet republics of Central Asia.[25] According to the Washington Treaty only European countries may join the Alliance. Hence, in the absence of a revision of the Washington Treaty it is inconceivable that enlargement would extend to another continent as occasionally suggested.[26] If every European country were interested in joining, the number of potential further entrants would be quite high. However, most European states which are not allies are not interested in NATO membership. Some of them have declared various forms of neutrality or non-alignment, like Moldova, Turkmenistan, and Ukraine. Some would not meet the political requirements of membership due to their authoritarian, if not outright dictatorial, political systems.[27] Last, but not least, there are a few states, which would be both interested in membership and would meet the criteria, but circumstances would not facilitate their aspirations.

Hence, the remaining potential candidates for NATO membership are a few states in the Western Balkans and eventually one or two non-aligned western democracies. Whereas some Western Balkan states will certainly represent the next tranche of NATO enlargement, it is far more doubtful that former neutral states would ever seek membership. They were hesitant when the Alliance was in better health than it is today. Bearing in mind the potential candidates, continuation of enlargement will most probably remain a routine matter and will not make major political waves. The Russian Federation, the single most important opponent of NATO enlargement, has feverishly opposed its continuation. It has focused its opposition upon the post-Soviet space so much that it may have inadvertently indicated that it does not oppose NATO enlargement continuing elsewhere, initially in the Western Balkans. Moscow still makes efforts to delay this process and discourage candidates, which have historically felt closer to it than to the West, and position itself for the moment when enlargement will take place. Nevertheless, a limited enlargement extending to states like Montenegro, Bosnia and Herzegovina, Serbia, and Macedonia, and in the very long run to Kosovo, will remain desirable. Those small states are already in NATO's orbit and in the long run they will have a prevailing interest to avoid standing on their own. Enlargement to include them would also help overcome regional divisions. It has to be taken into consideration that the strategically most important non-NATO member in the Western Balkans, Serbia, would have domestic political difficulties in pursuing a NATO integration policy. Serbia was the only European country (or the successor to it) in which NATO actually fought a war, in 1999. However, the May 2012 elections in Serbia have demonstrated that the country's establishment is not anchored in a NATO orientation. It is clear that Belgrade is strongly in favor of EU membership but in light of its history, understandably, remains ambiguous as far as its NATO prospects. How matters such as pending ethnic disputes or external territorial disputes, both mentioned in the NATO enlargement study of 1995,[28] will be taken into account when considering the prospects of accession is a separate issue.

The most optimistic scenario for NATO is accelerated enlargement with the accession of the countries of the Western Balkans followed by several countries in the post-Soviet space, with the prospect of further enlargement in the offing. NATO is unlikely to declare that the enlargement process is complete as such a declaration deprives the Alliance of leverage to influence states that one day may consider accession as an option. It would also be detrimental to delineate the territory that NATO may "absorb,"[29] as this would suggest NATO has given up on certain zones. It would also result in a situation in which Russia, as the main opponent of enlargement, would focus its attention on those states that may one day be in the position to join the Alliance and bring pressure to bear on them. This might take various forms, including the extreme ones demonstrated in 2008.

The most pessimistic scenario for NATO is that those currently interested in membership do not continue their efforts, and some existing members withdraw. This may be compensated by some increased emphasis on partnerships. The centrality of enlargement was conditional on a historical paradigm shift. With the end of the Cold War, the bipolar system dissipated, necessitating an active NATO policy towards its external environment in Europe and, as it turned out later, beyond. The large number of states seeking NATO membership and NATO's initially hesitant and then more and more positive attitude, made the matter central to alliance policy. The importance of the prospect of enlargement, and later accession to the Alliance proper, were important factors of legitimacy for the candidates. It is less often mentioned, if at all, that NATO has also benefited from the constant demand. It was then German Chancellor, Gerhard Schröder who pointed out that the "admission of new members is proof that NATO continues to be attractive."[30] Consequently, there could be mutual interest and potential benefit in the continuation of enlargement. Hence, in the abstract further enlargement of the alliance would be imaginable. Nevertheless, this is an unlikely scenario for two reasons. First, the continuation of the enlargement process would depend on candidates that are able and ready to meet the criteria and whom the Alliance would be willing to take as members. Second, it would require a NATO strategy that attributes strategic significance to enlargement, rather than paying lip service to it. As Ronald Asmus put it, "If the concept of enlargement is not to die, its supporters need to develop a new moral and strategic narrative for why further enlargement still matters and how policies should be modified to fit today's political realities."[31] In the absence of a push from candidates, enlargement may be stalled and eventually there might be member states which become hesitant in their commitments. Even though, for reasons outlined above, it is not likely that members would leave the alliance, enlargement may come to a standstill.

In light of the above three scenarios, and in particular the high likelihood this chapter attributes to the business as usual extrapolation, it is not surprising that it is regarded unlikely that enlargement would continue at a rapid pace or extend beyond the Western Balkans, to the post-Soviet space, or globally. The Russian Federation is held hostage by its own rhetoric and a *volte face* would be very difficult to engineer. Moreover, Russia could not position itself as a pole of a multipolar system if it aligns itself too closely with the West through integration into NATO. Indeed, Russia, as a pole of the multipolar system needs a group of loyal followers and hence will continue to attempt to block any post-Soviet state in practicing its sovereign right to join NATO. Last, but not least, global NATO is unlikely, as the global partners are satisfied with their current level of cooperation; globalization of the Alliance would require the changing of the Washington Treaty and result in a NATO not at all resembling the Alliance as we have known it. Even less, is it likely that the termination of enlargement could be declared? Such a declaration, as outlined briefly above, would be self-defeating for NATO as it would reduce the potential influence of the Alliance. Although ambiguity may not be favored by scholars and analysts, it is often rightly the preferred option of politicians and diplomats.

Conclusions

When measuring the achievements of NATO's eastern enlargement, the question emerges whether it has been a realistic expectation to unite Europe or an illusion pursued at the level of declarations. In the end, we know that the unification of the European security space has been only partly successful. It would be wrong to conclude, however that only the borders of the East-West divide have been redrawn. Namely, much more has happened. Even though European security in some sense remains divided, this division is not characterized by antagonism and confrontation. Actually, there are many areas where all-European security cooperation prevails, including the identification of the main sources of threat and the way to manage many of them.

The eastern enlargement of NATO following the end of the Cold War has effectively contributed to the modernization and Westernization of a large part of East-Central Europe, first and foremost of states, which involuntarily chose "socialism" after World War II. NATO has been part and parcel of the Western perspective. Through integration it helped prevent the renationalization of security that would have resulted in heightened political tension, uncertainty and, last but not least, higher defense spending through the nationalization of defense. NATO membership and its perspective, has also contributed to the transformation of the security sector of those states, many of which had to cope with the Warsaw Treaty legacy. Although NATO enlargement did not change the system, it has certainly contributed to a largely successful transformation of East to West. Enlargement has been a part of NATO history that has also contributed to the post-Cold War legitimacy of the Alliance.

Even though NATO enlargement will continue for some time in the foreseeable future, it will not regain the importance and public attention it had in the 1990s and in the first years of the 21st century. This is due to several reasons. Namely, the list of candidates is short and as far as the states of the Western Balkans are concerned, with the exception of Serbia, NATO integration would not cause any major political controversy and thus would not generate attention. It seems the Russian Federation has effectively "discouraged" NATO from enlarging into the post-Soviet space. This may be disappointing for some as it is a demonstration of a new political division of Europe but also because it demonstrates that the successor states of the former Soviet Union have limited sovereignty. This may also mean that the Brezhnev doctrine of 1968 on limited sovereignty, with certain modification, is again applicable in some parts of Europe. Before jumping to this conclusion, however, it is necessary to emphasize that there was no consensus among NATO member states about extending an accession invitation to any country in the former Soviet area.

Notes

1 M. Kramer, "The Myth of a No-NATO-Enlargement Pledge to Russia," *Washington Quarterly*, Vol. 32, No. 2, April 2009, pp. 39–61.

2 V. Rühe, "Shaping Euro-Atlantic Policies: A Grand Strategy for a New Era," *Survival*, Vol. 35, No. 2, Summer 1993, p. 135.

3 For a reliable account see G.B. Solomon, *The NATO Enlargement Debate, 1990–1997: Blessings of Liberty*, Westport, Conn., London, Praeger, 1998. The study of R.D. Asmus, R.L. Kugler and F. Stephen Larrabee, "NATO Expansion: The Next Steps," *Survival*, Vol. 37, No. 1, Spring 1995, pp. 7–33 was one of the first signs of the changing U.S. attitude.

4 See also Chapter 6 for further consideration of Russian views on NATO enlargement.

5 In the Permanent Joint Council, allies were seated alphabetically without Russia being integrated into the alphabetical order. In addition, allies agreed to an intra-alliance understanding to reach agreement among themselves before addressing issues with Russia. When the Permanent Joint Council was established, allies and Russia were seated in an integrated alphabetical order and the intra-alliance understanding was abandoned. In practice, however it seems that old reflexes prevail on some issues, at least. A Russian diplomat who attended a working group of arms control experts working under the NATO–Russia Council (much after 2002) said he made a presentation and

> was ready to take questions and to participate in the promised discussion. But ... I realized that something strange was happening. High-level experts from all NATO countries were sitting motionless, with their mouth shut as if they were full of water. Then the US representative took the floor ... She asked me to convey ... message to my capital. The chairman declared the meeting adjourned.
>
> V.L. Chernov, "The Collapse of the CFE Treaty and the Prospects for Conventional Arms Control in Europe," in W. Zellner, H-J. Schmidt, and G. Neuneck (eds), *The Future of Conventional Arms Control in Europe*, Baden-Baden: Nomos Verlag, 2009, pp. 186–187.

Let us assume that such structure of exchanges characterized only a certain period of the last decade and that sooner or later the parties will find the framework that is in concord with the underlying resolution.

6 NATO, "Summit Declaration," Issued by the Heads of State and Government participating in the meeting of the North Atlantic Council in Bucharest on 3 April 2008, para. 20. Online. Available: www.nato.int/cps/en/natolive/official_texts_8443.htm?mode_pressrelease (accessed 23 July 2011).

7 Accordingly, the "former Yugoslav Republic of Macedonia" requests the Court to order Greece to

> immediately take all necessary steps to comply with its obligations [... and] to cease and desist from objecting in any way, whether directly or indirectly to the Applicant's [the former Yugoslav Republic of Macedonia] membership of

the North Atlantic Treaty Organization and/or of any other "international, multilateral and regional organizations and institutions of which [Greece] is a member."

The Former Yugoslav Republic of Macedonia institutes proceedings against Greece for a violation of Article 11 of the Interim Accord of 13 September 1995, 17 November 2008. Online. Available: www.icj-cij.org/docket/files/142/14881.pdf.

8 International Court of Justice, Application of the Interim Accord of 13 September 1995 (The Former Yugoslav Republic of Macedonia v. Greece), 5 December 2011, para. 113, p. 38. Online. Available: www.icj-cij.org/docket/files/142/16827.pdf.

9 "NATO, Chicago Summit Declaration," Press Release (2012) 062, 20 May. 2012, para 26. Online. Available: http://www.nato.int/cps/en/natolive/official_texts_87593.htm?mode=pressrelease.

10 "NATO, Chicago Summit Declaration," paras 27 and 28.

11 Suffice to mention that several new NATO member states have purchased multi-purpose aircraft and then had financial and technical difficulties in employing them when it became necessary in the Libya operation of 2011. For example, Hungary, which leased half an air wing of Gripen planes, could not use them in North Africa as the pilots were not trained in air refueling and as the employment of high precision air-to-surface missiles would have been unaffordable.

12 The term was used by Celeste Wallander analyzing the first few years of the performance of some of the class of 1999, first of all Hungary. C.A. Wallander, "NATO's Price: Shape Up or Ship Out," *Foreign Affairs*, Vol. 81, No. 6, November–December 2002, pp. 2–8.

13 A survey conducted by the Atlantic Council in May 2012 asked the question "If you had to kick one country out of NATO which one would it be?" did not confirm that there would be significantly more problem with "new" members than with "old" ones. Namely, 18 percent of the respondents would get rid of Greece, 5 percent of Hungary, 4 of Turkey and 3 of Iceland. There is reason to assume that Hungary lost popularity not due to its performance as a NATO ally but as a country that gained some notoriety recently for its backtracking on democracy. See Atlantic Council, *Foreign Policy Survey: The Future of NATO*. Online. Available: www.acus.org/event/atlantic-councilforeign-policy-survey-future-nato.

14 North Atlantic Treaty, Art. 10. Online. Available: www.nato.int/cps/en/nato-live/official_texts_17120.htm?.

15 Actually, Russian documents reference NATO enlargement more generally. The national security strategy of 2009 highlighted NATO's eastern enlargement, or more accurately, the moving of the military infrastructure of the Alliance closer to Russia's borders, as a primary concern. See Russian Federation, "The strategy of national security of the Russian Federation until 2020 approved by the decree of the President of the Russian Federation on 12 May 2009." Online. Available: www.scrf.gov.ru/documents/99.html. The military doctrine approved in 2010 listed eleven external dangers. Among them "the attempt to give global reach to the military capability of the North Atlantic Alliance (NATO), in violation of international law, to bring the military infrastructure of NATO member states closer to the borders of the Russian Federation, including through enlargement of the Alliance" is noted first. See *Voyennaya Doktrina Rossiiskoi Federatsii*, 5 February 2010. Online. Available: www.scrf.gov.ru/documents/33html.

16 NATO, "Summit Declaration," Bucharest, para. 23.

17 H. Williamson, "Germany Blocks Ex-Soviet States," *Financial Times*, 1 April 2008, p. 4. The same article quotes Georgian President M. Saakashvili as saying "Anything that is not MAP is a great Russian victory." The Polish President also argued for granting MAP to the two states. See L. Kaczynski, "NATO has a duty to embrace Ukraine and Georgia," *Financial Times*, 31 March 2008, p. 9.

18 NATO, "Membership Action Plan (MAP) approved by the Heads of State and Government participating in the Meeting of the North Atlantic Council," 24 April 1999. Online. Available: www.nato.int/cps/en/natolive/official_texts_27444.htm.

19 Final Communiqué, "Meeting of the North Atlantic Council at the level of Foreign Ministers held at NATO Headquarters," Brussels, 3 December 2008, point 18. Online. Available: www.nato.int/cps/en/natolive/official_texts_46247.htm.

20 See R. Asmus, S. Czmur, C. Donnelly, A. Ronis, T. Valasek and K. Wittmann, "NATO, New Allies and Reassurance," *Centre for European Reform Policy Brief*, May 2010, p. 3.

21 NATO, Chicago Summit Declaration, paras 29 and 30.

22 "President Signed Law of Ukraine On the Foundations of Domestic and Foreign Policy," RISU, 15 July 2010, p. 2. Online. Available: www.risu.org.ua/en/index/all_news/state/legislation/36488/.

23 H.R. Clinton, "Remarks," Town Hall at Kyiv Politechnic Institute, Ukraine, 2 July 2010. Online. Available: www.state.gov/secretary/rm/2010/07/143941.htm.

24 Z. Brzezinski quotes Konstantin Kosachev, the chairman of the Duma's Committee on International Affairs. (Event transcript: Conference co-hosted by the Peterson Institute for International Economics, the Center on the United States and Europe at the Brookings Institution and the Atlantic Council, 7 July 2011, pp. 3–4.)

25 These 54 European countries are participating states of the OSCE.

26 The beginning of a "southern enlargement" extending eventually to MENA was highlighted by Russian former ambassador to NATO, Dmitry Rogozin.

27 The two groups have overlapping elements.

28 Study on NATO Enlargement, September 1995, point 6. Online. Available: www.nato.int/docu/basictxt/enl-9502.htm.

29 For such a proposal, see R. Biermann, "NATO Enlargement: Approaching a Standstill," *Security Insights of The George C. Marshall European Center for International and Security Studies*, No. 4, December 2009, p. 1. Online. Available: www.marshallcenter.org/mcpublicweb/MCDocs/files/College/F_Publications/secInsights/SecurityInsights_04_fullsize.pdf. He recommends: "This article proposes a 'package deal' that includes four elements: …A declaration that NATO enlargement has geographic limits and will stop in the Caucasus."

30 G. Schröder, Speech on the 41st Munich Conference on Security Policy, 12 February 2005, p. 2.

31 R.D. Asmus, "Is Enlargement Dead?" The German Marshall Fund of the United States, 10 May 2010, p. 2.

5 NATO partnerships

For peace, combat, and soft balancing?

Graeme P. Herd

1 Introduction

The end of the Cold War had a dramatic impact on NATO. In the London Declaration of 1990, allies recognized the need for building partnerships with former adversaries in order to ensure the security and stability of the Euro-Atlantic area. Allies agreed in London that:

> NATO must become an institution where Europeans, Canadians and Americans work together not only for the common defense, but to build new partnerships with all the nations of Europe. The Atlantic Community must reach out to the countries of the East which were our adversaries in the Cold War, and extend to them the hand of friendship.[1]

Extending this hand of friendship has developed into what some have characterized as a "partner industry," but it has also been one of NATO's most successful post-Cold War policies.

The May 2012 NATO Chicago Summit focused on partnership as one of the three key issues. Among other things, the Summit Declaration noted the key role that partners were playing in Afghanistan. NATO singled out 13 partners, who were invited to Chicago, for special attention, in light of recent significant financial, operational, and political contributions to NATO operations. These included Australia, Austria, Finland, Georgia, Japan, Jordan, Morocco, New Zealand, Qatar, the Republic of Korea, Sweden, Switzerland, and the United Arab Emirates.[2] In addition, meetings were held at the foreign minister level for all aspirant countries. Allies also highlighted the important role that Russia and other partners were playing in facilitating the transition to full Afghan responsibility for security at the end of 2014, ending the largest combat mission in NATO's history. Allies stated that:

> Our cooperation with Russia on issues related to Afghanistan – notably the two-way transit arrangements offered by Russia in support of ISAF,

our joint training of counter narcotics personnel from Afghanistan, Central Asia, and Pakistan, and the NRC (NATO–Russia Council) Helicopter Maintenance Trust Fund in support of a key ANSF (Afghan National Security Forces) need – is a sign of our common determination to build peace and stability in that region.[3]

From the inception of partnership, "regular diplomatic liaison," essentially meetings between NATO officials and Warsaw Pact members, NATO's partnership policies have grown to include the Euro-Atlantic Partnership Council and Partnership for Peace with 50 members (28 allies and 22 partner countries), regional partnerships such as the Mediterranean Dialogue and Istanbul Cooperation Initiative, bilateral partnerships with Russia (addressed in Chapter 6), Ukraine and Georgia, and close cooperation with countries outside these partnerships which contribute to NATO operations. NATO has also developed partnerships with other international organizations such as the UN, EU, OSCE, and African Union, as well as with a myriad of non-governmental organizations (which are dealt with in detail in Chapter 7 on a "comprehensive approach").

The importance of partnership was very clearly reflected in the 1999 NATO Strategic Concept which identified partnership as one of the Alliance's "fundamental security tasks," and described its objectives as "To promote wide-ranging partnership, cooperation, and dialogue with other countries in the Euro-Atlantic area, with the aim of increasing transparency, mutual confidence and the capacity for joint action with the Alliance."[4] Over the last decade, particularly following the accession of the Prague Seven in 2004, issues of how NATO can keep partnerships relevant and useful for the highly diverse partners have remained. The Comprehensive Political Guidance endorsed by NATO Heads of State and Government in Riga on 29 November 2006 called for strengthening and developing relations with partner countries: "to increase NATO's ability to provide practical advice on, and assistance in, the defense and security-related aspects of reform in countries and regions where NATO is engaged."[5] According to the assessment of former Secretary General Jaap de Hoope Scheffer in 2007, the EAPC and PfP "have also helped develop political and institutional interoperability between Allies and Partners" via "an impressive Euro-Atlantic network of political leaders, diplomats, soldiers and civil servants who can speak the same language, work together, and solve problems together." Decisions taken at the 2008 NATO Bucharest Summit were also designed to enhance partnership policies.

The EAPC and PfP have thus "contributed significantly toward a common, Euro-Atlantic, security culture – and most importantly, this culture is built on common values."[6] NATO's 2010 Strategic Concept states that partnership is open to "any nations that share our interest in peaceful international relations" and that NATO is open to consultations with any partner country on security issues of common concern.[7] In the NATO

Lisbon Summit Declaration, NATO signaled its openness to interaction with other international organizations and to develop new relations with "interested countries and organizations."[8] In addition, NATO agreed to promote an enhanced role for partners in "shaping strategy and decisions" for NATO operations to which they contribute. At an April 2011 Berlin ministerial, NATO allies also agreed to provide for enhancements for engaging partners across the globe.[9]

NATO's many partnerships, however, are very different from each other, in terms of membership composition, what kind of a relationship they want with NATO, the degree of institutionalization of the partnership, the resources dedicated to each by NATO – and by the partners – and of course the evolving political context for each partnership. It is clear, to take just one example, that the continuing lack of peace in the Middle East has been a severe impediment to achieving the objectives of the Mediterranean Dialogue, though the Arab Spring and overthrow of the Gaddafi regime in Libya have opened the door for Libya's membership.[10] At the Chicago Summit, allies said they were ready to "welcome Libya as a partner, if it so wishes."[11] Nevertheless, it is fair to say that PfP has been extraordinarily successful in achieving the following:

- in helping countries that wished to join NATO to prepare themselves;
- in enhancing support for, and participation in, NATO-led operations;
- in allowing countries that desired to do so, to draw closer to NATO;
- in drawing in additional assets, training and expertise from certain partner countries;
- in providing forums to address sensitive issues; and,
- in assisting countries to undertake broad reform efforts, including in defense and security reform, which they deemed in their interests.

Other partnerships have made contributions as well.

This chapter will briefly describe the key partnerships, how they have evolved over the last 20 years, the key policy challenges that they are facing and the parameters of the policy debates. It will then consider the degree to which NATO's new partnership policy, agreed upon by allies in June 2011 addresses some of these challenges and what some of the remaining issues are, before considering various scenarios.

2 The evolution of partnerships

Euro-Atlantic Partnership Council

Since the end of the Cold War, NATO has developed a multitude of partnerships with different objectives, members, programs, resources – and different degrees of success. The first of NATO's formal partnership programs was the North Atlantic Cooperation Council (NACC). This was replaced in 1997 by the Euro-Atlantic Partnership Council (EAPC). Both of these provided multilateral mechanisms for consultations on security issues of interest to allies and partners and for practical cooperation. The EAPC was intended to reflect "NATO's desire to build a security forum better suited for a more enhanced and operational partnership, matching the increasingly sophisticated relationships being developed with Partner countries."[12] It is a multilateral forum in which all allies and EAPC members can participate. It addresses a broad range of issues including KFOR (Kosovo Force), ISAF, Iraq, regional security cooperation, and international terrorism, among many others. It also provides a framework for all cooperation activities with EAPC/PfP members. While it has made important contributions to the development of a common security culture, as noted above, it has been criticized as a time-consuming talking shop, and declining interest – by allies and partners – has been reflected in reduced attendance by ministers at ministerial-level meetings. Among suggested solutions were more focused consultations and meetings with interested partners (not all partners) and non-partner contributing nations on topics of particular concern to them.

Partnership for Peace

The flagship partnership, both in terms of wide impact and general acclaim, is Partnership for Peace (PfP) which was established in spring 1994 as a program of bilateral cooperation between PfP countries and NATO. The objectives of PfP, as outlined in its framework document, are:

> facilitation of transparency in national defence planning and budgeting processes; ensuring democratic control of defense forces; maintenance of the capability and readiness to contribute, subject to constitutional considerations, to operations under the authority of the UN and/or the responsibility of the CSCE (Conference on Security and Cooperation in Europe); the development of cooperative military relations with NATO for the purpose of joint planning, training, and exercises in order to strengthen their ability to undertake missions in the field of peacekeeping, search and rescue, humanitarian operations, and others as may subsequently be agreed; the development, over the longer term, of forces that are better able to operate with those of the members of the North Atlantic Alliance.[13]

NATO summits in Prague and Istanbul took a number of steps to further enhance the EAPC and PfP by refocusing it and instituting new mechanisms. An important aspect of the new focus was an increased concentration on the Caucasus and Central Asia; there was also an increased emphasis on defense reform and interoperability. New mechanisms were developed at the Prague Summit in 2002, including IPAP (Individual

Partnership Action Plans). IPAP was intended "to ensure a comprehensive, tailored and differentiated approach to the Partnership"[14] to support the reform efforts of partners without them adopting a Membership Action Plan (MAP). In addition, the Partnership Action Plan against Terrorism (PAP-T), a framework through which allies and partner countries work to improve cooperation in the fight against terrorism through political consultation and a range of practical measures, was adopted. At the Istanbul Summit in 2004, a PAP-DIB (Partnership Action Plan on Defense Institution Building), which aimed to "build democratically responsible defense institutions" was initiated. Both the PAP-DIB and the PARP (Planning and Review Process), which is used to develop and evaluate forces and capabilities which partners could make available to NATO and helps promote effective, affordable, and sustainable armed forces and wider defense and security sector reform, received greater emphasis as tools to enhance defense reform and partnership efforts. In addition, a greater focus on the crucial role of education to enable transformation was stressed.

Once NATO invites interested countries to join the partnership, partners determine for themselves (the principle of self-differentiation) the pace and nature of their cooperation. This is considered one of the secrets of PfP's success. Self-differentiation has allowed some PfP partners to join NATO. Other partners have been able to use NATO's PAP process to receive practical advice on, and assistance in the defense and security-related aspects of reform which they considered to be in their interest. At the same time PfP provided an attractive framework through which the "neutrals" and "non-aligned" could interact closely and associate themselves with NATO while not aspiring to membership.[15]

The current Partnership Cooperation Menu consists of approximately 1,600 activities covering a very broad spectrum, which partners can choose from.[16] PfP has helped countries to democratize, reform their defense institutions and transform their military capabilities, in some cases so they could join NATO, and in others to contribute to NATO-led operations and associate themselves more closely with NATO. Since its inception, allies have developed a variety of tools designed to help achieve these objectives. While these have functioned successfully, they were complex, labor intensive, and not as robust, efficient or flexible as desirable.

Mediterranean Dialogue

The Mediterranean Dialogue (MD) was established in December 1994. Morocco, Tunisia, and Mauritania joined first, followed by Egypt, Israel, and Jordan, with Algeria joining in March 2000. Primarily political, it was intended to promote better mutual understanding and confidence, as well as good and friendly relations across the Mediterranean, and to help correct misperceptions in MD countries about NATO's policies and goals.[17] As with other partnerships, the MD has had both an increasing number and broadened scope of activities available to MD countries if they were interested. The MD reflects the allies' view that security in Europe is closely linked to security in the Mediterranean region and, as with PfP, MD countries are free to choose the extent and intensity of their participation.

Since 1997, high-level meetings – enabling "human interoperability"[18] – between NATO and MD countries have been taking place on a regular basis, and an annual MD Work Program (MDWP) has been established. Currently, the MDWP includes activities in the areas of information, civil emergency planning (CEP), science and environment (SEA), crisis management, defense policy and strategy, small arms and light weapons (SALW), global humanitarian mine action (GHMA), proliferation of weapons of mass destruction (WMD), terrorism, as well as a MD Military Program (MDMP). Political discussions have become more frequent and more intense.[19] In addition, a parliamentary dimension facilitates meetings between the NATO Parliamentary Assembly and MD country parliamentarians.[20]

Despite this progress, continuing conflict and tensions in the Middle East have undermined the MD's ability to achieve the desired objectives. Moreover, Dialogue countries have had different perceptions of what they expect from NATO and have devoted different resources to the process; these factors also help explain the relative underperformance of this partnership.[21]

Istanbul Cooperation Initiative

At the Istanbul Summit in 2004, allies launched a second Middle East initiative, the Istanbul Cooperation Initiative (ICI), which was intended to enhance security and regional stability through a new transatlantic engagement with the broader Middle East.[22] It was seen as complementary to, but distinct from other international initiatives, such as those of the European Union, the G8 or the OSCE. This initiative was offered by NATO to interested countries in the region, starting with the countries of the Gulf Cooperation Council (GCC),[23] to foster mutually beneficial bilateral relationships and enhance security and stability.[24] Of the six Gulf Coast Cooperation Council Members, Bahrain, Qatar, Kuwait and the United Arab Emirates have joined the ICI; Saudi Arabia and Oman have indicated interest.

Despite an active program of bilateral activities focused on the concrete integration of interests between GCC countries, the ICI has suffered from a number of difficulties that have impeded progress. First, GCC members had very different conceptions of what the initiative was and what it could do for them. Some saw it as a grand scheme to resolve all their problems, and for others it was "nothing more than a US presence in sheep's clothing;" that is to say, it was understood as being little more than the "foreign policy arm of the United States."[25] In addition, since it is largely a bilateral rather than multilateral program, it is not clear that it is the right instrument to develop regional cooperation.[26] Professor Abdullah Al Shayji of Kuwait University noted the range of GCC attitudes to the Initiative, including the perception of the ICI as an "imported security framework," which, more than fostering intra-GCC security cooperation, "risks undermining its already overdue achievement."[27] In addition, the current turmoil in the Middle East has complicated the relationship among GCC countries and further inhibited achievement of ICI objectives.

However, even within these two partnership models, two effective mechanisms can at least be identified. First, the adoption of a sub-regional forum and clusters of bilateral approaches can side-step divisive regional sore points. Second, the bottom-up approach based on needs MD and ICI states identify allows, as with PfP, for self-differentiation.[28] Indeed, the Albright Expert Group Report (published ahead of the Lisbon NATO Summit of 2010) offered a full chapter on partnerships and argued that a shift in thinking was needed to obtain optimum value, with new or revised partnership agreements, an expanded list of partnership activities (especially including those that lead to new operational capacities or enhance diplomatic cooperation on specific projects), a greater allowance made for more differentiation, and the modification of procedures to ensure the freest exchange of information.[29]

As noted in the introduction, in addition to the EAPC, PfP, the MD, and ICI, NATO has also developed bilateral partnerships with Russia, Ukraine, and Georgia. In Chapter 6 of this book, the conclusion notes that while the importance of the NATO–Russia strategic partnership is high and will remain so, the relationship is hampered by a trust deficit on both sides that is difficult to overcome. There are a number of sensitive issues upon which disagreement between Russia and NATO appears difficult to bridge by consensus, not least NATO relations with Ukraine and Georgia.

Ukraine's size, population, potential economic strength, military potential, and geostrategic location render it uniquely important, as the Charter on a Distinctive Partnership between NATO and Ukraine signed at the NATO Madrid Summit in 1997 reflects. While in 2002 it signed a NATO–Ukraine Action Plan and indicated its aspirations to join NATO, and in 2005 entered into an "Intensified Dialogue," public opposition to NATO membership, Russian sensitivities and current elite preferences all suggest close cooperation may be possible, but not membership in the foreseeable future. The NATO–Georgia bilateral strategic partnership presents a conundrum. Additionally, as one of the conditions for membership, set out in the 1995 Partnership Study, is to be on the way to resolving ethnic or territorial conflicts with neighbors peacefully, lack of progress on this front would further undermine the prospect of Georgian accession.[30] While its elites and public are ready and willing to join, and its interoperability and commitment to support NATO operations is clear, Russia's very strong objections to inclusion, as well as the strategic consequences of the Russo-Georgia conflict of 2008, all conspire to block Georgian membership in NATO.

3 Key contemporary policy debates

Impetus for reform

The impetus for reform of NATO's partnerships was derived from an overall NATO-wide reform effort to achieve greater effectiveness, efficiency and flexibility related, among other things, to increasing budgetary constraints, as well as issues specific to the partnerships themselves. As allies prepared for the Lisbon Summit they faced the basic challenge of adapting partnership to the changed strategic circumstances, not least the fact that by 2010 12 former PfP/EAPC members were allies and those that remained in PfP were extraordinarily varied in their level of political and economic development, defense reform, military capabilities, in what they wanted from NATO and what they could offer NATO. In addition, the large menu of partnerships had become increasingly unwieldy and difficult to deal with, both for partners and NATO. Another factor was the significantly different levels of institutionalization of the different partnerships and differing degrees of success that could be attributed to each. A key issue, therefore, was whether it would be possible to develop a more cohesive framework while retaining the specificity of each partnership. The decision by the North Atlantic Council in May of 2010 to establish a single committee to manage all partnership issues was a reflection of the effort to achieve greater coherence.[31]

Additional issues concerned the reach of partnership and updating the partnerships to address current security challenges. Some allies, particularly the U.S., feel that the focus of partnerships should be shifted from defense transformation (as an end in itself) to empowering partners who can provide forces for NATO operations (as a means to an end).[32] Secretary of State Hillary Clinton stated on 2 February 2010:

> NATO must also forge deeper partnerships with leading democracies beyond the Euro-Atlantic community. We are already working with many of these nations in Afghanistan. And we must find ways to build on these efforts and encourage more regular cooperation. We have already determined the need for a NATO that can operate at strategic distance. We need to cultivate strategic relationships in support of that goal.[33]

Such thinking recognizes that NATO is no longer self-sufficient – NATO's operational effectiveness is greatly assisted by partner contributions. "Partnerships" are understood to be essential for NATO through the provision of "troops, bases, over flights, intelligence, expertise..." and added political weight.[34] As a result, the U.S. sought to diminish the difference between partners and members by involving partners as much as possible in NATO activities. For example, as U.S. Ambassador to NATO Daalder stated: "while NATO reserves the right to make its own decisions, we also work hard at NATO headquarters to make sure that NATO's partners have a hand in shaping Alliance decisions that affect them."[35]

At his press conference on 15 September 2010, the Secretary General said that among the key axes of discussion in the run-up to the Lisbon Summit were how widely NATO's partnerships should reach and how to ensure they remain effective and practical, not just talk shops.[36] For some allies, the greatest importance of partnership was the participation in NATO-led operations. They therefore attached importance to addressing complaints by non-NATO troop contributing countries about the process of decision shaping for each operation.[37] Virtually from the inception of partnership participation in NATO-led operations, partners have complained about not getting enough information on a timely enough basis to make necessary decisions, particularly in cases where parliamentary oversight was required, and not having their views sufficiently taken into account. While allies appropriately reserve the final *decisions* on such matters to themselves, there has been an increasing effort to provide information to non-NATO troop contributors earlier and to take their views into account in shaping decisions. This was addressed in the 1999 Political-Military Framework for NATO-led operations, but not to partners' satisfaction. Andras Simonyi, former Hungarian ambassador to the U.S. and to NATO, has argued:

> Arrangements must be made for these willing and able partners to have access to NATO planning and intelligence-sharing on a continuous basis. In times of crisis and operation, the availability of these assets should be immediate and full. As much a matter of practicality as symbolism, when NATO builds its new headquarters, Sweden and other allies in this special group should have their offices right next to those of their allies. Perhaps the only difference in their access to NATO's facilities should be the color of the badges they wear.[38]

Another area of concern was finding a way to increase NATO's role in "training the trainers," which is seen as a cost-effective multiplier and a more efficient way to increase the capacity of partners to train others. Allies were also concerned, as already noted, in reforming partnerships to be more responsive to the needs of the Alliance and partners. An important aspect of this was an effort to include partners in NATO's increasing focus on emerging security challenges, for which a new division had been recently established. Another focus was on reforming partnership mechanisms to enhance their effectiveness and efficiency.

In addition, allies recognized the need to address the issue that the Secretary General had raised with regards to global connectivity: how far should NATO partnerships extend and what countries should be included? As noted below, the U.S launched a global partnership initiative in the run-up to the Riga summit in 2006 in an effort to develop an institutionalized framework for cooperation with partners around the world, but consensus could not be achieved on this proposal. A number of red flags had already been waved by both existing NATO members and the wider international community that suggested the reception of such an initiative would be turbulent.[39] NATO members have asked: what of the selection criteria? Is this a partnership of the rich, of the capable, in which democracies are privileged above key players/security providers? Does this result in the creation of a Global Security Network, a Security Providers Forum, or a Global Security Directorate that rivals the UN Security Council (UNSC) for influence? The argument in favor of partners all over the globe prior to the Lisbon summit in 2010 focused on the need for global relationships in order to address global threats, while making it clear that NATO was not and did not aspire to the role of global policeman or for global membership. NATO already had active partnerships with Australia, New Zealand, Japan, the Philippines, Thailand, Pakistan, and South Korea, but it seemed there was a need to increase this to include countries like India, China, and Brazil and to increase trust and encourage transparency.

NATO's new partnership policy (2011)

This impetus for reform placed a focus on the enduring question: what are NATO partnerships for? What do they provide for NATO that NATO cannot obtain otherwise? In the new Strategic Concept adopted in November 2010, allies highlighted the need to develop "a more efficient and flexible partnership policy," and the Summit Declaration noted that the "promotion of Euro-Atlantic security is best assured through a wide network of partner relationships with countries and organizations around the globe. These partnerships make a concrete and valued contribution to the success of NATO's fundamental tasks."[40] It is useful to look briefly at how allies implemented these objectives in the revised partnership policy adopted in April 2011, which will shape partnership for the foreseeable future but also to consider some of the issues which must now be addressed. The new policy consists of three documents: a new policy, a menu of cooperation and individual programs, and a revised political military framework for partners' involvement in NATO-led operations.[41]

The new policy identifies the following strategic objectives for all partnerships, an important innovation. These objectives, without any indication of priority ranking, are to:

1. New Policy
2. Menu
3. Revised PolMil Framework

Enhance Euro-Atlantic and international security, peace and stability; Promote regional security and cooperation; Facilitate mutually beneficial cooperation on issues of common interest, including international efforts to meet emerging security challenges; Prepare interested eligible nations for NATO membership; Promote democratic values and reforms; Enhance support for NATO-led operations and missions; Enhance awareness on security developments including through early warning, with a view toward preventing crises; Build confidence, achieve better mutual understanding, including about NATO's role and activities, in particular through enhanced public diplomacy.[42]

It also identifies a number of priority areas for dialogue, consultation and cooperation with partners, noting that other areas could be added with North Atlantic Council agreement.[43]

Allies also committed themselves to enhancing relations with other "relevant" international organizations, an area that is dealt with in detail in Chapter 7 on the Comprehensive Approach. In another major change which is consistent with the focus on broadening partnerships allies agreed to develop dialogue and cooperation with "any" nation across the globe that shares NATO's interest in peaceful international relations. A further significant change was the agreement to meet in "28+n" formats to focus on issues that could be thematic or event driven, with the North Atlantic Council approving the topic and participants.[44] In an important effort at streamlining and in another significant departure from past practice, allies agreed to develop a single "Partnership Cooperation Menu (PCM)" to be used for all partnerships and they agreed to open two key tools – IPAP and PARP – which had been restricted to EAPC/PfP members, to all partners.[45] Allies also agreed to prioritize the allocation of limited financial resources for partnership objectives, with a detailed set of considerations, starting with whether a partner aspires to join NATO. Although this innovation was foreseen in the founding documents of the EAPC-PfP, implementation of the 28+n formats is still being blocked by different countries (allies) for different reasons.

Finally, allies agreed upon a new "Political Military Framework for Partner Involvement in NATO-Led Operations" to replace the 1999 version. This document establishes a structural role for partners participating in NATO operations that formalized their participating in shaping strategy and decision-shaping from the planning through implementation of operations.[46] Among other things, the policy notes the requirement and provides procedures for consultation, cooperation, and transparency with operational partners and potential operational partners. It also provides a clear mechanism for taking partner views into account before allies make final decisions. In essence the procedure conveys provisional allied decisions to partners, with which partners can then formally associate themselves prior to final allied approval. These procedures are a significant advancement from the previous 1999 framework.[47]

The new policy provides for very significant advances but there are a variety of issues which will need to be addressed as it is implemented, including:

- the impact of resource constraints in the context of making more partnership activities available to more partners;
- a possible lesser commitment to the EAPC-PfP by partners, who may consider that the changes denote a watering down of the EAPC without benefits and framework of a wider and more focused partnership;
- the potential diminished focus on the bilateral partnership (Russia, Ukraine, and Georgia) when they become part of the more unified overall partnership process;
- which additional countries to include as partners; and,
- which international organizations allies will consider "relevant" as cooperation partners and what criteria will be used for the decisions. Is the Shanghai Cooperation Organization (SCO) relevant? The Cooperative Security Treaty Organization (CSTO)?

Thus, in 2011 NATO adopted an overall approach that applies to all partnerships. The implementation of this new partnership policy, with its far reaching changes, will be complicated, and additional policy issues are sure to arise. It is unclear which policy issues were difficult to reach agreement on and how consensus was reached on these difficult decisions. Constructive ambiguity and compromise must have been exercised. The decision by the North Atlantic Council (NAC), for example, to establish a single committee to manage all partnership issues cloaks the reality that while there is now one committee, it meets in six configurations, with different chairmen and different agendas.

Another possible future policy debate may well focus on the mismatch between the kind of internal systemic and structural sources of insecurity facing partner MD and ICI partner states, and the confidence building measures NATO partnerships are designed to provide. The Middle East and North Africa regions are characterized by relative deprivation – the gap between high expectations and diminishing opportunities – and uneven resource distribution governed by the logic of religious, ethnic, gender, or tribal allegiances and animosities. This is an agenda which concerns human and societal security concerns, best addressed through broad development policies – an agenda that NATO partnerships do not address.

4 Alternative scenarios

Given that the future pathway NATO pursues will shape the nature of NATO partnerships, their role and function, and vice versa; how partnerships evolve will affect how NATO develops, it is pertinent to pose the question: where is NATO heading? This is not easy to answer with any confidence, though it is possible to identify the extremes of the debate that unfold in the media, academia, policy, and practitioner circles. Counterintuitive outcomes may be possible and are difficult to ignore as they factor into any analysis. A first scenario that extrapolates from the present suggests that the future of partnerships will be marked more by continuity than change. A second scenario suggests that NATO's bilateral and regional partnerships will go global in order to undertake necessary crisis management operations and preserve the Global Commons, and so extend U.S. primacy. A third scenario suggests that NATO's regional and bilateral partnerships will seek to balance China in Central, South, and East Asia, a process driven as much by allies as by new partners.

A first scenario is to suggest that the future will in effect represent an extension of the present, reflecting more continuity than change, particularly in regard to gaps and blockages between what heads of states agree to at a policy level, commit themselves to rhetorically, and what is actually implemented in the practice of partnerships. If we extrapolate forward, then we would expect to see the same evolutionary trends in partnership over the next two decades as we have seen over the last two – that is, continuity in differentiated attitudes of allies and Partners towards Partnership, continuity in gradual incremental broadening of membership and partnership tools, and, the creation of new partnership programs and bilateral partnership relations.

According to this logic, NATO member state attitudes to partnerships would continue to be varied, governed by different expectations as to what partnerships can offer NATO. NATO member states which tend to be heavily involved in NATO operations (for example, the U.S., Canada, France, Netherlands, and UK) would look more at the utility of partnerships through this prism, placing a greater emphasis on global partners and perhaps institutionalizing a global partnership program. The same would continue to be true of partners – what partners want from NATO partnership will continue to be varied, ranging from viewing partnership as a stepping stone to full NATO membership, through to partnership as a means to other ends, such as strategic alignment with NATO and/or the U.S. through support for NATO operations, or partnership as a means to enhance ongoing internal defense and security sector reform efforts. Existing partnerships will incrementally broaden memberships (for example, Libya as a MD partner), and create additional partnership tools, with Individual Partnership Action Plans focused, for example, on border security or environmental security as this rises in strategic importance.

NATO could also slowly extend bilateral partnership relationships with key states outside of the Euro-Atlantic region, not least China, India, Pakistan, South Africa, Brazil, and Australia.

A second scenario would envisage NATO's cooperative security role being much more fully developed, with expanded global bilateral and regional partnerships enabling the management of shared threats. NATO would become the default global crisis management instrument of choice and so create additional partnership programs to facilitate UN-mandated operations to manage regional flashpoints. An "Addis Abbaba Initiative" focused on the Horn of Africa or the "Kampala-Kinshasa Dialogue," centered on the Great Lakes, might include Ethiopia, Kenya, Uganda, Tanzania, and South Africa as members, but also Ghana and Nigeria to give breadth.

A third scenario suggests that in response to the logic of power-shifts to China and growing interdependence and competition for finite energy resources and raw materials, NATO utilizes existing and creates new regional partnerships to balance China in Central, South, and East Asia. Here, the expectation is that China will exhibit behavior classic of other rising powers in the past. As noted in Chapter 1, Sino-U.S. competition may well be inevitable, as evidenced today by the rapid expansion of Chinese military, particularly naval, capability. States in East and South Asia would seek to balance China through stronger partnership agreements with NATO. Enhanced support for NATO operations (first humanitarian, then military) and even increased demands for membership, should soft balancing fail, would constitute a natural progression. Under such conditions, NATO crisis management operations would not be UN mandated. Regional partnerships would thus become as much political instruments to legitimize operations as militarily useful. This consideration would influence the composition of partnerships, suggesting *realpolitik* interests as much as normative compatibility will shape partnership memberships. Under such circumstances, for example, the NATO–Russia bilateral partnership would be much stronger, with a shared common strategic purpose – balancing China – forging enduring ties.

5 Conclusions

NATO's experience with partnership over the past dozen years has produced a mixed record of success and failure. Of course, it is simplistic and analytically dangerous to place all of NATO's partnerships under one microscope for scrutiny, as the PfP, MD, and ICI initiatives, NATOs partnerships with International Organizations, as well as bilateral relationships (Russia, Ukraine, and Georgia) all differ from one another in many respects. NATO will indeed need partners in the future for success, and it will continue to need different partnerships to achieve different Alliance objectives, as will the partners themselves. The prudent path for the

Alliance to take is to build in flexibility and achievable and practical goals into these partnerships, to treat each case on an individual basis, and to carefully select partners in the first place. This fluid and flexible approach holds the best promise for the future of a dynamic and relevant 21st century military alliance. This suggests that business as usual will be the order of the day, with an evolutionary approach to expanding partners and partnership programs, and implementation gaps between policy agreement and evidenced implementation.

Notes

1 NATO, "Declaration on a transformed North Atlantic Alliance issued by the Heads of State and Government participating in the meeting of the North Atlantic Council ('The London Declaration')," 6 July 1990. Online. Available: www.nato.int/docu/basictxt/b900706a.htm (accessed 31 October 2011). For an excellent recent addition to the meager literature on NATO partnerships, see H. Edström, J. Haaland, J. Matlary and M. Petersson (eds), *NATO: The Power of Partnerships*, Basingstoke: Palgrave, 2011.

2 U.S. Department of State, White House, Office of the Press Secretary, 21 May 2012.

3 NATO, "NATO Summit Declaration," Issued by the Heads of State and Government participating in the meeting of the North Atlantic Council in Chicago on 20 May 2012, Chicago Summit, 20 May 2012. Online. Available: www.nato.int/cps/en/natolive/official_texts_87593.htm.

4 NATO, "The Alliance's Strategic Concept, Approved by the Heads of State and Government participating in the meeting of the North Atlantic Council," Washington D.C., 23–24 April 1999. Online. Available: www.nato.int/cps/en/nato-live/official_texts_27433.htm (accessed 31 August 2011).

5 NATO, "Riga Summit Declaration," Issued by the Heads of State and Government participating in the meeting of the North Atlantic Council in Riga, 29 November 2006; Summit NATO–Russia Council [NRC], 28 May 2002. Online. Available: www.nato.int/docu/comm/2002/0205-rome/rome-eng.pdf. (accessed 20 August 2011). One proposal worth noting in passing was to revise Article 10 of the NATO Charter to allow a range of democratic states – from Argentina, Brazil, Australia, Brazil, New Zealand, Japan, and South Korea – to become NATO members, given that "global threats cannot be tackled by regional organizations." This "Alliance of Democracies" concept never gained traction and should not be confused with subsequent global partnership (rather than membership) initiatives. See I.H. Daalder and J. Goldgeier, "Global NATO," *Foreign Affairs*, September/October 2006, pp. 105–113.

6 Jaap de Hoop Scheffer, NATO Secretary General, Keynote address at EAPC Security Forum, Ohrid, 29 June 2007. Online Available: www.nato.int/docu/speech/2007/s070629b.html (accessed 1 August 2007). See also "If we sustain the momentum of our partnership policy, it can be a major strategic tool for coping with 21st century challenges." Jaap de Hoop Scheffer, "Speech given at 43rd Munich Conference on Security Policy," 10 February 2007. Online. Available: www.nato.int/docu/speech/2007/s070209d.html (accessed 20 August 2011).

7 "Active Engagement, Modern Defence," Strategic Concept for the Defence and Security of the Members of the North Atlantic Treaty Organization, Lisbon, 19 November 2010, para. 30. Online. Available: www.nato.int/lisbon2010/strategic-concept-2010-eng.pdf

8 NATO Lisbon Summit Declaration, Issued by the Heads of State and Government participating in the meeting of the North Atlantic Council in Lisbon, Press Release (2010) 155, 20 November 2011. Online. Available: www.nato.int/cps/en/natolive/official_texts_68828.htm?mode=pressrelease (accessed 20 August 2011).

9 NATO, Meeting of NATO Foreign Ministers, Berlin, Germany, 14–15 April 2011. Online. Available: www.nato.int/cps/en/natolive/official_texts_19552.htm (accessed 20 August 2011).

10 A.F. Rasmussen, NATO's Secretary General, has stressed the need for a "free, democratic and stable" outcome in Libya. He argues that NATO core values are "freedom, democracy and human rights" and that the intensification of political dialogue and new partnerships in North Africa are distinctly possible outcomes. A.F. Rasmussen, "NATO and the Arab Spring," *International Herald Tribune*, 2 June 2011, p. 6. See also A.F. Rasmussen, "NATO After Libya: The Atlantic Alliance in Austere Times," *Foreign Affairs*, Vol. 90, No. 4, July/August 2011, pp. 2–6.

11 NATO, Chicago Summit Declaration, para. 43.

12 NATO, "The Euro-Atlantic Partnership Council (EAPC)." Online. Available: www.nato.int/cps/en/natolive/topics_49276.htm (accessed 29 August 2011).

13 NATO, "Partnership for Peace: Framework Document," January 1994. Online. Available: www.nato.int/cps/en/natolive/official_texts_24469.htm (accessed 1 September 2011).

14 NATO, "Prague Summit Declaration issued by the Heads of State and Government participating in the meeting of the North Atlantic Council in Prague, Czech Republic," 21 November 2002, para. 7. Online. Available: www.nato.int/cps/en/natolive/official_texts_19552.htm (accessed 5 September 2011).

15 For a recent survey of such interaction, see M. Andrey, "Security Implications of Neutrality: Switzerland in the Partnership for Peace Framework," *Connections: the PfP Quarterly*, Vol. 9, No. 4, 2011, pp. 83–96.

16 NATO, "The Partnership for Peace Programme." Online. Available: www.nato.int/cps/en/natolive/topics_50349.htm (accessed 1 September 2011).

17 A.M. Rizzo, NATO Deputy Secretary General, Keynote address at conference on "NATO's Aims and Actions for the Mediterranean Dialogue and the Broader Middle East Region," Amman, Jordan, 26 June 2006. See also NATO, *Upgrading the Mediterranean Dialogue including on inventors of possible areas of cooperation*, official document approved at Prague Summit of NATO Heads of State and Government, November 2002. Online. Available: www.nato.int/meddial/2003/mdwp-2003.pdf (accessed 20 August 2011).

18 A.M. Rizzo, "NATO's Transformation and New Partnerships: The Mediterranean," *Mediterranean Quarterly*, Vol. 18, No. 3, p. 12. See also C. Mushi, "NATO's Mediterranean Dialogue: More than Just an Empty Shell," *Mediterranean Politics*, Vol. 11, No. 3, November 2006, pp. 419–424.

19 NATO, "A More Ambitious and Expanded Framework for the Mediterranean Dialogue," Policy Document, Istanbul Summit, pp. 28–29 July 1994. Online. Available: www.nato.int/docu/comm/2004/06-istanbul/docu-meddial.htm (accessed 20 August 2011).

20 In May 2005 the status of "Associated Mediterranean Delegation" was granted to Algeria, Israel, Jordan, and Mauritania. See A. Benantar, "NATO, Maghreb and Europe," *Mediterranean Politics*, Vol. 11, No. 2, July 2006, p. 170.

21 C. Donnelly, "Forging a NATO Partnership for the Greater Middle East," *NATO Review*, Spring 2004, p. 1. Online. Available: www.nato.int/docu/review/2004/issue1/english/art3_pr.html (accessed 20 August 2011). See also A. Benantar, "NATO, Maghreb and Europe," pp. 173–174.

22 NATO, "Istanbul Cooperation Initiative," Policy Document, NATO Istanbul

Summit, 28–29 July 2011. Online. Available: www.nato.int/docu/comm/2004/06-istanbul/docu-cooperation.htm (accessed 20 August 2011).

23 GCC members are Bahrain, Kuwait, Oman, Qatar, Saudi Arabia, and UAE.

24 NATO, "Istanbul Cooperation Initiative," para. 3.

25 NATO, STOPWATCH 2, "Bridging the Mediterranean, Special Interactive Video Forum series with Jamie Shea," 12 March 2005. Online. Available: www.nato.int/docu/speech/2005/s050311a.htm (accessed 20 August 2011). See also Mushi, "NATO's Mediterranean Dialogue," p. 424.

26 A. Sager, "The Gulf and NATO: Time to Revisit Relations," *NATO Review*, December 2008. Online. Available: www.nato.int/docu/review/2008/08/NATO_GULF_RELATIONS/EN/index.htm (accessed 31 December 2008).

27 "8–9 October 2008 – Report: Seminar in the UAE," NATO Parliamentary Assembly, Mediterranean and Middle East Special Group. Online. Available: http://natopa.ibicenter.net/default.Asp?CAT2=0&CAT1=0&CAT0=578&SHORTCUT=1655 (accessed 12 November 2008).

28 C. Donnelly, "Forging a NATO Partnership for the Greater Middle East," pp. 26–30.

29 NATO, *NATO 2020, Assured Security: Dynamic Engagement*, Analysis and recommendations of the group of experts on a new strategic concept for NATO, 17 May 2010, p. 23. Online. Available: www.nato.int/strategic-concept/expertsreport.pdf (accessed 20 August 2011).

30 NATO, Study on NATO Enlargement, September 1995, point 6. Online. Available: www.nato.int/docu/basictxt/enl-9502.htm (accessed 5 September 2011).

31 NATO, *NATO 2020, Assured security: dynamic engagement*, p. 22.

32 A.F. Rasmussen, Secretary General NATO, "First NATO Press Conference," 3 August 2009. Online. Available: www.nato.int/cps/en/natolive/opinions_56776.htm (accessed 20 August 2011).

33 H.R. Clinton, "Remarks at the NATO Strategic Concept Seminar," 22 February 2010, Washington, D.C. Online. Available: www.state.gov/secretary/rm/2010/02/137118.htm (accessed 20 August 2011).

34 J. Shea, in J. Ringsmose and S. Rynning (eds), *NATO's New Strategic Concept: A Comprehensive Assessment*, DIIS: Danish Institute for International Studies Report 2011: 02, p. 28.

35 I.H. Daalder, *Looking to Lisbon*, Ecole Militaire, Paris, 18 October 2010. Online Available: http://nato.usmission.gov (accessed 1 November 2010). See also I.H. Daalder, "A New Alliance for a New Century" (Commentary), *RUSI Journal*, Vol. 155, October–November 2010, pp. 6–10. Online. Available: http://photos.state.gov/libraries/lithuania/331079/pdf/Ivo%20Daalder%20-%20A%20New%20Alliance%20For%20A%20New%20Century.pdf.

36 A.F. Rasmussen, Secretary General NATO, "Monthly Press Briefing," 15 September 2010. Online. Available: www.nato.int/cps/en/SID-BCD82CEB-83B4AF4B/natolive/opinions_66220.htm (accessed 24 September 2010).

37 "Australia has consistently been the largest non-NATO contributor to ISAF and the 10th largest contributor overall. This more than entitled us to be heard and our views to be respected." K. Rudd, "NATO Partners Earn Respect," *The Australian*, 23 April 2011, p. 10. Online. Available: www.foreignminister.gov.au/articles/2011/kr_ar_110423.html.

38 A. Simonyi, "A Case for Overhaul of NATO's Partnerships; Organization should Seek Links with Capable Nonmembers," *The Washington Times*, 11 April 2012, p. 4.

39 Zbigniev Brzezinski, for example, warned that a global NATO would dilute and undermine the centrality of NATO's special transatlantic identity: Z. Brzezinski, "An Agenda for NATO," *Foreign Affairs*, Vol. 88, No. 5, September/October 2009, pp. 2–20.

40 NATO, "Lisbon Summit Declaration," Issued by the Heads of State and Government participating in the meeting of the North Atlantic Council in Lisbon, Press Release (2010) 155, 20 November 2011. Online. Available: www.nato.int/cps/en/natolive/official_texts_68828.htm?mode=pressrelease (accessed 20 August 2011). For a Russian perspective, see "Russia-NATO: After the Lisbon Summit," *International Affairs: A Russian Journal of World Politics, Diplomacy and International Relations* [serial online], Vol. 57, No. 2, March 2011, pp. 156–167.

41 NATO, "Policy for a more efficient and flexible partnership," PO(2011)0124, adopted 12 April 2011; "Improving the Management of our Partnerships – Menu of Cooperation and Individual programmes," Annex 1, PPC-M(2011)0024, adopted 12 April 2011; "Political Military Framework for Partner Involvement in NATO-Led Operations," PO(2011)0141, adopted 13 April 2011.

42 NATO, "Policy for a more efficient and flexible partnership," para. 4.

43 To paraphrase paragraph 5, these include: political consultations on regional issues, especially crisis prevention and management; cooperation in NATO-led operations and missions; defense reform in all aspects; counter-terrorism and -proliferation of WMD and their means of delivery; emerging security challenges, including related to cyber-defense, energy security and maritime security/counter-piracy; civil emergency planning. Allies agreed to further develop all existing partnerships while preserving their specificity with all partners to be offered deeper political and practical engagement, including consultations on topics of particular concern to them and developing policy approaches to common challenges. There is also a heightened focus on support for defense education, training and capacity building, "within existing resources." NATO, "Policy for a more efficient and flexible partnership."

44 J-J. de Dardel, *Whither the Euro-Atlantic Partnership? Partnership and NATO's New Strategic Concept*, Geneva Paper 10, pp. 35–36.

45 NATO, "Improving the Management of our Partnerships – Menu of Cooperation and Individual programmes."

46 NATO, "Political Military Framework for Partners Involvement in NATO-Led Operations."

47 NATO, "Political Military Framework for Partner Involvement in NATO-Led Operations."

6 NATO–Russia relations

Reset is not a four-letter word

John Kriendler[1]

Developing a reliable partnership with the Russian Federation has been one of NATO's highest priorities since the Cold War ended and remains high on the agenda as reflected in the Chicago Summit Declaration of 21 May 2012: allies reiterated their goal of a "true strategic partnership" with Russia.[2] As the Cold War ended, it was obvious that building security and stability in the Euro-Atlantic area would be much easier with Russia on board as a democratic, prosperous, stable country, positively engaged with NATO and the international community, and that few problems could be solved without Russia. As Dimitri Trennin noted, from the end of the Cold War the West understood that Russia was in a category by itself due to its nuclear weapons, its unbroken "great-power mentality," and its size.[3] Other factors that make it essential to engage Russia include its importance on the international stage, including its UN Security Council veto, its wealth and energy resources, the role it can play as an ally in combating terrorism, and its relationships with Iran and Pyongyang.[4] But if the imperative to cooperate was clear, like so many other issues on NATO's crowded agenda, allies had and still have significantly different views about Russia. Russia has proven to be a complicated interlocutor, and the results of these protracted efforts have been mixed.

Historical context and characteristics

NATO's interest in moving rapidly beyond Cold War hostility was reflected in Secretary General Manfred Woerner's July 1990 visit to Moscow to convey the Alliance's message of friendship and his personal support for enhanced cooperation,[5] and in NATO efforts to encourage the Soviet Union to join the North Atlantic Cooperation Council (NACC), predecessor to the Euro-Atlantic Partnership Council (EAPC), in 1991 and Russia to join Partnership for Peace (PfP) in 1994. NATO and Russia successfully put in place the institutions and mechanisms for cooperation. The Founding Act on Mutual Relations, Cooperation and Security between NATO and the Russian Federation, signed in Paris in 1997, expressed a joint commitment to build a lasting and inclusive peace in the Euro-Atlantic area and established the Permanent Joint Council (PJC). It provided on consultations virtually any issue that NATO and Russia wanted to discuss and on practical cooperation in a wide variety of issues. But the Permanent Joint Council did not meet either NATO or Russian aspirations and was suspended after the Kosovo air campaign; it was eventually replaced in 2002 by the NATO–Russia Council (NRC). Although there were various ups and downs, the relationship bottomed out with the Russian invasion of Georgia in August 2008, but then rebounded at the Lisbon Summit.

In considering the ups and downs of NATO–Russia relations, it is useful to focus on a number of key issues which remain important today and which will impact the evolution of NATO–Russia relations in the future. The full list of issues is a long one and many are interrelated, but some are of secondary importance or have faded. From the Russian perspective, key issues which have divided Russia and NATO include disappointment when NATO did not expire soon after the Warsaw Pact; NATO's involvement in the former Yugoslavia, including air attacks on Bosnia-Herzegovina in 1995 and the Kosovo crisis in 1999, which resulted in a Russian-imposed freeze on NATO–Russia relations; NATO enlargement, particularly the second echelon membership of the Baltic states; the 1999 Strategic Concept which highlighted NATO's role to ensure stability and security in the Euro-Atlantic Region; and Baltic air policing. From the NATO perspective, key concerns include Russia's failure to withdraw forces from Georgia and Moldova pursuant to the 1999 OSCE summit; its use of oil and gas as a political "weapon;" the suspension of Russian participation in the Treaty on Conventional Forces in Europe (CFE); the Russian–Georgian conflict; Russian recognition of and subsequently the increased Russian military presence in Abkhazia and South Ossetia; the decline of democracy in Russia; and less than desired cooperation on Iran. In addition, of course, Cold War stereotypes held and, in some cases, fostered on both sides impeded improvements in the relationship.

The intended basis for the development of a strong and durable partnership between NATO and Russia was the Founding Act signed in Paris in 1997, which expressed a joint commitment to "build together a lasting and inclusive peace in the Euro-Atlantic area on the principles of democracy and cooperative security" and established the NATO–Russia PJC.[6] NATO and Russia endorsed a broad range of topics for consultation and practical cooperation and joint action where there was agreement. The Founding Act also contained the three "nos:" the allies reiterated that they had "no intention, no plan and no reason to deploy nuclear weapons on the territory of new members . . . and do not foresee any future need to do so." They also stated that they had no plans for nuclear weapon storage sites in those states. But the PJC did not work; it did not fulfill the expectations or either NATO or Russia and Russia suspended participation following the initiation of the Kosovo air campaign.

President Putin's prompt offer of support for the U.S. war on terrorism following 9/11 triggered a process intended to "launch ... a new era in NATO–Russia cooperation" and a "qualitatively new relationship." By agreeing the Declaration on "NATO–Russia Relations: A New Quality," in Rome on 28 May 2002, NATO and Russia entered into a "second marriage."[7] They established the NRC, which replaced the PJC and which was to provide "a mechanism for consultation, consensus-building, cooperation, joint decision, and joint action for the member states of NATO and Russia on a wide spectrum of security issues in the Euro-Atlantic region."[8] In a variety of ways intended to give the relationship a new lease on life, the NRC differed significantly from the PJC. It met with 20 (now 29) members, rather than 19 plus Russia (19+1), so that Russia was on an equal status with allies. In addition, the Intra Alliance Understanding by which allies had previously agreed to reach common positions before discussing issues with Russia in the PJC was abandoned, although this obviously does not preclude allies consulting, in some cases in detail, on NRC issues. As former Secretary General Lord George Robertson optimistically described these changes, the difference between 19+1 and 20 was not one of mathematics but one of chemistry.[9] In fact, according to allied participants in both the PJC and NRC, the difference was one of "night and day."[10]

And there was progress in some of the areas of cooperation,[11] which allies and Russia identified and which included the struggle against terrorism, crisis management (peacekeeping), non-proliferation, arms control and confidence-building measures (CFE, open skies, nuclear experts' consultations), theatre missile defense, search and rescue at sea, military-to-military cooperation, defense reform, civil emergencies, new threats and challenges, scientific cooperation, cooperative airspace management, logistics, and a NRC pilot project for counter-narcotics training.[12] Of particular interest was Russian support for NATO-led operations as described by former Secretary General Jaap de Hoop Scheffer in early 2006: "[A]ll NATO's missions and operations since the launching of the NATO–Russia Council have been receiving either active or passive support from the Russian Federation."[13] And Russian soldiers had been engaged in NATO-led crisis response operations for more than seven years in the Balkans. Former U.S. Ambassador to NATO Victoria Nuland described successful practical cooperation between NATO and Russia and military-to-military contacts as the "untold story" which had an enormous impact on a whole generation of military offices.[14]

Despite these successes, it is fair to describe the NATO–Russia "partnership" as "ambivalent and incomplete," with the sharp break in relations following the Russo-Georgian War of August 2008 as the nadir of the relationship. While pronouncements of a new Cold Peace (or even at its most extreme a new Cold War) soon subsided, by 2011 and on the 20th anniversary of the ending of the Cold War, hostile historical legacies continue to influence contemporary perceptions and shape key contemporary NATO–

Russia policy debates. Vladimir Putin's return to the Presidency, bellicose rhetoric during the March 2012 elections and subsequently, and continuing sharp differences about NATO Ballistic Missile Defense have cast doubts on the U.S.–Russia and NATO–Russia resets and the future of NATO–Russia cooperation.[15]

Key current policy debates and drivers

The rationale for the U.S.–Russia and NATO–Russia resets was simple: relations had fallen to a post-Cold War low after the Russo-Georgian conflict, and there was a clear need to address issues of mutual interest without abandoning deeply held values or compromising relations with countries with whom Russia has difficult relations. Both the areas of common interest and those where there are significant differences are broad and many of the issues are interrelated, for instance, missile defense and arms control. As it would be overly ambitious to address all of the important policy debates and drivers, this chapter focuses on five sets of issues: areas for cooperation, enlargement, missile defense, Georgia and domestic political and economic developments in Russia. There are, of course, other important issues, but the above will all be with us for a long time and will have a direct impact on the evolution of NATO–Russia relations.

Areas for cooperation

To accentuate the positive and also reflect the logic behind the U.S. and NATO reset efforts, it is useful to start with areas where NATO and Russia have agreed that similar views and challenges make cooperation highly desirable – if not necessary. From the outset, in the Founding Act, NATO and Russia agreed to seek to cooperate in a wide range and number of areas, such as responses to civil disasters, military-to-military cooperation, cooperation in combating terrorism, nuclear safety, and submarine rescue, among others. Russian support for NATO-led operations in the Balkans was already noted above.

In endorsing at the Lisbon Summit the Joint Review of 21st Century Common Security Challenges, Russia and NATO agreed to undertake practical cooperation in a number of areas including Afghanistan; counter-narcotics; non-proliferation of weapons of mass destruction and their means of delivery; counter-piracy; counter-terrorism; and disaster response.[16] Many of these are areas which the PJC and NRC had in fact been focusing on. At Lisbon, NATO and Russia agreed to specific initiatives to advance cooperation in these areas, not least arrangements to facilitate ISAF transit arrangements. Successful cooperation can help address common challenges and build a more solid foundation of trust.

Enlargement

From the first mention of enlargement, the Soviet Union and then the Russian Federation were very unenthusiastic, and NATO's continued enlargement and the prospects for further enlargement have been a key and persistent irritant in NATO–Russia relations. As former NATO official Chris Bennett has written, "Dealing with Russia to avoid an anti-Western backlash and contribute to relations with Russia as a partner was one of the most difficult challenges of the enlargement process."[17] For NATO, enlargement was seen as making a major contribution to security and stability in the Euro-Atlantic area and, in the view of Ronald Asmus, a former senior Clinton administration official and architect of the NATO's enlargement policy, "Enlargement has created more democratic stability on Russia's western border than at any time since Napoleon."[18] But Russia certainly did not see it that way.

No less an expert on Russia than George Kennan, writing in 1997, said NATO expansion would be "the most fateful error of American foreign policy in the entire post-Cold War Era." Kennan based his argument on the notion that

> such a decision may be expected to inflame the nationalistic, anti-Western and militaristic tendencies in Russian opinion; to have an adverse effect on the development of Russian democracy; to restore the atmosphere of the cold war to East-West relations, and to impel Russian foreign policy in directions decidedly not to our liking.[19]

In addition to the loss of face and influence that enlargement engendered, Russia's negative reaction was rendered more acute by the perception that the U.S. and Germany had provided assurances that NATO would not extend further East[20] and rejection of Gorbachev's ideas about a pan-European security institution or suggestion of Soviet membership of NATO.[21]

Many Russian analysts argue that NATO should have followed the Warsaw Pact into disbanding and certainly should not have expanded to include states of the former Soviet Union. They saw NATO enlargement as designed to weaken and marginalize Russia.[22] President Yeltsin's angry outburst in response to the 1994 decision to undertake an enlargement study was evidence of continuing Moscow opposition to enlargement. Russia eventually learned to live with its discontent with the 1999 and 2002 rounds of enlargement. Although Russian opposition to the accession of the Baltic States was acute, it was nothing like the opposition caused by Ukrainian and Georgian progress towards NATO membership. Efforts to grant Ukraine and Georgia Membership Action Plan status, seen as a necessary stepping stone on the way to membership, at the Bucharest summit, and then agreement by allies that Georgia and Ukraine "will" become allies provoked strong Russian opposition. In the view of some analysts, Russia's successful provoking of Georgia in 2008 was intended to end Georgia's progress towards NATO membership, as it did. Evidence of the persistence of Russian concern about NATO enlargement was contained in the "Military Doctrine of the Russian Federation 2010," which identifies NATO as a

> military danger, specifically the "striving" to ascribe global functions to the force capability of NATO, implemented in breach of international law, and bringing the military infrastructure of NATO member countries closer to the borders of the Russian Federation, including by means of enlarging the bloc.[23]

And in any case it appears that Russian concern about enlargement has abated, in a statement in mid-June 2011, Russian Ambassador to NATO Dimitri Rogozin said "The war in Libya means the end of the alliance's eastward enlargement and the beginning of the southward enlargement."[24]

Missile defense

Measured by the vehemence of the Russian response, missile defense is another key driver of NATO–Russia relations. As Gustav Lindstrom has addressed the issue of developing Adaptive Missile Defense in detail in Chapter 11 of this volume, this chapter will focus on the Russian reaction: the obstacles to reaching agreement, why missile defense cooperation is seen in the West as a "game changer," and prospects for agreement.

Russia retains heightened Soviet sensitivity to anything it perceives as potentially undermining its strategic offensive capabilities and shifting the strategic balance. This concern has been accentuated by the continuing decline in Russian conventional military capabilities. As former Secretary of Defense William Gates noted, Russia has "a long history of hostility and wariness about missile defense."[25] The rationale for this sensitivity is that U.S. missile defense efforts are seen as part of a global system "to neutralize the offensive strategic potential of other nuclear powers, 'especially Russia.'"[26] A variety of bellicose statements threatening to target allied countries which hosted U.S. missile defense elements, to station short-range missiles in Kaliningrad, and to undertake a new arms race if a separate NATO system were developed which did not include Russia reflected this concern. In June 2004, President Putin reportedly threatened to take "retaliatory steps" in response to US missile defense plans, including "new targets in Europe" and a return to the Cold War era of hair-trigger confrontation.[27] President Medvedev later stated that the Kremlin sees a missile shield as a threat to Russian security[28] and, later, that Russia would install mobile Iskander missiles around Kaliningrad and use radio jamming equipment against the Western missile defense system.[29] These concerns were also reflected in language which Russia insisted be included in the preamble of the New START Treaty focusing on

> the existence of the interrelationship between strategic offensive arms and strategic defensive arms, that this interrelationship will become more important as strategic nuclear arms are reduced, and that current strategic defensive arms do not undermine the viability and effectiveness of the strategic offensive arms of the parties.[30]

Russia has been hesitatingly cooperating with NATO in the field of Theater Missile Defense (TMD) since consultations began in 1998. Already in 2000, President Putin proposed a joint system along the lines of what Russia is now supporting. The focus was on bridging gaps in technical standards and developing operational doctrine, an experimental TMD concept and a concept of operations to pave the way for possible future joint deployment. Cooperation was limited, however, by Russian interest in obtaining as much information as possible but not providing much in return. In any case, this limited cooperation did little to assuage Russian concern with the Bush administration's "third site" initiative,[31] which was to consist of ten silo-based long-range interceptors located in Poland, re-location of a narrow-beam, midcourse tracking radar from the U.S. Pacific test range to the Czech Republic, and fielding an acquisition radar focused on the Iranian threat from a forward position to provide detection, cueing, and tracking information.[32] The initial Russian reaction to the Obama Administration's European Phased Adaptive Approach was more positive as Gustav Lindstrom describes it, but cooled over time. Russian Ambassador to the U.S. Sergei Kislyak said in mid-2010 that "The new formula of the U.S. does not raise our old concerns. There is slightly more clarity and stability in the military sphere close to our borders."[33] But the old concerns had not been abandoned, and at a subsequent NATO–Russia Council meeting, Defense Minister Serdyukov was reported to have said that the NATO system would "neutralize Russia's strategic capabilities."[34]

In assessing progress in missile defense cooperation and the obstacles to progress, it is important to keep in mind the circumscribed nature of the agreements reached between NATO and Russia at the Lisbon Summit. While allies had agreed to "actively seek cooperation on missile defence with Russia,"[35] in the NRC Joint Summit Declaration, NATO allies and Russia agreed only "to discuss pursuing missile defence cooperation" and to resume Theatre Missile Defence Cooperation.[36] A report on how to cooperate in missile defense and progress was due at the June 2011 NRC meeting of Defense Ministers, but Secretary Gates noted limited progress: "While I had hoped we would be ready to move ahead on this subject in the NATO–Russia Council, it is clear that we will need more time."[37]

U.S. and NATO officials have repeatedly described the missile defense cooperation with Russia as a "game changer," and there would be obvious advantages if cooperation were achieved: increased transparency and better understanding of missile defense motivations, strengthened regional stability, increased dissuasion from proliferation, deploying or using ballistic missiles, leveraging of technical capabilities in NATO allies and Russia, and building a strategic partnership against a common threat. In addition to developing more effective ballistic missile defense capability for both NATO and Russia, Secretary General Rasmussen noted that

> Missile defence cooperation can create a virtuous cycle. It can help us to build the confidence and trust to tackle some of the more difficult issues in our relationship. It provides a unique opportunity for us to build greater security and stability across the entire Euro-Atlantic area. And it could lead to a sea-change in the way we look at our relations.[38]

From the Russian perspective, missile defense is seen as a "test" of NATO's willingness and ability to cooperate with Russia.

Despite these advantages, there are serious obstacles to ballistic defense cooperation. The most important is that Russia and NATO have contradictory visions on what such cooperation should entail. NATO has proposed separate systems which would allow cooperation in exchanging early warning information tracking data and assessments and even coordinating responses. Russia, on other hand, advocated a joint missile defense system in which Russia would be an equal participant with NATO, an approach that NATO has repeatedly rejected. Subsequently Russia sought agreement on a treaty which would provide "legal guarantees" that NATO would not be the target of Russian missiles, as well as detailed limitations such as "the maximum amount and types of interceptor missiles, their speed as well as locations for missiles and radars" which should be spelled out in the treaty.[39]

Hopes that agreement on missile defense cooperation would be achieved in time for the Chicago Summit, which President Putin could then attend, were not realized, and the Russian reaction to NATO Ballistic Missile Defense (BMD) became more acrimonious. As anticipated, NATO declared interim operational capability for its BMD system but also noted that if the threat, which was explicitly not Russia, diminished, plans for the NATO system could be adapted.[40] allies also repeated their commitment to missile defense cooperation with Russia, including establishment of a joint Missile Defense Data Fusion Center and a joint Planning Operations Center. Increasing Russian pressure on NATO missile defense efforts was reflected in: (1) General Nikolai Makarov's statement at a missile defense conference in Moscow prior to the Chicago Summit that Russia could carry out pre-emptive strikes on NATO missile defense bases, and (2) the successful test of a new Russian long-range missile on 23 May designed, the press reported, to improve its capability to penetrate NATO missile defenses.[41]

Georgia

Because it was the proximate cause of the worst drop in NATO–Russian relations, which still roil and will for the foreseeable future, it is important to understand the repercussions of the 2008 Russo-Georgian conflict. As on so many other issues, allies had different perceptions of what happened and how to respond, which framed the responses that allies agreed on. The depth of NATO concern was reflected in the decision by NATO foreign ministers on 19 August supporting the sovereignty and territorial independence of Georgia and stating that further ties with Russia would be dependent on Moscow making good on a pledge to pull its troops back to pre-conflict positions in Georgia. Furthermore, allies suspended meetings of the NRC, reaffirmed that Georgia could one day join the alliance,[42] and, on 27 August 2009, condemned Russia's decision to recognize the South Ossetia and Abkhazia regions of Georgia and called upon Russia to reverse its decision. As further evidence of support, in September 2008, during a visit to Tbilisi, Secretary General de Hoop Scheffer and NATO Ambassadors established the NATO-Georgia Commission.[43]

The Russian reaction included ending military cooperation with NATO and an announcement by Russian Ambassador to NATO Dmitry Rogozin that Russia would not participate in peacekeeping operations with NATO for six months, would suspend participation in Partnership for Peace, and would delay sending its chief military representative to NATO.[44] President Medvedev said that Moscow was ready to break with NATO,[45] and recalled Ambassador Rogozin "for consultations." Interestingly, Rogozin said Russia was not planning to cease its cooperation with NATO for transit of non-lethal materiel for ISAF. Medvedev emphasized that NATO needs Russia more than Russia needs NATO, and it would be "nothing frightening" if the Western alliance were to sever all ties.[46]

Western insistence on restoration of Georgia's territorial sovereignty and territorial integrity, and Russia's continuing efforts to conclude state-to-state agreements with Abkhazia and South Ossetia, refusal to fully implement the 2008 Ceasefire Agreement, events on the ground, and the lack of progress in the Geneva talks highlight the likelihood of difficulties that these issues are likely to cause for the foreseeable future.[47] From the standpoint of NATO–Russia relations, however, the fact that Georgian membership in NATO is dead in the water, also for the foreseeable future, at least removes that irritant.

While the Chicago Summit was explicitly not an "enlargement" summit, Georgia figured importantly at Chicago. It attended all the configurations of partner meetings at Chicago, including a meeting of aspirant country foreign ministers with Secretary of State Clinton, and was the focus of two substantial and largely positive paragraphs in the Summit Declaration which, among other things, reiterated that Georgia would join NATO.[48]

Democracy and modernization

The Founding Act provides that NATO and Russia will build "a lasting and inclusive peace in the Euro-Atlantic area on the principles of democracy and cooperative security." In addition, Russia and NATO agreed to base their relations on a commitment to a number of principles including "acknowledgement of the vital role that democracy, political pluralism, the rule of law, and respect for human rights and civil liberties and the development of free market economies play in the development of common prosperity and comprehensive security."[49] Unfortunately, "sovereign democracy" as practiced in the Russian Federation differs fundamentally from Western conceptions of democracy, and the trend lines for democratic governance in Russia go in the wrong direction. As Fred Hiatt described it in July 2010,

> Inside Russia, meanwhile, Putin has constructed a system without room for real political opposition, and the state continues to narrow the space for independent action. Most recently, the last arena of contested elections in municipalities is being curtailed, and Medvedev is steering through parliament a law that further strengthens the successor to the KGB.[50]

Despite decreased Western public emphasis on Russian governance issues, concerns about the state of democracy in Russia are and will remain a continuing irritant to relations between NATO and Russia.

Another facet of the Russian domestic scene, economic weaknesses and the related drive for modernization, provide significant impetus to improving relations with the West in general and with NATO allies in particular. Russia was particularly hard hit by the economic crisis, with significant declines in the value of the ruble, foreign direct investment, industrial production, employment, stock market values, and GDP.[51] Moreover, Russian dependency on energy and commodity prices, problems with Russia's energy and transportation infrastructure, and a high level of corruption have all been recognized as serious problems.[52] Although Russian leaders reacted very negatively to Vice President Biden's July 2009 criticism of Russia's failing economy, corrupt banking system and backward looking leadership, Russian leaders have echoed some of these concerns, including President Medvedev. On 10 September 2009 President Medvedev published an article entitled "Russia, Forward!" in which he criticized Russia's "humiliating" dependence on raw materials, as well as its "inefficient economy, a semi-Soviet social sphere, an immature democracy, negative demographic trends, unstable Caucasus."[53] In more recent remarks, in Saint Petersburg, on 17 June 2011, which Prime Minister Putin subsequently endorsed, Medvedev emphasized the need to "move quickly to reform and modernize [Russia's] economy and decentralize political power from the Kremlin."[54]

If pursued, the drive to reform and modernize would place a premium on cooperation with the West which could provide the investment capital and technology that Russia needs. With the new Russian government dominated by Putin loyalists, Medvedev's push for reform is likely to be constrained, and it is not clear to what degree modernization will continue to be emphasized.[55] Moreover, the U.S. Department of State's Human Rights report for 2011, released on 24 May 2012, highlights serious human rights problems including violations of democratic processes, issues related to the administration of justice, and limitations of freedom of expression among many others.[56] It is by no means clear that the new Russian administration will be disposed to address these and other human rights issues.

Possible futures for NATO–Russia relations

The evolution of a large number of complex, interrelated variables will determine how NATO–Russia relations evolve; weighing the possible evolution of these variables and their likely impact is immensely difficult. The following three scenarios are hopefully "coherent, credible stories about alternative futures"[57] which can provide useful strategic insights. The first scenario is predicated on the notion of strategic dissonance: although NATO and Russia agree on the strategic threats, consensus as how best to address these threats is lacking. The second scenario suggests that not only do NATO and Russia identify the same strategic threats, but there is general agreement on how these threats might best be cooperatively addressed – strategic alignment is the outcome and a move towards integration. The third scenario centered on increased hostility suggests strategic divorce as the outcome: NATO and Russia can neither agree on identified strategic threats nor the means to address them.

The first scenario is the most likely and offers a combination of continued progress in a number of areas but little in others, resulting in essential stasis in the relationship, and is underscored by the assumption that NATO–Russian relations reflect underlying structural tensions in Russia-Euro-Atlantic relations, rather than vice-versa. In light of the clear benefits to Russia of a stable Afghanistan and increased counter-narcotics efforts there, one could expect that Russian cooperation in U.S. and ISAF transit would continue as long as required, as described above. Continuation of cooperation in other areas highlighted in the Joint Review of 21st Century Common Security Challenges (detailed above) would be another positive factor.

Improved Russian governance could result from the re-election of President Putin in the March 2012 elections and could impact positively on

NATO–Russia relations. However, in the view of some observers, in particular Andrew Monaghan of the NATO Defense College, whoever is elected is unlikely to bring about major change in Russian domestic or foreign policy in the short or medium term because of the emergence of a unified team with essentially similar views and also because decisions are so poorly implemented.[58] In any case a continuing denial of the right to free, fair, and competitive elections would diminish western trust and the likelihood of enhanced NATO–Russia relations.

From the Russian perspective, continued emphasis on NATO's open door policy is likely to be only a minor irritant as prospects for Georgian integration in the near or mid-term are dim. Concerning Ukraine, despite reports of serious Ukrainian-Russian differences and of Ukrainian interest in significantly increased cooperation with NATO, no change in Ukraine's non-block policy can be anticipated.[59] Continuing emphasis on the fact that Georgia "will" become an ally and Ukraine, too, if it were to decide it wanted to, will remain as irritants. A lack of a Russian commitment to resolving the unresolved conflicts of Nagorno-Karabakh or Transnistria and consequent lack of progress would further sour the relationship. Also on the negative side, agreement on deepened cooperation on missile defense would appear unlikely in light of the substantially mutually contradictory natures of the NATO and Russian proposals and the continuing sensitivity of the issue for Russia. This will contribute to continuing distrust on the part of Russia.

The second scenario is the most favorable and would result in significant benefits for NATO, Russia, other Euro-Atlantic partners and beyond. In light of Russian concerns about its southern flank and for increased counter-narcotics trafficking efforts in Afghanistan, Russian assistance in Afghanistan, in particular with transit of ISAF materiel and personnel, is likely to increase. Assuming that training and materiel will continue to be provided to the Afghan National Army and Police, this cooperation will remain important as ISAF transitions to Afghan responsibility for security. In addition, if NATO and Russia reach agreement on cooperative missile defense, which would assure substantial technology, information, and intelligence transfer to Russia and possible joint consideration of responses to ballistic missile attacks, while retaining NATO's full autonomy and freedom of action to protect allies, such cooperation would have a significant impact on a range of other issues. Further benefit would derive if Russia increased its present role in seeking resolution of the unresolved conflicts in Moldova and Nagorno-Karabakh. In addition to other areas, increased cooperation could be expected in counter-terrorism, counter-narcotics, non-proliferation, counter-piracy, and disaster response, where there are broad common interests. Although unlikely to lead to any significant agreement, allies could discuss in detail Russian proposals for a European Security Treaty.

The increased trust resulting from the cooperation described above, could also lead to efforts to reach an agreement with Georgia on a settlement that would recognize Georgian sovereignty in Abkhazia and South

Ossetia while providing for extensive autonomy for both regions. Russian concern about China could be another factor that would engender greater cooperation with NATO. Obviously, Russian success in obtaining a satisfactory agreement in Libya, which it has offered to try to broker would be a significant step forward, both for NATO objectives in Libya and NATO–Russian relations. The Russian approach, however, has been critical of NATO. In response to a question about a UN resolution for Syria, President Medvedev responded, "I am not ready to support … a dead-ringer for Resolution 1973 on Libya, because I am firmly convinced that a good resolution was turned into a scrap of paper to cover up a pointless military operation."[60]

Another positive development would be an indication by allied heads of state and government that Russia could become a NATO ally if it wished to do so, met all the requirements for membership, and if all allies were in agreement. The issue of Soviet/Russian membership has arisen a number of times since the start of "Khrushchev's thaw" in 1954, when the Soviet Government proposed entry into NATO and the signing of a collective security treaty.[61] In 1995 Russia said if there was enlargement, Russia should be the first member; then shifted views.[62] On the other hand, while indicating opposition to NATO enlargement in a statement in early 2005, President Putin said that that Russia could not join NATO because to do so would threaten its sovereignty and restrict its freedom of action.[63] More recently, when the issue has arisen, U.S. officials and the NATO Secretary General said they did not rule Russian membership out if it sought membership, met the requirements and all allies agreed, but Russian authorities said they were not interested.[64] On 29 July 2010, Secretary Clinton is reported to have said that "if Russia wants to join, and meets the qualifications for joining, NATO's door is open."[65] If the U.S.–Russian and NATO–Russian "resets" continue to be successful, the idea attributed to Michael McFaul, one of President Obama's top Russia advisers and recently nominated to be the new U.S. Ambassador to Moscow, of offering Russia a path toward NATO membership, could attract support, despite the likelihood that Russia would reject the offer.[66] When queried about possible Russian membership in a mid-May 2011 Newsweek interview, the Secretary General said, "We haven't seen an application from the Russian side and I don't think we will."[67] A perspective of integration could address continuing Russian concerns that it is excluded from the role and influence it merits in Euro-Atlantic Security institutions.

The third scenario is the most negative. It assumes increasingly sharp differences on key issues, declining trust, lack of cooperation even on issues where cooperation is imperative and an increasingly hostile and acrimonious relationship. This would pose serious problems for NATO for a variety of reasons, such as the need for Russian cooperation to address important transnational issues, including Afghanistan; Russia's influence as a permanent member of the UN Security Council; and increasing European dependence on Russian energy resources, among many other issues.

The major factors that could contribute to this scenario, some of which have been touched on above, include:

- Continuing progress on NATO missile defense and lack of progress in missile defense cooperation between NATO and Russia;
- Threats or actual withdrawal by Russia from the new START treaty;
- Lack of progress in other arms control negotiations including those dealing with non-strategic nuclear weapons;
- Lack of progress in moving towards some modus operandi with Georgia;
- Continuing Russian dissatisfaction with the present European security architecture;
- Withdrawal of Russian support for Afghanistan transit;
- Continuing Russian violation of accepted norms of democracy governance, the rule of law and basic human rights;
- A neo-imperial foreign and defense policy;[68]
- A revived government campaign of anti-American and anti-NATO rhetoric;
- Worsening Russian relations with Ukraine and Ukrainian interest in a closer relationship with NATO;
- Continuing resentment and suspicion of Russia by NATO allies.

Conclusions

While speculation about the future is a treacherous endeavor at best, there are some conclusions about NATO–Russia relations that can be made with confidence. The importance of Russia and of NATO–Russian cooperation will not diminish. The trust deficit, on both sides, remains high and will not be easy to overcome. NATO and Russia will continue to disagree on a number of sensitive issues. Allies will continue to have significantly different views about issues related to Russia, and it will continue to be difficult to reach agreement by consensus. Russia is and will remain a difficult partner and divining Russian intentions will continue to be a very difficult task. Both the U.S. and NATO will continue to seek improvement in their relations with Russia, which were better but clearly require further essential improvement.

Notes

1 The views expressed in this chapter are those of the author and do not reflect the official policy or position of the George C. Marshall European Center for Security Studies, the Department of Defense, or the U.S. Government.
2 NATO, "NATO Summit Declaration: Issued by the Heads of State and Government participating in the meeting of the North Atlantic Council in Chicago on 20 May 2012," Chicago Summit, 20 May 2012, para. 36. Online. Available: www.nato.int/cps/en/natolive/official_texts_87593.htm.

3 D. Trennin, "Russia Leaves the West," *Foreign Affairs*, Vol. 85, No. 4, July/August 2006, p. 87.
4 See J. Collins and M. Rojansky, "Why Russia Matters: Ten Reasons Why Washington Must Engage Moscow," *Foreign Policy*, August 2010. Online. Available: www.unc.edu/world/2011Seminars/Why_Russia_Matters.pdf (accessed 19 June 2011).
5 R. Hendrickson, "Manfred Woerner: NATO's Visionary," *NATO Review*, Autumn 2004.
6 NATO, "Founding Act on Mutual Relations, Cooperation and Security between NATO and the Russian Federation," signed in Paris, France, 27 May 1997. Online. Available: www.nato.int/cps/en/natolive/official_texts_25468.htm (accessed 19 June 2011).
7 NATO, "NATO–Russia Relations: A New Quality," Declaration by Heads of State and Government of NATO Member States and the Russian Federation, 28 May 2002. Online. Available: www.nato.int/cps/en/SID-7FFC1EC0–7FB6DEA1/natolive/official_texts_19572.htm (accessed 19 June 2011).
8 NATO "NATO–Russia Relations: A New Quality."
9 Summit NATO–Russia Council [NRC], 28 May 2002. Online. Available: www.nato.int/docu/comm/2002/0205-rome/rome-eng.pdf.
10 Author's interview with NATO official.
11 "Council on Foreign Relations NATO At 60 Symposium: Session II: NATO, Russia AND Eastern Europe," Transcript, 26 February 2010.
12 Briefing by NATO official September 2006.
13 Press conference by NATO Secretary General Jaap de Hoop Scheffer following the meeting of the NATO–Russia Council, 10 February 2006. Online. Available: www.nato.int/docu/speech/2006/s060210c.htm (accessed 10 Feb 2006).
14 Council on Foreign Relations, "NATO at 60 Symposium: Session II: NATO, Russia and Eastern Europe." Online. Available: www.cfr.org/nato/council-foreign-relations-nato-60-symposium-session-ii-nato-russia-eastern-europe/p18692 (accessed 28 June 2011).
15 See for example: A. Racz, *Good Cop or Bad Cop: Russian Foreign Policy in the New Putin Era*, Transatlantic Academy, Analysis, January 2012; "Russia and NATO: Rethink the Reset," *The Economist*, 19 May 2012; A.C. Kucins and I.A. Zevelev, "Russian Foreign Policy: Continuity and Change," *The Washington Quarterly*, Winter 2012, pp. 147–161.
16 NATO, Lisbon Summit Declaration, para. 19.
17 C. Bennett, "Building Effective Partnerships," *NATO Review*, Autumn 2003, p. 2.
18 R. Asmus, "Europe's Eastern Promise: Rethinking NATO and EU Enlargement," *Foreign Affairs*, Vol. 87, No. 1, January/February 2008, pp. 95–106.
19 G. Kennan, "A Fateful Error," *The New York Times*, 5 February 1997.
20 For both sides of the issue see M. Sarotte, "Perpetuating U.S. Preeminence: The 1990 Deals to Bribe the Soviets Out and Move NATO In," *International Security*, Vol. 35, No. 1, Summer 2010, pp. 110–137; M. Kramer, "The Myth of the No-NATO-Enlargement Pledge to Russia," *Washington Quarterly*, Vol. 32, No. 2, Spring 2009, pp. 39–61.
21 Sarotte, "Perpetuating U.S. Preeminence."
22 A. Pushkov, "Missed Connections," *The National Interest*, May/June 2007, p. 55.
23 Section II.8a, cited in K. Giles, *The Military Doctrine of the Russian Federation 2010*, Research Review, Research Division, NATO Defense College, Rome, February 2010, p. 1.
24 "Libyan Operation Starts NATO's Southward Enlargement – Russia's envoy," *Russia Today*, 16 June 2011.
25 P.E. Gates, " 'Genuine interest' in Russia on missile defense," *DOD Buzz*, 9 June

2011. Online. Available: www.dodbuzz.com/2011/06/09/gates-genuine-interest-in-russia-on-missile-defense/#ixzz1QYX9lus7 (accessed 29 June 2011).

26 S. Kortunov, "'Hard Power' Imperative: The High and Lows of the New Russian-U.S. Treaty," *Russia in Global Affairs*, July 2010. Online. Available: http://eng.globalaffairs.ru/number/Hard_Power_Imperative-14890 (accessed 12 June 2012).

27 S. Stolberg and D. Sanger, "Bush to Seek a Bit of Unity with Putin," *The New York Times*, 5 June 2007.

28 J. Dempsey and D. Bilefsky, "U.S. and Czechs Sign Accord on Missile Shield," 9 July 2008.

29 E. Barry and S. Kishkovsky, "Russia Warns of Missile Deployment," *New York Times*, 6 November 2008.

30 Kortunov, "'Hard Power' Imperative."

31 See Chapter 11 by Gustav Lindstrom for a more detailed description of a range of missile defense issues.

32 P. O'Reilly, Deputy Director, Missile Defense Agency, Speech at Atlantic Council, 19 April 2007.

33 "New U.S. missile defense plans less worrying – Russian ambassador," *Interfax* (Moscow), 21 June 2010.

34 M. Corder, "NATO, Russia Clash Again on Missile Defense Plan," Associated Press, 8 June 2011.

35 NATO, "Active Engagement, Modern Defence," Strategic Concept for the Defense and Security of the Members of the North Atlantic Treaty Organization, Lisbon Summit, November 2010. Online. Available: www.nato.int/lisbon2010/strategic-concept-2010-eng.pdf.

36 NATO–Russia Council Joint Statement issued at the meeting of the NATO–Russia Council held in Lisbon, 20 November 2010. Online. Available HTTP: www.nato.int/cps/en/natolive/news_68871.htm.

37 V. Gienger and P. Donahue, "Gates Laments Delay in Missile-Defense Agreement with Russia," Bloomberg, 9 June 2011.

38 A.F. Rasmussen, NATO Secretary General, "Speech to RUSI on how NATO can defend against ballistic missile attack," Twelfth RUSI Missile Defence Conference, Whitehall, London, 15–16 June 2011.

39 "Russia Softens Stance on Missile Defence," Associated Foreign Press, 6 June 2011.

40 NATO, "NATO Summit Declaration," Chicago, 21 May 2012, paras 58–62.

41 S. Gutterman, "Russia Tests New Missile, in Warning over U.S. Shield," Reuters, 23 May 2012.

42 P. Ames, "NATO: Russia halts military cooperation," Associated Press, 22 August 2008.

43 D. Brunnstrom, "NATO Chiefs to Underline Georgia Support with Visit," Reuters, 11 September 2008.

44 "Russia freezes peacekeeping operations with NATO for 6 months," RIA Novosti, 26 August 2008.

45 "Stuck in Georgia," *New York Times*, 27 August 2008.

46 B. Feller, "Bush Calls on Russian Leadership to Reject Independence for 2 Breakaway Regions of Georgia," Associated Press, 26 August 2008.

47 Press Statement, Mark C. Toner, Acting Deputy Spokesman, Office of the Spokesman, Washington, D.C., 30 April 2011.

48 NATO, Chicago Summit Declaration, paras 29 and 30.

49 NATO, Founding Act.

50 F. Hiatt, "Can Reset Push Russia toward Democracy?" *Washington Post*, 18 July 2010.

51 R. Andreychuk, "Resetting Relations with Russia," NATO Parliamentary Report 032 PC 09 E, May 2009, p. 4.

52 Ibid.

53 President Dmitry Medvedev, "Forward, Russia!" *Gazeta*, 10 September 2009. Online. Available: www.gazeta.ru/comments/2009/09/10_a_3258568.shtml (accessed 29 June 2011).

54 B. Whitmore, "Medvedev Talks Reform in St. Petersburg," *Radio Free Europe/ Radio Liberty*. Online. Available: www.rferl.org/content/medvedev_talks_ reform_in_st_petersburg/24238558.html (accessed 22 June 2011).

55 G. Bryanski and D. Busvine, "Putin to dominate new Russian government," Reuters, 21 May 2012.

56 U.S. Department of State, "Country Reports on Human Rights Practices for 2011: Russia," 24 May 2012. Online. Available: www.state.gov/j/drl/rls/hrrpt/ humanrightsreport/index.htm?dynamic_load_id=186397 (accessed 26 May 2012).

57 I. Wigert, "Civil and Military Defence Planning and Scenarios Techniques," CRN Workshop Report, 2004, p. 1.

58 A. Monaghan, *The Russian* Vertikal*: the Tandem, Power and the Elections*, Russia and Eurasia Programme Paper (REP) 2011, NATO Defence College, June 2011.

59 "Ukraine Secretly Ramps up Ties with NATO," Agence France-Presse, 21 June 2011.

60 "Interview with President Dmitry Medvedev," Transcript, *Financial Times*, 19 June 2011.

61 A. Fedyashin, "NATO Reaching out to the Black Sea," RIA Novosti, 10 July 2008.

62 Interview with NATO Official, 2006.

63 Cited in S. Blank, "The NATO–Russia Partnership: A Marriage of Convenience or a Troubled Relationship?" Strategic Studies Institute, U.S. Army War College, Carlisle, Pennsylvania, November 2006, p. 2.

64 On 29 July 2010.

65 K. Degnan, "Bulgaria Exemplifies Approaches for NATO's New Strategic Concept," Hungarian Newswire, 29 July 2010.

66 C. Young, "From Russia with Loathing," *The New York Times*, 21 November 2008.

67 W. Schreiber, "The NATO Secretary-General Speaks on the Significance of the Alliance's Libya Mission and how bin Laden's Death will Affect Afghanistan," *Newsweek*, 15 May 2011.

68 For an interesting analysis of Russian views see Blank, "The NATO–Russia Partnership," p. vii.

7 NATO and the Comprehensive Approach

Weak conceptualization, political divergences, and implementation challenges

Thierry Tardy[1]

Introduction

The increasing complexity of conflict management has led policymakers to identify some key parameters that, if given sufficient attention, could improve the overall effectiveness of institutional responses to crises and conflicts. Among those parameters is the coordination of the different stakeholders that participate in conflict management activities. The underlying assumption is that the effectiveness of conflict management is inherently undermined if the main actors involved plan and implement policies without coordinating with others. Conversely, inter-institutional coordination is meant to help achieve strategic objectives in areas in which no singular institution can make a lasting difference on its own.

Several levels of this imperative coordination can be identified. First, at the level of the (intervening) state, where different departments within the same administration need to coordinate their activities to make the state's response coherent and effective. It is at this level of coordination that the notions of Whole-of-Government Approach (WGA), the "3-Ds" (Defense, Diplomacy, Development), or "3-Cs" (Coherent, Coordinated and Complementary) have emerged. A second level is that of international institutions' internal coordination, which is a mere reflection of the national approach at the international organization's level. Within a given organization, overall coherence is derived from the coordination of its different components (political, military, development, humanitarian, etc.). This has given birth to the concept of "integrated mission" at the United Nations. Third, the coordination of conflict management stakeholders also carries an external dimension, with the need to bring together the wide range of national, local, international, and nongovernmental actors.

Elaboration on the concept of Comprehensive Approach by NATO has taken place in this third, broader framework. Drawing upon the lessons of NATO operations in the Balkans and Afghanistan, the military Alliance

1. State intervener
2. UN
3. NATO (Broadest)

has come to the conclusion that non-Article Five missions cannot be implemented successfully through an exclusively military approach. The military component of any NATO mission needs to be complemented by a civilian dimension, which is central to the achievement of strategic objectives. The military can of course, try and establish a certain degree of security, but this can only be sustained if progress is made simultaneously in other key areas of stabilization, such as the establishment of the rule of law or economic recovery. As NATO does not have any particular expertise in these other areas, it needs to coordinate with actors that do.

This chapter presents and offers a critique of the NATO conception of Comprehensive Approach (CA). The first section looks at the conceptual development, from the recognition by NATO that the military cannot cover the entire conflict management spectrum to the process of defining the Comprehensive Approach. The second section examines the various obstacles to the implementation of the Comprehensive Approach, from the low consensus among NATO allies on its very meaning and implications to its narrow conceptualization, making the Comprehensive Approach more a NATO-centered approach that is primarily interested in achieving NATO military objectives rather than a method to improve multi-actor crisis management policies. Finally, the third section tries to identify possible scenarios for the future. At the heart of this debate is the nature of future NATO operations and the level of coercion that will characterize them. While mutually beneficial inter-institutional cooperation is arguably easier in permissive conflict management-type settings, a situation of open conflict like the one in Afghanistan makes the Comprehensive Approach more difficult to implement. Interestingly enough, is it not precisely the non-permissive nature of the Afghan environment that made the need for a Comprehensive Approach so important? In any case, how central to NATO's identity will the Comprehensive Approach be in the post-Afghan phase remains an open question.

Origin and definitions of the Comprehensive Approach

The need to go beyond military power

The NATO conception of Comprehensive Approach finds its origin in the much narrower U.S. military approach to Effects-Based Operations (EBO), which became NATO policy under the term Effects-Based Approach to Operations (EBAO). Presented as a methodology for using non-military power and for thinking in terms of the effects that can be delivered in operations rather than through the lens of "platforms or unit numbers," EBO has been considered, by virtue of its logic, as forming the basis for a military-civilian integration process.[2] EBAO is defined as the "coherent and comprehensive application of various instruments of the Alliance combined with the practical cooperation along with involved non-NATO actors, to create [the] effects necessary to achieve planned objectives and ultimately the NATO end-state."[3] The idea is to move beyond the sole role of the military to developing a new way of planning and running operations that ensure the cooperation of non-military actors.

Although the Comprehensive Approach is conceptually derived from EBAO, the link between the two concepts is ambiguous in NATO language. EBAO is presented as a tool that can help in the conceptualization and implementation of the Comprehensive Approach,[4] and definitions of the two notions are similar. Also the two terms are sometimes used interchangeably in NATO military circles.[5] Yet, neither the Riga nor the Bucharest NATO Summit Final Declarations – that define the Comprehensive Approach – explicitly make the relation between the two ideas or mention the term EBAO, which has been a source of confusion within NATO. This being said, Comprehensive Approach is a more generic term and describes a political process that subsumes the narrower and more technical, effects-based approach. EBAO is also more NATO-centered – it is fundamentally about ultimately achieving "the NATO end-state" – while Comprehensive Approach is supposed to achieve a better balance between the military and the civilian components. Finally, the evolution of definitions reflects political sensitivities and diverging interpretations of the terms (see below). In a way, the Comprehensive Approach definition is more diplomatic, so as to accommodate NATO member states that have different views on what embracing Comprehensive Approach implies. Notwithstanding, what is important in these developments is how military increasingly makes the point that the nature of contemporary conflicts alters that of their management so as to acknowledge the key role of non-military power in achieving planned objectives.[6]

The Comprehensive Approach was first introduced within NATO policy circles through a Danish initiative in late 2004.[7] Six other countries – Canada, Czech Republic, Hungary, Netherlands, Norway and Slovakia, and lastly the United States – later endorsed the Danish idea before the Comprehensive Approach was officially put on the Agenda of the Alliance's Riga Summit in November 2006. A mandate was then given to the Senior Political Committee to develop the Action Plan identifying "pragmatic proposals to improve [the] coherent application of NATO's own crisis management instruments as well as practical cooperation at all levels with partners, the UN and other relevant international organizations, Non-Governmental Organizations and local actors in the planning and conduct of ongoing and future operations."[8] The Action Plan was then developed[9] and endorsed at the 2008 Bucharest Summit, which also attempted to define further the Comprehensive Approach concept.

The military-civilian interface

The military nature of NATO determines its conception of the Comprehensive Approach. One starting point of the Comprehensive Approach is the fact that in most crisis response operations, the military are the only ones with the capacity to deploy rapidly. In hostile environments, this comparative advantage makes the military the de facto filler of gaps – i.e. they conduct civilian tasks – in the immediate aftermath of conflicts. Apart from the fact that this shows a structural weakness of civilian peacebuilding actors,[10] this kind of gap-filling function raises several questions. One is whether NATO should acquire its own civilian assets which would allow it to be better equipped in meeting the diversity of needs of stability operations. The Riga Summit declaration recognizes that "NATO has no requirement to develop capabilities strictly for civilian purposes."[11] Yet, the New Strategic Concept concedes that NATO will "form an appropriate but modest civilian crisis management capability to interface more effectively with civilian partners," which will be "used to plan, employ and coordinate civilian activities until conditions allow for the transfer of those responsibilities and tasks to other actors."[12] The desire to strengthen the civil-military interface appears as a priority, but debates about NATO civilian assets have also led to confusion about the ultimate objective of the Comprehensive Approach, as it was sometimes understood as reflecting the will of NATO to develop new capabilities, and by doing so to duplicate what already exists in other institutions, the EU in particular.

Another question raised by the gap-filling activities is the appropriateness and possible consequences for a military organization involved in civilian activities, both in terms of NATO purpose and identity and in terms of the impact on the recipient populations of these military-led but civilian programs. In the development and humanitarian fields, the fact that NATO runs its own programs, as in the case of the Provincial Reconstruction Teams (PRTs) in Afghanistan for example, begs the question of the function of NATO in crisis response operations and of the relevance of combining military and civilian tasks carried out by the same organization.[13] This question feeds the general debate on burden-sharing of security governance in the 21st century and on the role of NATO in the evolving security architecture; but it also sheds light on national views about the function of NATO as a defense and security actor (see below).

This leads to a third level of debate, that of cooperation and co-ordination of NATO with civilian actors, be it in parallel programs (NATO and civilian actors deployed simultaneously) or in a transition between NATO-led and civilian-led activities. NATO involvement in humanitarian or development projects puts the issue of coordination with humanitarian or development actors in a different light than when NATO missions remain purely militaristic in nature. Not only does it raise the question of inter-institutional coordination, but it also puts the coordination debate in the broader context of the role and added-value of the military in non-military tasks, the legitimacy and long-term effectiveness of such actions, and their impact on the humanitarian space and its related principles.[14]

Definitions of the Comprehensive Approach

It is a characteristic of many new concepts that are supposed to encapsulate the activity of an institution to be ill-defined and/or the object of diverging interpretations from the main actors implementing them. Such is the case with Comprehensive Approach which has remained a rather vague and non-consensual notion. The 2006 NATO Riga Summit Final Declaration first talked about the need for a "Comprehensive Approach by the international community involving a wide spectrum of civil and military instruments."[15] In the meantime, the Comprehensive Political Guidance adopted in Riga, although not explicitly mentioning the Comprehensive Approach, defined as a top priority, "the ability to draw together the various instruments of the Alliance brought to bear in a crisis and its resolution to the best effect, as well as the ability to coordinate with other actors." Two years later, the 2008 NATO Bucharest Summit Final Declaration was more explicit and underlined that

> Many of today's security challenges cannot be successfully met by NATO acting alone. Meeting them can best be achieved through a broad partnership with the wider international community, as part of a truly comprehensive approach, based on a shared sense of openness and cooperation as well as determination on all sides.[16]

It then stated that

> Experiences in Afghanistan and the Balkans demonstrate that the international community needs to work more closely together and take a *comprehensive approach* to address successfully the security challenges of today and tomorrow. Effective implementation of a *comprehensive approach requires the cooperation and contribution of all major actors, including that of Non-Governmental Organisations and relevant local bodies.* To this end, it is essential for all major international actors to act in a coordinated way, and to apply a wide spectrum of civil and military instruments in a concerted effort that takes into account their respective strengths and mandates.[17]

The 2010 New Strategic Concept uses similar language and further stresses the desire of the Alliance "to engage actively with other international actors before, during and after crises to encourage collaborative analysis, planning and conduct of activities on the ground, in order to maximize coherence and effectiveness of the overall international effort."[18] In the same vein, the May 2012 Chicago Summit Declaration confirms the previous NATO commitments.[19]

Those different definitions are rather wide, and allow for a broad interpretation by the actors that are supposed to implement the Comprehensive

Approach. They, however, acknowledge the limited role of NATO in the larger conflict management field and, therefore, the necessity to work with other actors – including non-governmental organizations (NGOs) and local bodies – to achieve overall coherence and effectiveness of the broader crisis response.

The difficult operationalization of the Comprehensive Approach

NATO began work on the issue of inter-institutional cooperation a few years ago, and has since developed a genuine awareness of the need for better coordination with non-military actors. However, the Comprehensive Approach has suffered from important flaws that have hampered its development as a concept as well as its implementation in the field. The academic and policy literature abounds on the shortcomings that NATO is facing.[20] Four of these obstacles are addressed below.

Weak consensus amongst allies

The Comprehensive Approach is first the victim of diverging views among member states on what the Approach is really about. Several levels of debate can be distinguished here. One pertains to the understanding of what Comprehensive Approach is about in relation to the Afghan context, and the extent to which the Comprehensive Approach is perceived to be a tool of counter-insurgency or as a broader conflict management method. The U.S. view is largely shaped by the Iraqi and Afghan operations, in which working with others is primarily motivated by the need to support the military objectives. In contrast, other countries that are not involved in combat in Afghanistan tend to have a less military-focused view of the Comprehensive Approach and see it in the broader context of peace consolidation. At a more political level, the debate over the Comprehensive Approach raises a series of questions on the role of NATO in non-Article Five missions; the impact of the development of Comprehensive Approach on the internal organization of the Alliance, in relation to its civilian capabilities in particular; or the type of the military-civilian interface that NATO is promoting. As noted by David Yost, for some of the NATO allies such as France, Belgium, Germany, or Spain, the Alliance must primarily remain a military institution.[21] They therefore express reluctance about a Comprehensive Approach that would lead to the development of civilian capabilities, or simply the implication of NATO in development activities. In the same vein, discussions over the Comprehensive Approach are connected with those about the broader role of NATO in world security governance and the issue of its "global vs. regional" remit. Here again, for member states that oppose the idea of a "global NATO," the concept of Comprehensive Approach is perceived as a tool to broaden the geographical scope of NATO activities.

All these divergences have hindered the consensus on the idea of Comprehensive Approach, and undermined its implementation on the ground.[22]

Weak conceptualization

Second, the Comprehensive Approach as a NATO tool has remained under-conceptualized and under-developed. This chapter has briefly described the process that led NATO to develop and endorse the concept of the Comprehensive Approach; the policy literature and internal debates have abundantly addressed the issue. Yet, in reality, the implementation of the Comprehensive Approach has been the responsibility of NATO member states rather than that of NATO as an institution. In Afghanistan in particular, where the Comprehensive Approach has led to some policy developments, and has been to some degree implemented in the PRTs, it has largely been done through national mechanisms and according to national standards. This has resulted in heterogeneity of the policies. While some member states – such as the UK, Canada, Norway, or Denmark – have endorsed the idea of comprehensiveness and tried to develop it on a national scale, others – such as France, Germany, or most of the Southern and Eastern European NATO members – have lagged behind for political or technical reasons and, therefore, made little progress in implementing it. In all cases, the national conceptions have prevailed over the theoretical NATO approach. This makes it difficult to talk about a genuine NATO Comprehensive Approach that would bring together the member states, and make it substantially distinct from that of other international institutions. The disconnect between the national and the institutional levels has undermined the cohesion of the Alliance, thus negatively impacting on the ability of NATO to liaise with other international organizations or local actors in the name of the Comprehensive Approach.[23]

Military focus: winning the peace vs. winning the war?

Third, the military identity of NATO combined with its strength and means in Afghanistan have given the Comprehensive Approach an ostensible military color, contradicting the official narrative and at the expense of its overall coherence.

The involvement of NATO member states in Afghanistan, i.e. in a situation that falls between a post-conflict environment and a war zone, has led some of them to see the Comprehensive Approach as being part of a broader counter-insurgency effort. As mentioned before, countries that are the most involved in combat operations in Afghanistan tend to see the Comprehensive Approach as a way to make counter-insurgency more effective by bringing in the civilian reconstruction and humanitarian dimensions.[24] The U.S. Counter-insurgency (COIN) Manual makes this explicit when stating that

COIN is an extremely complex form of warfare. At its core, COIN is a struggle for the population's support. The protection, welfare, and support of the people are vital to success. Gaining and maintaining that support is a formidable challenge. *Achieving these aims requires synchronizing the efforts of many nonmilitary and host nation agencies in a comprehensive approach.*[25]

Such vision of the Comprehensive Approach is fundamentally different from the one previously presented in this chapter. While the former is about bringing together different actors and activities of the conflict management effort in order to increase the effectiveness of international action, and therefore the chance to establish sustainable peace, the latter is about how to integrate the civilian actors so as to buttress the military objectives. The difference is not just one of semantics; it refers to the distinction between war-fighting and conflict management. Comprehensive Approach as a tool of COIN is about how to win a war, whereas Comprehensive Approach as a method of multidimensional conflict management is about how to win the peace. The two approaches lead to very different types of activities, coordination mechanisms, and degrees of hierarchical subordination between different actors. The Comprehensive Approach a tool of COIN de facto leads to a militarization of development and humanitarian affairs for military objectives rather than to a truly holistic approach that would combine the military and development/humanitarian components of the same multidimensional mission so as to optimize both activities and positively affect the feasibility and sustainability of peace.[26]

Without necessarily being an instrument of counter-insurgency, the PRTs have also demonstrated a military dominance of the Comprehensive Approach.[27] This is expressed not only by the very limited number of civilians in each PRT and the lack of balance in the origin of funds (that predominantly come from the defense budgets) allocated to development programs, but also by the way in which development objectives come in support of the military operation. Most importantly, the civilian dimension of PRTs has tended to be watered down as stabilization turned into counterinsurgency, making the role of civilians even more constrained.

Beyond these debates, what is at stake is whether the Comprehensive Approach is designed to help improve the effectiveness of conflict management policies or rather that of NATO policy in stability operations. Is the Comprehensive Approach NATO-centric or does it reflect a desire to improve conflict management on a larger scale? All institutions are confronted with this question, and NATO official discourse makes the point that "NATO does not own a Comprehensive approach."[28] Yet the NATO narrative on the Comprehensive Approach and its own role in its implementation – as illustrated in the PRTs in Afghanistan and the "winning hearts and minds" policy – tend to reveal a NATO-centered approach that is primarily interested in achieving NATO military objectives.

Inter-institutional cooperation dilemmas

Fourth, the idea of a Comprehensive Approach leads to the inherent challenges of coordination and cooperation among different kinds of actors.[29] Inter-institutional cooperation takes place for reasons that pertain to materialist and ideological motives. They can find their rationale in reciprocal needs (and benefits), as well as in a sense of common understanding – or even shared values – among partnering institutions. Cooperation relates to political, technical as well as cultural reasons.

NATO is relatively well placed insofar as materialist motives are concerned, as it displays comparative advantages – such as manpower, robust military capabilities, logistics, rapid reaction units – that can be of interest for other conflict management actors and therefore induce cooperation. On the other hand, the military identity of NATO tends to be detrimental to both its ability to work with others and the propensity or desire of others to partner with it. For example, if the UN Office for the Coordination of Humanitarian Affairs (OCHA) recognizes the necessity to work with NATO, it also expresses concerns about the impact on the humanitarian space and insists on the fact that "Humanitarian workers must never present themselves or their work as part of a military operation."[30] The relationship between NATO and NGOs is even more complex, and if the two types of actors can draw upon 20 years of simultaneous presence in conflict management settings, the political and cultural divergences remain important and in the end, constitute a major obstacle to the implementation of the Comprehensive Approach.[31] For some NGOs, even the relevance of cooperating with NATO is not intuitively a necessary or positive thing, given the associated risks to the integrity of the humanitarian space. NATO Secretary-General Rasmussen acknowledged these difficulties, in a speech made at the University of Chicago in 2010:

> The lack of communication with non-governmental organizations is also striking. I recently suggested publicly that we needed to work more closely with NGOs, so that their "soft power" could complement our hard power. Their reaction, I can tell you, was not very receptive. I think they are worried about becoming a party to a conflict. They wish to remain neutral. Therefore, they are often reluctant to work under military protection.[32]

In this context, the PRTs in Afghanistan offer a mixed assessment. While they are sometimes presented as having helped in bridging the gap between the military and the development and humanitarian actors,[33] they are also the object of criticism from NGOs that underline the threat that they have constituted to the independence of humanitarian and development workers while questioning their added-value in establishing peace.[34] On the NATO side, a related issue is that of the general reluctance of the Alliance or of the military to be coordinated by others – be they civilians, the United Nations, or local parties – while the very concept of the Comprehensive Approach is supposed to allow for such coordination.

Overall, in the debate on inter-institutional cooperation in conflict management operations, NATO tends to be perceived as a dominant actor that conceives its relations with others in hierarchical terms – with NATO at the top – rather than in terms of a network in which all actors are theoretically placed on an equal footing. In the same vein, NATO's Western membership, the United States role in NATO, and the politicization of the Alliance's policy that follows, tend to complicate the establishment of partnerships or cooperation mechanisms with other crisis management actors. The political tensions that accompanied the signature of the UN-NATO Joint Declaration in September 2008 provide an example, with some large countries such as China and Russia expressing deep concerns about the rationale of partnering with NATO (not to mention the critique over the ability of the UN Secretary-General to engage the UN without consulting the member states).[35]

What is the future of the Comprehensive Approach?

The broad conflict management realm has gone through a series of fundamental evolutions over the last two decades. In terms of mandates, actors, and methods, the peacekeeping/peacebuilding field in 2012 is very different from the early 1990s. In the meantime, one can also observe continuity in the type of challenges with which conflict management actors are confronted. Issues such as clarity of mandates, lack of resources and institutional overstretch, legitimacy, and effectiveness of the operations, or coordination among the actors involved have been with us for a while. As far as coordination is concerned, there is little doubt that it will remain on the agenda for the foreseeable future and that NATO will, therefore, have to deal with it. In other words, the debate on the Comprehensive Approach (or another term that will cover the same *problématique*), its rationale and constraints, is here to stay.

At the same time, the future of the Comprehensive Approach as a concept and as a method depends on at least three related developments: the evolution of conflict management and its level of coercion; the evolution of NATO itself and the way it – and its member states – see its role in conflict management; the evolution of other actors' policies and capabilities and of the interaction between NATO and these other actors. The various combinations of these three parameters lead to a high number of possible scenarios that cannot be systematically examined in the framework of this chapter. The intention here is rather to look at the three evolutions in sequence and to see how they can affect the development of the Comprehensive Approach.

The mission determines the Comprehensive Approach

The future of the Comprehensive Approach first depends on the evolution of NATO's policy vis-à-vis conflict management. The broad spectrum of conflict management constitutes the context in which inter-institutional cooperation can take place, and the conditions of such cooperation vary according to the nature of the operations, and in particular, their level of coercion. As seen before, the Comprehensive Approach in a COIN environment is conceptually different from the Comprehensive Approach in a more traditional peace consolidation context. While both types of operations require coordination of the actors involved – a Comprehensive Approach is presumably as important in Afghanistan as it is in Kosovo – mutually beneficial inter-institutional cooperation is arguably easier in permissive environments, allowing military and non-military actors to develop partnerships based on comparative advantages, reciprocal needs, and a minimum level of trust. In contrast, a context characterized by a situation of open conflict, especially when fighting involves the military component of the external interveners (as is the case in Afghanistan), makes a comprehensive approach more difficult to achieve, because it tends to exacerbate the political and cultural divergences among the main external actors. In Afghanistan, for example, inter-institutional co-ordination has been hindered by the military domination of the Comprehensive Approach that characterized COIN operations, with the development/humanitarian dimension coming in support of the military objectives.

Looking ahead, whether Afghanistan and Libya prefigure the type of operations that NATO runs or whether it is rather Kosovo, will shape the nature of, as well as the obstacles to, inter-institutional coordination. A return to more traditional peace consolidation missions might well be the favored option for quite a few countries which do not wish to repeat the Afghanistan experience.[36] Paradoxically then, although CA is theoretically easier in peacekeeping contexts, the necessity to develop further the Comprehensive Approach might lose its momentum, as the coordination with others might appear, from a military perspective, less essential to the success of peacekeeping-type operations.

In the meantime, for some NATO member states, one lesson from Afghanistan and the difficulty of establishing links with non-military actors means that NATO should revisit the way it handles the relationship with civilian actors and, in particular, the idea of acquiring some civilian capabilities. Jamie Shea notes that "The experience of Afghanistan will undoubtedly lead over time to the U.S. and other allies investing more in civilian reconstruction expertise and rapid response civilian capabilities able to operate for long periods in dangerous areas."[37] The debate will then be centered on the nature and scope of these civilian capabilities, whether they should necessarily be developed within NATO, as well as on the extent to which they would alter the role of NATO as a conflict management organization. This would lead back to the broader debate over the purpose of NATO, its function as a collective defense organization, and national divergences on the type of conflict management actor that it should become.[38] It is then likely that the divergences and the different types of obstacles that have been analyzed in this chapter will come up, at the expense of a more coherent Comprehensive Approach.

The Comprehensive Approach losing momentum in a post-Afghan era

This in turn leads to the level of activity of NATO in conflict management, which will largely determine how much the Comprehensive Approach remains a priority. Presumably the Comprehensive Approach can only be a priority if, following the Afghan and Libyan operations, NATO maintains its presence in non-Article Five operations, including at least one of significant size. In contrast, a situation in which NATO would become, either by design or by default, a relatively low-key conflict management actor, with operations that do not necessitate any kind of long-term inter-institutional coordination, would most likely undermine the relevance of the Comprehensive Approach as a method of conflict management. In this context, the extent to which NATO manages to institutionalize the Comprehensive Approach, as opposed to member states developing it (or not), will be equally important. Given the financial constraints that all NATO members face, combined with a general reluctance to repeat the Afghan scenario, the option of a withdrawal is not to be ruled out. In other words, although the 2011 developments in the Middle East and North Africa (MENA) region should lead to the utmost prudence when it comes to predicting conflict management trends, the scenario of another NATO-led Afghan-type mission that would maintain the idea of a Comprehensive Approach at the top of the agenda, is not the most likely. In the same vein, as the Comprehensive Approach was born and developed in the Afghan context, there is a risk that the momentum over its utility can be lost after NATO's withdrawal from Afghanistan. Even if NATO remains present through the "provision of training, advice and assistance to the Afghan National Security Forces (ANSF)" as well as "long-term political and practical support through [the] Enduring Partnership with Afghanistan,"[39] activities that will all require some degree of inter-institutional coordination, it is difficult to imagine the same narrative on the necessity to "maximise coherence and effectiveness of the overall international effort" once the combat units are withdrawn.

Towards more inclusiveness

Third, as the Comprehensive Approach should not be an exclusive NATO policy but on the contrary a method of conflict management that is shared by other stakeholders, the policies and own capabilities of these other actors will be essential in determining the role of NATO in implementing the Comprehensive Approach. This is important as it means that the level of success of a NATO Comprehensive Approach is only partially in NATO's hands, and very dependent on its "future partners." In particular, the kind of security actor that the EU will become, and therefore its capacity in the military field, will no doubt have an influence on what NATO is doing and how the two institutions will coordinate.[40] The prospect of the EU being able to project the kind of military power that NATO can project in the coming years is low. Reciprocally, NATO will not be able to compete with the EU in the civilian sphere. This should create some complementarity that would make coordination of the two actors a priority, yet not necessarily politically feasible.[41] What is certain is that the framework of their cooperation, with the ill-designed and now obsolete Berlin Plus agreement,[42] will have to be revisited and adapted to the new environment.

Similarly, the situation of overstretch that the UN is facing and will most likely continue to face in the future years creates a certain dependence vis-à-vis military actors, NATO among others. There is no doubt that the UN is the institution that has gone the furthest in thinking about inter-institutional coordination and the need for system-wide coherence. Notwithstanding the above-mentioned political tensions between the two organizations, the UN Secretariat is *a priori* willing to cooperate with (and coordinate) any conflict management actor provided they meet certain conditions relating to the legal framework of the operations. But when it comes to the development or humanitarian dimensions of the UN response (with UN agencies, such as UN Development Program (UNDP) or UN High Comissioner for Refugees (UNHCR), or departments of the Secretariat, such as OCHA), the interaction with the Atlantic Alliance is not automatic and raises the traditional questions of the impact of cooperation with the military on the integrity of development and/or humanitarian activities.

Inter-institutional cooperation in crisis management has improved a lot over the last 20 years; institutions know each other far better in 2012 than in the early 1990s. The debate over the security-development nexus has also helped in bringing closer two types of actors that initially, and that still to a large extent, belong to different worlds. Yet, the main conflict management actors, including the NGOs, continue to have different mandates, cultures, and timeframes that make their coordination operationally complex.

In this context, although it has a lot to offer, because of its military focus and U.S. influence, NATO is not the easiest partner for other organizations. In comparison, the EU has managed to institutionalize its relationship with the UN and its agencies, the African Union and NGOs in a way NATO has not, but could try to draw on. This touches upon the kind of institutional mechanisms that can facilitate dialogue among organizations as much as the long-term establishment of a culture of cooperation. In a way, it is the mere idea of a NATO Comprehensive Approach that is a contradiction in terms. If the Comprehensive Approach is about interinstitutional coordination, in particular with the civilian actors, if it is, as NATO Secretary-General said, "not about hierarchy," but "all about synergy,"[43] then the entire process – beginning with conceptualization – should be more inclusive, and give the civilian actors a say in the debates. To summarize, if the need for a Comprehensive Approach is theoretically here to stay, there also exist strong obstacles that make that progress, if any, can only be slow, incremental, and therefore less visible in the short term.[44]

Conclusions

The need for NATO to better coordinate with other conflict management actors at present is well understood and has led to some efforts to conceptualize and operationalize the idea of Comprehensive Approach. In the meantime, the development of the Comprehensive Approach has not taken place in a political vacuum. It has in reality, suffered from a mix of endogenous and exogenous obstacles, ranging from NATO's internal coherence (or lack thereof) about the meaning of the Comprehensive Approach, states' divergences about the relevance and implications of the Comprehensive Approach, to the inherent dilemmas of civil–military relations and inter-institutional cooperation.

The idea of a Comprehensive Approach is, as understood in NATO circles, about how to facilitate coordination with non-military actors so as to make the NATO response more effective. However, the Comprehensive Approach also belongs to a broader debate about inter-institutional cooperation in conflict management settings with the objective of improving the overall international response to conflicts. There is more than a nuance between these two approaches; the dichotomy not only informs about the nature of NATO's conception of comprehensiveness, but also begs the question of the ultimate purpose of acting in a coordinated way: the success of NATO policy versus that of the international community. Herein lies the problem. As long as the NATO approach is distinct from broader considerations, it is likely that little progress in inter-institutional cooperation will be achieved. For NATO, going beyond a NATO-centric approach is both a question of effectiveness and legitimacy.

Notes

1 The author is grateful to Victoria Porell for her research assistance and help in copy-editing this chapter.
2 See D. Korski, "British Civil-Military Integration. The History and Next Steps," *The RUSI Journal*, Vol. 154, No. 6, December 2009, p. 17.
3 "Military Committee Position on an Effects-Based Approach to Operations," NATO Military Committee, MCM 0052–2006, June 2006.
4 See NATO Defence College, "10 Things You Should Know about a Comprehensive Approach," November 2008, p. 1.
5 See B. Smith-Windsor, "Hasten slowly. NATO's Effects Based and Comprehensive Approach to Operations," *Research Paper*, No. 38, NATO Defense College, July 2008, p. 1.
6 In line with earlier NATO documents, the Chicago Summit Declaration states that "Our operational experiences have shown that military means, although essential, are not enough on their own to meet the many complex challenges to our security." NATO, "NATO Summit Declaration: Issued by the Heads of State and Government participating in the meeting of the North Atlantic Council in Chicago on 20 May 2012," Chicago Summit, 20 May 2012, §18. Online. Available: www.nato.int/cps/en/natolive/official_texts_87593.htm.
7 See F. Arne Petersen and H. Binnendijk, "The Comprehensive Approach Initiative: Future Options for NATO," *Defense Horizons*, No. 58, Center for Technology and National Security Policy of the National Defense University, September 2007.
8 NATO, "Riga Summit Declaration," Issued by the Heads of State and Government participating in the meeting of the North Atlantic Council in Riga on 29 November 2006, §10.
9 The adoption of the Action Plan was difficult due to states' divergences on the definition of the CA.
10 See M.J. Williams, "(Un)Sustainable Peacebuilding: NATO's Suitability for Postconflict Reconstruction in Multiactor Environments," *Global Governance*, Vol. 17, No. 1, 2011, pp. 115–134.
11 NATO, "Riga Summit Declaration," §10. The two documents on the CA circulated by two groups of countries in the spring of 2006 (written by Canada, Denmark, Czech Republic, Netherlands, Norway, and Slovakia) and in September 2006 (previous countries plus the United States) indicate that NATO should not develop its own civilian capabilities.
12 NATO, "Active Engagement, Modern Defence," Strategic Concept for the Defense and Security of the Members of the North Atlantic Treaty Organization, §25, Lisbon Summit, November 2010. Online. Available: www.nato.int/lisbon2010/strategic-concept-2010-eng.pdf.
13 See M. Dziedzic and M. Seidl, "Provincial Reconstruction Teams: Military Relations with International and Nongovernmental Organizations in Afghanistan," *Special Report*, 147, USIP, Washington, D.C., September 2005; M. Hofman and S. Delaunay, *Afghanistan: A Return to Humanitarian Action*, Médecins sans Frontières, March 2010.
14 See S. Cornish, "No Room for Humanitarianism in 3-D Policies: Have Forcible Humanitarian Interventions and Integrated Approaches Lost their Way?" *Journal of Military and Strategic Studies*, Vol. 10, Issue 1, Fall 2007, pp. 1–48.
15 NATO, "Riga Summit Declaration," Issued by the Heads of State and Government participating in the meeting of the North Atlantic Council in Riga on 29 November 2006, §10.
16 NATO, "Summit Declaration," Issued by the Heads of State and Government participating in the meeting of the North Atlantic Council in Bucharest on

3 April 2008, §4. Online. Available: www.nato.int/cps/en/natolive/official_texts_8443.htm?mode_pressrelease (accessed 23 July 2011).

17 NATO, "Summit Declaration," Bucharest, §11.

18 NATO, "Active Engagement, Modern Defence," §21.

19 See NATO, "Summit Declaration," Chicago, §§5, 18.

20 See in particular C. Wendling, "The Comprehensive Approach to Civil-Military Crisis Management. A Critical Analysis and Perspective," IRSEM, Paris, 2010; "Comprehensive Approach. Trends, Challenges and Possibilities for Cooperation in Crisis Prevention and Management," Seminar Publication, Crisis Management Initiative, Helsinki, 2008; P. Viggo Jakobsen, "NATO's Comprehensive Approach to Crisis Response Operations. A Work in Slow Progress," *DIIS Report 2008*, No. 15, October 2008.

21 D.C. Yost, *NATO and International Organizations*, Forum Paper 3, NATO Defense College, September 2007, p. 155. On France, also see Viggo Jakobsen, "NATO's Comprehensive Approach to Crisis Response Operations," pp. 11–13.

22 See Yost, *NATO and international organizations*, pp. 155–158; Viggo Jakobsen, "NATO's Comprehensive Approach to Crisis Response Operations."

23 See C. de Coning *et al.*, "Norway's Whole-of-Government Approach and its Engagement with Afghanistan," *NUPI Report*, 2009, pp. 40–42.

24 See P. Dahl Thruelsen, "Implementing the Comprehensive Approach in Helmand: Within the Context of Counterinsurgency," Royal Danish Defence College, 2008.

25 "Counterinsurgency," Field Manual 3–24 (MCWP 3–33.5), Headquarters Department of the Army, United States, December 2006, 1.28.

26 On the role of the CA in war-type situations, see J. Lindley-French, P. Cornish and A. Rathmell, *Operationalizing the Comprehensive Approach*, Program Paper ISP PP 2010/01, Chatham House, March 2010; D. Berlijn, "Continuously Transforming to Fit in Comprehensive Approached Operations," *NATO's Nations and Partners for Peace*, 2008.

27 M.J. Williams, "Empire Light Revisited: NATO, the Comprehensive Approach and State-building in Afghanistan," *International Peacekeeping*, Vol. 18, No. 1, 2011, pp. 67–68.

28 NATO Defense College, "10 Things You Should Know about a Comprehensive Approach."

29 See R. Paris, "Understanding the 'coordination problem' in postwar statebuilding," in R. Paris and T. Sisk, *The Dilemmas of Statebuilding: Confronting the Contradictions of Postwar Peace Operations*, London: Routledge, 2009; K. Haugevik, *New Partners, New Possibilities: The Evolution of Inter-Organizational Security Cooperation in International Peace Operations*, NUPI Report, Oslo, 2007; T. Tardy, *Cooperating to Build Peace: The UN-EU Inter-Institutional Complex*, Geneva Papers – Research Series, No. 2, GCSP, May 2011.

30 OCHA, "Civil-Military Relationship in Complex Emergencies. An IASC Reference Paper," 28 June 2004, p. 9.

31 See L. Borgomano-Loup, *Improving NATO-NGO Relations in Crisis Response Operations*, Forum Paper No. 2, NATO Defense College, March 2007; A. Gheciu, "Divided Partners: The Challenges of NATO-NGO Cooperation in Peacebuilding Operations," *Global Governance*, Vol. 17, No. 1, 2011, pp. 95–113.

32 A.F. Rasmussen, "Afghanistan and the Future of Peace Operations," Speech by NATO Secretary-General at the University of Chicago, 8 April 2010. Online. Available: www.nato.int/cps/en/natolive/opinions_62510.htm; See also Dr Unni Karunakara, Address by International President of Médecins sans Frontières, to NATO Deputy Permanent Representatives Committee, Brussels, 14 December 2010.

33 See "Policy Options for State-building in Afghanistan: The Role of NATO PRTs

in Development in Afghanistan," SAIS, May 2009, pp. 9–12; C. Malkasian and G. Meyerle, *Provincial Reconstruction Teams: How do we Know they Work?* U.S. Army War College, Strategic Studies Institute, March 2009.

34 See *Provincial Reconstruction Teams and Humanitarian-Military Relations in Afghanistan*, Save the Children, 2004; *Quick Impact, Quick Collapse. The Dangers of Militarized Aid in Afghanistan*, Paper by a coalition of NGOs, January 2010; and Hofman and Delaunay, *Afghanistan*.

35 See M. Harsch and J. Varwick, "NATO and the UN," *Survival*, Vol. 51, No. 2, 2009, pp. 5–12.

36 See P. Rotmann, *Built on Shaky Ground: The Comprehensive Approach in Practice*, Research Paper No. 63, NATO Defense College, December 2010, p. 7.

37 J. Shea, "NATO Strategy: Building the Comprehensive Approach," in *Afghanistan: Now You See Me?* IDEAS Strategic Updates, London: LSE, March 2009, p. 8.

38 See D. Yost, "NATO's Evolving Purposes and the Next Strategic Concept," *International Affairs*, Vol. 86, No. 2, 2010, pp. 489–522; NATO, *NATO 2020: Assured Security; Dynamic Engagement*, Analysis and Recommendations of the Group of Experts on a New Strategic Concept for NATO, NATO Public Diplomacy Division, Brussels, 17 May 2010. Online. Available: www.nato.int/strategic-concept/expertsreport.pdf.

39 NATO, "Chicago Summit Declaration," 20 May 2012, §§6–7.

40 See S. Biscop, *From Lisbon to Lisbon: Squaring the Circle of EU and NATO Future Roles*, Security Policy Brief No. 16, Egmont, Brussels, January 2011.

41 On the difficulties of NATO-EU relations, see Yost, *NATO and International Organizations*; N. Lachmann, "The EU-CSDP-NATO Relationship: Asymmetric Cooperation and the Search for Momentum," *Studia Diplomatica*, Vol. 63, No. 3–4, 2010, pp. 185–202.

42 The Berlin Plus arrangement was signed in 2003 by NATO and the EU. It was aimed at allowing the EU to draw on NATO planning assets for EU-led crisis management operations. Only two (operations Concordia in Macedonia and Althea in Bosnia and Herzegovina) of the six EU-led military operations were conducted under the Berlin Plus agreement. The agreement is the only framework for inter-institutional dialogue between the two organizations; it does not allow for institutional cooperation in places where the EU operation is autonomous or of a civilian nature, as in Kosovo or Afghanistan. Its implementation, notably in the field of classified information exchange, is also impeded by the Turkey-Cyprus relationship. See S. Duke, "The Future of EU–NATO Relations: A Case of Mutual Irrelevance through Competition?" *Journal of European Integration*, Vol. 30, No. 1, 2008, pp. 27–43.

43 A.F. Rasmussen, "The Future of Peace Operations," Speech by NATO Secretary-General at the University of Edinburgh, 17 November 2009.

44 See C. de Coning and K. Friis, "Coherence and Coordination: The Limits of the Comprehensive Approach," *Journal of International Peacekeeping*, Vol. 15, 2011, pp. 243–272.

8 Pulling together?

NATO operations in Afghanistan

Julian Lindley-French

As a bottom line up front, it is ISAF's assessment that the momentum achieved by the Taliban in Afghanistan since 2005 has been arrested in much of the country and reversed in a number of important areas. However, while the security progress achieved over the past year is significant, it is also fragile and reversible. Moreover, it is clear that much difficult work lies ahead with our Afghan partners to solidify and expand our gains in the face of the expected Taliban spring offensive. Nonetheless, the hard-fought achievements in 2010 and early 2011 have enabled the Joint Afghan-NATO Transition Board to recommend initiation this spring of transition to Afghan lead in several provinces.

General David Petraeus, Commander, ISAF NATO, 15 March 2011[1]

Introduction

The purpose of this book is to consider the role, shape, and structure of NATO in order to understand NATO in the 21st century. One thing is clear: NATO will not be in Afghanistan in any strength over the medium to longer term. Indeed, the May 2012 NATO Chicago Summit declaration states that the "irreversible transition of full security responsibility from the International Security Assistance Force (ISAF) to the Afghan National Security Forces (ANSF) is on track for completion by the end of 2014, as agreed at our Lisbon Summit."[2] However, there will be many lessons from what has proven to be the most challenging of stability operations. The period 2012–14, whilst dressed up in the language of "transition" to Afghan rule, is in fact the beginning of a retreat that will accelerate given the critical pressures on national exchequers as a result of the 2008 and 2011 financial crises. The lesson for NATO 2030: do not start what cannot be finished.

This is not without irony, much of it tragic. By late 2010 the U.S.-led NATO coalition had roughly the right force levels to prosecute the campaign effectively and thus create the conditions for some semblance of political stability in the country. In spite of expanding Taliban activity in the north of Afghanistan, significant success was achieved in rooting out

Taliban safe havens, with the Taliban leadership suffering major losses. Indeed, as General Petraeus, the former Commander of NATO's International Security Assistance Force (ISAF) pointed out in his March 2011 testimony to Congress, some 700 former Taliban had officially "reintegrated" whilst some 2,000 were at various stages of reintegration. Moreover, major advances had been realized in the development of the capability of the Afghan National Security Forces (ANSF) to such an extent that the Joint NATO-Afghan Transition Board recommended that President Karzai and NATO leaders transition control to Afghans in several provinces.

NATO's May 2012 Chicago Summit confirmed the November 2010 Lisbon framework for transition and agreed on an interim milestone by mid-2013 that would confirm progress toward the transition goal. The mid-2013 milestone would mark the point at which the ANSF assumes the lead for combat operations across the country.

The two stage/five tranche transition process was announced by President Karzai on 22 March 2011 and would require the progressive transition of security responsibility to the Afghan National Security Forces. The process began in May 2011 and saw ISAF forces adopt a support and advisory role whilst the ANSF took the lead in decision-making, planning, and the conduct of security operations. In phase one seven districts and provinces would be handed over. These are Bamyan province, Kabul province, with the exception of Surobi district, Panjshir province, Herat City (capital of Herat province), Lashkar Gah (capital of Helmand province), Mazar-e-Sharif (capital of Balkh province), and Mehtar Lam (capital of Laghman province).

Phase two was announced by President Karzai on 27 November 2011 and involved the hand-over of power in Balkh, Day Kundi, Takhar, Samangan, Nimroz, and the remainder of Kabul province. The cities of Jalalabad, Chaghcharan (Ghor province), Sheberghan (Jawzjan province), Feyzabad (Badakhshan province), Ghazni (Ghazni province), Maidan Shahr (Wardak province), and Qala-e Now (Badghis province) would also be handed over together with a host of districts in some of the more challenged areas of Afghanistan. By the end of 2013 all of Afghanistan will have begun the process with the aim that by the end of 2014 the ANSF will lead and conduct security operations across the whole of Afghanistan.

The AFPAK strategy

The goal of the U.S. Afghanistan-Pakistan (AFPAK) strategy, which has framed NATO operations since it was announced by President Obama on 27 March 2009, was to disrupt terrorist networks in Afghanistan and Pakistan in order to degrade their ability to launch international terrorist attacks; promote a more capable, accountable, and effective government in Afghanistan; develop self-reliant Afghan security forces that could lead the counter-insurgency with reduced U.S. assistance; and involve the international community to actively assist in addressing these objectives by establishing an important leadership role for the United Nations Assistance Mission in Afghanistan (UNAMA).

Whilst progress has undoubtedly been made towards such a goal, these "achievements" are clearly not irreversible and remain fragile. In effect, the period 2011–14 is in many ways a race between Kabul and its Coalition allies, and the insurgents to establish/prevent some basic form of acceptable government/governance before the bulk of western military forces are withdrawn. Although the strategic imperative strongly suggests that U.S. and NATO (sadly, one must make that distinction these days) forces will remain in some strength well beyond 2014, there exists neither the political will nor the financial resources to sustain such operations.

The core message of this chapter and the key lesson for future NATO operations is thus simple: if extended stabilization and reconstruction operations are to be successful, real unity of effort and purpose must be established at the outset of a NATO campaign based on a truly multinational approach to operations, which must be established on a willingness to share political and military risk. The U.S. view that NATO was from the outset a sideshow to their main effort helped to condemn the Alliance to self-fulfilling failure (although NATO did not need much help in that regard) as it prevented the necessary level of ambition both in terms of political scope and civilian and military resources vital to succeeding in a theatre of operations such as Afghanistan. Specifically, the European effort was not commensurate with mission success in Afghanistan; neither in terms of scale, effective organization or shared rules of engagement across the mission. Indeed, the political ambition of many NATO allies seemed to be to do *just enough* to keep the U.S. paying for much of Europe's parochial security and defense. As such, a "Bosnia-plus" approach was adopted by all Europeans, except the British, until 2010. Consequently, NATO Europeans by and large sent small forces to large places without the proper political and resource support of capitals that viewed Afghanistan as an obligation to an ally rather than a NATO operation vital to their own security and defense.

NATO operations Afghanistan: the basic facts

NATO's ISAF in Afghanistan was sanctioned by United Nations Security Council Resolution 1386 on 20 December 2001 in the wake of the September 2011 attacks by Al Qaeda on the United States and as envisaged by the Bonn Agreement of the same month.[3] Resolution 1386 aimed to free the Afghan people from oppression and terror, and reaffirmed the responsibility of Afghans to provide security, as well as law and order. Commensurate with that aim, the ISAF mission set out first to protect the seat of government in and around Kabul so as to permit the establishment of the Afghan Transitional Authority under Hamid Karzai. In October 2003, the

UN agreed to the expansion of the ISAF mission across Afghanistan. Stage One expansion to the north was completed by October 2004. Stage Two in the west was completed by September 2005. Stage Three expansion in the dangerous and predominantly Pashto south of the country was completed by July 2006, and Stage Four expansion across the whole of the country by October 2006.

As of June 2012, there were 50 Troop Contributing Nations (TCN) operating under the Integrated Joint Command (IJC), totaling some 150,000 troops under the command of U.S. Army General John Allen. The U.S. is by far the largest troop contributor with some 90,000 troops in theater. The United Kingdom comes in distant second with 9,500 and Germany is in turn a distant third, with 4,800. At NATO's Chicago Summit France announced it would withdraw its forces prematurely by the end of 2012.

The ISAF mission is as follows: "In support of the Government of the Islamic Republic of Afghanistan, ISAF conducts operations in Afghanistan to reduce the capability and will of the insurgency, support the growth in capacity and capability of the Afghan National Security Forces (ANSF), and facilitate improvements in governance and socio-economic development in order to provide a secure environment for sustainable stability that is observable to the population."[4]

On 22 June 2011 U.S. President Barack Obama announced "The Way Forward in Afghanistan." By 31 December 2011, U.S. force levels dropped by 10,000 personnel, and then by a further 23,000 in summer 2012. This reduced U.S. force levels to the same level as prior to the 2010 surge. It is envisaged that all U.S. combat troops will be withdrawn from Afghanistan by 2014. The British have announced a similar intention.

The focus of NATO operations

There are two main lines of operation which provide the context for NATO stability operations in Afghanistan: national and regional political stability and capacity-building of local security forces. In light of attempts to strengthen both the writ and purview of Kabul and ANSF capacity-building, a meaningful partnership with Pakistan has been and remains vital. The partnership with Pakistan is particularly important for reintegration and reconciliation and underlines the centrality of a regional approach.

However, the relationship with Pakistan is complex and dangerous. This has become more so since the May 2011 killing of Osama bin Laden by U.S. Navy Seals during a raid on a compound in Pakistan. Moreover, Pakistan's military intelligence, the Inter-Services Intelligence (ISI) remains unhappy that the U.S. has been allowed to hunt independently for members of the Haqqani network, which is responsible for much of the violence in Afghanistan, and the use by the U.S. of drone strikes to degrade the Al Qaeda leadership remains contentious. In June 2012 just such a strike killed Al Qaeda Number Two Abu Yahya al-Libi.

The second line of operation is the creation of an effective and accepted Afghan National Security Force (ANSF) that will provide the foundation for a functioning Afghan state. Certainly, efforts to construct a 250,000 strong Afghan National Army (ANA) are proceeding, although the extent to which they will be ready to operate by 2014 as a force independent from mentors and trainers is a moot point. However, it is the effort to create an Afghan National Police force worthy of the name that will perhaps offer the best barometer of progress. At present the NATO Training Mission-Afghanistan (NTM-A) is seeking to establish a police force across all 385 police districts. Progress has been patchy to say the least. For example, some 700 or so police trainers are still needed across the country.

This has not been helped by the travails of the European Union Police Mission (EUPOL) which has singularly failed to establish sound strategic planning. This in turn has frustrated efforts by NTM-A to establish a close working relationship with EUPOL. Even though it is late in the campaign, EUPOL has only recently begun developing a vision of what civilian policing in Afghanistan should comprise and involve.

The solution may be close to home. President Karzai's local police initiative has been an important step forward because it creates a form of community-based policing that reduces the ability of the Taliban to intimidate and extort. There are some 70 districts identified for Afghan local police with each totaling around 300 personnel, with 27 districts now cleared for full operations; 43 others are in various stages of being established. More needs to be done and urgently, but with the prospect of western forces leaving, it may be that Kabul will finally begin to act more effectively. It is not before time.

At the very least, a renewed political commitment is needed (both at home and in Kabul) to see the campaign through. Sadly, NATO's successful conduct of Operation Unified Protector in Libya has not overcome the Afghanistan-fatigue that is all too painfully apparent in many NATO capitals. Such fatigue is undermining – possibly fatally – the tight political-military relationship essential both at the strategic and theater levels if an all-important comprehensive peace settlement is ever to be eventually realized. The claim that NATO nations will stay beyond the end of 2014 in any role beyond the merely token looks increasingly hollow, something not lost on the Taliban leadership in Peshawar and Quetta.

Equally, progress has been made in critical areas such as security, economic governance, life quality, and relations between the government and people. Moreover, over the past year the Taliban have suffered profound setbacks, not least in and around their spiritual home of Kandahar. Lt. Gen. William Caldwell IV, who heads NATO's Training Mission in Afghanistan, said in a recent article that

As Afghan forces are readied to assume more security responsibility, combined NATO-Afghan operations are also clearing insurgent strongholds in Helmand, Kandahar, and Kunduz and normalcy is slowly returning to areas that only knew war. Local militias are integrating into the formal security structure; commerce is returning; and schools are opening. GDP has increased from $170 under the Taliban to $1,000 per capita in 2010; almost all Afghans now have increased basic health services (only nine per cent did in 2002); school enrolment has increased from 900,000 (mainly boys) to almost seven million (37 per cent girls); and women now serve in government.[5]

However, progress is still painfully slow and with the clock now ticking, the tension between the minimum level of stability sought and the situation on the ground is clear. At the very least the coalition will need to intensify efforts to talk, while fighting with the insurgents with a new set of political and reconciliation initiatives launched to improve the conditions for serious transitional negotiations. To that end, much more needs to be made of Track II processes, including proxy negotiations for the leaderships of the parties to the conflict.

Consequently, tactical and local level reconciliation can only be seen in the context of efforts to achieve national political reconciliation. Without that linkage, local steps will always be vulnerable. In fact, political momentum will only be achieved if host nation stakeholders are at the forefront of the political process and the Karzai regime steps to the front quickly. External mediation is of course vital and will remain so, but needs to be led by a powerful political figure. However, since the loss of Richard Holbrooke, no figure of comparable stature has emerged.

Ultimately, however, the success of the campaign now depends on the Afghan Government, which not only remains profoundly corrupt but must surely understand that it cannot be propped up indefinitely by NATO and the wider West. Frankly, poor governance and official corruption continues to drive too much of the conflict and the performance of the Afghan Government and this must improve. It might thus be useful if the government in Kabul began to properly enunciate its own vision of a future pluralistic and complex Afghanistan – that would be the true start of transition.

Making the Comprehensive Approach[6] a reality

The nature of Alliance stability operations demands three critical partnerships: first, close partnership with the UN and other international organizations to provide political legitimacy; second, a close working partnership is still needed with the Kabul Government for all its many failings; third, a close, coherent, and effective civil-military partnership is needed across the policy as well as a task list generated for stability operations. The 2010

NATO Strategic Concept placed a particular premium on operationalizing the Comprehensive Approach.[7]

However, the Comprehensive Approach is dependent on the efficient generation and use of political will, strategic patience, and necessary resources. Operations in Afghanistan reinforce the need to grip the fundamentals of operational effectiveness in hybrid conflict situations. Lessons from Afghanistan suggest that effective hybrid operations must be centered on a four-star theater command, supported by rotatable High Readiness Forces (Land) (HRF (L)) able to fight and maintain the tactical battle.[8] Ideally, a bespoke Comprehensive Approach Command under the Deputy Supreme Allied Commander, Europe (DSACEUR) would ensure that civil-military integration takes place from top to bottom and from the strategic to the tactical level, with the initial role of strategic headquarters to ensure that campaign planning is sound, and above all, the assured organization and delivery of forces and resources to theater.

Operations within the compass of the Comprehensive Approach must, from their inception, be based on a holistic view of the strategic objectives, which has not always been the case in Afghanistan. This particularly concerns the impact of actions on mission success and that assessments of such actions are shared by all partners. Influence is the medium through which the Comprehensive Approach is most clearly manifested. It is the central organizing concept for hybrid operations, among elements (campaign planning, targeting policy, and strategic communications) that form a holistic approach to mission management.

Naturally, continuity at the politico-military level is vital. NATO is best equipped to develop mechanisms such as policy steering groups and civilian planning elements. However, they must be developed for all headquarters and fully integrated into the best practices of Supreme Headquarters, Allied Powers, Europe (SHAPE) and strategic headquarters, such as Brunssum and Naples, so that all partners critical to mission success are brought into the process (physically as well as figuratively) and thus embrace both concept and design early in the operational cycle. Moreover, too often variances between U.S. approaches and structures and those of NATO allies have undermined the unity of effort and purpose vital to mission success.

In hybrid operations, NATO strategic commands must be rigorous in their application of a standard model of effective and flexible command and control. Strategic command must be able to embrace key civilian partners (member and partner nations, International Organizations (IOs) and Non-Governmental Organizations (NGOs)), supported by HRFs that are able to operate at the tactical level as a rotatable planning and command nexus for sustained operations in such domains. Too often NATO has failed this test.

The aspiration of the Comprehensive Approach has been a whole-of-government approach centered on the Alliance with structures built in accordance with the sustained backing of nations to support the theater-level effort. However, the Alliance has tended to over-bureaucratize the process, and the campaign in Afghanistan has suffered accordingly. Specifically, NATO has failed to harmonize headquarter practices and Standard Operating Procedures (SOP), which demands the establishment of more systematic relations between partner institutions and states engaged on and in hybrid conflict. This would promote a better understanding of realizable aspirations and thus enhance all-important campaign planning and performance monitoring.

Experience gained in Afghanistan suggests regular meetings and exercises would lead to a better understanding of the opportunities (and constraints) for cooperation. Additionally it would lead to a better understanding of achievable goals over time, which is a central tenant of effective stability operations. Therefore, building on NATO's Mid-Term Exercise Program, a more systematic set of exercises is needed with a detailed audit process and results that are shared with all partner institutions and partner states. A broad understanding of civilian capacity and capability development is also vital. NATO lacks capability beyond short-term infrastructure development, which is in itself limited to the direct support of deployable forces. NATO, therefore, requires mechanisms that can afford the Alliance a broader understanding of capacity and capability development together with assured access to resources (together with a determination to become involved in these sectors) that are, usually, on a direct path to the strategic objectives of a mission.

Afghanistan operations also suggest far more NATO Subject Matter Experts are needed both at the center and within operational headquarters. Certainly, NATO needs to build civilian capability within structures using seconded civilian experts at SHAPE, Joint Force, and HRF levels. This is different from merely looking after people it has applied to a mission; rather it combines the creation of specific command and control structures to support such efforts with systematic access on short notice, to relevant expertise prior to other actors taking the lead. Civilian expertise will also need to be positioned to support deployed headquarters. A more systematic approach to training and education is thus needed for military and civilians alike. There ought to be a particular focus on how to operate in a multinational military organization, better understand the contemporary operating environment, build effective and durable networks with civilian organizations, and understand the different planning methodologies and doctrines of a multiplicity of critical partner organizations.

Furthermore, all of NATO's deployable headquarters must be able to effectively "plug and play" with a cadre of expert civilians built around a dedicated Civilian Planning Element (CPE) embedded in civil-military planning and the civil support elements of a headquarters. The CPE must be able to pass on knowledge and know-how to successors to ensure campaign momentum.

NATO experience in Afghanistan has reinforced the vital importance of effective strategic communications. Strategic communications explain why actions are necessary and effective targeting policy must always be able to justify such actions in terms of both mission and public opinion. Broad consultation regarding policy with key civilian partners; a wider understanding of what comprises a strategic communications target; and a strategic communications strategy that places all actions within a broad context would all promote enhanced synchronization and reduce conflict of efforts by partners.

Certainly, NATO headquarters have become much more effective at achieving synergies between action and message but the response times still too often lag that of the Taliban. Small command groups now support NATO commanders in real time and now include as standard a strategic communications advisor, who is often a civilian from outside the formal structure to work in support of the public affairs officer or an experienced military practitioner. The advisor works in close conjunction with the political advisor and cultural advisor and often liaises with academics via a commander's initiative group. The advisor is part of a civilian cluster designed to test all planning assumptions as well as reach out to external expertise, possibly under a "super-advisor" who acts as a Chief of Advisory Staff.[9]

20 military-strategic lessons from Afghanistan for future NATO operations

There are 20 military-strategic lessons from NATO operations in Afghanistan, all of which relate back to the need for unity of effort and purpose in hybrid conflict. All of the lessons emphasize the need for a truly multinational approach to operations, from campaign design to completion based on a willingness to share political and military risk. It is NATO's planning capabilities and SOPs that not only make such synergy possible but unique the world over. Indeed, it is NATO's unique selling point in the first decades of the 21st century. The lessons can be summarized as follows.

1 Take a strategic approach to campaign planning and performance

A strategic approach to campaign planning and performance avoids the tendency to confuse values with interests apparent in NATO's campaign. Use of NATO armed forces should always be commensurate with the national interests of its members. Naturally, Counter-Insurgency (COIN) by definition requires a pact with the people. However, specific criteria that define minimum success should be established at the outset and adhered to throughout the campaign to avoid mission creep.

2 Establish strategic unity of effort and purpose at the outset of a campaign

The division between the U.S.-led Operation Enduring Freedom (OEF) and ISAF led to a division of effort that compromised the relationship between counter-terror and COIN operations. Too often, this led to a perceived imbalance on the part of Afghans as to the nature of the foreign presence. OEF was by definition very "kinetic," which too often countered ISAF efforts to establish all-important trust at the community level. This was compounded with the lack of a truly multinational command approach. Too often deployed forces simply imported national doctrines reinforcing the friction at the heart of NATO operations.

3 Harmonize the political strategy with local politics and custom

Most fractured or failed states have never known and/or are probably incompatible with Jeffersonian democracy. In such societies stability comes first, for it is that commodity upon which survival is made possible. Political strategy must from the outset be utterly sensitive to, and build upon local traditional structures if national and sub-national efforts at capacity-building are to be realized.

4 Place reconciliation and rehabilitation as a central tenet of the political strategy

Insurgencies are rarely monolithic. The Taliban is a loose grouping comprised of four distinct elements. Indeed, evidence suggests that many attacks on coalition forces often took place by local elements angry at the presence of foreigners. By making reconciliation central to campaign planning, not only will this assist in dividing insurgents, it can also lead to critical intelligence about the nature and motivations of adversaries.

5 Avoid linking transition to withdrawal

Transition to host nation governance must not become synonymous with withdrawal in the mind of the people. This not only exacerbates popular uncertainty, but also encourages adversaries. Critical to success will be sufficiently robust and accountable governmental bodies, able to perform a full range of governance. This requires a determined focus on government capacity-building, which must necessarily provide the bedrock for stability during any drawdown.

6 Establish a sound relationship between strategy and resources from the outset of a campaign

The COIN strategy in Afghanistan was badly under-resourced, fractured, and ill-conceived from the outset. This led to disconnect between the political goals and the military effort. Indeed, even when sufficient resources were made available, the ability of the Afghan Government to absorb support was inadequate. This compounded the corruption which has plagued the effort from the outset.

7 Create a clear command chain

For the sake of political politesse non-U.S. forces were nominally under NATO, i.e. SHAPE command. In fact, the preponderance of U.S. forces, allied to a lack of respect for the Alliance amongst the American political and military leadership resulted in a situation in which, for all intents and purposes, U.S. Central Command really ran the show. This created unnecessary levels of friction and complexity in an already byzantine command chain. In the future, SHAPE should lead and be properly prepared for the task.

8 Establish transition at the outset of a campaign

This means a clear focus early to hand over/back power and responsibility to host governments at the earliest opportunity. This places particular emphasis on capacity-building of host nation security forces.

9 Match forces to mission

Ideally the main bulk of force is needed at the outset of a campaign, allied to shared rules of engagement across the theater to promote unity of effort and purpose. This is vital if campaign momentum is to be established.

10 Prepare early for the long haul

The Bosnia-plus mind-set of many NATO allies prevented the early establishment of a shared level of ambition commensurate with the challenge in Afghanistan. This colored all subsequent actions, which were often too little, too late. Even when the combat capability has been removed, training and support will likely be needed over a long period. Who will undertake such missions and how they will be protected is a critical issue that was never satisfactorily addressed in Afghanistan. The critical shortage of expert civilians was compounded by an inability to properly protect them. This created an imbalance in the effort and as such, civilians could rarely venture into the areas where they were critically needed.

11 Ensure the force to task to space ratio is balanced

There have never been a sufficient number of troops to assert control across Afghanistan. This has been compounded by a lack of ability to rapidly reinforce forces under pressure. The lack of reserves was enhanced by (1) the lack of tactical mobility, i.e. insufficient numbers of helicopters; (2) numerous national caveats, preventing effective force mobility and rotation; and (3) varying national caveats which prevented the efficient use of the force and which in effect rendered it far smaller as a force than numbers would suggest.

12 Do not parcel out regions to states

The creation of Provincial Reconstruction Teams (PRT) was based on U.S. practice in Iraq. However, in Iraq the overwhelming majority were U.S.-led. In Afghanistan nationally led PRTs led to a complex mass of different approaches, methodologies, doctrines, and metrics which undermined the campaign.

13 Treat the enemy with respect

The Taliban is a sophisticated enemy that continually changes both tactics and methods. For example, their use of Improvised Explosive Devices (IED) and electronic communications has become steadily more sophisticated since 2001. Too often, NATO forces were deployed with ineffectual tactics and equipment, leading to increased casualties or simply withdrawn from the field due to excessive risk, stalling the campaign.

14 Focus on balanced security force capacity-building

Fighting power is critical to any force, particularly the ANA. However, due regard must be given to the moral component. This involves working with host forces to develop leadership, discipline, culture, ethics, and anti-corruption if the capability of a force is to be ensured over the longer term.

15 Consider civilian casualties in all operational planning

NATO forces must at all times consider the possibility of civilian casualties, how to avoid them, and how best to respond when regrettably such casualties are incurred. Only in the last year or so has the number of civilian casualties begun to drop. However, by this time a significant amount of trust had been lost. To better understand the impact of such casualties, both on the population and the strategy, better monitoring is needed, as well as a greater level of understanding about the difference between casualties inflicted by the coalition and those by the insurgents.

16 *Harmonize macro and micro-planning in campaign planning*

At the macro-economic level, the U.S. has calculated Afghan mineral resources to be worth some $1 trillion. Such natural resources not only enable development to be funded, but also help to re-integrate national economies into the regional and global economy. At the micro-economic level the support of local tribes and clans is vital to establishing order and governance. To that end, the development of a legitimate local economy is critical because it would help to undermine support and sanctuaries for adversaries.

17 *Create seamless strategic communications early in the campaign plan*

Culturally focused strategic communications via television and radio help to ensure words and deeds match: strategic communications seek to change behavior and perceptions for the better. As such, strategic communications are central to a coordinated influence and information campaign. Communicating strategically demands that such campaigns are led from the center under a high level of political leadership. Moreover, such communications necessarily demand a high degree of understanding of local and national communities. Access to Subject Matter Experts (SME) both deployed and at home will be vital.

18 *Place a greater emphasis on language-training*

Sufficient numbers of deployed civilian and military personnel must be able to converse in local languages and dialects.

19 *Establish a conditions-based approach to force levels*

When initial stability has been established, force-levels should be commensurate with conditions on the ground. This is particularly important during withdrawals. If carried out without due regard to the conditions, host governments and forces will be placed in a very difficult position. By their very nature such forces will be relatively brittle and thus support of them will be critical to the strategy.

20 *Develop an Alliance-wide concept of civil-military operations*

The effective operationalization of the Comprehensive Approach is central to the future utility of NATO, and the Alliance is vital to the effective, legitimate conduct of the Comprehensive Approach if mission success is to be achieved in future hybrid operations. Effective civil-military operations are dependent on (1) sufficient numbers of deployable civilians; (2) the development of a real civil-military partnership culture; and (3) consistency of effort in developing such partnerships up.

Alternative futures for operations

The NATO Chicago Summit declaration notes that after 2014 full security responsibility will be transferred to Afghan authorities and the NATO-led combat mission will have ended, though NATO will

> continue to provide strong and long-term political and practical support through our Enduring Partnership with Afghanistan. NATO is ready to work towards establishing, at the request of the Government of the Islamic Republic of Afghanistan, a new post-2014 mission of a different nature in Afghanistan, to train, advise and assist the ANSF, including the Afghan Special Operations Forces.[10]

In a world in which current change – its pace and scope – are virtually unrivalled in history, any analyst should approach future scenarios with extreme caution. The options range from World War III at one end of the scale to a political and economic settlement at the other. Therefore, having established an author's health warning, the three scenarios are thus: *plus ça change, plus c'est la même chose*, a tighter but still informal network approach; or a NATO Comprehensive Approach Command.

Scenario one envisages an Alliance that has learned a lot from operations in Afghanistan but which lacks the political will to turn lessons into structures. Allied Command Transformation (ACT), or whatever its successor command is called (reorganization is the only sure thing in a failing organization), and the Joint Assessment and Lessons Learned Center will offer a multitude of lessons which will be disseminated across both commands and nations. Some of the more engaged international states, such as Britain and France, will consider them. Other Europeans will examine them and then discard them on the grounds that if one lacks the capability *and* the capacity, neither the Americans nor the UN will ask one to do anything. The Americans, of course, will have to learn their own lessons and much time will be lost in conferences between the Americans and Europeans discussing the failures of Afghanistan, each blaming the other. Consequently, there will be little unity of effort and purpose, and certainly no structure. As such, increasingly as we move into the future all those with experience in Afghanistan will either be dead, retired, or will have forgotten.

Scenario two envisages an alliance that has indeed taken the lessons from above and distilled them into NATO Standards and Standard Operating Procedures (SOPs). Nevertheless, whilst Allied Command Operations and its component high readiness joint and land forces have exercised new headquarters structures for deployment, the emphasis remains on coalitions of the willing, rather than an Alliance-wide structure. As some states will be more willing than others, the exercise program will reflect this, with the usual military and civilian suspects populating events such as, let us imagine, Exercise ARRCADE FUSION 2020. The Americans, British, and French will be in the lead, possibly with Dutch, German, and Italian support. However, because the funding lines for operations stem from capitals, the danger remains that as soon as a crisis which requires a stabilization and reconstruction campaign design emerges, the nations will withdraw control from the Alliance. NATO will be reduced to coordinating a series of security and development fiefdoms across the "new Afghanistan." NATO will have grasped how to make such an effort more efficient but nevertheless, the effort will remain essentially flawed.

A third scenario could anticipate a NATO that has learned the lessons of Afghanistan. More importantly, so have the nations. Consequently, in 2015 at the Strategic Concept Mid-Term Review Summit, NATO member states decide to build on the 2010 Strategic Concept and its call for improved crisis management structures. They construct an Alliance Comprehensive Approach command. Supreme Allied Commander Transformation (SACT) is invited to submit a report within a year to the North Atlantic Council and then given the go-ahead to develop a program of experimentation, exercising, and gaming that will lead to the formal creation of a certificated NATO Comprehensive Approach Command with national civil and military "forces" rotating through the command. NATO commanders, informed by the Secretary-General, will be given freedom to establish the necessary rules of engagement with all national caveats removed. A common operational fund will be established in parallel with new outreach structures established to ensure access to the necessary expertise. The focus of campaigns will be on a four-star headquarters in theater with NATO strategic headquarters, such as Brunssum and Naples playing an enabling and supporting role.

Conclusions

NATO has faced many challenges in Afghanistan and many of them have been self-inflicted. No matter what happens by the end of major combat operations in 2014, there is no question that the Alliance's ability to shape and influence the strategic landscape has been damaged by the poor quality of campaign planning and performance in Afghanistan. That said, both NATO members and others are exaggerating Alliance "weakness." The simple fact is that the Afghanistan campaign never crossed the threshold between peace and war in many NATO capitals to justify the investment of forces and resources in order to succeed. One can design the most elaborate of campaigns but without the necessary resourcing from the outset, underpinned by political legitimacy and above all, sound and consistent high-level political leadership, any such effort risks failure.

Notes

1 Statement of General David Petraeus, U.S. Army, Commander, International Security Assistance Force, before the Senate Armed Services Committee, Washington, 15 March, 2011.

2 NATO, "NATO Summit Declaration," Issued by the Heads of State and Government participating in the meeting of the North Atlantic Council in Chicago on 20 May 2012, Chicago Summit, 20 May 2012. Online. Available: www.nato.int/cps/en/natolive/official_texts_87593.htm.

3 The Agreement on Provisional Arrangements in Afghanistan Pending the Re-Establishment of Permanent Government Institutions, otherwise known as the Bonn Agreement, aimed at re-creating a State of Afghanistan which is today known as the Government of the Islamic Republic of Afghanistan (GIROA).

4 ISAF website. Available: www.isaf.nato.int/troop-numbers-and-contributors/imdex.php.

5 W.B. Caldwell, "NATO and the Afghan Surge," blog posted 15 August 2011. Online. Available: www.acus.org/new_atlanticist/nato-and-afghansurge.

6 The Comprehensive Approach is the generation and application of security, governance and development services, expertise, structures, and resources over time and distance in partnership with host nations, host regions, allied and partner governments, and partner institutions, both governmental and non-governmental. See Chapter 7.

7 Paragraph 21 of the 2010 NATO Strategic Concept states: "The lessons learned from NATO operations, in particular in Afghanistan and the Western Balkans, make it clear that a comprehensive political, civilian and military approach is necessary for effective crisis management. The Alliance will engage actively with other international actors before, during and after crises to encourage collaborative analysis, planning and conduct of activities on the ground, in order to maximise coherence and effectiveness of the overall international effort." See the "Strategic Concept For the Defence and Security of The Members of the North Atlantic Treaty Organisation" Adopted by Heads of State and Government in Lisbon at the NATO Summit, 19 November, 2010.

8 The seven HRF (L) HQs of NATO's Force Structure include, in addition to the ARRC, the Eurocorps, the 1st German-Netherlands Corps, the NATO Rapid Deployment Corps-Italy, the NATO Rapid Deployment Corps-Spain, the NATO Rapid Deployment Corps-Turkey, and the Rapid Reaction Corps-France.

9 The author is Head of the Commander's Initiative Group of NATO's Allied Rapid Reaction Corps (ARRC).

10 NATO, "NATO Summit Declaration," Chicago.

9 NATO and nuclear weapons

Michael Rühle[1]

As long as nuclear weapons exist, NATO will remain a nuclear alliance.
NATO's Strategic Concept, November 2010

Introduction

To a considerable extent, questions of nuclear weaponry and deterrence are questions of faith, beyond "hard" empirical science. The overriding rationale of nuclear weapons is to deter conflict. Yet since one can never prove with certainty why an event has *not* occurred, the role of nuclear weapons in preventing war remains a mere assumption. The same holds true for the more specific political and military functions attributed to nuclear weapons: they are more or less plausible assertions, without definitive proof.

However, the absence of empirical evidence does not mean that each and every view on nuclear matters carries equal weight. If anything, questions that cannot be "proven" require an even greater amount of intellectual discipline. This is all the more true when it comes to pondering the future of nuclear weapons in NATO. Since its inception, NATO has been struggling with the challenge of how best to integrate nuclear weapons into its defense posture and strategy. Throughout NATO's history, allies have argued about the relationship between nuclear and conventional weapons, about the credibility problems of extended deterrence, about preventing the proliferation of nuclear weapons, and about granting non-nuclear allies influence over U.S. nuclear planning and employment.

Despite the controversial aspects that surround nuclear weapons, the U.S. willingness to use them in case of a major attack on its allies has become a central pillar of Western security policy and indeed of the European political order. Given the new debate about nuclear abolition, in which key tenets of nuclear deterrence – and in particular extended deterrence – are being revisited, it is instructive to examine NATO's nuclear history and its implications for alternative futures.

NATO's nuclear history

The beginning of the Cold War and the advent of the nuclear age were two seminal events that occurred simultaneously. The world became bipolar and nuclear at the same time. This symbiotic relationship between the Cold War and nuclear weapons lasted for four decades and shaped NATO to a considerable degree.

Almost since its inception NATO has been a nuclear alliance. Faced with the dilemma of providing military reassurance for a demoralized postwar Western Europe on the one hand while balancing the budget on the other, the U.S. made nuclear weapons a centerpiece of its strategy for NATO. Unlike major conventional re-armament, nuclear weapons were affordable, and, due to U.S. nuclear superiority, a credible means of war prevention. Since the Soviet Union had no means to threaten the U.S. homeland, the strategy of "massive retaliation," which envisaged the early use of nuclear weapons, even in case of a purely conventional Soviet attack, had a certain logical consistency. Accordingly, the U.S. introduced nuclear weapons into Europe as early as 1952. By the end of the decade, about 3,000 nuclear weapons (missiles, artillery, and mines) were deployed in Europe.

Throughout the 1950s, allied consensus regarding "massive retaliation" was strong. A nuclear-centered defense strategy allowed the European allies to avoid a massive conventional buildup and focus on their economic recovery. Moreover, NATO's lack of strategic depth in Western Europe would have required a conventional defense on a level that seemed elusive, and the recent experience of World War II had convinced many observers that even a large-scale conventional war would devastate this densely populated region. "Massive retaliation," therefore, appeared like the optimal solution, as it seemed to reconcile political-military credibility and economic affordability.[2]

With the advent of Soviet intercontinental ballistic missiles in the late 1950s, the transatlantic consensus on NATO's nuclear dimension started to unravel. When the United States became vulnerable to Soviet long-range nuclear weapons, a NATO strategy of early and massive nuclear use in the European theatre appeared increasingly risky, as it could lead to counterattacks on the U.S. homeland. Consequently, the new Kennedy administration sought to modify NATO's strategy by arguing in favor of a more selective use of nuclear weapons and by putting a greater emphasis on conventional defense measures.

Despite its emphasis on enhancing U.S. credibility, "flexible response" met with skepticism and even outright resistance by the European NATO allies, who continued to prefer "massive retaliation" as a far less costly alternative. As a result, "flexible response" was not officially adopted by NATO until 1967. Even after this formal endorsement, however, the strategy was never fully implemented. While European allies began to absorb the conceptual logic of "flexible response," they were not willing to provide the necessary conventional means to translate this strategy into practice. As a result, NATO's conventional defense posture in Europe never fully corresponded with the ambitious strategy it was supposed to underpin. Moreover, despite Washington's emphasis on bolstering NATO's conventional defense, the 1960s and 1970s witnessed the introduction of even more nuclear weapons into Western Europe, eventually peaking at 7,000 warheads.

The unwillingness of the European allies to put more emphasis on conventional defense was not the only dilemma that burdened NATO throughout the 1960s. Two other developments had come to the fore that required addressing by the U.S. and NATO: preventing nuclear proliferation among the allies as well as globally, and finding a way for the allies to participate in U.S. nuclear planning. Both issues were intertwined. With the UK and France developing their own nuclear arsenals and France leaving NATO's military structure due to disagreements with the U.S., Washington could only hope to contain further proliferation among the allies by granting them a degree of political and military participation in U.S. nuclear planning. While the proposal for a sea-based multilateral nuclear force (MLF) failed for political, military and financial reasons,[3] the Nuclear Planning Group (NPG), set up in 1967, finally provided the appropriate forum for the allies (except France) to discuss nuclear matters and develop agreed guidelines on nuclear employment.[4]

This political evolution mirrored developments in the military domain. When starting to introduce nuclear weapons into Western Europe in the early 1950s, the United States had offered that the conventional forces of all willing allies be made "dual-capable" with the provision of U.S. nuclear warheads under bilateral programs of cooperation. The warheads were to remain under the positive control and physical custody of the United States, but in wartime would be released for employment by certified allied units. In the 1960s, a major element of these nuclear sharing arrangements was embodied by European dual-capable aircraft (DCA) that were deployed in several European NATO countries and armed with U.S. nuclear gravity bombs. These sharing arrangements were also meant to ease European – notably German – worries with regard to signing the 1968 Non-Proliferation Treaty (NPT) as Non-Nuclear Weapons States (NNWS). The notion of "sharing" would at least ameliorate the NTP's inherent discriminatory character by suggesting, at least in intent, a tendency towards equalizing the status of nuclear and non-nuclear allies. In conformity with the logic of the NPT, the U.S. would retain control of its nuclear arsenal, yet European allies would participate in the nuclear mission, both materially and conceptually.

While the discrepancy between NATO's ambitions and military reality was a recurring theme in Western defense expert circles, it did not become a matter of public debate. On the contrary, the second half of the

1960s saw notions of détente and arms control gaining prominence, cul-minating in NATO's 1967 "Harmel Report" that laid out a dual approach of defense and détente. In 1972, the United States and the Soviet Union agreed limitations on strategic nuclear missiles as well as missile defenses – agreements that were interpreted by many observers as a willingness of both superpowers to enshrine strategic nuclear parity and mutual vulnera-bility as the benchmarks of their nuclear relationship. As fears of Soviet military power subsided, the dilemmas of NATO's nuclear strategy did not feature in the public discourse.

Developments below the strategic nuclear level, however, remained problematic. When the Warsaw Pact began to pursue a strategy that seemed to aim at a rapid conventional offensive intended to undercut NATO's nuclear response options, the mismatch between NATO's declar-atory policy and actual posture became all the more apparent. The allies sought to counter this strategy by introducing advanced conventional strike weapons with longer ranges, yet financial constraints made these measures appear half-hearted. In addition, the debate over NATO's vul-nerabilities and the costs of reducing them also acquired a public dimen-sion. Public criticism of concepts such as "Air Land Battle" or "Follow-on Forces Attack" as being too offensive for a defensive alliance highlighted another dilemma of NATO: unlike the Warsaw Pact, NATO's democracies had to pursue security policies that would reassure rather than alarm their electorates.

NATO's 1979 decision to deploy intermediate-range nuclear forces in Europe sparked a series of events that almost led to a breakdown of reas-surance. The decision had been a reaction to the introduction of a new generation of medium-range Soviet nuclear missiles, which would have provided Moscow with a "eurostrategic" option, i.e. the option to hold Western Europe at nuclear risk without necessarily involving the United States. European allies became concerned that Moscow was seeking to acquire the option of limiting a nuclear exchange to the European theatre and raised the specter of transatlantic "de-coupling." However, the deploy-ment of nuclear ballistic missiles and cruise missiles by the U.S., intended to redress this growing nuclear imbalance and provide for better "cou-pling" with U.S. nuclear forces, led to massive public protests in Western European countries. The sense of alarmism and outright panic that per-meated the public debate was not least a result of the fact that for a long time NATO nations had managed to avoid a public debate about nuclear issues. Thus, European publics were largely unprepared when they were confronted with concrete deployment issues.

In retrospect, the fact that NATO governments stood firm in the face of public opposition appeared like the beginning of the end of the Cold War. Moscow's willingness to enter into negotiations on intermediate-range nuclear forces (INF) – an agreement that eventually led to the elimination of this entire weapons category – contributed to a profound change in the political dynamic of East-West relations that foreshadowed the end of the Cold War a few years later. However, NATO governments had learned the lesson that any debate about nuclear issues was to be avoided at all cost.

NATO's nuclear dimension after the Cold War

The end of the Cold War took nuclear weapons out of the European debate. With the withdrawal of Soviet troops from Central and Eastern Europe, nuclear weapons became disentangled from the conventional sphere. Consequently, NATO's July 1990 London Declaration described nuclear weapons as "weapons of last resort,"[5] indicating that they were no longer regarded as warfighting weapons to augment NATO's conventional defense. This new rhetoric was soon followed by deep cuts in European-based nuclear weapons. Sweeping unilateral reductions by the United States in 1991, echoed by similar Russian commitments, led to the removal of all U.S. nuclear artillery shells and short range ballistic missile warheads from Europe, leaving only U.S. gravity bombs mounted on European DCA. The fact that Russia never fully lived up to her own commitments was not considered to be a serious cause for concern.

As NATO's agenda shifted the emphasis on facilitating Europe's transformation into an undivided democratic security space, nuclear issues faded into the background. A potential political crisis that could have emerged from the nuclear aspects of NATO enlargement was defused preemptively by NATO's so-called "three no's," according to which NATO had "no intention, no plan, and no reason to deploy nuclear weapons on the territory of new members nor any need to change any aspect of NATO's nuclear posture or nuclear policy."[6] Moreover, NATO's post-Cold War military missions – from the Western Balkans to Afghanistan – had no nuclear dimension whatsoever. And the EU's efforts to become an autonomous foreign and security policy actor deliberately excluded the potentially controversial nuclear element.

For almost two decades NATO's nuclear policy remained virtually unchanged. Only small adjustments were made to the force posture, notably by withdrawing U.S. nuclear weapons from Greece and the United Kingdom, and by further reducing the alert levels and readiness criteria for those dual capable aircraft that were earmarked for nuclear missions. None of these measures were made public; they became known only long after they had been implemented. However, the allies repeatedly issued statements according to which the principle of broad allied participation in nuclear matters was considered to remain essential for their security. The new NATO members also joined the NPG, where they would be familiarized with NATO's nuclear "acquis."

Throughout the Cold War, nuclear weapons had been a centerpiece of NATO's deterrence and defense policy and posture. Accordingly, allies had been deeply involved in the debate. While some of these debates were highly controversial, there was a clear understanding about the importance of the nuclear dossier, and about the need for joint strategy development. However, given the diminishing relevance of nuclear weapons for European security after the end of the Cold War, the interest of many European allies in this issue seemed to wane. The strategic communities reoriented themselves towards other subjects. With the exception of France and the UK, NATO's European nuclear powers, the interest in and expertise on nuclear weapons and strategies declined markedly. If there was any debate at all, it was among the non-proliferation community, which looked at NATO's nuclear weapons and sharing arrangements in the context of their implications for global non-proliferation and disarmament.

The second nuclear age

Unlike in Europe, where the fading interest in nuclear matters was a direct result of an improving regional security situation, the United States' perception of nuclear developments was far less sanguine. From the point of view of many Europeans, the end of the Cold War also meant the end of nuclear worries. For the United States, however, with a web of security commitments reaching far beyond Europe, the end of the nuclear stand-off with the Soviet Union provided only partial relief. As early as the mid-1990s the term "second nuclear age" entered the discussion, implying that the end of the Cold War had only marked the closing of one particular chapter in the history of nuclear weapons, and that another was just about to begin.[7]

One early indication of this second nuclear age was the 1991 Gulf War. To deter Iraq from using chemical weapons against coalition forces, Washington warned Saddam Hussein that such an action would mean the end of his regime. This implicit nuclear threat did not amount to an abrogation of the so-called negative security assurances, which prohibit nuclear states from threatening non-nuclear states with nuclear weapons. However, it did underline that biological and chemical weapons of mass destruction had to be included in the U.S. nuclear calculus. As future opponents of the United States might be armed with such weapons, the option of a nuclear threat had to be retained – at least rhetorically.

The discovery of Iraq's secret nuclear program immediately after the Gulf War revealed a massive verification failure – a failure that would later contribute to overestimating Iraq's capabilities in the run-up to the 2003 Iraq war. In 1993, North Korea's nuclear ambitions could only be contained through massive U.S. political and military pressure, yet there was little international support. Several years later, North Korea left the NPT and in 2006 conducted a nuclear test. In 1998, the nuclear tests by India and Pakistan raised questions of how to discourage non-NPT members from seeking nuclear weapons, but also how to bring wayward outsiders into the NPT. That same year, the withdrawal of the UN Special Commission (UNSCOM) from Iraq further underscored the limits of traditional multilateral approaches to non-proliferation.

The terrorist attacks against the United States on 11 September 2001 gave the non-proliferation question a new sense of urgency and dramatically decreased U.S. tolerance vis-à-vis proliferating states (the "axis of evil"). The attacks also raised the specter of terrorist non-state actors armed with WMD, thereby creating a new challenge for the inter-state nature of the NPT regime and invalidating many assumptions of rationality and restraint that were considered central for maintaining a stable deterrence regime. Finally, the debate on the eventual "Talibanization" of Pakistan raised the nightmare of a fundamentalist nuclear power emerging literally overnight.

The uncovering of the nuclear smuggling network of the Pakistani scientist A.Q. Khan in early 2004 invalidated yet another widely shared assumption on which the classical NPT regime was based: the dependence of would-be nuclear powers on support by traditional nuclear weapons states (NWS). Khan's network had supplied Iran, Libya and several other states with technology and know-how. It thus demonstrated that proliferation was increasingly proceeding outside the inter-state NPT regime. It also underscored the danger posed by "second-tier proliferation," an acceleration of the spread of nuclear weapons might lead to more "turnkey states" able to rapidly convert their civilian nuclear programs into military ones.

However, the most severe development was the uncovering of Iran's nuclear program in 2002. Although Iran claimed that the program was entirely for civilian purposes, numerous characteristics indicated a distinctly military focus. Unlike the North Korean challenge, which could be contained, a nuclear Iran was considered by many Western experts to be a "game changer" — faced with the prospect of a nuclear Iran, Saudi Arabia, and other neighbors in the Middle East and the Gulf might also decide to go nuclear. Indications of such a potentially destabilizing "nuclear cascade" were the decisions of many countries in the region to start civilian nuclear programs. As these decisions were taken shortly after the Iranian program had become known, they seemed to be aimed at creating "hedging" options for an uncertain future.

In the view of the George W. Bush administration, these developments were clear indications of the endemic weakness of the international non-proliferation regime. Accordingly, it put the emphasis on unilateral or selective approaches, ranging from voluntary coalitions of states to interdict suspicious shipments (the Proliferation Security Initiative) to UN Security Council Resolution 1540, which obliged all states to pass legislation to tighten non-proliferation efforts. However, the climax of this robust approach in dealing with the second nuclear age was the 2003 war on Iraq. This conflict, which deeply divided the NATO allies, achieved its aim of regime change, yet Iraqi WMD – the major official reason for going to war – could not be found, thus undermining the credibility of the United States and reinforcing European notions that the U.S. was giving too much importance to nuclear issues. By contrast, traditional reciprocal non-proliferation approaches received far less attention during the Bush Administration – a fact that invited charges of pursuing a self-serving and ultimately counter-productive agenda.

The Bush administration's support for a strong U.S. nuclear arsenal also led many observers, notably in the media, to confuse means and ends. A typical example was the discussion on the use of force against future proliferators. Although the administration had produced an ambitious Nuclear Posture Review that sought to further reduce the role of nuclear weapons, parts of the media were creating the false impression that Washington was contemplating the pre-emptive use of nuclear weapons against would-be nuclear powers. Such caricatures served to reinforce European notions that the United States was embarking on a course that Europe was best advised not to follow. Accordingly, the U.S. debate about the "second nuclear age" and its potential implications for Western security received little attention in Europe.

The vision of a nuclear-free world

It was therefore to be expected that the end of the Bush administration would lead to a revival of traditional non-proliferation policies. However, the way in which this revival manifested itself was not. The degree to which the Obama administration appeared willing to subordinate U.S. foreign and defense policy to non-proliferation concerns caught many by surprise. The Obama administration's analysis about the dangers of a second nuclear age did not deviate substantially from those of its predecessor. However, the conclusions were diametrically opposed. Rather than championing selective approaches, the Obama Administration sought to revive the "grand bargain" between the NWS and the NNWS enshrined in the NPT: in order to make progress on non-proliferation, the Nuclear Weapons States had to take their disarmament commitments seriously. In a speech in Prague in April 2009, Barack Obama unveiled his vision of a nuclear-free world and committed the United States to this long-term goal. In early 2010, a new U.S.-Russia treaty on the reduction of strategic nuclear arms was signed, followed by a Nuclear Security Summit in Washington, and the publication of a Nuclear Posture Review that reduced the role of nuclear weapons in U.S. defense strategy. By investing a lot of political capital, the U.S. administration also achieved a successful conclusion of the 2010 NPT Review Conference. All these steps were meant to create the impression of an irresistible political force – a charismatic U.S. president leading the world on a project that seemed both morally appealing and politically necessary.

Not surprisingly, President Obama's vision of a nuclear-free world found a positive reception among many European leaders and non-proliferation experts. Much of this enthusiasm was due to the disappointment about the deterioration of transatlantic relations during the George W. Bush era rather than a result of a concrete analysis of the nuclear landscape. Still, many Europeans were pleased with the de-emphasis of nuclear issues by an administration that promised a different and more benign kind of leadership.

The way in which the U.S. administration qualified its vision of a nuclear-free world made it clear that it was at best a declaration of intent rather than a serious policy guideline for U.S. security policy. The administration was at great pains to reassure allies, notably in Asia, that U.S. extended deterrence commitments would be upheld. U.S. officials also admitted that the logic of the U.S. "nuclear umbrella" – to provide reassurance for allies and thus prevent them from seeking their own nuclear options – had not changed, and that these arrangements might even be extended to the Middle East and the Gulf region should Iran go nuclear. Hence, the 2010 Nuclear Posture Review, despite its overarching message of a reduced salience of nuclear weapons in U.S. defense policy, put a strong emphasis on the U.S. role as a provider of extended nuclear deterrence. Moreover, the decision to modernize both the existing nuclear arsenal as well as the nuclear infrastructure indicated that the U.S. was expecting to stay in the nuclear business for the foreseeable future.

NATO's nuclear dimension at a crossroads

Notwithstanding these qualifications, however, the renewed focus on non-proliferation was bound to direct attention to NATO's nuclear policy and posture. Since the end of the Cold War, repeated appeals by individual European politicians and NGOs to withdraw the remaining U.S. nuclear weapons from Europe had failed to gain support. However, with the U.S. championing the goal of a nuclear-free world, such calls appeared to acquire new significance. In the wake of President Obama's Prague speech, several NATO governments, including from countries that host U.S. nuclear weapons, demanded withdrawal of these weapons. While all allies agreed that changes in NATO's nuclear posture should be decided by consensus, thus ruling out purely national solutions, the debate that NATO had been avoiding for almost 20 years had finally arrived. Unlike previous nuclear debates, however, the key issue was not how to restore the credibility of NATO's nuclear deterrent in light of an adversary's military buildup. On the contrary, the new debate was dominated by the desire to minimize, if not outright terminate, certain aspects of NATO's traditional nuclear policies and arrangements.

Whether a nuclear-free world will actually be a safer world need not be discussed here, as the complete elimination of nuclear weapons is likely to take more than a generation, if it can be achieved at all. Hence, the focus will be on the process rather than the desired end-state. Still, the way in which the debate has unfolded since President Obama's Prague speech indicates that this process will confront NATO with several challenges, in particular with respect to the specific contributions that NATO could or should make, as well as their timing. The ambiguity of the U.S. approach, which seeks to marry a long-term "abolitionist" vision with the continued reliance on nuclear deterrence in the short and medium term, invites different interpretations of the implications for NATO's policy. Not surprisingly, NATO's November 2010 Strategic Concept endorsed the vision of a nuclear-free world, yet not without caveats.[8]

A fundamental discussion about global military developments and their implications for NATO's defense posture did not take place until after the release of the Strategic Concept in November 2010. The Deterrence and Defence Posture Review (DDPR) sought to take a fresh look at NATO's conventional and nuclear requirements, including in light of developments outside of Europe. The Review, which introduced missile defense as a separate category next to conventional and nuclear weapons, was given the mandate to re-visit the "appropriate mix" of forces and thus refine the general guidelines offered by the Strategic Concept. NATO's willingness to engage in such an exercise created high expectations, notably by the NGO community, as to fundamental changes in NATO's nuclear posture and declaratory policy. However, given the widely known differences in allied views, the DDPR, which was published at the May 2012 Chicago Summit, contained more evolutionary than revolutionary elements.[9] The fundamentals of NATO's nuclear policy and posture were reaffirmed. However, although with heavy caveats, negative security assurances were introduced, and eventual further reductions in Tactical Nuclear Weapons (TNWs) were envisaged. Moreover, the decision to continue an arms control committee that had only been established in the run-up to the DDPR could also be interpreted as a greater emphasis on the arms control and non-proliferation dimensions. The emphasis on Russian reciprocity, however, underscored the need for NATO to also take external developments into account. Once again, as with the 2010 Strategic Concept, considerations of alliance cohesion and reassurance prevailed over national de-nuclearization agendas and non-proliferation arguments.

The modest results of the DDPR brought home that the approach that had been pursued by many arms control and non-proliferation advocates, notably from the NGO community, was deficient at least in one important respect: the emphasis on non-proliferation, often complemented by claims that TNW and nuclear sharing arrangements were relics of a bygone era, missed the very essence of NATO as a security and defense alliance. Still, the DDPR could not be expected to end the debate for good. The document's ambiguous wording was a clear sign that the debate would continue, and that the proposals put forward by the NGO community would remain on the international agenda.

The most obvious short-term challenge for NATO's nuclear dimension pertains to nuclear sharing.[10] In the view of "global zero" supporters, the withdrawal of U.S. nuclear gravity bombs from Europe would send a powerful message that the NATO allies were giving non-proliferation precedence over outdated nuclear dogmatism. Such proposals tie in with arguments that had long been made by the anti-nuclear activists among the NGO community, who maintain that nuclear sharing arrangements were violating the Nuclear Non-Proliferation Treaty. However, the end of a U.S. nuclear presence in Europe would have serious ramifications. As a result of NATO enlargement, several nations that have joined the alliance continue to harbor doubts as to Russia's benign long-term evolution. As these nations are also geographically the most exposed, they have consistently sought a high degree of U.S. and/or NATO visibility with respect to their defense. While NATO's "three no's" rule out nuclear deployments in these countries except for the most serious of circumstances, these allies nevertheless regard U.S. nuclear systems in Europe as an important symbol of U.S. commitment. Consequently, the removal of these systems would constitute a security "minus" and possibly increase doubts about the level of U.S. willingness to protect NATO's most vulnerable members.[11]

In addition, the degree of European influence on U.S. nuclear planning might diminish should European allies no longer be willing to share nuclear burdens. Finally, the palpable nervousness in Japan and South Korea (where there are no sharing arrangements of any kind) about the level of U.S. nuclear commitment suggests that NATO's nuclear sharing arrangements based on DCA are still valuable and thus are not likely to be relinquished early in the process towards a nuclear-free world. Accordingly, NATO's 2010 Strategic Concept states that NATO will "ensure the broadest possible participation of allies in collective defense planning on nuclear roles, in peacetime basing of nuclear forces, and in command, control and consultation arrangements."[12] In the short term at least, the reduction of the number of nuclear weapons in NATO Europe may thus appear to be more feasible than their complete withdrawal.

Another contribution that NATO could make is a "sole purpose" declaration along the lines of the 2010 U.S. Nuclear Posture Review. However, the NPR conditions this declaration in ways that appear impractical for a multinational alliance.[13] Moreover, such a declaration, if deemed desirable, would need to require the consent of the other nuclear powers in NATO, as both Britain and France – albeit to different degrees – currently ascribe functions to their nuclear weapons that go beyond merely deterring the use of other nuclear weapons.

Yet another contribution to maintaining the momentum of non-proliferation would be transparency measures, notably with respect to Russia's opaque stockpile of tactical nuclear weapons. These measures would be the first step in a process that could eventually lead to the abolition of this weapons category, along the lines of the 1987 INF agreement. Although Russia has demonstrated a lack of interest in such negotiations, given both its conventional inferiority vis-à-vis NATO and concerns about China, the possibility of a negotiated outcome will remain attractive to allies and thus remain on the U.S.-Russian agenda.

Another contribution to global non-proliferation – albeit an indirect one – would be the introduction of missile defenses. NATO's decision to build an alliance-wide missile defense system has been understood by some observers as marking a shift from deterrence by punishment to deterrence by denial, thus reducing the salience of nuclear weapons in NATO's strategy. Whether this argument is serious or merely another alibi for de-nuclearization can only be determined once the planned missile defense system is in place. Moreover, the allies' preference for an agreement with Russia regarding missile defenses may require the acceptance of quantitative and qualitative limits that would constrain the system's effectiveness.

All these proposed measures have one common characteristic: their focus is on political and military contributions to nuclear non-proliferation rather than on military requirements of nuclear deterrence. With the arguable exception of missile defense, which – at least in the U.S. view – is a means to defend against Iran as well as future nuclear aspirants, the post-Prague debate about nuclear weapons in NATO appeared detached from global military developments. Attempts during the DDPR process to connect NATO's deterrence requirements to new nuclear developments outside of Europe, notably the Middle East, have proven difficult. As a result, some aspects of the nuclear debate seemed focused on the past, as evidenced by the frequent references to Russia's TNW arsenal. Throughout these nuclear debates it had become obvious that despite its military and political engagement on several continents, NATO has not yet developed a collective mindset that fully takes account of global security developments.

Three scenarios

Whether the emphasis on non-proliferation over deterrence is likely to remain a defining characteristic of NATO's approach to the nuclear issue will depend on the broader international context. Just as the renewed focus on non-proliferation is largely due to a distinct U.S. view on how to approach global security challenges, any further change in U.S. views due to new global developments will, by definition, change the political dynamic within NATO. The three distinct scenarios that are presented here are intended to illustrate the range of change that could affect NATO's nuclear dimension in the next two decades. All three scenarios proceed from the assumption that the United States will maintain its internationalist posture, and that it will continue to play the role of a major pillar of global order, including through its security commitments. By contrast, if the U.S. were to opt for a policy of retrenchment, none of the three scenarios would apply – nor would NATO have a future.

1.   The first scenario – moving towards the global elimination of nuclear weapons – has already been analyzed in considerable depth, since it has become a major part of the nuclear discourse at the end of the first decade of the 21st century. Several NGOs have proposed timetables and action plans which seek to provide sensible roadmaps for achieving the desired goal of a nuclear-free world. While the timetables vary, most of these studies converge on a number of key steps that need to be taken if the abolition of nuclear weapons is to be realized at the latest by the middle of the century. These steps include a process of gradual denuclearization by changing political rhetoric, military strategies, and procurement of weapons systems. Examples of such steps are a no-first-use declaration by the nuclear powers and their alliances; a "sole purpose" declaration, according to which the only purpose of nuclear weapons is to deter the use of other nuclear weapons; the end of the development of nuclear weapons; and the elimination of entire categories of nuclear weapons. Other elements include the establishment of further Nuclear-Weapons-Free-Zones (NWFZ) or similar agreements; the end of NATO's nuclear sharing arrangements; and the introduction of missile defenses to reduce the salience of nuclear weapons.[14]

A major assumption that underlies these proposals is the feasibility of sparking a virtuous cycle of gradual progress in non-proliferation and disarmament and increased confidence-building. As nations become confident that nuclear reductions and other measures will not compromise their security, not least because of strengthened verification regimes, they will also become more open to effecting further changes. This process is supposed to lead to the universally agreed legal prohibition of nuclear weapons, augmented by measures to deal with eventual cases of noncompliance.

For NATO, such a scenario would mean to embark on a balancing act between contributing to the "global zero" momentum while maintaining its cohesion as a defense alliance. Finding a way to reconcile the goal of delegitimizing nuclear weapons in the long term with the continued interest in nuclear deterrence in the shorter term might prove extremely difficult, all the more so as allies would disagree on the respective emphasis that should be given to both aspects. Moreover, NATO's European-based nuclear posture is too small to allow for continuous arms control gestures, while the arms control benefits offered by changes in NATO's nuclear rhetoric (e.g. a no-first-use declaration) would be largely symbolic. In short, as NATO's contribution to the arms control and non-proliferation momentum will be limited, U.S. leadership in this process will be crucial. As the originator of the vision of a nuclear-free world, the U.S. must maintain control over how this vision is to be implemented, including with respect to its alliances and bilateral security relationships. Maintaining leadership also requires that the U.S. successfully impose its own vision in a way that does not allow other actors, be it the NGO community or its own allies, to reinterpret this vision in line with their own narrow preferences.[15]

It is moot to speculate about NATO's role once a nuclear-free world has been achieved. If the vision were just about abolishing one specific weapons category, one might simply conclude that NATO's security situation would improve further, as the allies would enjoy global conventional military superiority over any conceivable opponent. However, the vision of a nuclear-free world means much more than the mere abolition of a particular kind of WMD. As even its most ardent supporters admit, a nuclear-free world is only conceivable once the political relationships between the major powers have been profoundly transformed. Hence, the vision is both highly ambitious and highly tautological: if the major problems that lead nations to acquire nuclear weapons were removed, the world would be by definition largely peaceful. In such a cooperative global order NATO might no longer be needed except as an insurance policy in case the system were violated, in order to address smaller, non-existential conflicts, or to manage humanitarian relief operations. *Multinuclear*

2 The second scenario – prevailing in a multinuclear world – proceeds from the assumption that the nuclearization of certain countries, notably Iran, would indeed constitute the frequently mentioned "tipping point" which would lead to a breakdown of the international non-proliferation regime and to a cascade of proliferation. This scenario might unfold with an underground test by Iran, followed by the nuclear "outing" of Israel and accelerated nuclear programs by several other countries in the Middle East and the Gulf. In Asia, a similar cascade might unfold, although most probably not resulting from North Korea's nuclear program but rather from concern over Chinese policies in the region. Such an "anarchic" scenario would also have to include the possibility of certain states reversing their previous decisions to denuclearize, thus sparking new arms competitions in their respective regions. Finally, the emergence of a fundamentalist-controlled nuclear-armed state could not only lead to heightened tensions in its own region, but also trigger a wave of WMD terrorism, ranging from "dirty bombs" all the way to nuclear blackmail or even the deliberate detonation of a nuclear device.

Irrespective of its origins, this multi-nuclear, non-cooperative world order would be characterized by an increasing preference for national over regime-based approaches. Moreover, it would not just lead to a re-emphasis on nuclear weapons but also on other WMD (e.g. biological weapons). The lack of transparency measures due to the breakdown of arms control and non-proliferation regimes would add to a climate of mutual mistrust which in turn would lead nations to rely on preventive and pre-emptive military strategies that could increase the risk of miscalculation in a crisis.

For NATO, such a scenario of nuclear anarchy would mean a significant change in the theory and practice of its nuclear strategy. The need for U.S. nuclear assurances would grow, both with respect to NATO Europe and other allies. In order to contain eventual nuclear temptations of some allies (even in NATO Europe) the U.S. would have to return to a far more robust extended deterrence approach. This would include a re-emphasis on elaborate nuclear sharing arrangements in NATO, but also the extension of these arrangements to other allies, notably Japan and South Korea. NATO's general "to whom it may concern" deterrence would have to give way to tailored deterrence messages to specific countries. The breakdown of arms control agreements might allow NATO to introduce new long-range weapons systems, yet most allies would most likely prefer to refrain from such "provocative" steps. The same holds true for the option of retracting the "three no's" regarding the non-deployment of nuclear weapons in those countries that became NATO allies after the end of the Cold War. While legally possible, the political drawbacks of such a step, in particular vis-à-vis Russia, might far outweigh the military gains.

Whether such a "nuclear anarchy" scenario would lead to more alliance cohesion is doubtful, however. Even if all allies were to perceive a greater threat, they would not necessarily follow similar approaches in dealing with it. While the U.S. and some of its allies would opt for a more robust approach, some European allies would prefer a conciliatory policy and thus seek to prevent NATO from adopting strategies that they would perceive as counterproductive. Indeed, the risk of allied divergence appears greater in this scenario than in any other, as a confrontational environment would trigger national reflexes in accordance with national "strategic cultures," making allied consensus more difficult to achieve. It is for this very reason that NATO, despite the low likelihood of such a scenario, will at least have to consider it in its political consultation process.

The third scenario – muddling through – proceeds from the assumption that efforts to eliminate nuclear weapons will falter, yet that this will not result in a major push towards general nuclearization. By 2030 "global zero" efforts will have lost much of their initial momentum, both due to a lack of interest of the existing nuclear powers and, above all, due to other issues occupying the international agenda. The traditional non-proliferation and arms control agenda will continue, yet without the sense of urgency that underlies the "abolitionist" logic. However, even without non-proliferation occupying center stage, the number of Nuclear Weapons States (and those possessing other WMD) will remain small, as most nations will continue to consider a nuclear option to be politically, militarily, and financially unattractive. This scenario also assumes that, mainly due to U.S. extended deterrence commitments, no regional "cascading" effects will occur and the (few) new nuclear nations can be prevented

Trajectory

from transferring nuclear technology to others. In concrete terms, this would mean that by 2030 the number of NWS (official and unofficial) will have grown to about a dozen at most. However, due to their growing civil nuclear expertise, well over 60 states will remain at the level of "virtual" NWS.

Assuming that no specific country or group of countries would emerge as a distinct adversary to NATO, such a scenario would allow the U.S. and NATO to continue to relax the requirements for extended nuclear deterrence. By 2030, the various life extension programs of dual-capable aircraft will have reached their limits and, assuming that the nuclear gravity bombs in Europe have not yet been eliminated by a U.S.-Russian arms control agreement, the DCA mission might end. This would tie in with the general technological trend of phasing out manned aircraft due to their diminishing militarily usefulness. The U.S. would provide extended nuclear deterrence offshore, for example through submarine-launched ballistic missiles, but it would also put a far greater emphasis on conventional strike options and missile defenses, which will have become an integral part of NATO's posture.

In such a scenario, NATO would also put elements of a preventive nonproliferation approach on its agenda, such as the alliance's formal participation in the Proliferation Security Initiative or similar arrangements. Allies might also take a harder line vis-à-vis countries suspected of WMD ambitions, for example by militarily implementing UN-mandated embargoes against certain proliferators. The allies would continue to discuss nuclear matters in dedicated fora, although the influence of the non-nuclear allies – and perhaps also their interest – in this issue may wane. Without shared hardware and without allied participation in the nuclear strike mission, nuclear sharing in the traditional understanding would cease to exist. However, the presence of allied officers in U.S. nuclear command posts would maintain a semblance of "sharing" that nations may still deem politically desirable. In essence, the nuclear dimension of NATO would become less visible, almost to the point of being a mere "virtual" U.S. security guarantee. The key question will be whether the U.S. body politic will accept such devolution as natural and desirable, or whether it will be regarded as yet another sign of European "burden-shedding."

Conclusions

Over a period of 60 years, NATO's nuclear dimension has undergone profound changes. Initially the centerpiece of NATO's defense strategy, nuclear weapons were increasingly understood as being political weapons with limited military utility. The end of the Cold War further reduced the salience of nuclear weapons. However, largely for reasons of alliance cohesion, NATO maintained a minimal posture of dual-capable aircraft and U.S. gravity bombs that allowed for the continuation of its nuclear sharing arrangements and thus underlined the sharing of nuclear risks and burdens.

NATO's nuclear dimension is now again under review. However, this review is less a result of new developments that directly affect the alliance – such as the end of the Cold War and the collapse of the Soviet Union – but rather of a changing U.S. perception about global nuclear developments. Hence, eventual changes in NATO's nuclear dimension are supposed to support broader political efforts to reduce the salience of nuclear weapons worldwide.

It would not be the first time that NATO used adjustments of its nuclear policy and posture to help facilitate positive political change: the "weapons of last resort" formula of the 1990 London Declaration, for example, was intended to signal to Moscow that NATO was no longer a military antagonist and that it was not going to militarily exploit the political changes that were unfolding within the Soviet Union's crumbling empire. However, that context had been a highly specific one. By contrast, today's debate is about the relationship between NATO's nuclear dimension and global non-proliferation requirements – a much more ambiguous context.

Another difference compared to the past is the U.S. stance on nuclear weapons. Notwithstanding its consistent call for stronger conventional forces, the U.S. used to be a vocal supporter of nuclear deterrence and the leader in nuclear strategy development in NATO. However, the new emphasis on non-proliferation forces the U.S. to argue for the de-legitimization and eventual abolition of the very weapons it considers essential for today's security requirements, notably with respect to providing extended deterrence for allies and friends. Managing this balancing act in a multilateral alliance will require firm U.S. leadership, or else it will risk serious friction within the alliance.

NATO's greatest historical achievement was to define Europe and North America as one single security space. Almost since NATO's founding, this message was understood to apply both to the conventional and the nuclear domain. For the allies, therefore, the key question is whether they can now safely change this traditional understanding by ending European participation in NATO's nuclear mission and reduce NATO's nuclear dimension to what essentially amounts to a unilateral U.S. nuclear promise. For some, this would mean a step towards nuclear enlightenment; for others it would simply mean less alliance solidarity and security.

Notes

1 Head, Energy Security Section, Emerging Security Challenges Division, NATO. The views expressed are solely the author's own.

2 J. Stromseth, *The Origins of Flexible Response: NATO's Debate over Strategy in the 1960s*, Oxford: Macmillan Press, 1988; I. Daalder, *The Nature and Practice of Flexible Response: NATO Strategy and Theater Nuclear Forces Since 1967*, New York: Columbia University Press, 1991.

3 H. Brands, "Non-Proliferation and the Dynamics of the Middle Cold War: The Superpowers, the MLF, and the NPT," *Cold War History*, Vol. 7, No. 3, 2007, pp. 389–423.

4 A 1974 message by the U.S. Mission to NATO provided a concise summary: "The U.S. fostered the establishment of the NPG to satisfy the desire of most of our allies – and particularly the FRG [Federal Republic of Germany] – to have a voice in the formulation of alliance nuclear policy; to reassure allies of U.S. nuclear commitment; to foster a better understanding among allies of uses and limitations of nuclear weapons; to blunt proliferation pressures; and to mitigate concern over ultimate U.S. control over use of nuclear weapons." Message from the U.S. Mission to NATO to the Secretary of State and Secretary of Defense, "Future of NPG," 30 November 1974, declassified 30 June 2005, quoted in D.S. Yost, *The U.S. Debate on NATO Nuclear Deterrence* (unpublished manuscript).

5 NATO, "Declaration on a Transformed North Atlantic Alliance, Issued by the Heads of State and Government participating in the meeting of the North Atlantic Council ('The London Declaration')," 6 July 1990. Online. Available: www.nato.int/cps/en/natolive/official_texts_23693.htm.

6 NATO Final Communiqué, Meeting of the North Atlantic Council in Defence Ministers Session held in Brussels, Press Release M-NAC(DM)-3(96) 172, Issued on 18 December 1996. Online. Available: www.nato.int/cps/en/natolive/official_texts_25057.htm?mode=pressrelease.

7 F. Iklé, "The Second Coming of the Nuclear Age," *Foreign Affairs*, Vol. 75, 1996, pp. 119–128. P. Bracken, "The Second Nuclear Age," *Foreign Affairs*, Vol. 79, January/February 2000, pp. 146–156.

8 "We are resolved to seek a safer world for all and to create the conditions for a world without nuclear weapons in accordance with the goals of the Nuclear Non-Proliferation Treaty, in a way that promotes international stability, and is based on the principle of undiminished security for all." NATO, "Active Engagement, Modern Defence: Strategic Concept for the Defense and Security of the Members of the North Atlantic Treaty Organization," November 2010, para. 26. Online. Available: www.nato.int/lisbon2010/strategic-concept-2010-eng.pdf.

9 See NATO, "Deterrence and Defence Posture Review," Press Release (2012) 063, 20 May 2012. Online. Available: www.nato.int/cps/en/natolive/official_texts_87597.htm?mode=pressrelease.

10 M. Chalmers and A. Somerville, *If the Bombs Go: European Perspectives on NATO's Nuclear Debate*, Whitehall Report, 2011, 1–11. Online. Available: www.rusi.org/downloads/assets/IFTHEBOMBSGO.pdf.

11 M. Rühle, "NATO and Extended Deterrence in a Multinuclear World," *Comparative Strategy*, Vol. 28, January 2009, pp. 10–16.

12 NATO, "Active Engagement, Modern Defence."

13 The NPR conditions the strengthening of its long-standing "negative security assurance" by declaring "that the United States will not use or threaten to use nuclear weapons against non-nuclear weapons states that are party to the NPT and in compliance with their nuclear non-proliferation obligations." The NPR also notes that "[g]iven the catastrophic potential of biological weapons and the rapid pace of bio-technology development, the United States reserves the right to make any adjustment in the assurance that may be warranted by the evolution and proliferation of the biological weapons threat and U.S. capacities to counter that threat." U.S. Department of Defense, Nuclear Posture Review Report, April 2010. Online. Available: www.defense.gov/npr/docs/2010%20nuclear%20posture%20review%20report.pdf.

14 See G. Perkovich and J.M. Acton (eds), *Abolishing Nuclear Weapons: A Debate*, Carnegie Endowment for International Peace, Washington, D.C., 2009. Online.

Available: www.carnegieendowment.org/files/abolishing_nuclear_weapons_ debate.pdf.

15 Unlike several NGOs, which have published disarmament timetables, the U.S. Government has refrained from publishing either specific timetables or specifying conditions for achieving a nuclear-free world. This makes the U.S. politically less vulnerable to eventual setbacks in the process, yet it also perpetuates ambiguity with regard to U.S. sincerity.

10 NATO and cyber security

Jeffrey Hunker

Introduction

National and alliance security topics prefaced with cyber – war, security, defense, deterrence, attack, power, doctrine, operations – are all evolving, so to say inchoate, fields. NATO can and should have a major security presence in cyberspace,[1] acting as a credible deterrent against cyber attack aimed at Alliance members or interests. That role, however, will not come without very significant changes to NATO's current roles and capabilities. If NATO is not proactive in developing these new postures, other institutions will assume the responsibility. One should not be ambivalent about these alternative outcomes.

Perhaps unique to the security issues facing NATO, NATO's choices about key cyber technologies on which it relies, could reshape – to NATO's advantage – the terrain of cyberspace. The Internet itself is highly insecure, and by cyber standards a very old technology. While NATO is not a Research and Development (R&D) institution, within the timeframe of this book it likely could have the opportunity to be among the early adopters of a network technology superior to today's Internet in both functionality and security. Such early adoption could reshape cyberspace and significantly enhance NATO's defense and deterrence posture in cyberspace.

Current characteristics shaping cyber

Several realities shape our discussion of NATO's future role in cyberspace:

> *Self-evident is the near ubiquitous dependence of Western nations on the dependable functioning of information systems and networks.*

Cyberspace is almost all interconnected through the Internet.[2] The Internet is literally an interlinking of separate networks. Individual "networks" so connected may range from, say, your home computer or e-book reader to very large-scale networks such as the SIPRNet (Secret Internet Protocol Router Network operated by the U.S. Department of Defense).[3] Obviously, individual networks restrict access in a variety of ways (e.g. firewalls, intrusion detection systems) but only those networks physically "air-gapped" from an Internet connection can be said to be unconnected to the larger cyberspace.

Cyberspace is insecure: Even physical "air-gapping" does not fully protect a network from being attacked from the outside. In 2010 the Stuxnet worm[4] was reported to have caused the destructive malfunctioning of centrifuges critical to the Iranian nuclear program. According to press reports, these computer-controlled centrifuges were not connected to the Internet or any outside networks. The Stuxnet worm was reportedly introduced through a physical memory device that someone connected to the internal plant system.[5]

Cyber attacks are defined as any illicit action that seeks to steal data from or disrupt the operation of a computer, system, or network. Flaws and vulnerabilities, mostly in software, make these systems open to exploitation and disruption by malefactors. There is no sign that systems and networks will be dramatically more secure in the future, and little indication that the relative superiority of offense over defense will change.

Information systems can be attacked from within or from the outside. The Internet itself is insecure, and the infrastructure that operates the Internet is vulnerable to attack; the Internet can also be used to attack individual systems.[6] A Distributed Denial of Service (DDoS attack) is a common attack method which uses other computers on the Internet to "flood" a particular network with messages, and thus force it off the Internet.

Note, however, that the simplest way of breaking into a network is through an attacker that already possesses legitimate access. The recent release by WikiLeaks of U.S. diplomatic cables illustrates the possible damage from "insider threats;" a U.S. soldier with legitimate access to classified government networks has been charged with downloading the cables.[7]

Cyber attacks can be "passive" or "disruptive" and come from a wide range of sources: An attack can intend to copy and then remove data without disrupting the systems or data (without being noticed by the operators) or to disrupt cyberspace systems by corrupting or changing data, affecting system or network service, or denying or preventing use of systems or networks.[8] A growing and transmogrifying constellation of cyber "bad guys" is behind such attacks. Until recently the most serious malefactors have been highly sophisticated cyber criminal networks, and cyber espionage, possibly by nations. A passive cyber attack could either be a cyber crime[9] (e.g. theft of credit card data) or cyber espionage or intelligence collection. A disruptive cyber attack could be cyber crime, for greed, vandalism, revenge, extortion, or as an act by political "hactivists." To date, no publicly reported disruptive attacks have come from terrorists.

Nations are active in cyber attack: Many nations are reportedly active in espionage through passive cyber attacks, while also developing disruptive

cyber attack capabilities. China, for instance, talks of "winning informa-
tionized wars by the mid twenty-first century" and is, according to U.S. analysis, developing "an advanced information warfare capability, the stated
goal of which is to establish control of an adversary's information flow and
maintain dominance in cyberspace."[10]

Now, NATO must concern itself with the possibility of destructive
attacks launched over information networks by nation-states and non-state
actors – popularly but inaccurately called "cyber war."[11] Almost certainly,
we have already seen disruptive cyber attacks by one nation against
another nation. Of note, in 2007, during a period of tension with Russia,
Estonian Government, commercial, and private organizations, notably
banks, were the subject of three weeks of DDoS attacks. Other DDoS
attacks occurred against Georgia in 2009, prior to kinetic military action
with Russia. Most recently the Stuxnet attack is widely believed to have had
U.S. involvement. Governments have not acknowledged any responsibility
in any of these cases. Illustrating the difficulties of attack attribution, the
cyber attacks against Georgia were orchestrated from a control computer
in Brooklyn, New York!

Characteristics shaping security, conflict, and defense in cyberspace

Cyber weapons, once used, often lose their effectiveness: Many cyber attacks
depend on exploiting vulnerabilities unknown or not yet fixed. If the
operators of the attacked network know that they have been attacked
(often this does not happen), most likely the operators will fix or "patch"
that particular vulnerability. Much of cyber defense is about a race
between attackers and defenders as to who will find the next vulnerability
first.

The effects of a cyber attack can be highly uncertain or unexpected: Cyber
attacks seek to directly change the performance of highly complex cyber
systems, which in turn may affect the behavior of also highly complex physical systems, like infrastructures. The behavior of complex systems is, in
general, not well understood. Or cyber tools can spread in unexpected
ways; the first ever cyber worm, the Morris worm of 1988, unintentionally
shut down much of the then nascent Internet when launched; that was
certainly not the intent of the then-graduate student developer.

The Law of War has a bearing on this: on legal and humanitarian
grounds unexpected collateral damage could be viewed as indiscriminate
attacks.

Technical attribution of the source of the attack is very difficult: Because the
Internet's creators never envisioned the need, the Internet has no reliable
means for tracing where a packet comes from. Usually network attack
techniques employ a series of stepping stones, using compromised intermediate hosts to "launder" packets sent. Some of the best though
inadequate means of technical attribution require "hacking back" through

intermediate systems. A hack back may itself result in significant violations of the Law of War because it most likely would require literally breaking into these intermediate "hops" without permission. If done repeatedly, or if there is significant collateral damage that results, such hack backs might be considered "attacks."

Accidents can happen: Even with proper command and controls in place, accidental cyber attacks can occur. For instance, similar to accidentally sending an e-mail, the wrong code could be relayed to a target.

Key policy debates and drivers

NATO's focus on cyber defense dates back at least to 2002, when implementation of a Cyber Defense Program – "a comprehensive plan to improve the Alliance's ability to defend against cyber attacks by improving NATO's capabilities" – was approved by the North Atlantic Council.[12]

The cyber attacks on Estonia in April/May 2007 transformed the scope of NATO cyber defense activities. Prior to that time, NATO efforts were primarily concentrated on protecting the communications systems owned and operated by the Alliance. During the DDoS attacks against Estonia, responding to a historic request by a NATO member to assist in the defense of its digital assets, NATO members, including the U.S., provided technical assistance. As a result of the Estonian attacks, "practical cooperation on cyber defense" with NATO partners is being developed in accordance with the "Council Guidelines for Cooperation on Cyber Defense with Partners and International Organizations" (August 2008) and the "Framework for Cooperation on Cyber Defense between NATO and Partner Countries" (April 2009). Estonia, Slovakia, Turkey, the UK, and the U.S. have signed agreements with NATO to facilitate cooperation in the event of a cyber attack.

Operationally NATO cyber defense activities comprise and are now governed (from bottom to top as listed) as follows:[13]

- The NATO Computer Incident Response Capability (NCIRC), created in 2002, handles and reports cyber security incidents and disseminates important incident related information to systems/security management and users. NCRIC is part of the NATO Communications and Information Services Agency.
- The Cyber Defense Management Board (CDMB) maintains sole responsibility for coordinating cyber defense across the Alliance. Also, in August 2010 the Emerging Security Challenges Division (ESCD) was created within the NATO International Staff to address non-traditional risks and challenges, including cyber defense.
- The Defence Policy and Planning Committee in Reinforced Format, and above that the North Atlantic Council.
- Officially separate from NATO but also referenced officially as supporting NATO capabilities[14] is the Cooperative Cyber Defense Center

of Excellence (CCDCOE). It is an Estonian center which NATO has accredited. It was established in 2003, and accredited as a NATO Center of Excellence (COE) in 2008. It conducts research and training on cyber warfare. The Center is an international effort that currently includes Estonia, Latvia, Lithuania, Germany, Hungary, Italy, Slovakia, and Spain as Sponsoring Nations.

NATO's cyber policy today

The framework for NATO's cyber policy was first outlined in the language of the Strategic Concept adopted November 2010 at the Lisbon Summit:

Strategic Concept

12 Cyber attacks are becoming more frequent, more organized and more costly in the damage that they inflict on government administrations, businesses, economies, and potentially also transportation and supply networks and other critical infrastructure; they can reach a threshold that threatens national and Euro-Atlantic prosperity, security, and stability. Foreign militaries and intelligence services, organized criminals, terrorist, and/or extremist groups can each be the source of such attacks.

13 All countries are increasingly reliant on the vital communication, transport and transit routes on which international trade, energy security and prosperity depend. They require greater international efforts to ensure their resilience against attack or disruption.

The concurrent Lisbon Summit Declaration called for a series of actions including for the Council to develop an in-depth NATO cyber defense policy by June 2011[15] and to prepare an action plan for its implementation.

Most recently, in the meeting of the North Atlantic Council in May 2012, in its Chicago Summit Declaration,[16] the Council reiterated the cyber strategies outlined in Lisbon, specifically:

- as called for, have developed and adopted a Cyber Defence Concept, Policy, and Action Plan;
- bringing the NATO Computer Incident Response Capability (NCIRC) to Full Operational Capability (FOC) by the end of 2012;
- committed to provide the resources and complete the necessary reforms to bring all NATO bodies under centralized cyber protection;
- to integrate (Alliance member) cyber defense measures into Alliance structures and procedures;
- as members, to remain committed to identifying and delivering national cyber defense capabilities to strengthen Alliance collaboration, including through the NATO defense planning processes;

- committed to engage with relevant partner nations and with international organizations;
- to take full advantage of the expertise offered by the Cooperative Cyber Defence Centre of Excellence in Estonia (as noted earlier in this discussion).

Providing further detail, the *NATO Policy on Cyber Defence* and the accompanying *Action Plan*[17] make clear that NATO's focus is on the protection of its own communication and information systems. The underlying policy principles are based on prevention, resilience, and non-duplication. Certain threats will persist despite all efforts to eliminate them. Prevention is about mitigating risk. Resilience is about facilitating rapid recovery after an attack.

Coordinated defense across Alliance member and NATO networks is key; the Plan calls for the NATO Defence Planning Process (NDPP) to guide the integration of cyber defense into national defense networks. Furthermore, NATO will develop minimum requirements for national networks that are connected to or process NATO information (although, from the author's perspective, how this policy will be developed and furthermore enforced may prove very difficult).

Response is the third element of the Plan. NATO will maintain strategic ambiguity as well as flexibility on how to respond to different types of crisis that include a cyber component (the importance of such strategic ambiguity in response is discussed later in this chapter). Furthermore, there is the commitment that NATO will provide coordinated assistance if an ally or allies are victims of a cyber attack and request assistance.

This Plan represents a good start. Foundational to moving forward will be decisions that NATO ought to make about the nature of the threat and the basis for NATO response. The choices made will serve as key drivers of future direction, so it is worth looking at them in detail.

What is the threat?

Characterizing the threat is very difficult in cyberspace. It does not take a large well funded national effort to pose a threat. If well informed, clever, and lucky, small teams can be quite effective.[18] I would suggest that NATO members need to consider a future where one or more of the following will occur:

- *Cyber as a component in a major all-out conflict:* Though this scenario appears highly unlikely, if the Alliance is involved in a kinetic conflict involving major powers, cyber attacks intended to disrupt, disable, or infiltrate both military and civilian targets will be used.
- *Cyber as a tool of major state power used during periods of tension:* Cyber attacks are a likely choice as one instrument among several aimed at

achieving political and strategic goals short of outright conflict.[19] Attacks can be tailored to a wide range of impacts (large, small, noticeable to the general population or not, etc.) and targets. For the attacking state, there is the fiction of deniability.

The above two scenarios are the closest we will see to what has been popularized as "cyber war." Unlike popular writings, here, at least, I define the term: Cyber war is sustained state-on-state conflict carried out exclusively and publicly in cyberspace for the primary purpose of compelling the other side to accede rather than face the prospect of continued or greater pain.[20] The second scenario is perhaps more plausible than the first, and fits the definition of "cyber war." However, as the following more likely scenarios suggest, a NATO focus on cyber war diverts focus away from more likely uses of cyber in conflict.

- *Cyber attacks in response to NATO limited engagements:* A rogue country – say the future equivalent of the Gaddafi Government of Libya – faced with the imminent prospect of attack or invasion has something to gain and little to lose in launching cyber attacks against NATO.[21]
- *Cyber attacks against a smaller Alliance member:* It is very difficult to envision Russia launching a conventional military attack against a small NATO state; it is much easier to see serious cyber attacks.[22] Alternatively, there is the prospect that "irritating" cyber attacks would be launched against some of the smaller Alliance members as part of retaliatory measures against NATO operations or posture.
- *Terrorist or political extremist attacks:* The political/hacker group Anonymous has already shown that extremist political groups will launch disruptive cyber attacks. We can expect to see much more of this as groups gain sophistication. It is unclear whether terrorist groups would have the sophistication to launch attacks against critical infrastructures – if so "cyber terrorism" may come closer to becoming a reality.
- *Accidents:* As noted before, accidental attacks can happen in cyberspace, perhaps with greater ease than other forms of attack.
- *Egregious cyber espionage:* The Law of War does not recognize espionage as a *casus belli*. Some suggest that a good case for changing this has yet to be made,[23] but the speed and quantity of information it is possible to acquire through cyber espionage raises the issue of whether and if the line between espionage and cyber attack might blur.

Note, too, that more attention needs to be given to the combination of cyber with physical attacks in the future. Particularly in critical infrastructures, the interdependencies between physical elements and cyber controls are not well understood.

How serious can the threat be?

In the kinetic world, analysts can match the characteristics of a weapon against target characteristics, in most cases on the basis of computational models based on physics. There is no comparable formalism for understanding the effects of cyber weapons. Furthermore, hard information about the cyber threat posed by adversaries is scarce and hard to obtain. As noted earlier, the behavior and interdependencies of targeted complex cyber and associated physical systems, for example the electric power grid, is poorly understood. The net result is that cyber threat assessments cannot totally rule out the possibility that a cyber attack will result in worst case assessments. In the absence of a more bounded threat assessment, policy makers need to resort to "level of effort" decisions based on assessments of likelihood and consequences.[24]

Deciding when a cyber attack merits NATO consultation or collective action

The action NATO undertakes when a cyber attack occurs will depend upon how allies perceive a particular event and the development of the necessary consensus on how to respond. There will be an Article 5 response when allies agree to it, depending on the particular circumstances. Several considerations may weigh on this deliberation.

First, a great deal of attention has been devoted to the question of whether and under what circumstance a cyber attack constitutes an act of war, or can be considered an attack under Article 5 of the North Atlantic Treaty. This extensive discussion[25] has been inconclusive. Perhaps it should remain so; ambiguity as to likely responses to a cyber action may be very useful (a point discussed later in this chapter).

Attacked member states may also face internal conflicts between their defense/NATO perspectives and those of their national law enforcement authorities. Because attribution of cyber attacks is difficult, it may be unclear to the attacked nation whether a cyber attack is a criminal action or a national security issue. In a less than perfect world, the possibility of bureaucratic infighting exists. This internal friction may or may not be of consequence.

With the opportunity for consultation, these issues can be sorted out. It may be that there are circumstances under which an "automatic" defense response is called for. Events in cyber space happen quickly (though this does not always mean that an automatic response is called for). Under these conditions, the unsatisfactory reality is that NATO would have to develop protocols that allow it to act, even if uncertain.

How much effort at cyber security is enough?

Metrics for "how secure" a system is against cyber attack are highly imperfect. One approach is to audit the system using security criteria; the other is to test the system by repeatedly trying to break in ("red teaming" is the term of art). Neither provides for a reliable measure of security (for instance, the effectiveness of red teaming depends critically on the skill of those doing it). The conclusion therefore is that budget and resource constraints, rather than some measure of adequacy, may be the determining factor in NATO cyber security.

Possible future pathways

NATO will "enhance our cyber defense capabilities" according to the Lisbon Summit Declaration, but the Declaration in subsequent language notes, "we will take into account the cyber dimension of modern conflicts in NATO's doctrine." This phrase is, I would suggest, key to outlining future pathways for NATO. In the future NATO members will almost certainly face the prospect of disruptive cyber attacks coming from adversary states, state-sponsored actors, and other non-state entities. NATO will need a policy of deterrence to dissuade its adversaries from doing so.[26]

A framework for NATO cyber deterrence

Deterrence has three components:

- Defensive: denying the ability of the adversary to succeed;
- Declaratory and diplomatic: encouraging restraint on the part of the adversary by making clear that some courses of action will result in unacceptable consequences to the adversary and (possibly) that more jointly acceptable courses of action are available;
- Responsive: imposing costs or punishing the adversary for its actions.

In cyberspace the concept of deterrence lacks the foundations that it has in nuclear and conventional conflict.[27] As one analyst has noted:

In the Cold War nuclear realm, attribution of attack was not a problem, the prospect of battle damage was clear, the one-thousandth bomb could be as powerful as the first, counterforce was possible, there were no third parties to worry about, private firms were not expected to defend themselves, any hostile nuclear use crossed an acknowledged threshold, no higher level of war existed, and both sides always had a lot to lose.[28]

The lessons of nuclear deterrence are not uniformly applicable to cyber power. With cyber weapons, less confidence can be imputed to their performance on demand. Furthermore, it is difficult to effectively stage demonstrations of cyber power without reducing the very effectiveness of the cyber arsenal. Basing deterrence on other modes of response, e.g. kinetic responses, may further worsen a situation and certainly raises its own legal and diplomatic issues. Cyberspace deterrence may thus have to rely on new formulations, just as nuclear deterrence evolved from concepts different from those common to conventional military power.

Defense

Defending cyber networks is the focus of the Lisbon Summit Declaration, and the most politically palatable cyber role for NATO. While defending NATO's own proprietary networks might seem straightforward, it is worth noting by comparison that securing the U.S. Defense Department's networks occupies a major portion of the effort by U.S. Defense Department agencies, including the National Security Agency and the Defense Information Systems Agency. The technical challenges and the resources required are considerable. Furthermore, in securing NATO's networks there are some important political level decisions to be made that will shape NATO's future in cyber.

Even if NATO only used its own networks, the task of securing them would be both technically and organizationally daunting. Security also requires specifically defining how and under what circumstances NATO's own networks interconnect with Alliance member networks, and the mechanisms for changing (perhaps rapidly) that interconnection. This is a highly technical challenge, but the fundamental questions are those of network design: in the future exactly how interconnected do Alliance members want to be with NATO networks? This is a very important political level issue – should NATO be the vehicle for a unified defense information network among Members? (The implications of this issue are discussed in the later subsection, "Role in the deployment of a new more secure network in parallel to the existing Internet").

Additionally, NATO functionalities also depend on other non-military government networks (e.g. the U.S. State Department) and private sector networks (e.g. telecommunications companies). These different network providers differ in their capabilities and motivations for security (this is a vastly oversimplified way of stating a very complex problem, since "security" is difficult to measure).

Because NATO depends critically on inter-connected networks, most of which are not under its direct control, NATO cyber defense is really a matter of (1) determining the key components of NATO's mission that must be protected; (2) identifying the networks and cyber assets that critically support those components; and (3) working with the various network operators to ensure an adequate level of security. If it is the case (as it may very well be, especially in private sector networks) that critical NATO

components depend on networks with inadequate security, then alternative arrangements will have to be found.

Securing networks requires more than installing a set of technical protocols. Insider threats arising from disloyal NATO-cleared individuals are a
particularly dangerous threat and very hard to defend against.[29]

As noted in the Lisbon summit Declaration, NATO will need to work
closely with other actors, especially with the EU and the global network of
Computer Emergency Response Teams (CERTs). European national cyber
security policies either do not exist (also the case in Canada) or are only now
being developed. Not all NATO members have yet adopted legislation that
would make it mandatory for the private sector to protect their data and networks.[30] Closer relationships with the EU are needed, because it is the EU
that issues laws on comprehensive standards for cyberspace.[31] There has been
progress in developing the network of CERTS that are now established in all
NATO countries. Close operating relationships between NATO and these
CERTs is needed to bolster NATO's situational awareness and to strengthen
the Alliance's ability to respond to and repair damage from cyber attacks.

Declaratory policy

For deterrence to work it needs to be understood by potential adversaries.[32] NATO needs a declaratory policy that provides a credible, convincing explanation of why NATO takes cyber threats seriously and intends to
respond with decisive actions.[33] The point is not just to warn, but to influence the psychology and motivations of potential adversaries.

In establishing its policy for cyber deterrence, NATO has the unique
opportunity to shape the international standards by which cyber attacks
are viewed. I would suggest that there are three principles it is essential to
make clear:

- Disruptive cyber attacks will be evaluated, in part, according to their
  equivalence to any other form of attack. A cyber attack disrupting electric power would be viewed as equivalent to its kinetic counterpart.
- Other nations will be held accountable for the actions of those within
  its borders.[34]
- Other nations have the obligation to vigorously assist in the apprehension of non-state linked cyber adversaries.

This declaration of cyber deterrence policy ought to be an essential component of NATOs overall security policy.

Response for deterrence

Cyber defenses will not be impregnable. NATO will require a response
(retaliatory) capability if a posture of cyber deterrence is to be credible.

Note, however, that NATO's options for response to a cyber attack may be limited. Responding to a cyber attack in kind may have problematic results – as noted, cyber attacks have uncertain impacts, and many cyber attack tools cannot reliably be reused. A kinetic response to a cyber attack may break new ground. Other options, such as sanctions,[35] or criminal prosecution, are outside of NATO's direct purview. The key point is that any response to a cyber attack will require that NATO integrate its actions with other instruments of national power perhaps being exercised by individual allies.[36]

Value of "constructive ambiguity"[37]

I would suggest that an explicit cyber deterrence policy – one that spells out exactly for what types of events particular responses will incur – is not in NATO's interests. An explicit deterrence posture that deals with a cyber attack, with obvious effect from a non-obvious source, creates a dilemma between responding publicly (and possibly getting it wrong) or refraining (and losing credibility).[38] The scope of potential cyber attack targets and intended consequences is vast; further complicating this picture is the gap between the actual and intended impact of any particular attack. NATO should not unduly limit its scope of action by making its policies for cyber deterrence too explicit.

Ambiguity of policy increases NATO's cyber deterrence. An "armed attack" on one or more is seen as an attack on all, and allies are committed to respond. However, it may be that NATO members experience a cyber attack that does not meet the threshold of an "armed attack," but where the Alliance concludes that a response is required. In such circumstances it might be appropriate for other Alliance members with greater cyber response capabilities to take action, while keeping the identity of which member nation has acted in response anonymous. In other words, cyber deterrence can be enhanced if attackers believe that even a "minor" attack on any ally might have deleterious consequences, regardless of whether the attacked ally is believed to have its own response capabilities.

There should be, however, a creative tension between flexibility and ambiguity on one hand, and planning on the other (admittedly, such "creative tension" is often easier said than done). A catalog of response options that could be invoked when required and agreed upon would be very useful. Cyber elements could be included in the Catalog of Military Response Options that is part of the NATO Crisis Management System.

An evolving doctrine of cyber power

In building its security presence in cyberspace, NATO must focus not only on preventing cyber attacks, but on how nations and non-state actors might use their presence in cyber space to influence events – in other words to exert power. To date, almost all discussion of cyber in an Alliance context has been about defense, and less so about war. Yet foundational to both of these concepts is the concept of power. Cyber power is an undeveloped concept, but I would suggest that while undeveloped now, it may serve as the framework for events that shape NATO's environment in 2030.

Stated differently, one focus of NATO doctrinal development should be on understanding the consequences of cyber power, and not just on fighting a cyber war or defending against cyber attack. Cyberwar or cyber attacks are just facets of the potentially larger exercise of cyber power between nations or non-state actors.

Capabilities required for cyber deterence

The Alliance needs to create new capabilities and address new agendas.

Policy coordination/command and control in cyber response

Credible deterrence mechanisms need to work even under great stress.[39] At the same time, effective response will require new ways for allies to coordinate their actions. Cyber attack tools are often highly specialized one-use instruments. An ally who has developed a new attack tool may wish to keep its existence secret; even revealing generalized information about possible ways the tool might be used risks revealing the nature of the tool. In that case, NATO might need procedures for allies to reveal and coordinate the use of previously secret cyber response capabilities. This transfer and use is not comparable to, say, transferring a national air wing to NATO command, where at least the existence and general capabilities of the force are known to all beforehand. Creating this process of cyber attack tool "show me" among allies, so that cyber response can be coordinated, may be tricky, since it is in the self-interest of any nation (including allies) to withhold secret information while other nations reveal their secrets.

Coordinating response will be further challenging because cyberspace is inherently a technical subject and remains arcane to most military and political leaders. Much of what technically knowledgeable staff may report or recommend runs the risk of being lost in translation. Recommendations to senior political/military leadership may be based on highly technical factors but have to be communicated in ways that are both understandable and accurate.

I would suggest that support for coordinated Alliance action in cyberspace merits building a specialized senior operational cadre of NATO officials[40] who have:

- access to cyber attack and defense tools in the arsenals of Alliance members;

- the ability to evaluate the potential role of these tools in any contemplated NATO action;
- the ability to accurately and succinctly advise senior military and political leadership of the options, and the benefits and costs of their deployment, broadly defined to include psychological, economic, and political ramifications.

This is an extremely tall order, but a necessary function. Senior NATO leadership needs to be able to weigh the use of cyber modes versus other means available for any particular situation, and need a highly expert staff that is both informed about the range of cyber options available and able to present the options crisply to decision makers.

Ensuring backup capabilities in the event of network failure

The general rule is that any system can be successfully attacked given sufficient effort. NATO needs, therefore, to invest in capabilities to ensure that the functions being supported by cyber capabilities can continue to function even under the worst case scenario. Simply put, ensuring this capability may be costly.

Engagement with private industry and relevant national authorities for critical infrastructure protection

An important related component of defense is Critical Infrastructure Protection (CIP). Critical infrastructures include electric power, banking and finance, and telecommunications networks – systems vital to the economic and social functioning of a nation. These infrastructures are cyber dependent. Implicitly, prime responsibility for critical infrastructure protection is with national governments. Some nations (U.S., UK) have explicit policies, others do not (e.g. Canada), while yet others (e.g. Germany) foresee a role for NATO to establish standards.[41] NATO has the opportunity, working in conjunction with the EU, to develop and support security standards and protocols for critical European regional infrastructures. Ties might also be strengthened with the U.S. Department of Homeland Security, which coordinates U.S. CIP policies.

NATO will need the capability to assess the reliability of the critical infrastructures on which it relies. In the case that certain infrastructures are judged insufficiently secure and reliable, mechanisms for correction – by working with member governments – or investing in alternative back-ups are going to have to be in place. Such corrective mechanisms may either be costly, administratively fractious, or both. Fortunately, expertise for developing these capabilities may already exist in the Civil Emergency Planning (CEP) at NATO, where industry experts support NATO through the planning boards and committees. Civil Emergency Planning plays an important role by serving as an interface between a variety of ministries (as diverse as health, agriculture, transport) and military planning. In addition to a network of civil experts in the countries which are members of the Senior Civil Emergency Planning Committee (SCEPC), the Planning Boards and Committees provide inter-agency support to NATO's military bodies.

Promoting international agreements

NATO should also seek to advance international agreements that generally limit the use of cyber attack tools. A start would be, as a matter of Alliance policy, to encourage all members and partners to become signatories to the Convention on Cybercrime. NATO should also seek to ensure that the principles of its own cyber deterrence policy are enshrined in international law and enforced.

Russia has proposed an international treaty to ban the use of cyber weapons.[42] International agreements that create some ground rules are appropriate but the topic has to be considered carefully in light of technical implications and issues of verification. Defining a threshold above which attacks constitute an act of war would be difficult to establish; it might also perversely encourage the private sector critical infrastructure owners/operators to under-invest in network security if "serious" attacks become acts of war outside of their responsibility.[43]

Greater cyber intelligence capabilities

Because of its collective defense and security responsibilities, NATO requires enhanced "situational awareness." International watch and warning networks are needed. Cyber defense arguably should be tightly integrated with cyber espionage capabilities to allow defenders to see threats coming before they have done damage. More controversial would be capabilities for "active response" so that NATO could "reach into" the systems of attacking adversaries in order to disable attacks or otherwise stop them.

Role in the deployment of a new more secure network in parallel to the existing Internet[44]

For technical reasons, today's Internet cannot ever provide the security needed for sensitive uses. NATO could advance its cyber deterrence agenda if it were among the first adopters of a new network protocol that provides much greater security and reliability than today's Internet. This is not to suggest that NATO should develop a new network technology. A more or less globally trusted initiative should develop the new protocols (there are multiple of these underway); NATO can be one – and perhaps the – critical early adopter.

The idea is as follows: the NATO C3 Agency working with allied R&D capabilities could choose a new networking protocol among the various protocols being developed in Western research initiatives.[45] With appropriate prototyping, a new network protocol, providing far greater security and reliability than the current Internet configuration could be adopted as the basis for the NATO network. Interoperability with existing networks would of course be a prime issue.

NATO is not an R&D institution. Adopting a new network protocol would therefore require technical support from Alliance members. Such a proposal is not "pie in the sky" – it could be achieved and the advantages would be significant. However, the actual cost of a new network would not be excessive; the existing infrastructure of buried cables would not be replaced.

Scenarios for the future

This chapter began by noting that most security topics prefaced by "cyber" are inchoate in their development. Cyberspace is also transmogrified by what is perhaps the fastest pace of technological change of any human endeavor. This, however, does not mean that looking 20 years in the future is an exercise in futility – but we should expect that the future might be surprising. Consider if this chapter were written in 1991 looking forward. It might be entitled "Information Technology," but that belies the fact that most of the major elements that shape today's cyber environment were already in place and well known, at least to the expert community – the Internet, the World Wide Web, hackers and security threats, personal computers, distributed computing. So too, today, most of the major elements of cyberspace are in place.

There are, however, two facets of cyberspace which represent "wild cards" in predicting the future. One facet we already have great familiarity with – social networking. But who in 1991 would have predicted Facebook, or Twitter, and the possibly consequential impact of these impacts on political discourse and even regime change? Most social networking technologies do not in themselves represent great technological leaps – they are social innovations using slight modifications of existing technologies. I would argue that these "social innovations" may prove one of the great "wild cards" of the future.

A second possible – though more unitary – transformative agent would be the widespread adoption of a more secure, more reliable, "new network" to replace the Internet. As noted above, the technologies for such a new internetworking are already developed, or close to development. The Internet's lack of some desirable qualities – like attribution – now implicitly supports cyber crime and sophisticated cyber attacks. It is entirely possible to imagine the "new network" in large scale rollout in 20 years, though certainly the Internet would continue to function in parallel, just as telegraph continued for decades after the introduction of the telephone. The "new network" might fundamentally transform cyber-space, and most particularly, it would certainly provide the basis for a much more secure cyberspace than can be otherwise envisioned. The choice of whether this "new network" emerges, however, is largely a matter of political will. Just as the Internet was launched through the commit-ment of the U.S. DOD, so too, the "new network" would require the com-mitment of some meta-organization. NATO could, and I argue should, play a significant role in introducing this network.

Even with these caveats, there is a wide range of uncertainty about the role of cyber in multilateral security relations.

Scenario one: business as usual

In this most positive scenario, we see the intensification of current trends in 20 years. The increasing economic and social dependence on cyberspace-based systems continues. Mobile devices and sensor networks (including in cars) make the efficient functioning of Western economies completely dependent on cyber-based networks. Cyber crime continues to grow in sophistication, though the consequent financial losses are absorbed (and largely hidden from public view) by the private sector. The continual arms race between cyber security and cyber attackers continues; security costs increase in both private sector and military/government organizations. There are occasional events, some mildly disruptive to smaller nations, which are believed to be linked to nation-state action, though none are acknowledged. Some smaller NATO members in Central/Eastern Europe might become targets. Intelligence estimates con-tinue to point towards increasingly sophisticated cyber attack capabilities by technologically sophisticated nation-states. "Cyber war," however, remains something which is theorized about but not observed. Smaller third world states are not successful in developing effective cyber attack capabilities, nor are terrorists. Cyber espionage – both industrial and nation-state – causes significant and embarrassing losses.

Scenario two: emergence of a competitive multipolar world

With the large number of sophisticated hackers/computer scientists in most countries, sophisticated attack capabilities are commonplace among a number of less developed nations, as well as among terrorist and radical political/religious groups. Cyber attacks against national and multilateral institutions become routine. Except in the most sophisticated cyber systems, cyber attack capabilities now have the capacity to overwhelm cyber security. At least one major cyber criminal group has adopted a strong anti-Western political agenda, while continuing to finance itself through sophisticated cyber crime activities. Consequently, disruptive cyber attacks occur against both computer systems and against some critical infrastructures like transportation, although the latter, while successful, cause only disruption and irritation. Most of these attacks are from nihilistic anti-Western political groups. NATO systems, however, are attacked and some command systems have been disrupted for a consequential amount of time by a small nation-state where NATO forces have been committed. As NATO and other high end systems invest increasing amounts in security, sophisticated insider threat attacks against these systems – including NATO's – become an increasing concern. ID theft through theft of personal data becomes a commonplace technique for disrupting the lives of mid-level NATO and other military staff.

In addition, China and perhaps Iran – authoritarian regimes – also launch a long term systematic effort to replace the U.S. and other Western democracies in controlling the various technical bodies (e.g. Internet Engineering Task Force, Internet Corporation for Assigned Names and Numbers, the Internet Society) whose decisions ultimately shape how open and unrestricted the Internet remains. Increasingly there develops conflict – often expressed in less than obvious technical terms – between alternative views of how global networks should operate.[46] At issue are technical choices that would make global censorship and restrictions on the free flow of information easier to implement.

Network attacks that disrupt large portions of the Internet in Western Europe occur, and are believed to be trial runs for sophisticated first-tier nation-state capabilities, most probably Russian, although by this point there is also an increasing fusion of cyber crime groups with the Russian state. A bit later, there is one acknowledged disruption of NATO networks by Russia in a period where there is a dispute over Serbia.

In addition, NATO operations in a Muslim country could result in a Jihadist war against NATO, which includes widespread use of insiders (contractors, support personnel) who successfully poison a number of NATO computer systems. Smaller states may routinely use cyber attack in their own conflicts, and with the increasing world-wide dependence on cyber networks, these attacks often cause significant disruption of critical infrastructures. The use of cyber attack by radical political groups could also become routine, e.g. radical environmentalists opposing Western chemical and oil interests on environmental grounds routinely attack chemical and refinery operations by implanting cyber attack tools into the computer controlled plant operations. Resulting explosions would cause significant loss of life.

Scenario three: emergence of a cooperative multipolar world order

This world in many ways is similar to the "business as usual" case – cyber crime in particular continues to grow in sophistication and impact, and offensive cyber skills become widespread.

However, cooperative arrangements for managing the risks of cyberspace start to become functionally important in limiting risk. The Council of Europe Convention on Cybercrime is ratified by all Western nations, and some other countries (but flagrant violating countries like Nigeria remain non-signatories); equally, or more importantly, international law enforcement over cyber crimes starts to become effective.

A modest beginning is made in multilateral negotiations between major states (U.S., Russian, other NATO signatories, China) in limiting the use of offensive cyber attack tools, although verification remains a challenge, and much work remains. In parallel, however, a coalition of Western states (with implicit NATO participation) begins to coordinate network management policies so as to retaliate against or punish cyber malefactors; the coalition maintains what is in effect a network embargo against traffic from certain points of origin. These information embargos are at best only modestly effective, but they illustrate an increasing willingness by Western democracies to use their implicit cyber-power to enforce appropriate behavior in cyberspace. Joint legal prosecutions in country-specific or world courts also start to become an accepted tool; in other words cybercriminals begin to be treated as pariahs in the world order.

Financial instruments for managing risk emerge from their current boutique status. A major insurance and reinsurance market for underwriting cyber related risk becomes a motivating factor for Western companies to invest more in network security – and also to learn how to cooperate with law enforcement and national security interests, including NATO.

In other words, threats in cyberspace continue to grow, both from sophisticated criminal enterprises and increasing comfort among terrorist groups to consider cyber as a theatre for action. However, mechanisms for common defense and cooperative deterrence – both among Western nations and also major corporations – keep pace with these threats.

Summary and conclusion

NATO's future role in cyberspace illustrates how the mission of the Alliance is shifting. Many of the capabilities NATO will need to provide for collective cyber security do not now exist. If NATO is to continue to serve as the transatlantic security alliance against all threats, NATO needs to make itself relevant for issues of collective security in cyberspace.

Enhancing NATO's cyber defense capabilities, as called for in the Lisbon Summit Declaration, is conceptually simple and politically appealing. It is also technically difficult, resource intensive, and may raise questions of network integration among allies. "Enhanced defense" will also require new partnerships, most notably with key private sector infrastructure providers.

Beyond that, however, NATO should begin to develop and implement a doctrine of cyber deterrence. This will require new doctrine and new capabilities for response. Cyberspace is a nuanced and incipient environment, and much work – technical, organizational, and conceptual – remains to be done. At some point in the future, nations and other actors will begin to understand how to project power through cyberspace, and not just launch attacks. Understanding that environment and creating the capabilities to operate within it is a further challenge.

While cyber creates the need for new capabilities and new roles for NATO, it also offers the opportunity for the Alliance to continue its work of maintaining a framework for peace in the North Atlantic. It is important that Alliance members provide the commitment and the resources needed to step into this new role.

Notes

1 Cyberspace is the notional environment in which digitized information is stored or communicated over information systems and networks. Equally important to what cyberspace *is* is what it *does*. The information in cyberspace *controls* directly a wide variety of physical and electronic activities (e.g., so called Supervisory Control and Data Acquisition (SCADA) networks control many industrial processes); cyberspace data also i*nforms* decisions that people make.

2 A little more technically, the Internet is a set of technical protocols (Transport Control Protocol and Internet Protocol, TCP/IP for short) that transform data from one computer (say an e-mail message) into a large number of small data "packets"; each packet travels to its destination following its own independent path. At the destination computer the packets are reassembled into the original e-mail.

3 NATO Parliamentary Assembly, "074 CDS 11E – Information and National Security – draft general report by Lord Jopling," 2011 Spring Season.

4 A worm is a self-replicating malicious computer program.

5 NATO Parliamentary Assembly, "074 CDS 11E."

6 For a further discussion, see J. Hunker, *Creeping Failure: How We Broke the Internet and What We Can Do to Fix It*, McClelland and Stewart/Random House, 2010.

7 R.H. Anderson, *Research and Development Initiatives Focused on Preventing, Detecting, and Responding to Insider Misuse of Critical Defense Information Systems: Results of a Three-Day Workshop*. RAND CF-151-OSD, 1999.

8 A fuller definition of nation-state disruptive cyber attack: the unauthorized penetration, use, or denial of use by a nation-state (or its proxies) of another nation's cyber systems (whether government or private) for the purpose of causing the disruption of or damage to these systems or their use, or the systems (including physical infrastructures) which these systems control. This definition is mine, but is based on elements of other definitions.

9 Total cyber-related business losses in 2009 are estimated to be USD 42 billion for the United States, and USD 140 billion globally. However, estimated losses due to cyber crime are highly unreliable; many businesses prefer not to report cyber crime. Cyber crime has exploded since 2000 and has become a form of organized crime. D.C. Blair, "Annual Threat Assessment of the Intelligence Community for the House Permanent Select Committee on Intelligence," Washington, Director of National Intelligence, 2009. Online. Available: http://intelligence.senate.gov/090212/blair.pdf (accessed 27 September 2010).

10 A thorough recent discussion of Chinese capabilities is: S. DeWeese *et al.*, *Capability of the People's Republic of China to Conduct Cyber Warfare and Computer Network*

Exploitation, Report prepared by Northrop Grumman Corp. for the U.S.-China Economic and Security Review Commission, Washington, 17 February 2010. Online. Available: www.uscc.gov/researchpapers/2009/NorthropGrumman_ PRC_Cyber_Paper_Final_Approved Report_16Oct2009.pdf (accessed 27 September 2010). See also "War in the Fifth Dimension: Briefing on Cyberwar," *The Economist*, 3 July 2010, pp. 25–28.

11 See R.A. Clarke and R. Knake, *Cyber War: The Next Threat to National Security and What to do About It*, New York: Harper Collins, 2010; or for a more balanced view, J. Hunker, *Cyber War and Cyber Power: Issues for NATO Doctrine*, Research Paper No. 62, Research Division, NATO Defence College, Rome, November 2010, pp. 1–12.

12 NATO, "Defending against Cyber Attacks." Online. Available: www.nato.int/ cps/en/natolive/topics_49193.htm?selectedLocale=en (accessed 27 September 2010). Unless noted, material in this and following paragraphs is drawn from this report.

13 This reflects the most recent (May 2012) evolution of NATOs cyber defense posture. See NATO, *Defending the Networks: The NATO Policy on Cyber Defence*, 4 October 2011. Online. Available: www.nato.int/cps/en/natolive/search.htm.

14 NATO, "NATO Summit Declaration: Issued by the Heads of State and Government participating in the meeting of the North Atlantic Council in Chicago on 20 May 2012," Chicago Summit, 20 May 2012, para. 42. Online. Available: www. nato.int/cps/en/natolive/official_texts_87593.htm.

15 The Policy was developed and approved by the NATO Defence Ministers on 8 June 2011 and is coupled with an Action Plan which has specific tasks and activities for NATO's own structures and allies' defense forces. A public summary is at NATO, *Defending the Networks*. See also NATO, "NATO Defense ministers adopt new cyber defense policy," 8 June 2011. Online. Available www.nato.int/ cps/en/SID-001632DA-6B60591F/natolive/news_75195.htm (accessed 27 July 2011).

16 NATO, "NATO Summit Declaration," Chicago.

17 NATO, *Defending the Networks*.

18 M. Libicki, *Conquest in Cyberspace*, New York: Cambridge University Press, p. 257.

19 R. Kugler, "Deterrence of Cyber Attacks," in Franklin D. Kramer, Stuart H. Starr, and Larry K. Wentz, *Cyberpower and National Security*, Washington, D.C.: Potomac Books, 2009, p. 320.

20 R. Mesic, M. Hura, M. Libicki, A. Packard, and L. Scott, *Cyber Command (Provisional) Decision Support*, RAND Project Air Force, 2010.

21 Kugler, "Deterrence of Cyber Attacks," p. 328.

22 J.M. Goldgeier, *The Future of NATO*, Special Report No. 51, Council of Foreign Relations Press, February 2010, p.7.

23 M. Libicki, *Cyber Deterrence and Cyber War*, Santa Monica, California: RAND, p. 24. Online. Available: www.rand.org/pubs/monographs/MG877.

24 H. Lin, "Thoughts on Threat Assessment in Cyberspace," in P. Shane and J. Hunker, eds., *Cybersecurity: Shared Risks, Shared Responsibilities*, Carolina Academic Press, forthcoming 2012.

25 See for instance: D.E. Graham, "Cyber Threats and the Law of War," *Journal of National Security Law and Policy*, Vol. 4, No. 1, 2010, pp. 87–102.

26 Deterrence is anything that dissuades an attack.

27 Libicki, *Cyber Deterrence and Cyber War*, p. 5.

28 Libicki, *Cyber Deterrence and Cyber War*, p. xvi.

29 This is not a slight upon NATO. Disloyal American citizens have done more damage to U.S. security interests than any other recent threat. See: Anderson, *Research and Development Initiatives*.

30 NATO Parliamentary Assembly, 074 CDS 11 E, p. 8.

31 NATO Parliamentary Assembly, 074 CDS 11 E, p. 8.
32 A point made clear in Stanley Kubrick's movie *Dr. Strangelove*.
33 Kugler, "Deterrence of Cyber Attacks," p. 332.
34 Note that this is not saying "accountable for cyber attacks launched from within their borders." Technically cyber attacks can as their final point before the attack be "launched" from an otherwise innocent third country. The intent is to trace the chain of culpability back to the originators of the attack.
35 Kugler, "Deterrence of Cyber Attacks," p. 330.
36 Kugler, "Deterrence of Cyber Attacks," pp. 320–321.
37 Clarke, *Cyber War*, uses the term "constructive ambiguity," p. 177.
38 Libicki, *Cyber Deterrence and Cyber War*, p. xvii.
39 Kugler, "Deterrence of Cyber Attacks," p. 324.
40 These NATO officials might be members of the international staff in the newly created Division on Emerging Security Challenges, where there is a Cyber section (though it is currently a small section whose role is still being defined). Such staff might be complimented by allied military officers assigned to NATO and serving in the International Military Staff of headquarters or allied officers who are assigned to their delegations to NATO.
41 "We are in favor of the Alliance's commitment to establishing uniform security standards, which Member States may also use for civilian critical infrastructures on a voluntary basis, as foreseen in NATO's new Strategic Concept." Federal Ministry of the Interior, Germany, *Cyber Security Strategy for Germany*, Alt-Moabt 101 D, 10559, Berlin, February 2011, p. 11.
42 Specifically: 1) a ban on secretly embedding malicious code that could later be activated; 2) application of humanitarian laws banning attacks on noncombatants; 3) a ban on deception in operations in cyberspace (e.g. as in anonymous attacks); and 4) broader international government oversight of the Internet. See John Markoff and Andrew E. Kramer, "U.S. and Russia Differ on a Treaty for Cybersecurity," *New York Times*, 27 June 2009, p. A1.
43 NATO Parliamentary Assembly 074 CDS 11E.
44 For a fuller discussion, see Hunker, *Creeping Failure*, Chapter 9.
45 See for instance www.geni.net. GENI is the Global Environment for Network Innovation.
46 See Z. Brzezinski, *Strategic Vision: America and the Crisis of Global Power*, New York: Basic Books, 2012, pp. 112–113 for an interesting discussion of this potential in the face of declining U.S. power.

11 NATO

Towards an adaptive missile defense

Gustav Lindstrom

Origins and nature of missile defense

Defending against incoming missiles dates back to the late stages of World War II, when British planners devised a basic missile defense system based on anti-aircraft artillery to defend London against German V-2 missiles. With the advent of nuclear weapons, the concept of missile defense took on new importance in the 1950s and 1960s. Among the better known examples of missile defense systems developed in the 1960s was the U.S. Safeguard system to protect the silos housing the Minutemen intercontinental ballistic missiles (ICBMs) and the Soviet "Galosh" system to protect Moscow from incoming ICBMs.

The logic behind missile defense remained relatively static during the Cold War era. In its simplest form, it represented one of several elements in the deterrence toolkit. The deterrence factor was formed by protecting the "survivability" of a second strike capability. The thinking was that neither the United States nor the Soviet Union would risk launching an all-out ICBM attack with the knowledge that a substantial second strike capability might remain which could be then be used as a response to the initial attack.

The end of the Cold War, coupled with developments in missile defense technology, resulted in a broadening of the missile defense concept in two ways. First, greater emphasis was placed on countering ballistic missiles of varying ranges, including short-range tactical missiles with a reach of less than 1,000 kilometers. A manifestation of this trend was visible during the First Gulf War, when U.S. Patriot missiles were employed to counter Iraqi Scud missiles launched against Israel and Saudi Arabia. Second, and related to the first point, policymakers moved beyond the deterrence mantra for missile defense, exploring the possible protective benefits of missile defense at the operational and tactical levels.

With the end of the bi-polar world order, and western troops becoming more deployable abroad, policymakers saw the need for theater missile defense systems that could protect military personnel serving in areas of instability – in particular given the recognition that multiple countries were either developing or enhancing existing missile programs. An indication of this trend was manifested in the first half of 2001, when NATO launched two feasibility studies in parallel to gauge the prospects for a NATO Theater Missile Defense (TMD) system. Another, and less frequently observed expression of this trend, was the growing interest in TMD systems in different parts of the world. A number of countries – such as Israel, Japan, and India – started to explore missile defense systems to protect their populations. Israel, for example, gradually developed the Arrow and Iron Dome defense system with U.S. support to achieve a TMD zone.

The uses of missile defense were further extended after the September 11th terrorist attacks. Missile defense was increasingly considered an insurance policy against non-state actors and regimes that might seek ballistic missiles of varying ranges to threaten the United States and its allies. Under such a scenario, missile defense could provide a key protective component against an attacker that might not be deterred via traditional means, such as the threat of a return strike. Some policymakers also saw missile defense providing non-proliferation benefits as it might discourage some actors from pursuing missile technologies in the first place. A final advantage of developing existing missile defense systems would be that it could protect against accidental missile launches.

Missile defense in Europe

Although missile defense efforts in the United States continued throughout the Cold War and thereafter, efforts were reinvigorated during the Presidency of George W. Bush. Among the two most notable actions during the Bush administration was the formal withdrawal of the United States from the 1972 Anti-Ballistic Missile (ABM) Treaty in 2002 – which facilitated the push for a territorial missile defense system – and the initiative to establish a missile defense system in Europe (also known as the "third site") to counter the missile threat from Iran.[1] The third site would consist of a radar system in the Czech Republic and ten interceptors emplaced in Poland.[2] The initiative met with resistance from several fronts, among them European public opinion and Russia which felt such a system could be used to intercept their nuclear missiles – tipping the nuclear missile balance in favor of the United States. As a result, Russia threatened among other things to place short-range Iskander missiles in Kaliningrad as a response to missile defense in Europe.[3]

With the election of President Barack Obama in 2008, many believed that missile defense in Europe would be discontinued given the controversies it had stirred, including some that were likely to arise in the horizon, such as negotiating a follow-on START treaty with Russia. The weak outlook for missile defense was supported by several Obama officials who early on indicated the need for reviewing the plans for missile defense.[4]

Consistent with these signals, on 17 September 2009, the Obama Administration announced that it would discontinue the Bush era plan for missile
defense. What caught many observers by surprise was the simultaneous
announcement that the United States would readjust its efforts in the
missile defense arena. On the same day, President Obama announced a
modified approach for ballistic missile defense in Europe. The new system,
known as the European Phased Adaptive Approach (EPAA), would be
based on a "proven, cost-effective system using land- and sea-based interceptors against Iran's short- and medium-range missile threat." Under the
new arrangement, the Department of Defense (DoD) would deploy

Table 11.1 The phased adaptive approach for Europe

Phase	Objective	Key Components
I (by 2011)	Initial capacity against SRBMs, MRBMs, and IRBMs	• Aegis BMD 3.6.1 ships equipped with SM-3 IA • AN/TPY-2 (FBM) • C2BMC AOC
II (by 2015)	Robust capability against SRMBs and MRBMs	• Aegis BMD 4.0.1/5.0 ships with SM-3 IB • Aegis Ashore 5.0 with SM-3 IB (one site) • HAAD • C2BMC updates • ALTBMD Lower Tier • Enhanced sensors
III (by 2018)	Robust capability against IRBMs	• Aegis BMD 5.1 with SM-3 IIA • Aegis Ashore 5.1 with SM-3 IB/IIA (two sites) • THAAD • Precision Tracking Space System • ABIR • C2BMC updates • ALTBMD Upper Tier • Enhanced sensors
IV (by 2020)	Early intercept capability against MRBM and IRBMs, as well as ICMBs from today's regional threats	• Aegis BMD 5.1. with SM-3 IIA • Aegis Ashore 5.1 with SM-3 IIB (two sites) • THAAD • Precision Tracking Space System • ABIR • Enhanced C2BMC • Enhanced sensors

Notes
SRBM = short-range ballistic missile; MRBM = medium-range ballistic missile; IRBM = inter-
mediate-range ballistic missile; AN/TPY = Army Navy/Transportable Radar Surveillance;
C2BMC = Command, Control, Battle Management, and Communications; ALTBMD = Active
Layered Theatre Ballistic Missile Defence System; THAAD = Terminal High Altitude Area
Defense; ABIR = Airborne Infrared (capacity).

increasingly capable elements and interceptors – with many of the components being mobile and adaptable to current threats. Like its predecessor, it would require physical assets on the European continent.

The EPAA consists of four phases, with the final phase reached around 2020. Among the key selling points of the system is that it will give the United States an initial capability to counter missiles incoming from a country such as Iran six to seven years earlier than would have been possible under the Bush era "third site" programme. Another selling point is the mobility of the system which yields a missile defense architecture that is flexible and can be adapted as the threat picture evolves.[5]

As shown in Table 11.1, the system will rely on a variety of platforms, ranging from converted Aegis ships equipped with different variations of the Standard Missile 3 (SM-3) to a Precision Tracking Space System. Going from an initial capability against short-range, medium-range, and intermediate-range missiles in 2011, the system is envisioned to have early intercept capability against medium-range, intermediate-range, and intercontinental missiles from "today's regional threats" by 2020.[6]

Another important characteristic of the EPAA is its integration into NATO's ballistic missile defense architecture. NATO is currently developing its Active Layered Theatre Ballistic Missile Defence (ALTBMD), which was initiated in September 2005 to enhance NATO's command and control as well as strengthen communication networks between NATO and national missile defense systems.[7] At the May 2012 NATO Chicago Summit, Heads of State and Government declared an Interim NATO BMD capability. Looking ahead, the NATO ALTBMD system will be combined with the EPAA during the EPAA's second phase. This represents a departure from the Bush Administration's missile defense plans for Europe which did not take a strong position on the synergy between the two evolving systems. With these developments in mind, the next section examines some of the principal policy debates regarding developments in missile defense.

Key policy debates

With the development of an EPAA, as well as other regional missile defense efforts, there are several on-going debates concerning missile defense. These relate to the value of missile defense and the possible unintended consequences that may arise in the mid- to long-term. The unintended consequences may range from impacted bilateral relations (e.g. between the United States and Russia) to the development of alternative means to circumvent the protective benefits of a missile defense architecture.

The costs of missile defense

A persistent issue of contention with respect to missile defense is whether or not it "is worth it." Policymakers tend to base their opinions on some form of cost-benefit analysis to defend their positions: those who are against missile defense argue that the costs outweigh the benefits and those who are for missile defense see the benefits outpacing costs. Complicating this policy debate, however, are the complexities of fully capturing the costs and benefits associated with missile defense.

On the cost side, most analysts tend to focus on the dollar amounts spent on acquiring a missile defense system. Given diverging methodologies and different starting points to start the calculations, most studies provide different cost calculations. Table 11.2 below provides an illustration of such variations, where figures are often presented in a range format. As seen, the study by the Center for Arms Control and Non-Proliferation provides a substantially higher estimate for the now defunct layered missile defense plan compared to those of other studies.

A possible explanation for the divergence between official and non-official figures is that government calculations tend to focus on development and acquisitions costs and underestimate more intricate cost categories such as operations and support costs.[8] In line with this argumentation, a 2004 report by the U.S. General Accounting Office noted that there was limited reporting to the U.S. Congress on the life-cycle costs of missile defense.[9]

Table 11.2 Examples of missile defense cost estimates

Study	Date/System range	Low estimate	High Estimate
Center for Arms Control and Non-Proliferation (2003)	Layered missile defense (George W. Bush Plan)	$785–825 billion*	$1.1–$1.2 trillion*
CBO Study (2002)	2002–2015	$23 billion	$64 billion
GAO Study (2008)	2002–2008	$57 billion	
Selected Acquisition Report to Congress (2003)	2002–2009	$62.9 billion**	
CBO Report (2006)	2006–2024	$247 billion	

Sources
R. F. Kaufman (ed.), *The Full Costs of Ballistic Missile Defense,* Center for Arms Control and Non-Proliferation, January 2003; U.S. Congressional Budget Office, *Estimated Costs and Technical Characteristics of Selected National Missile Defense Systems,* January 2002; U.S. General Accounting Office, *Missile Defense: Actions Needed to Improve Planning and Cost Estimates for Long-Term Support of Ballistic Missile Defense,* Report to the Subcommittee on Strategic Forces, Committee on Armed Services, House of Representatives, GAO-08-1068, September 2008; D. Ruppe, "Pentagon Sees $20 Billion Cost Growth for National Defense System," *Global Security Newswire,* 16 April 2003 (quoted by the Center for Defense Information); U.S. Congressional Budget Office, *The Long-Term Implications of Current Defense Plans and Alternatives: Detailed Update for Fiscal Year 2006,* January 2006.

Notes
*Calculated in constant 2003 dollars and includes deployment and maintenance costs;
**Covers solely R&D, testing and evaluation.

From a different angle, examples of controversial cost categories include the technical feasibility of missile defense and the threat it is supposed to address. While some would argue that technical challenges add both costs and uncertainty regarding the viability of the entire project (thus a cost), others respond that technical challenges are a minor issue – especially when current systems are built on proven technologies – and that the eventual technical advances will produce benefits to industry and society at large.[10]

A cost that is frequently left out of policymakers' calculations is the opportunity cost of missile defense – the potential benefits that could be derived by spending missile defense money elsewhere. In other words, how could the billions of dollars spent on missile defense to date have brought more benefits to security by funding other activities? While there is no clear answer to this question, it will continue to spawn debate on whether or not missile defense is worth it.

The benefits of missile defense

On the benefits side, the advantages of missile defense are usually not quantifiable in dollar terms. The inability to attach even a ballpark monetary figure to the benefits side complicates the cost-benefit analysis. Commonly listed benefits of missile defense include:

- *Physical protection*: Missile defense can protect a specific geographic area against incoming ballistic missiles of different ranges. The benefit of physical protection increases as more countries express an interest in missile technology or examine ways to improve their existing stocks of missiles. According to a 2004 Congressional Research Service study, over 30 countries have or are pursuing missiles that could be used to carry either conventional payloads or weapons of mass destruction.[11] Of principal concern to the West are missile developments in Iran and North Korea, for example Iran's testing of its Safir and Simorgh ICBM/SLV (Space Launch Vehicle) and North Korea's ICBM/SLV tests in 2006, 2009, and 2012.
- *Psychological security*: Although a missile defense system cannot guarantee full protection, civilian populations are likely to derive a feeling of security from it. This psychological benefit was on display during the First Gulf War when the Patriot Missile received strong praise among populations that were protected, even though its record was not always stellar.
- *Technological benefits*: A range of benefits may accrue, spanning the development of new breakthrough technologies to the application of missile defense technologies in other domain areas (e.g. civilian). It may also encourage technical cooperation and advances by key allies and partners.

- *Economic benefits:* Missile defense is beneficial to many high-technology firms. Beyond the direct benefits of employment, it supports key industrial sectors that may help produce other key technologies in the future that will result in both technological and economic benefits.
- *Collective defense benefits:* As stated in NATO's Deterrence and Defence Posture Review, adopted at the May 2012 Chicago Summit, missile defense represents a core component of NATO's overall capabilities for deterrence and defense. Missile defense is expected to "become an integral part of the Alliance's overall defense posture, further strengthen the transatlantic link, and contribute to the indivisible security of the Alliance."[12]

As noted earlier, missile defense is also sometimes said to provide a non-proliferation "benefit" as it may discourage others from pursuing ballistic missile technology. This benefit is controversial. Some take the opposite view, arguing that missile defense is more likely to encourage proliferation as some countries see the necessity to boost their missile capabilities to maintain a deterrent capability.

Lastly, some costs and benefits associated with missile defense may come in the form of unintended consequences that do not appear immediately. The next section examines these in greater detail. While the unintended consequences may provide either positive or negative outcomes, it focuses primarily on those of a challenging nature.

The unintended consequences of missile defense

There is a growing recognition that missile defense may result in a host of unintended consequences – some of which may take several years to manifest themselves. At least four issues stand out: U.S.–Russia relations, implications for disarmament, the potential for non-ballistic missile proliferation, and changes in the strategic use of outer space.

U.S.–Russia relations

There are many questions over how Russia will respond to NATO's evolving missile defense architecture and how it will affect U.S.–Russian relations. There have already been several signals that Russian policymakers perceive the EPAA as being targeted against Russia and are keen to stop or limit its progress.

Among Russian concerns is that EPAA will go ahead with phases III and IV regardless of the status of Iran's missile and nuclear programme. At those stages the interceptors (SM-3 IIA and SM-3 IIB) are likely to achieve speeds of 5 kilometers per second or higher. According to Russian military officials, these high velocity interceptors would be able to intercept U.S.-bound Russian ICBMs, thereby impacting Russia's strategic deterrent.[13]

Exacerbating this concern is the possibility that the U.S. places Aegis-based interceptors in strategic locations such as the Arctic Ocean which would shorten the time needed to intercept Russian ICBMs.

U.S. policymakers have unsuccessfully tried to argue that the EPAA is unable to negate Russia's strategic deterrent. For example, they have pointed out that in spite of their high velocity, the SM-3 IIA and IIB would still not be fast enough to intercept Russian ICBMs. According to U.S. officials, one reason is that the missile defense system needs an incoming missile to achieve burnout before a "firing solution"/interception trajectory can be calculated. With an ICBM achieving burnout anywhere from 130 to 180 seconds after launch, combined with the time needed to achieve a firing solution, an SM-3 launch is most likely to take place anywhere from 190 to 240 seconds after an ICMB launch.[14] Given this time lapse, even the fastest EPAA interceptors would be unable to catch up to a Russian ICBM. Russia's ability to deliver nuclear weapons from land, air, and sea further complicates the EPAA's capacity to negate Russia's strategic deterrent.

Regardless of these and other explanations, Russian concerns remain. If the EPAA is not targeted at Russia, why can't there be a legally binding agreement to that effect? U.S. officials have countered that such assurances can be (and have been) provided via political statements.[15] Resorting to more specific agreements, which might also contain criteria such deployment sites and technical performances, is considered too far reaching and unlikely to attain political traction in the U.S. and among NATO allies. As a result, Russian decision- and policymakers have outlined a number of proposals in response to the EPAA. In November 2011, then President Medvedev outlined several steps, including:[16]

- Placing the missile attack early warning radar station in Kaliningrad on combat alert;
- Commissioning new strategic ballistic missiles to be equipped with advanced missile defense penetration systems and effective warheads;[17]
- Drawing up measures for disabling missile defense system data and guidance systems;
- If the above are insufficient, deploying modern offensive weapons systems in the west and south of the country – an initial move being the deployment of Iskander missiles to the Kaliningrad Region.

Sometimes known as "phased adaptive response," other Russian retaliatory measures include increasing the defense of fixed launched sites, maximizing the concealment of strategic nuclear force mobile launchers, and ensuring the destruction or disruption of opposing ballistic missile defense infrastructure assets such as interceptors, launchers, command and control posts, and outer-space detection means.[18] With little doubt, a move in this direction would have negative implications for U.S.–Russian relations.

Disarmament considerations

A second unintended consequence concerns disarmament trends. For example, while there is no direct mention of missile defense in the "New START" Agreement, the preamble states that there is an "interrelationship between strategic offensive arms and strategic defensive arms" and "that this interrelationship will become more important as strategic nuclear arms are reduced." With missile defense falling into the category of strategic defense arms, Russian policymakers make an implicit link between current and further reductions in nuclear arsenals and the status of missile defense efforts. As a consequence, future arms reduction treaties may be more difficult to negotiate due to missile defense developments. The New START agreement faced some of these challenges and it is likely that the successor treaty (New START expires in 2021) will be more difficult to secure. In his November 2011 speech on missile defense, then President Medvedev noted that Russia could consider withdrawing from the New START agreement should missile defense not evolve in Russia's favor.[19]

While U.S. policymakers do not regard the text in the preamble having any impact or constraining effect on missile defense efforts, several steps have been taken to assuage Russian concerns. Principal among them is exploring cooperation opportunities in the missile defense arena. At the third NATO–Russia Council Summit held in Lisbon in late 2010, Heads of State and Government gave NATO and Russia the green light to carry out a joint ballistic missile threat assessment and to renew theatre missile defense cooperation. To ensure momentum, they likewise "tasked the NRC [NATO–Russia Council] to develop a comprehensive Joint Analysis of the future framework for missile defense cooperation."[20]

Proliferation of non-ballistic missiles

A third unintended consequence may be that some countries become increasingly interested in acquiring and relying on other types of missiles to ensure their security needs.[21] Given their low-signature targets and relatively cool exhausts, cruise missiles might become particularly attractive as a means to circumvent missile defenses. As missile defense plans evolve, so will the search for alternative or more advanced means to penetrate the system. To illustrate, countries may place greater emphasis on procuring shorter-range missiles that do not have a ballistic trajectory, thereby avoiding the defensive properties of missile defense. Some countries may even consider rudimentary means of delivery such as sea-based delivery vessels from which a nuclear tipped short-range missile could be fired.

Such effects may also occur regionally, where some countries (e.g. Israel) are pursuing theatre missile defense systems. Thus, there may be effects in regional security calculations that spawn localized arms races.

Encouraging such a trend is the general rule that it costs more to protect oneself against incoming missiles than finding alternative means to probe chinks in the armor (such as advanced decoys). As a result, over the long run, it may become even more expensive to maintain an effective defense shield – adding fuel to the debate on the costs and benefits of missile defense.

Strategic use of outer space

Missile defense may also have an impact on the strategic use of outer space. Some countries may see missile interceptors as potential kinetic anti-satellite weapons. To date, there have been a limited number of cases when missiles were used to shoot down a satellite. Among the most recent examples are the Chinese destruction of a Feng Yun 1C polar orbit weather satellite in 2007 and the U.S. destruction of its USA-193 satellite with a SM-3 missile in early 2008. While no other satellite has been shot down since then, there are concerns that some countries will take proactive efforts to protect their space-based assets from missile interceptors, possibly opening the door to a space arms race. In the longer term, efforts to protect satellites that provide critical information services may become more elaborate, encouraging the weaponization of space. This in turn might affect long standing international treaties such as the 1967 Outer Space Treaty. It may also provide new impetus to initiatives such as the Prevention of an Arms Race in Outer Space (PAROS) item on the Agenda of the Conference on Disarmament and the draft Treaty on the "Prevention of the Placement of Weapons in Outer Space and of the Threat and Use of Force Against Outer Space Objects" (PPWT) introduced by Russia and China in 2008. With these factors in mind, the next section considers how NATO missile defense may evolve in the future.

Possible future pathways

Regardless of stumbling blocks such as technical viability, system coverage, or threat picture, current trends suggests that NATO missile defense efforts will continue over the long term. Indeed, the EPAA already identifies system objectives until 2020 and beyond. With the European Phased Adaptive Approach set in motion as a contribution to NATO's missile defense architecture – combined with the need to address Russian concerns over missile defense – three distinct scenarios seem plausible over the medium to long term:

1　A cooperative NATO–Russia missile defense effort;
2　A separate NATO–Russian missile defense system characterized by limited cooperation;
3　A joint NATO–Russian missile defense system.

The first scenario in many ways reflects current reality. Both the United States and Russia recognize that there are benefits from missile defense cooperation. For example, U.S. officials have identified advantages ranging from operational benefits via data sharing and fusion to political benefits (e.g. both sides gain insights into BMD plans and capabilities while sending a clear message to other countries that proliferation will not go unchallenged).[22] Russian officials see cooperation as a means to protect their strategic deterrent while facilitating access to advanced technology. Reflective of this cooperative spirit, Heads of State and Government participating in the 2012 NATO Chicago Summit noted their commitment to "cooperation on missile defense in the spirit of mutual trust and reciprocity."[23]

Under this scenario, cooperation will commence in areas such as joint analysis, joint exercises, and the sharing of early warning data. An example of such cooperation was the NATO–Russia Council Theatre Missile Defence Exercise held in Ottobrun (Germany) in January 2008. The computer-assisted command post exercise was preceded by three preparatory stages held between December 2003 and October 2006. While the exercise had certain limitations – such as no links to actual geography or limited to incoming missiles with a range of less than 3,000 kilometers – it marked a starting point for future exercises.[24] NATO and Russia successfully conducted a computer-assisted missile defense exercise in April 2012. With respect to information sharing, there is momentum for the establishment of a future joint NATO–Russia Missile Data Fusion Centre and a joint NATO Russia Planning and Operations Centre.[25] With respect to early warning, Russia has offered access to data from its Gabala and Armavir radars. According to a Russian official, the Gabala radar is able to spot and track up to 75 percent of ICBM launches from the "south" while Armavir can provide 100 percent coverage and tracking capacity over the same region.[26]

The key question for this scenario is how far reaching NATO–Russia cooperation can go. Presently, U.S. and Russian officials seem to have different visions, with the U.S. emphasizing low-key cooperative measures while Russia seeks greater cooperation that may eventually lead to a joint system. Thus, while the prospect for this scenario is quite likely over the medium term, the viability of the cooperative model is much weaker in the long term. From a Russian perspective, the evolution of the EPAA will present a greater threat to its strategic deterrent. As such, levels of cooperation would need to grow substantially to offset the (perceived) increased capacity of the EPAA in phases III and IV – especially in the absence of legally binding guarantees. Looking ahead, cooperative efforts would give way to a more confrontational view – something which is already visible. From a U.S. perspective, too much cooperation could open the door to a "joint" system which is not in its strategic interest and could also lead to an overflow of technology transfers. Moreover, some other NATO members are likely to object to strong cooperation with Russia on missile defense given their suspicion of Russian foreign and defense policy.

Under a second scenario, NATO and Russian missile defense efforts would be characterized by limited cooperation. While the political statements made at the November 2010 NATO–Russia Council Summit call for NATO–Russian collaboration on missile defense, the scenario of limited cooperation and separate NATO–Russia systems is likely over the long term. What speaks in favor of this scenario over the longer term is that policymakers on both sides can accommodate some basic levels of cooperation while pursuing a separate system – an appealing option as Cold War mentalities are still prevalent on both sides when it comes to missile defense.

A development that gives credence to this scenario was NATO's decision against a "sectoral missile defense" approach. Proposed by then President Medvedev during the 2010 Lisbon Summit, a sectoral approach would have created overlapping sectors of responsibility in which both the U.S. and Russia would have had equal footing under a common system. The proposal, which would have called for substantial levels of cooperation with respect to information exchange and target distribution, was rejected as it would have outsourced NATO's security to a non-NATO country.

Over the long run, a worst case scenario might be the need for NATO missile defense to adjust to a Russian phased adaptive response. This would most likely negate some of the cooperative steps taken early on and could modify the evolution of NATO missile defense. For example, it could open the door to a more global NATO missile defensive system that links elements from the EPAA with evolving missile defence infrastructures in other regions – notably the Middle East and Asia. This is unlikely although some Russian policymakers would like to push in this direction. Since a joint system would theoretically follow a period of strong cooperation and collaboration, the prospects for a joint system is only feasible in the long term. Some of the key elements leading to a joint system have already been identified. For example at the political level, Russian policymakers would like to have a formally and legally binding agreement between NATO and Russia declaring that neither side would target the other's offensive missiles with missile defense interceptors. At the operational level, both sides would collaborate in areas such as early warning, joint analysis, and other areas identified under the first scenario.

Beyond this point, there are different views on how "joint" the system could be. As noted earlier, there is willingness on both sides for a joint NATO–Russia Missile Data Fusion Centre and a joint NATO Russia Planning and Operations Centre. However, a truly joint system would imply a single ballistic missile defense architecture with both sides having access to the interceptor kill switch – a low probability prospect. As was the case under the second scenario, unmet expectations on both sides could eventually lead to decreases in cooperative levels and a movement towards U.S.–Russian friction.

In summary, NATO–Russia missile defense is likely to be trademarked by low- to mid-level cooperation. Over the long term, such cooperation is likely to hit a plateau and give way to a more competitive relationship in which both sides seek to exploit comparative advantages to maintain their strategic deterrent while addressing perceived missile threats.

Conclusion

While there is no single vision for how missile defense architectures will evolve, there are clear signals that missile defense efforts will be sustained over the long run. Notwithstanding concerns over technical feasibility and costs, missile defense has found new grounding with the introduction of a phased adaptive approach that will feed into on-going NATO missile defense efforts.

However, there are still several key issues that will need to be addressed to better understand how NATO missile defense develops in the future. Examples of such questions include: (1) the degree to which NATO and Russia cooperate on missile defense efforts, (2) the degree to which the PAA extends to regions beyond Europe, including the degree of synergy between different platforms and sensors, and (3) how the missile threat picture evolves. The answers to these questions will invariably impact the evolution of NATO missile defense and the types of unintended consequences that arise.

The degree to which the Phased Adaptive Approach (PAA) extends beyond Europe is particularly important. As noted in the 2010 Ballistic Missile Defense Review, the U.S. will "pursue a phased adaptive approach within each region that is tailored to the threats unique to that region."[27] Regions beyond Europe that may see a PAA to ballistic missile defense include East Asia and the Middle East.[28] While the regional architectures require a different approach, the potential for synergies and connections between the different systems could theoretically open the door to a more global missile defense system.

Such a trajectory would be of concern Russia, in particular as the EPAA matures in 2020. While U.S. policymakers insist that the PAA will be appropriately tailored, phased, and adaptive (and therefore unlikely to result in a global missile defense system), the perception in itself will have implications for U.S.-Russia relations and the evolution of NATO missile defense. Looking ahead, the evolution of NATO missile defense and regional missile defense architectures are also likely to impact China. In the longer term, it may see its deterrent capability threatened – especially as it has a limited number of long-range ballistic missiles and does not have alternative means of delivery, such as advanced submarine-launched ballistic missiles.[29] These perceptions, especially if inaccurate, should be addressed as early as possible to limit the movement towards a more competitive multipolar world order.

Notes

1 The two other sites hosting interceptors were located in the United States (Fort Greely in Alaska and Vandenberg Air Force Base in California). Currently, they represent the backbone U.S. homeland missile defense.

2 These would be complemented by existing missile defense assets such as Fylingdales Ballistic Missile Early Warning Radar System in the United Kingdom.

3 For more on Russian technical concerns see Y. Butt and T. Postol, *Upsetting the Reset: The Technical Basis of Russian Concern over NATO Missile Defence*, Federation of American Scientists, FAS Special Report No. 1, September 2011.

4 See for example S.A. Hildreth and C.I. Ek, "Long-Range Ballistic Missile Defense in Europe," *Current Politics and Economics of Europe*, Vol. 22, Issue 1, 2011.

5 P. O'Reilly, "Phased Adaptive Approach to Missile Defence in Europe: Overview for the Atlantic Council," Presentation by Lieutenant General Patrick O'Reilly, 7 October 2009. Online. Available: www.acus.org/files/OReilly%20 Powerpoint%20Atlantic%20Council%20Missile%20Defense%20Conference. pdf.

6 O'Reilly, "Phased Adaptive Approach to Missile Defence in Europe."

7 For more information on ALTBMD, see NATO information available at www. tmd.nato.int.

8 R.F. Kaufman (ed.), *The Full Costs of Ballistic Missile Defense*, Center for Arms Control and Non-Proliferation, January 2003.

9 U.S. General Accounting Office, *Missile Defense: Actions are Needed to Enhance Testing and Accountability*, Report to Congressional Committees, GAO-04–409, April 2004.

10 For examples of technical challenges, see Y. Butt, "Re-examining the Conceptual Basis of Strategic Missile Defense," *Bulletin of the Atomic Scientists*, 3 December 2010. Online. Available: www.thebulletin.org/web-edition/features/ re-examining-the-conceptual-basis-of-strategic-missile-defense.

11 A. Feickert, *Missile Survey: Ballistic and Cruise Missiles of Foreign Countries*, CRS Report for Congress, RL30427, March 2004. See also www.nato.int/cps/en/ natolive/topics_49635.htm.

12 See NATO, "Deterrence and Defence Posture Review," Press Release (2012) 063, 20 May 2012, p. 4. Online. Available: www.nato.int/cps/en/natolive/offi-cial_texts_87597.htm?mode=pressrelease.

13 See for example the presentation of Colonel-General V.V. Gerasimov, "Assessment of BMD Global Capabilities," presented at the international conference "Missile Defence Factor in Establishing New Security Environment," 3–4 May 2012. Online. Available: www.mil.ru/conference_of_pro/news/more.htm?id= 11108033@egNews.

14 R. Hendrickson, *European Phased Adaptive Approach (EPAA) Ballistic Missile Defence: A Technical Overview*, Missile Defence Agency, 12-MDA-6723, 30 April 2012.

15 This was most recently stated in the NATO Chicago Summit Declaration: "We today reaffirm that the NATO missile defence in Europe will not undermine strategic stability. NATO missile defence is not directed at Russia and will not undermine Russia's strategic deterrence capabilities." NATO, "NATO Summit Declaration," Issued by the Heads of State and Government participating in the

meeting of the North Atlantic Council in Chicago on 20 May 2012, Chicago Summit, 20 May 2012, para. 62. Online. Available: www.nato.int/cps/en/nato-live/official_texts_87593.htm.

16 D. Medvedev, "Statement in connection with the situation concerning the NATO countries' missile defence system in Europe," 23 November 2011. Online. Available: http://eng.kremlin.ru/news/3115.

17 On 23 May 2012, Russia test-fired a new Topol ICBM which includes "capabilities for overcoming missile defences." "Russia Test Fires New Ballistic Missile," RIA Novosti, 23 May 2012. Online. Available: http://en.ria.ru/mlitary_news/20120523/173620397.html.

18 N. Makarov, "Views of the Ministry of Defense of the Russian Federation on Missile Defence Issues," presentation at the international conference 'Missile Defence Factor in Establishing New Security Environment," 3–4 May, 2012. Online. Available: www.mil.ru/conference_of_pro/news/more.htm?id=11108033@egNews.

19 D. Medvedev, "Statement in connection with the situation concerning the NATO countries' missile defence system in Europe."

20 NATO–Russia Council Joint Statement issued at the meeting of the NATO–Russia Council held in Lisbon, 20 November 2010. Online. Available: www.nato.int/cps/en/natolive/news_68871.htm.

21 For an overview of the cruise missile challenge, please see D.M. Gormley, *Cruise Missiles and NATO Missile Defense: Under the Radar?* Proliferation Papers No. 41, Spring 2012. Online. Available: www.ifri.org/?page=contribution-detail&id=7082.

22 M. Creedon, "U.S. Ballistic Missile Defense," presentation at the international conference "Missile Defence Factor in Establishing New Security Environment," 3–4 May, 2012. Online. Available: http://photos.state.gov/libraries/russia/231771/PDFs/ASD_Creedon_MD_Conference_Remarks.pdf.

23 NATO, "NATO Summit Declaration," Chicago, para. 62.

24 I. Sheremet, "Russia's Assessment of NATO–Russia Theatre Missile Defence Exercise," presentation at the international conference "Missile Defence Factor in Establishing New Security Environment," 3–4 May 2012. Online. Available: www.mil.ru/conference_of_pro/news/more.htm?id=11108033@egNews.

25 NATO, "NATO Summit Declaration," Chicago, para. 62.

26 E. Ilyin, "Coordination in BMD Area as an Element of Military Cooperation," presentation at the international conference "Missile Defence Factor in Establishing New Security Environment," 3–4 May 2012. Online. Available: www.mil.ru/conference_of_pro/news/more.htm?id=11108033@egNews.

27 U.S. Department of Defense, *Ballistic Missile Defense Review Report*, February 2010.

28 U.S. Government Accountability Office, "Ballistic Missile Defense," GAO-11–220, January 2011.

29 Although testing seems to be ongoing. See, for example http://english.chosun.com/site/data/html_dir/2011/01/31/2011013100702.html.

12 NATO and energy security
Defining a role

*Phillip Cornell**

Introduction

It should not come as a surprise that energy has been gaining in importance lately within security circles. A tight global oil market, substantial and sustained price increases, a new era of resource nationalism, rapidly rising demand from emerging markets, and heightened concerns about terrorism and conflict around infrastructures and supply lines, all lead to serious concerns about the availability of stable and sufficient supplies at reasonable prices. At the same time, such questions are by no means new, and while the issue is mainly an economic one, its military and security dimensions have been historically significant. Many of the current debates about energy security infrastructure and supply line protection, as well as producer-consumer political relationships, also have long histories. However, the regional dynamics in NATO's neighborhood are fluid, and the blurred lines between traditional security and globalized economic interchange (and especially energy flows) present new challenges.

This chapter will seek to explain the debate surrounding the role of NATO regarding energy questions and their evolution. It examines those regional energy security issues which are of particular importance to NATO, and concludes with some possible paths for the development of energy scenarios that the Alliance may have to face in the next 20 years. Arguably, the reasons why security policymakers have become so interested in energy questions have more to do with fundamental shifts in the global energy market than with those in the security landscape. Therefore, using scenarios developed by the International Energy Agency to help us understand how energy markets may develop between now and 2035 can shed some light on how the market evolution might impact security issues over that timeframe.[1]

The energy security debate within NATO

Defining a role for NATO in energy security is tricky, for both political and practical reasons. NATO's potential role can range from the direct protection of critical infrastructure for energy production and transport, to training, crisis reaction, and even facilitating political dialogue among consumers and suppliers about security issues. Thinking more broadly, NATO's possible roles can quickly become controversial.

In March 2006, the Polish foreign ministry proposed an "energy Article V" that would require all signatories to pledge assistance to a country facing supply disruption. The reference to NATO's founding charter, the unspoken target of that initiative (Russia), and the support proffered at the 2006 Riga Summit by Senator Richard Lugar, implied a deterrent role for the organization when it comes to energy. Even though this moment helped to kick-start the NATO debate, support among members was never widely shared, and Poland's proposal was viewed as extreme within the spectrum of options.

Indeed, the political arguments *against* NATO's assumption of a substantial role, particularly with ambiguous and potentially military ramifications, were always compelling. "Militarizing" a fundamentally economic issue would have distortionary effects on the markets, discouraging investments to expand capacity precisely at a time when they are so necessary. It could sour relations with producing countries by adding an apparently confrontational dimension, further politicizing energy trading and at the same time casting a shadow over various other political issues. In short, a leading NATO role would be counter-productive to the end-goal of political and security risk reduction. While a coordinated international approach to energy security is certainly necessary, the policies which would have the greatest impact – liberalizing the European market, facilitating greater connectivity between national energy networks, encouraging reserve and supply chain capacity, supporting the development of alternative energy sources, and encouraging conservation and efficiency – are decidedly outside NATO's purview.

Yet in January 2006 when the annual drama of Russian-Ukrainian gas negotiations turned particularly sour and caused a supply shortage to Europe, NATO began in earnest to look at how it could contribute to solving a problem with so many political and security impacts. Suggestions about NATO's role, starting with the Polish proposal, subsequently spanned the spectrum of political possibility. In November 2006 Jamie Shea, then the director of NATO's in-house policy think tank, proposed a collection of monitoring and assessment mechanisms at NATO, including Article IV assistance to allies (such as joint consultation and response, without Article V triggers), maritime surveillance, and even possible interdiction operations.[2] In 2007, former SACEUR James Jones (later U.S. President Barack Obama's National Security Advisor) alluded to NATO's possible contribution to stability in the Niger Delta, where sporadic attacks consistently kept national output at 20 percent below full production levels.[3] Others pointed to the fact that through NATO, Europe could bring U.S. political pressure to bear on Russia. Turkey could be institutionally involved in European energy security, and engagements with producer countries on energy concerns through the Mediterranean Dialogue (MD), the Istanbul Cooperation Initiative (ICI), and the Partnership for Peace (PfP) could occur within those existing frameworks.[4] Assistance towards critical energy infrastructure protection (CEIP) – through communications, surveillance, and training support – held out most promise of consensus. More ambitious proposals envisioned direct CEIP support, but a scenario in which NATO troops are stationed on platforms or along pipelines was always unlikely. Indeed, many of the above suggestions were politically unpalatable. There was a recognized risk that well intentioned over-involvement could ultimately undermine the security it seeks to enhance – either the security of energy supply by impeding investment, or geopolitical security by militarizing energy flows and the sensitive regions in which they tend to originate. That is not to say that NATO cannot add value. CEIP, around which consensus within NATO built early, is a good example. Improving energy infrastructure security measures by providing tools that the private sector cannot, including capital-intensive surveillance (air, sea, or space-based reconnaissance) and training support to the security sectors of producing and transit countries, can mitigate risks which otherwise drive up costs and discourage investment. In civil security circles, there is a crucial security gap where public services are expected to operate, for instance to avert catastrophic debilitation. The international network-centric nature of enormous and complex energy supply chains means that the quality of such publicly supplied security varies along the chain. Therefore, there is clear potential for militaries (perhaps under the aegis of NATO) to identify the weakest links and assist in ameliorating public security provision at those points. There is also a question about whether the elements of public security provision that already exist (e.g. American maritime patrols or surveillance support) might benefit from internationalization, for purposes of enhanced legitimacy and access.

However, the relationship between international security policy and energy policy is not a one-way street. Just as tools of hard power may be able to play a supporting role to improve energy security, energy policy can have a significant impact on the international security environment. In some cases, for example, additional transport capacity, diversification, or energy access may not be commercially viable, but may be of significant benefit to the security environment. Decreasing regional dependence on a few export routes in order to encourage policy independence in the southern Caucasus was at least part of the political logic in the 1990s to support the construction of the Baku-Tbilisi-Ceyhan (BTC) pipeline, and similar arguments have been raised with respect to the Nabucco gas pipeline from Baku to Europe. To the degree that it is responsible for that security environment, NATO could add value to those debates.

Over the course of 2007–08 the NATO International Staff completed a report entitled "NATO's Role in Energy Security," which was noted by the Heads of State at the 2008 Bucharest Summit. It identified the following areas where NATO can add value:

- information and intelligence fusion and sharing;
- projecting stability;
- advancing international and regional cooperation;
- supporting consequence management; and
- supporting the protection of critical infrastructure.

Despite the identification of these areas, discussion and concrete action remained limited. The first three areas are broad objectives that certainly impact positively on energy security, but whose pursuit (at least within NATO) is only marginally driven by energy concerns. Concretely, value-added in these areas generally mean using existing fora as talking shops. As for consequence management, exercises organized by the Euro-Atlantic Disaster Response Coordination Centre (EADRCC) at NATO duly included energy aspects in 2008, and some energy infrastructure specialists were added to their emergency contact lists. But otherwise implementation was sparse.

So in the run-up to the Lisbon Summit in November 2010, and particularly in the formation of the new Strategic Concept, CEIP and information sharing around it remained at the centre of discussions on potential NATO contribution. This includes cyber-security, an "emerging challenge" often spoken in the same breath as energy security within NATO circles (with institutional implications in terms of NATO Secretariat organization – both now fall under the same department). The challenges of cyber-security and energy infrastructure, in a world of interconnected supervisory control and data acquisition (SCADA) systems, are closely linked. The 2010 Stuxnet virus which affected Iranian nuclear operations is one publicly visible example. But as the implementation of smart electricity grids increases with more variable renewable technology integration and efficiency concerns, data control systems will be increasingly important to maintain the delicate grid balance that keeps the lights on.

It is not surprising then, that when the new Strategic Concept was unveiled at Lisbon, cyber security garnered particular attention and CEIP (loosely defined) stood out as the cornerstone of NATO's future energy security endeavors. Noting that energy supplies are "increasingly exposed to disruption" and therefore require "greater international efforts to ensure their resilience,"[5] NATO committed itself to

> develop[ing] the capacity to contribute to energy security, including protection of critical energy infrastructure and transit areas and lines, cooperation with partners, and consultations among allies on the basis of strategic assessments and contingency planning;[6]

At the Chicago Summit two years later, NATO leaders gave a more substantive nod to energy.

> In order to further NATO's contribution to energy security, we will work towards significantly improving the energy efficiency of our military forces; develop our competence in supporting the protection of critical energy infrastructure; and further develop our outreach activities in consultation with partners, on a case-by-case basis. We welcome the offer to establish a NATO-accredited Energy Security Centre of Excellence in Lithuania as a contribution to NATO's efforts in this area.

Commitment to the energy efficiency of NATO forces may seem a novel addition to this discussion, and indeed the task is vital. Militaries remain by far the largest public consumers of energy in most countries, and by some measures the US Air Force is the world's greatest consumer of fossil fuels. But the effort is not a new one in NATO, and blurring military fuel policy and NATO's contribution to its members' energy security may be slightly disingenuous.

On the other hand, Lithuania's plan to establish a Centre of Excellence (CoE) is indeed new. A CoE is an education and research centre accredited within the NATO training and education system, and a similar Estonian one was established for cyber-security in 2008. At the least, such a centre could function as a substantive focal point for education and knowledge exchange. It may also be able to offer innovative contributions to NATO's possible role. That would be welcome – it is unlikely that a broader mandate for NATO at the nexus of energy and security can be recognized unless policymakers begin to think outside the CEIP box. In order to begin to do that, it is important to understand the political and historical context in which energy and security politics combine, and indeed what we mean by energy security.

A new century of concerns: historical and contemporary political issues

Over the past 200 years, abundant supplies of energy have driven economic growth and sustained economic activity in industrial and post-industrial societies. Securing access to energy resources has consequently long been crucial to keeping factories humming and transport links running. But it is also key to keeping militaries moving, and it is that requirement which has always made energy resources special – and a commodity category so closely linked with national security.

This was less of an issue in the 19th century, when the great powers generally possessed sufficient domestic coal deposits to fuel their factories, trains, and ships. But it was Winston Churchill's 1912 decision to switch the British Royal Navy to oil which proved critical, and is widely regarded as the birth of international energy security concerns.[7] Political relationships with (or control of) producing regions became key, as well as secure supply lines to them. In a stroke, strategic energy security went global. This was exemplified in the role of hydrocarbons in defining strategic military objectives during World War II, as well as in post-war Middle East politics from Mossadegh to the nationalization of regional oil production and the creation of OPEC. In 1974 the consuming nations formed the International Energy Agency (IEA) to collectively promote energy security by providing statistics, sharing technology, and crucially by coordinating emergency response measures (which eventually focused on the use of strategic oil stocks).

But with a new wave of globalization and liberalized financial and commodity markets from the 1980s, OPEC lost much of the power it had held to influence price by fiddling with the taps. These changes had an impact on price volatility, and also on the sensitivity of the market (in the short and medium term) to perceived risks to supply. Volatility could cause price spikes which threaten growth and feed headline inflation, but also price collapses that sting producers and discourage investment.

While still dominant, oil and coal have been increasingly complemented by other energy sources. Natural gas, used in lamps since the 19th century, is so difficult and expensive to transport that it was often simply burned off during petroleum extraction.[8] With the steady expansion of distribution networks and shippable liquefied natural gas (LNG) from about the 1970s, and especially with the recent unconventional gas revolution taking hold in North America and elsewhere, demand for gas has increased for both consumer (e.g. heating and cooking) and industrial use (e.g. electricity production). But the cost of transport means that gas markets and prices continue to be more regionally specific than oil, and politics often center on particular supply/demand dependencies, as well as transport routes.

Rising global demand and competition for energy on the back of economic growth are therefore nothing new. In the 21st century, however, a confluence of factors combine to intensify those issues, and fundamental changes in the world economic balance are significantly changing energy trading patterns. Indeed, Asia's economic rise is most likely to be the dominant story of energy markets in the coming decades.

With regard to demand, rapid industrialization and economic growth in much of the developing world, and particularly in Asian emerging markets led by China and India, are driving sky-rocketing demand for energy even after the global economic crisis. The effect of that crisis was to dramatically widen the gap between demand changes in OECD countries where it was flat or falling, and those in emerging economies where it surged ahead. In 2000, China's primary energy demand was only half that of the United States, but in 2011 it became the largest consumer of energy in the world. Currently, Asia accounts for about 35 percent of global demand, but that percentage is expected to increase to 44 percent by 2035 under the IEA's baseline "New Policies Scenario."[9] Indeed, 93 percent of all energy demands growth to 2035 is expected to come from emerging economies and 36 percent from China alone. Industrial consumption continues to be pushed by growing manufacturing production, and an expanding middle class drives personal consumption of new televisions, air conditioners, and cars. The global car fleet is projected to grow from just under 800 million vehicles today to close to 1.6 billion by 2035 – of which more than 40 percent will be in Asia, from 18 percent today.

Global oil suppliers have struggled to meet such demand rises over the past decade, partly because of disruptions and security problems. But supply is especially constrained by chronic underinvestment, both from nationalized oil companies (NOCs) and private international oil companies (IOCs). Such conservatism was driven by fear of a price collapse after 1998, but also by fewer opportunities. Declining output from mature fields (largely in OECD countries) and limited access to the world's remaining reserves (largely in OPEC countries) means that oil production is becoming ever more concentrated.

Investment by NOCs and other nationalized energy producers continues apace, but can be constrained by lack of access to capital or technology, or by political developments. The 2011 Arab Spring elicited new risk concerns about Middle Eastern production, even if Libya was the only significant producer to be drastically affected. Also, the 2011 Iranian presidency of OPEC revealed deep fissures inside the organization, which prevented an increase in production quotas in June, even in the face of disrupted Libyan production.

The result of such constricted supply expansion and runaway demand in emerging economies is a tightening oil market. The 2008 price correction and the economic crisis that followed offered a brief respite, but from September 2010 the tightening trend continued well into 2012. A tighter oil market without ample spare production capacity creates precisely the conditions in which disruptions, including those caused by security events, can have even more drastic effects on the global oil market.

Supply concentration and regional politics: Russia

The political debate about the reliability of Russian energy supply was reignited in January 2006 when Gazprom, the Russian state monopoly, signaled its intention to raise the price of previously subsidized gas exports to Ukraine from USD 50 to USD 230 per 1,000 cubic meters. Besides demanding Western European prices for its natural gas, Gazprom also asked that contracts be settled in cash. Ukraine refused to pay the higher prices, and before a compromise was reached at USD 95, Russia reduced the flow of gas through the country and accused Kiev of stealing supplies intended for Europe.[10] Through the year, a succession of similar disputes with Georgia, Azerbaijan, and even over oil with Belarus, a close Russian ally, stoked European fears that Russian political spats with transit countries could endanger Western supply. Among security experts, these events raised questions about Russia's willingness to use the "energy weapon" in its political dealings, and thus also about the wisdom of the heavy dependency of many European countries (mostly in Central and Eastern Europe) on Russian energy supplies. Although Gazprom was demanding Western "market" prices from Ukraine, the move was seen by some to put pressure on President Viktor Yushenko after his success over the Kremlin's preferred candidate in the 2005 "Orange Revolution." It was following the Ukrainian crisis that Poland released its proposals for an "all-for-one" energy pact. Political rumblings from mainly Eastern quarters lamented the lack of European solidarity in the face of Russian energy power and depicted a growing security problem. The undersea Nord Stream pipeline from Russia directly into Germany (bypassing Poland) and the Italian diversification toward, rather than away from, Russian gas in 2006 served as examples of such division.

After averting a repeat in 2007, relations soured again in 2008, finally resulting in another disruption starting 7 January 2009. Slovakia, Bulgaria, and Moldova were among the most impacted by severe cut-offs in gas supply, with some civilian heating being interrupted in the dead of winter. In addition, various other countries from Hungary to the North Sea also experienced significant pressure drops and service interruptions. A deal was made and gas supplies were restored on 21 January 2009. Russian public messaging had improved significantly since 2006. While the crude portrayal of an antagonist/victim relationship that drove security concerns in 2006 was tempered, trust in both Russia and Ukraine as stable suppliers and transporters was certainly affected. The annual kabuki theatre of Russian-Ukrainian gas disputes continue, and the story's political legacy in Kiev includes the ongoing imprisonment of Yushenko's prime minister for striking the Russian deals.

The mix of sources of imported oil and gas is indeed dominated in Europe by a substantial reliance on Russia for both commodities. The European Union imports 60 percent of its natural gas demand, almost 50 percent of which is supplied by (or via) Russia.[11] However, there is a significant variation across European importers when it comes to reliance on Russia. Hungary, for instance, is particularly dependent with over 90 percent of its imports coming from the East (including 100 percent of oil imports),[12] but Northwest Europe, on the other hand, receives comparatively little Russian oil or gas. Globally, Russia's increasing importance as mature North Sea production dwindles and Middle Eastern uncertainty continues, is undeniable. The country possesses 6 percent of proven oil reserves globally, and 25 percent of gas reserves.[13]

The creeping "shady-nationalization" of Russia's energy industry is a tricky business. Unlike outright state control in other countries, Russian companies are tangled in a web of subsidiaries and joint ventures that bring the state in through the back door and render the entire sector notoriously opaque. Government agents or individuals representing their interests may sit on the board of one or more entities within these complex webs, which often extend well beyond Russian borders. But the state also exerts pressure via personal connections, regulatory pressure, contractual ambiguity, and a host of public-private arrangements that may represent significant conflicts of interest. The nature of state control in the Russian energy sector is worrying to the degree that energy sales and transport may be employed as political tools; but the trend is uneven and often opaque. While the extent to which the state intends to exercise its influence and the degree to which energy plays a broader role in Russian foreign and security strategic thinking may be unclear in practice, it is unambiguous in official doctrine. The 2009 Russian report on its National Security Strategy to 2020 describes energy resources as both tools and objectives of security policy.

> The change from bloc confrontation to the principles of multi-vector diplomacy and the [natural] resources potential of Russia, along with the pragmatic policies of using them has expanded the possibilities of the Russian Federation to strengthen its influence on the world arena.[14]

But the generally rising profile of the state also raises political-economic questions about how policy will be affected by the importance of energy to the Russian economy. Corruption, already a significant problem, is exacerbated by the flow of resource assets into state pockets. Moscow's reliance on energy income does not appear likely to be going away soon. Its dependence on high prices susceptible to volatility was felt acutely when the price collapsed in 2008, causing Russia to suffer a massive reduction in its capital reserves and a particularly sharp recession. Over the longer term, the problem of Dutch-disease (whereby petrodollars crowd out development in other sectors) is showing signs of afflicting the Russian economy in which a large state-dominated energy sector threatens diversification. The heavy reliance of the Russian economy on oil and gas combined with the political-economic effects of creeping state control combine to make fluctuating energy prices key to Russian stability.

But the irony of the Russian gas security question in Europe, particularly given its important role in sparking the energy security debate in NATO, is that events have largely overtaken the issue. Since 2009 natural gas markets have been turned on their head with the spread of hydraulic fracturing to cheaply access unconventional gas, particularly American shale gas. Tumbling prices in the United States and expanding supply created a knock-on effect in LNG markets where massive capacity expansions in anticipation of exports to the U.S. market (particularly from

Qatar) came online in 2009 just as unconventional gas production was exploding. Investments in European regasification infrastructure and the availability of LNG (sometimes even on a cheap spot-price basis), as well as large expansion of gas storage in Europe and the improvement of regional interconnections, have helped to mute concerns about Russian dependency.

How long this will continue is unclear as voracious Chinese demand moves into gas – a policy confirmed by the unveiling in 2011 of its Twelfth Five-Year Plan. That may end the "unexpected" gas glut sooner than many realize. This expectation is partly borne out in unprecedented regional divergences in U.S., UK/European, and Asian gas prices. In a recent scenario, the IEA has raised the specter of a possible "Golden Age of Gas."[15] But a golden age is certainly not assured, and the gas glut may offer only breathing space for those countries that were caught with particularly dependent gas sectors. The time should be seized to invest in longer term solutions.

Supply concentration and regional politics: the Middle East

As a region, the Middle East dominates energy production and global distribution. Over the longer term, OPEC (whose members are predominantly but not totally based in the region) will account for an ever increasing share of global oil production. Supply concentration will render the entire market ever more dependent on regional stability. Saudi Arabia alone contains about 20 percent of global oil reserves and serves as the "central bank" of oil via OPEC.[16] What little spare capacity exists in global oil production is overwhelmingly in Saudi Arabia, but deepening and more liquid financial markets (and the speculation which occurs within them) have increased absolute volatility and diminished the country's ability to control prices over the past 20 years. The second and third largest oil reserves in the region are in Iraq and Iran, both of which present political and security problems as reliable suppliers.

The region is also a leader in gas production. Indeed, Iran is second only in the world to Russia. However, the political jigsaw map of the region impedes sufficient overland transport infrastructure to bring much of it to the European market. Thus Qatar is the largest producer of LNG globally and undersea pipelines bring North African (primarily Algerian) gas to Europe via Spain and Italy. While none of the three major oil producers have formal relations with NATO as an organization, the Alliance does have official ties with many of the major gas players in the region, including Algeria, Egypt, and Qatar. Middle Eastern political and security concerns loom large, potentially impacting energy supplies from a region which will substantially increase its share of global exports over the next decades. The 2011 Arab Spring raised the specter of major producers falling prey to domestic political upheaval, though for the moment Libya is the only significant producer to have faced disruption as a result. With over USD 1 trillion expected to be transferred for the first time from non-OPEC to OPEC countries in 2011,[17] countries may be tempted to buy off dissent. But the habit among some of those countries under domestic pressure of distributing largesse to placate the people can effectively lock in higher oil prices by raising the price necessary to balance national budgets and by raising the political "price floor" sought by producers. Comments from officials in major producers, like Saudi Arabia, about optimal oil prices have steadily risen since the Arab Spring from USD 70–80 to USD 100-plus per barrel.

The "risk premium," which derives from ongoing uncertainties through-out the Middle East, had been priced in for years – but its rise was partly to blame for price hikes through 2011. Particularly in an environment of such political jitters, individual incidents can still spook markets and send prices rocketing. Understanding those security issues is crucial if one is to identify how NATO can help to mitigate threats to energy supply and resultant market risks. In 2005 Patrick Clawson and Simon Henderson cited five major potential sources of an oil supply disruption in the region which still loom today: terrorist attacks on energy facilities; an exodus of oil workers prompted by fears of unrest; domestic political instability (such as Arab Spring movements); the spread of Iraqi instability into other producers; and confrontation with Iran and subsequent threats to the Strait of Hormuz.[18]

Saudi Arabia

The first three apply separately across a range of countries, but come together to threaten Saudi Arabia. The Kingdom alone possesses what excess production capacity exists in the global system and contains almost a quarter of global reserves. J. Robinson West, Chairman of the U.S. Institute for Peace and founder of PFC Energy, places concerns about Saudi Arabia's stability as a supplier into three broad categories: regime stability (including terrorist threats); foreign policy and external alignment; and production capabilities.[19] An external security organization can do little to affect production capabilities, particularly when Saudi Aramco monopolizes domestic production and investment decisions are not particularly affected by security risk assessments, but rather by price management targets and backroom negotiations (often with the United States). This is not to say that security risks are not negligible. Indeed since May 2003 a wave of Islamic militancy has targeted Westerners and energy infrastructures with the explicit aim of undermining the Saudi regime by disrupting oil revenues. After the 2004 Khobar Towers attack succeeded in killing many Western oil workers and impacting the world oil market by precipitating fears of a foreign exodus and production drop, the Saudi government passed various measures to tighten security. However, divisions exist within the ruling family about balancing security crack-downs, political reform, and appeasing popular sentiment (which can include elements of religious extremity and anti-Western opinion). The Kingdom has also been very mindful in the past to construct numerous systemic redundancies and maintain excess capacity to mitigate the effects of attacks. But especially when spare capacity is very low (as in 2008), it can be difficult to convince the market of Saudi Arabia's ability to withstand future attacks with only negligible effects on output. In 2005 Saudi Arabia embarked on a program to increase production capacity, causing new infrastructure to come online since 2009. However, many are skeptical of the Kingdom's assurances that its reserves are as vast and easily tapped as it claims.[20] That being said, during the 2011 Libyan disruption, Saudi Arabia still proved a responsible producer in raising production as rising demand rendered the disruption particularly acute.

But its reaction to the Arab Spring in announcing almost USD 130 billion in increased public transfers raised its preferred oil price. The budget break-even point rose from USD 68 to USD 88 per barrel. At the same time, Saudi markets have quickly moved East, with China becoming Saudi Arabia's primary customer by a significant margin. The orthodox political-security logic which has linked Saudi Arabia to the West (and particularly the United States) has been one in which the Saudis maintain significant spare capacity and cooperate to manage reasonable oil prices, while the United States provides security cover as well as a primary export market whose economic health serves Saudi interests. Given current economic trends, that logic could begin to fall apart. Such a decoupling would represent one of the most significant shifts in regional and global security in 20 years, leaving serious uncertainties.

Libya

Libyan production has been reviving after a total shut-in during the 2011 civil war. NATO air-strikes brought similar scrutiny on European enthusiasts as had Iraq eight years earlier. Though there were very legitimate arguments for providing military support to prevent civilian deaths (and also to support a fledgling movement for liberation, if not democracy), the truth remains that Libya is also a major energy supplier to Europe. That is not to say that energy was ever a major or even significant objective, but stability on Europe's energy producing periphery certainly is.

With the fighting, 1.6 million barrels per day of oil were taken off the market in March 2011.[21] Because this came at a low-point in the annual demand cycle, the impact on the physical market could be withstood. But sufficient OPEC production increases to make up for the shortfall failed to materialize through the spring. After a particularly acrimonious June 2011 OPEC Meeting failed to agree to lifting official production quotas, Saudi Arabia announced it would pump more oil unilaterally. But with summer demand already rising, the IEA countries chose in June to release strategic stocks and serve as a bridge to increased production.

The entire episode demonstrated that while major security lapses in producing member states on Europe's periphery could severely impede production, existing IEA measures can function to maintain liquidity in the market. However, that may not be enough to curb rising oil prices, which are driven not only by the physical market but also by speculation, fears, and expectations – including about the security situation that NATO is influencing. The NATO operation and the IEA action are obviously not connected. In fact the degree to which NATO airstrikes drew out the conflict in Libya extended production stoppages. However, if stability in producing regions can be improved with the introduction of greater political legitimacy in the long run, the result can only be positive for energy security.

Iraq

Iraq represents a serious uncertainty with the potential to serve as a game-changer in global oil production over the coming years. On the high-end of estimates, the government announced plans to raise production from three million b/d (barrels per day) to 12 million b/d in the next decade. This will be an extremely ambitious target, but few doubt that outputs will nonetheless rise substantially.

On the other hand, the security situation is still unsure and could yet deteriorate. Domestic political developments following the U.S. withdrawal dictate the security situation, and by consequence, impact the pace of production expansion. Production has only just recovered to pre-war levels, more than nine years after the invasion, and for most of the decade it hovered at 25 percent below pre-war output. Today the principal constraints to expanding production are infrastructure bottlenecks, but attacks on installations are still not unheard of. During the height of violence in 2007 a U.S. Defense Department report on Iraq security assessed that "the timing and location of more recent attacks [on infrastructure] resulted in greater disruption of service. In addition, weak ministerial oversight, ineffectual rapid-repair teams, and criminal harvesting of infrastructure assets have proved to be major impediments."[22] Indeed in January 2007 production dropped 300,000 b/d below the 2006 average.[23]

Having divided the allies in 2002–03, Iraq is a highly sensitive and essentially taboo subject notwithstanding the compounding controversy of NATO and energy. However, if the encouragement of sustained security can help to realize even half of Iraqi production targets by 2020, this will represent a huge boost to global supply and energy security.

Iran

Iranian political tensions with the West over its nuclear program and suspected involvement in Iraq have raised the specter of military confrontation.
The country is a major player in the market as the third oil producer and
first gas producer in the Middle East and North Africa region. It also holds a
strategic coastline along the Strait of Hormuz, through which 20 percent of
the world's oil supply passes. Stated Iranian military strategy has long envisioned affecting this traffic to target either producer or consumer adversaries. In 1982 it targeted ships exporting Iraqi oil and was met with American
air attacks on its vessels. More recently, in 2006 the supreme commander of
Iran's Revolutionary Guards, Major General Yahya Safavi, threatened repeatedly Iran's intention to block the straits if the country were to come under
UN sanctions due to its nuclear program. Similar threats were issued in
2011 by Revolutionary Guards Naval Commander Ali Fadavi, who warned
that "the Islamic Republic has the ability to block the Strait of Hormuz if
threatened."[24] 2012 saw these threats escalate further, especially in the face
of crippling sanctions which significantly reduced oil exports through the
year. In the unlikely event of a successful closure of the strait, IEA stocks
would be able to cover the enormous resultant oil supply shortfall for many
months until the security situation could be resolved, perhaps with NATO
or Western intervention. However, both interventions would be crucial elements of the policy response.

Supply concentration and regional politics: the Caucasus and Central Asia

At the beginning of the last century, the area around the Caspian Sea, and
particularly the coastal city of Baku in Azerbaijan, was a leader in energy
production. Under Soviet rule, Caspian basin and Central Asian deposits
were under-utilized in favor of Siberian reserves. Thus as the region
emerged as a collection of independent states after 1991, there were high
hopes that it would provide a new alternative to Middle Eastern and
Russian suppliers. Transportation from this relatively inaccessible region
has historically constituted the greatest hurdle to large-scale export.
Indeed, the Nobel brothers financed an entire Transcaucasian Railway
line in order to bring their Baku oil to market in the 19th century. Unsurprisingly then, energy concerns in the region tend to revolve around a
complex interplay of "pipeline politics." Under the Soviet Union, the
region was fully integrated into the Soviet pipeline system. As a result,
post-independence exports were subject to the high transit fees charged
by Transneft and Gazprom or extremely low prices for gas and oil purchased directly. Even given high fees, underinvestment in the Russian
transit systems meant that pipelines were often working to capacity,
restricting exports and forcing them onto higher-cost, lower-capacity trans-

port means (such as railways). By monopolizing the export networks, the Russian state-controlled transit companies thus subjected exports to potential political interference. However, the same was true of imports, causing oil-rich Azerbaijan to rely on Transneft to export Caspian oil and on Gazprom to import necessary gas supplies. Other states in the region are reliant on the two entities to different degrees depending on their oil and gas endowments. While this was the case, Caucasian and Central Asian states were held virtually hostage to Russian energy cooperation, and by extension, to Russian political pressure.

The Caucasus

It was in order to circumvent Russian distribution systems that Western public financing was granted through the International Finance Corporation (IFC) and the European Bank for Reconstruction and Development (EBRD) towards the building of trans-Caucasian routes. An initial oil pipeline to the Georgian port of Supsa offered an alternative from Baku but still required shipping through the clogged Bosphorus. The South Caucasus gas pipeline provided an export route for Caspian gas through Turkey. But most importantly, since the completion in 2006 of the Baku-Tbilisi-Ceyhan (BTC) oil pipeline from the Azeri-Chirag-Guneshli (ACG) field to the Southern Turkish coast, the political implications of a viable alternative oil export route have already become apparent in the region. In the wake of the Russian-Georgian row of 2008, the newly completed BTC line allowed Azerbaijan the political freedom to support its avidly pro-Western neighbor and compensate for Georgian gas shortages. When Gazprom tried to apply pressure in turn on Baku by doubling the price of Southern gas exports, Azerbaijan refitted some power generators to run on oil (thus eliminating its need for gas imports) and halted all oil exports north through Russia. The move was a symbol of new-found Azeri energy independence from Russia, which, along with high oil prices, has helped to bolster the Azeri regime's confidence. Such confidence impacts the security of a region rife with frozen conflicts with mixed results. Revenues from Azeri energy are financing a new railroad to bring goods through Georgia to Turkey and on to Europe, but a military build-up is also threatening to renew violence in Nagorno-Karabakh. President Aliyev's efforts to court the West seemed to be gaining in 2007. While less vocal than Georgia, Azerbaijan was undoubtedly orienting itself towards the Euro-Atlantic community. Building direct energy interdependence and serving as a realistic option for European energy diversification were both integral parts of this process. In the case of both Georgia and Azerbaijan, new-found energy independence and tightening regional cooperation were providing room to maneuver in foreign and security policies. In the case of Georgia, however, this new sense of confidence was undoubtedly a factor in Tbilisi's reckless diplomacy, which helped trigger the 2008 war with Russia. But even in its significant bombing campaign, Russia made a point of avoiding the pipeline. Since that conflict, the politics in the Caucasus have been more fluid and Azeri energy ties with Russia have warmed significantly. But on the whole, there is no doubt that investments in regional energy production and transport infrastructure have granted a political independence to the Southern Caucasus countries, which they did not enjoy in the decade after independence.

Central Asia

Across the Caspian, Turkmen and Kazakh oil and gas also seek transport routes to market, resulting in what seemed to be a geopolitical tussle between Russia and the West in the last decade. However, Chinese energy demand is rising quickly, and Beijing has shown its capacity to complete huge international pipeline projects in a fraction of the time which Western consortia require to dither over financing, equity, and political support. That has allowed Central Asian producers to triangulate between Moscow, Europe, and China.

For its part, Kazakhstan was keen to emphasize its cooperation with Russia despite significant investment by Western majors. During a March 2007 meeting with Vladimir Putin, President Nursultan Nazarbayev reaffirmed his country's energy commitment to Russia and intention to export most of its resources through Russian pipelines. In 2007, 50 million tons of oil and 54 bcm (billion cubic metres) of gas (including 48.1 bcm of Turkmen gas) were exported via Russia.[25] This is unlikely to change without new and very large transport infrastructure projects since substantial Kazakh oil deposits are located near the Northern border and are well connected to the Russian network. However, Russian anxiety about a Kazakh reorientation is not wholly unfounded. Kazakhstan has been receptive to Chinese moves to strengthen bilateral energy relations. The completion of the Kazakhstan-China oil pipeline in 2009, which reached full capacity in 2011, offers a new export route East. But more relevant for European supply and regional security interests, Astana has been less receptive to any trans-Caspian pipeline (TCP) plan, relying on Russian transit networks to sell to Europe.

In the world of Central Asian energy, Turkmen gas has been sought after by Europe and China and the country has used this as a principal bargaining chip in its Russian diplomacy. The political proclivities of its new leadership, following the death in December 2006 of autocratic ruler Saparmurat Niyazov, appear more opportunistic and pragmatic than ideological. Gurbanguly Berdymukhammedov, confirmed in February 2007 as Niyazov's successor, at first appeared committed to promoting the diversification of Turkmen export options away from Russian dependency. Indeed, Niyazov had already been actively pursuing such a course in the months before his death, promoting new export routes to

China and through Afghanistan to South Asia and negotiating a 54 percent price increase in gas sold to Russia. But soon after coming to power, Berdymukhammedov signed a deal with Putin to expand export capacity through Russia and construct the first gas pipelines in the country since the 1970s.

In 2009, a pricing dispute with Moscow caused Gazprom to block the gas flow North eventually resulting in a dramatic pipeline explosion. Exports resumed only in 2010 after a nine-month hiatus. Previously, such a dispute would have been unthinkable, effectively starving the country of crucial revenue. But the completion in 2009 of new gas lines to China and Iran, as well as a swamp of Chinese loans to tide over the country during the stoppage, allowed Ashgabat to turn the screws. It lost no time in doing so.

As for NATO, its standing in Central Asia is somewhat mixed. After 11 September 2001, Central Asian countries gained significant standing on the security agenda and intensified partnership programs have assisted with defense institution building and strengthened armed forces. However, across the board significant entrenched business interests continue to bind the region to Russia, and Central Asian governments are cautious of political interference while welcoming both the legitimacy and enhanced military capabilities that ties with NATO bring.

The lesson to take from Caspian energy politics is that they are the legacy of over a century of Russian political dominance meeting with the 21st century reality of Chinese demand and new European export routes. Caspian neighbors have been (variously) keen to escape from under Russian dominance once manifested in an energy export stranglehold that commanded political and strategic subservience. Russia is anxious to lose lucrative transit fees, sources of cheap gas, and to see competition from Europe and in Asia. From NATO's point of view, whether the energy goes East or West, new markets and export options can have major impacts on the strategic independence of Caspian countries. Accessing Asian energy and encouraging political and economic regional development are two sides of the same coin.

Possible futures – energy driving security challenges

As mentioned in the opening of this study, the more independent variable in the security-energy nexus going forward is likely to be the energy side. Fundamentally changing patterns of production, consumption, and technology deployment are likely to alter security relationships long based on relatively static producer-consumer ties built around legacy technologies. The Russian-European and Saudi-American relationships have already been mentioned and key to both has been a long-standing producer-consumer interdependency. The question then arises as to the role of NATO in response to these challenges, and in particular the type of energy scenarios that the Alliance may have to face in the next 20 years.

IEA New Policy Scenario: Pacific NATO

The IEA New Policy Scenario (NPS) assumes cautious implementation of climate change targets already announced up to the Copenhagen Accords.[26] While world energy demand rises by 36 percent as we approach 2035, the growth is uneven in terms of location and fuels. Demand for oil and coal drops significantly in the OECD countries but raises 18 percent overall on the back of non-OECD demand growth. On the supply side, oil production will also shift geographically and OPEC's global market share rises from 44 percent today to over half by 2035. So as supply is steadily reduced to a few OPEC producers (Saudi Arabia sees the largest marginal production increase, followed by Iraq), their market also shifts decidedly East.

At the same time, gas demand increases by 44 percent between 2008 and 2035, led by China and the Middle East, with China accounting for almost one-quarter of the increase in global demand. Demand in the Middle East, which is well endowed with relatively low-cost resources, increases almost as much. In terms of production, the Middle East leads the expansion of gas production over the outlook period with its output almost doubling to 800 bcm by 2035. Two-thirds of this increase is consumed locally.

From a strategic orientation point of view, this scenario sees a much stronger relationship develop between Middle Eastern producers and Asian emerging economies in both oil and gas. The decoupling of the Saudi-U.S. relationship would be more likely and happen more quickly, with real impacts on oil prices. Unless industrialized countries were to significantly reduce oil dependence, such a scenario could seriously impact medium-term economic recovery in the West – and portend an extended period of austerity with impacts on defense spending at just the time of rising Asian powers. The focus of European and American strategists will certainly be on the Pacific region and on maritime traffic in the Indian Ocean and around Southeast Asia – whether or not NATO expands its own area of responsibility so far afield. China and India, on the other hand, are unlikely to leave such vital supply routes unprotected and increasing military presence in the region may well be a consequence. How NATO develops its relationships with the Pacific countries will be crucial under any scenario, but in this case existing cooperation in the context of anti-piracy actions in the Western Indian Ocean holds significant scope for expansion. Concerns over the protection of Gulf waters and especially the Strait of Hormuz (through which almost 16 million barrels of oil currently pass daily) will become more pressing to Asian strategists. Whether or not the U.S. Fifth Fleet will remain the primary guarantor is unclear.

IEA "Golden Age of Gas" Scenario: pipelines and home waters

The IEA "GAS" Scenario assumes lower gas prices;[27] pricing mechanisms which are projected to become more reflective of market conditions; Chinese gas demand which is expected to rise along the lines of its Twelfth Five-Year Plan; 10 percent less nuclear energy additions, particularly after the Fukushima crisis; and a rise in natural gas vehicle (NGV) use (70 million NGVs in 2035 vs. 30 million in NPS). Gas demand increases from 3.3 tcm (trillion cubic meters) in 2010 to 5.1 tcm in 2035 – an increase of over 50 percent – with the average rate of increase in gas demand being nearly 2 percent per year. Unsurprisingly, natural gas sees the strongest demand growth of all energy sources in absolute terms in the GAS Scenario.

Under this scenario, the share of natural gas in global energy consumption increases to account for 25 percent in 2035, compared with 22 percent in the baseline NPS. The combined effect of a strong increase in natural gas demand throughout the outlook period and a decline in global coal demand from around 2020 onwards results in global demand for gas overtaking coal before 2030 to become the second-largest fuel in the primary energy mix.

How would this production be distributed? High investment in unconventional exploration, along with minimal regulatory oversight blocking extraction under this scenario, could lead to large increases in gas production in various parts of the world including Asia, Latin America, Australia, and Africa. While Europe has some potential for unconventional production (for example in Poland), regulatory and legal hurdles (from European sub-soil ownership laws to strong political resistance to the technology in places like France) make for a relatively poor medium-term outlook on the continent.

With most Middle Eastern and Pacific LNG going to Asian markets, and more of rising global demand being met by local unconventional production, rising European gas demand could reignite questions of gas security. Particularly, rising demand to replace coal could renew the specter of competition over Russian gas under this scenario, with the Arctic also becoming a key zone for European economic activity in a new gas bonanza. NATO has already begun to consider the growing strategic value of the Arctic and a high-level Alliance conference in Reykjavik in January 2009 examined the issues. Given crucial unresolved boundary issues and multiple overlapping claims to shipping and resource exploitation rights, the potential for stiff competition over Arctic resources and territory exists.

North African security and the protection of the Mediterranean could also be key areas with the renewed importance of piped gas from Algeria and Libya and new gas plays being developed off Cyprus and Israel. Finally, Turkey's growing importance as a regional energy hub could come into play and a more active Turkish policy in its region could prove a boon for European energy needs. While overtures in recent years in the context of its "no problems with neighbors" policy have sometimes been met with media suspicion or even whispers of "losing Turkey," it is largely Turkish policy that will help determine whether supplies are there to feed Europe's current "grand project," the Nabucco pipeline. Europe should leverage its close ties with Turkey, through NATO, to encourage its energy hub ambitions and nurture close relations with the only NATO country with concurrent political and strategic interests whose growth rates and economic dynamism put it squarely into the camp of emerging economies on par with India, Brazil, and others.

IEA "450" Green Scenario: pacified NATO

The 450 Scenario goes beyond the New Policies Scenario in terms of action to tackle climate change with the aim of achieving long-term stabilization of the atmospheric concentration of greenhouse gases at 450 parts per million (ppm) – a level that, according to the International Panel on Climate Change, gives the world a 50 percent chance of limiting global average temperature increase to 2 °C. This is the IEA's "greenest" scenario and is one of the most ambitious remaining in terms of achieving emissions targets (scenarios from other major institutions are beginning to see 550 ppm or even 650 ppm as the most optimistic outcomes). Even the IEA appreciates that it is becoming increasingly unrealistic.

The "450" target is based on the high-end of pledges, announced in association with the Copenhagen Accord, on strong implementation of the commitments made by the G-20 to phase out fossil-fuel subsidies and on strong action after 2020 to rapidly reduce emissions from all sectors. Gas still plays an important role for countries making the transition to a lower-carbon power sector, but overall, fossil fuelled electricity generation will fall to only around 20 percent by 2035, from almost 70 percent today. Already in the NPS, renewable-based electricity generation will triple in absolute terms between 2008 and 2035 – the increase coming primarily from wind and hydropower. But in the 450 Scenario, this is set to grow almost four-fold or 30 percent higher than in the NPS. Renewable sources (including hydro) and nuclear power are projected to account for 45 percent of total global power generation by 2035, a sum increasing from the 32 percent that exists today. We see a marked shift occurring in OECD countries where this share will reach 56 percent by 2035. Non-OECD countries also move towards low-carbon technologies in the power sector. In absolute terms, China sees the biggest increase in generation from both renewable sources and nuclear power between 2008 and 2035 at almost 2,000 TWh (terawatt-hour per year[28]) and 830 TWh respectively.

From a strategic point of view, the 450 Scenario represents significant benefits for energy security in both developed and emerging economies, as well as security benefits from limiting ballooning wealth transfers to the Middle East and reducing dependence on fossil fuel imports (with their implications for protecting foreign regimes or trade routes). Annual spending on oil imports in 2035 by the five largest importers – China, the European Union, the United States, India, and Japan – is around USD 560 billion, or one-third lower than in the NPS. This also implies a declining level of spending on oil imports as a share of GDP in all major importing countries. That is not to say that OPEC countries would suffer – cumulative oil revenues in 2010–35 amount to USD 27 trillion, or a little over USD 1 trillion per year. While this is 16 percent lower than in the NPS, it is more than a three-fold increase compared with the last quarter century. For those parts of the economy still dependent on oil, the price would stay flat over the long term from about 2020. Even while the greenest IEA scenario continues to see huge increases in absolute fossil fuel demand, it also predicts global oil demand to peak before 2020 at 88 million b/d – helped by more than 4 million b/d reduction in OECD oil demand by that peak date and 14 million b/d reduction by 2035.

Under the 450 scenario, the strategic landscape in the 2030s could look significantly different for NATO and the world. With oil demand less than that of today and falling by 2035, we can begin to see a trajectory that finally moves the entire world away from oil dependence over the long term. Supply will still be concentrated, and the Middle East in particular will retain its strategic importance, but especially in the OECD reinvestment into the low-carbon high-tech sector of the domestic economy displaces huge wealth transfers abroad. Massive electrification of the economy, including in transport (where 70 percent of new cars will run on low-emission power sources by 2035), largely refocuses much of the concern on electricity security (with new implications for grid technology and security). In terms of environmental endowment, international transfers of energy will still be important in the electricity sector, for example, in dreams to cover the Sahara with photovoltaics (such as the Desertec project) or to send solar power from Greece to Germany (the Helios project).[29]

But overall, for the first time since the industrial revolution, developed economies can reverse the trend of increasing reliance on foreign sources of energy. Just as this trend initiated the growing importance of energy to international security concerns, so its reversal could begin to decouple that link.

Conclusion

This chapter has attempted to offer only background insights into the major issues regarding energy within NATO and on the European periphery. As European states seek to promote diversification of suppliers especially for gas, the political relationships between Europe and those alternative suppliers will remain at the forefront. A "Golden Age" of gas could reinforce that situation, despite upheavals in the market and a recent gas "glut." NATO's political-security agenda in a rapidly changing economic environment therefore offers significant scope for influence. But over the longer term, technological and economic changes, and especially concerted government policy choices in terms of investment, could lead to different energy scenarios with very different implications for NATO. As a general rule, reducing dependence on foreign imports, particularly on those fossil fuels such as oil whose production will quickly be concentrated in fewer countries, will greatly benefit the security environment. In the meantime, the focus will surely move rapidly east, with huge increases in fossil fuel imports from developing Asia off-setting flat or declining energy demand in the developed economies. This will have major implications for long-standing security relationships, as producers untangle themselves from historic dependencies with the same enthusiasm as consumers. Though the point may finally sound glib, NATO will have to decide how it evolves to embrace a Pacific century – because energy concerns will only accelerate that trend.

Notes

* The views expressed in this chapter are those of the author and do not reflect the official policy or position of the International Energy Agency.
1 Note that there is no attempt here to assess the probabilities of these scenarios, which would have to be considered, mostly based on expert opinions, in actual decision situations.
2 J. Shea, "Energy Security: NATO's potential role?" *NATO Review*, Autumn 2006. Online. Available: www.nato.int/docu/review/2006/issue3/english/special1. html.
3 J. Jones, Comments at the Brussels Forum, "Do we Need a Transatlantic Energy Policy," 30 April 2006.
4 A. Monaghan, *What role for NATO?* NATO Defence College Research Paper No. 29, October 2006, pp. 2–7.
5 NATO, "Active Engagement, Modern Defence," Strategic Concept for the Defense and Security of the Members of the North Atlantic Treaty Organization, November 2010, para. 13. Online. Available HTTP: www.nato.int/lisbon2010/strategic-concept-2010-eng.pdf.
6 NATO, "Active Engagement, Modern Defence," para. 19.
7 E. Dahl, "Naval Innovation: From Coal to Oil" *Joint Force Quarterly*, Vol. 27, Winter 2000–01, pp. 50–56.
8 This continues to be a problem in places like Russia and Africa, and is addressed through schemes such as the World Bank Global Gas Flaring program.
9 The IEA New Policy Scenario (NPS) assumes cautious implementation of national pledges made in Copenhagen to reduce greenhouse-gas emissions by 2020, even if detailed polices to achieve these cuts may not have been implemented. The NPS also assumes that the new measures introduced after 2020 are continued in such a fashion to maintain the pace of decline in carbon intensity.

10 See "Murky Deal Ends the Russian Gas Row," *The Economist*, 4 January 2006. Online. Available: www.economist.com/node/5353164.
11 See IEA, *World Energy Outlook 2010*, pp. 193–194. Online. Available www. worldenergyoutlook.org/media/weo2010.pdf. Note that EU net imports are only 40 percent.
12 IEA, "Energy Policies of IEA Countries: Hungary 2011," *In-Depth Review Series*, 2011, p. 14.
13 IEA, *Russia Country Analysis Brief*, November 2010. Online. Available: www.eia. gov/cabs/Russia/pdf.pdf.
14 See Russian Federation, *National Security Strategy of the Russian Federation to 2020*, May 2009, p. 9.
15 IEA, "Are We Entering a Golden Age of Gas?," Special Report, *2011 World Energy Outlook*, June 2011. Online. Available: www.iea.org/weo/docs/weo2011/ WEO2011_GoldenAgeofGasReport.pdf.
16 IEA, *Saudi Arabia Country Analysis Brief*, June 2010. Online. Available: www.eia. gov/countries/country-data.cfm?fips=SA.
17 See F. Birol, Interview with IEA Chief Economist, *Financial Times*, 29 March 2011.
18 P. Clawson and S. Henderson, "Reducing Vulnerability to Middle East Energy Shocks: A Key Element in Strengthening US Energy Security," *Policy Focus*, No. 49, November 2005, pp. ix–x.
19 J.R. West, "Saudi Arabia, Iraq, and the Gulf," in J.H. Kalicki and D.L. Goldwyn (eds), *Energy and Security: Toward a New Foreign Policy Strategy*, Woodrow Wilson International Center for Scholars, 2005, p. 201.
20 This includes U.S. government officials, as revealed by the 2011 Wikileaks release as well as many independent analysts (as compiled by the Oil Drum website). See www.guardian.co.uk/business/2011/feb/08/saudi-oil-reserves-overstated-wikileaks and www.theoildrum.com/node/7465.
21 IEA, *Monthly Oil Market Report*, 13 July 2011, p. 3. Online. Available: http://omr-public.iea.org/omrarchive/13jul11full.pdf.
22 U.S. Department of Defense, "Measuring Security and Stability in Iraq," Washington, D.C., March 2007, p. 20.
23 IEA, *Monthly Oil Market Report*, 18 January 2007, p. 12. Online. Available: http:// omrpublic.iea.org/omrarchive/18jan07full.pdf.
24 "Iran's Revolutionary Guards Ready to Close Strait of Hormuz Linking Gulf to International Markets," *Al Arabiya* news agency, 4 July 2011. Online. Available: www.alarabiya.net/articles/2011/07/04/156120.html.
25 IEA, *Perspectives on Caspian Oil and Gas Development*, Working Paper Series: International Energy Agency, December 2008. Online. Available: www.iea.org/ papers/2008/caspian_perspectives.pdf.
26 IEA, *World Energy Outlook 2010*, p. 46.
27 Natural gas prices in the GAS scenario are between USD 1.5 per million British thermal units (Mbtu) and USD 2.5/Mbtu lower than the NPS – so USD 8/ Mbtu in 2035 vs. 10.4 NPS, Europe 10.9 vs. 13.3 and Japan 12.9 vs. 15.3.
28 1 TWh/year = 114 MW.
29 See T. Gropp (Director of the Desertec Foundation), "Multi-Euro Project Helios," 6 September 2011. Online. Available: www.desertec.org/en/press/ press-releases/110906–01-multi-billion-euro-project-helios/.

13 "Good enough is better than good"

Towards a third "Transatlantic Bargain"?

Graeme P. Herd and John Kriendler

Introduction

The difference between "dead-alliance walking" or a NATO in robust and rude health has profound implications for the national security strategies of Alliance members, regional security architecture and, indeed, the management of global security. For security policymakers and policy implementers, the fact that NATO will continue to exist is not in doubt, but what kind of NATO – its roles, functions, and membership – will reflect future judgments and negotiated strategic calculi that will be very difficult to predict. Can we, in considering possible alternative future scenarios, lazily conclude that NATO's future will be like the past, only more so? If past is prologue, NATO's utility will be viewed differently by different allies, but these differences will be acknowledged and a *modus vivendi* struck and sealed in a new "Transatlantic Bargain." This bargain, if it can be struck, will reflect a workable equilibrium between what is considered acceptable to the societies of member states, appropriate to a shared understanding of strategic stability in the context of power-shifts and interdependence and affordable given financial constraints and opportunity costs. Irrespective of which candidate wins the next U.S. presidential election, if we accept as a given that the U.S. will seek to maintain its primacy on the international stage within a changing global power structure, then it follows that the U.S. will continue to judge NATO's utility through the prism of its wider global responsibilities and obligations. Where the balance falls will be determined by the perceived needs of U.S. grand strategy – to maintain primacy does the U.S. need an alliance that can conduct military operations efficiently and effectively or one that can provide politico-strategic legitimacy for operations – or some combination of both?

The speed and direction of structural change are key to our understanding of its strategic effects. A central issue is whether the system will be bipolar or multipolar and whether emerging powers will be status quo or revisionist international actors. A new bipolar world order appears to have a greater potential to generate a more competitive strategic environment; new multipolarity a more multilateral and cooperative one. On this basis, two alternative types of structural change can be posited: first, rapid structural change from a uni-polar to a bipolar competitive world order based on Sino-U.S. rivalry; second, a less rapid structural change in which China emerges alongside other BRICS and Next-11 states, such as Indonesia, Turkey, and Mexico, to create a multipolar cooperative world order to replace uni-polarity. Each variant would generate a different U.S. grand strategy, and each grand strategy would seek to instrumentalize NATO to best effect. As Rob de Wijk, a prominent European strategic analyst, notes: "The Americans are instrumental multilateralists, because they use international organizations to win international support, but if support is not gained Americans end up going it alone in unilateral support of their grand strategy of primacy."[1] Hence structural change engenders different strategic effects. In either case, U.S. grand strategy would seek to maintain primacy and to instrumentalize NATO's support to that end. Let us examine possible scenarios of structural change in turn and the potential "transatlantic bargains" that they might engender.

U.S.-China new Cold War scenario: implications for a Transatlantic Bargain?

The overarching strategic framework of U.S. engagement with the Asia Pacific region rests on three pillars: stability through bilateral alliances and partnerships, prosperity through open markets, free trade and investment, and the prevention of emergence of a dominant rival.[2] The current U.S. strategic posture appears to be based on the premise "integrate but hedge" (perhaps an equivalent of Reagan's Cold War notion of "trust but verify"), and this finds contemporary expression in U.S. Secretary of Defense Leon Panetta's announcement that the 60:40 split in U.S. naval assets (carrier groups, destroyers, cruisers, submarines, littoral combat ships) between the Atlantic and Pacific will by 2020 be 50:50 in favor of the Pacific.[3] In a best case scenario, the U.S. would leverage relations with regional partners to further strengthen its bilateral relationship with a *status quo* China and so better integrate it into a U.S.-led global normative order as a "responsible stakeholder." In the worst case, enhanced alliances and partnerships in the region would enable the U.S. to better counterbalance and contain a rising China that is revisionist and aggressive.[4]

The issues assume particular importance in the case of China as analysts seek to decide: "Is China, and will it be, a *status quo* power?"[5] Realist theorists are quick to answer in the negative, and the notion that China and the U.S. are heading for a "new Cold War" or "second Cold War" is gaining traction. Stephen Walt, a leading U.S. realist international relations theorist, argues that China's economic rise renders security competition with the U.S. "virtually inevitable," citing the rapid Chinese military expansion, particularly naval capability as "a classic manifestation of great power status": "Beijing is seeking to build its economy, then expand its military capacity, achieve a position of regional dominance, and then exclude other major powers from its immediate neighborhood."[6] Yuriko Koike, former Japanese Defence Minister, supports this contention arguing China seeks regional hegemony: "by working to exclude the U.S. from the region and preventing regional partnerships from flourishing."[7] As a result, East Asian integration on Chinese terms will take place: "The Pacific era will be led by China – and no one else."[8] John Mearsheimer contends that there is no difference between containment and balancing – they are the same thing:

> If China grows in the next 30 years as it has over the last 30 years, it will seek to dominate Asia the way America dominates the western hemisphere. If China turns into a greater Hong Kong, it will try to push the United States out of Asia and develop its own Monroe Doctrine. I think that China cannot rise peacefully and that this is largely pre-determined.[9]

Richard Rigby suggests that key current debates in China are about regime survival, whether the U.S.'s decline is structural or temporary, and whether to abandon permanently Deng Xiaoping's advice to keep a low profile internationally: "Observe carefully; secure our position; cope with affairs calmly; hide our capacity and bide our time; be good at maintaining a low profile, and never claim leadership."[10] While China officially rejects Cold War thinking, "circles within China's own foreign policy community have such thinking. They talk about win-win, but the zero sum game is deeply embedded within the system."[11] In this competitive paradigm, the previous durable, tolerable hegemony exercised by a single state – the U.S. – is understood to be "decreasingly sustainable."[12]

According to Joseph Nye, the U.S.'s ability to hedge against China is directly conditioned by the perception of Chinese intentions and actions by its neighbors: "only China can contain China – though its behaviour."[13] ROK president, Lee Myung-bak, underscores this contention with his comment: "I am not sure if China's performance over the past year or so has drastically improved the marketability of the 'peaceful rise' or the image of a benevolent hegemon."[14] He may refer, among other points of tension, to the detention by Japan of a Chinese fishing boat captain, the arrest of Japanese businessmen in China, the embargo of rare earths to Japan, the announcement (later rescinded) of China's foreign Minister which extended China's core national interests to place the Spratly Islands on par with Tibet and Taiwan, (that is, in the non-negotiable category despite the territorial claims of five other states), and the growing China-DPRK-Cambodia-Laos-Bangladesh-Myanmar-Pakistan Axis.

Within the new Cold War bipolar paradigm, the U.S. struggles with China for leadership of the global strategic agenda – not least in the global commons, though U.S. and Chinese polar opposite approaches to Syria and sanctions through 2012 indicate that normative splits may already have become unbridgeable when it comes to dealing with regional crises in a cooperative manner. "If neither the United States nor some form of 'world government' can provide the leadership to tackle the world's common political problems" then, according to Gideon Rachman, a "third alternative" will emerge, with China and Russia spearheading an "axis of authoritarianism."[15] According to this conceptual framework, politico-ideological rivalry is based on the promotion of divergent modernity paradigms: a Beijing versus a Washington, or post-Washington consensus.

The U.S. would champion the liberal international order based on free trade, social advancement and market-democratic states, with a more explicit military-security dimension based on two pillars: a renewed engagement with Europe through a new "Transatlantic Bargain," and a neo-containment policy in the Asia-Pacific, based on revitalized trade partnerships and defense alliances.

In the event of a bipolar global paradigm in which security threats in the Asia and Pacific region substantially increased, one could envisage that the U.S. would look to its European (as well as Asian and Pacific) allies to provide a forum for consultations, political support, and legitimacy and, only in extremis, which appears difficult to imagine, military support for a non-Article 5 NATO-led mission. According to Michael Rühle (Chapter 9) the U.S. would return to a more robust extended deterrence approach, which would: "include a re-emphasis on elaborate nuclear sharing arrangements in NATO, but also the extension of these arrangements to other allies, notably Japan and South Korea." He warns that: "the risk of allied divergence appears greater in this scenario than in any other, as a confrontational environment would trigger national reflexes in accordance with national 'strategic cultures,' making allied consensus more difficult to achieve." As Jeffrey Hunker (Chapter 10) notes, conflict between the U.S. and China could occur in virtual cyber-space using proxy forces:

> The unprecedented discovery of a cyber espionage program against U.S. defense interests could well result in significant public tension between the U.S. and China. After the U.S. threatens to affect Chinese economic interests, there is wide scale disruption of U.S. cyber and critical infrastructures by 'patriotic Chinese citizens.'

In response to the logic of power-shifts to China and growing interdependence and competition for finite energy resources and raw materials, NATO utilizes existing and creates new regional partnerships to balance China in Central, South and East Asia, as Graeme P. Herd suggests in

Chapter 5. One could envisage, for example, Thailand, Japan, Republic of Korea, Australia, New Zealand, Vietnam, or even India creating alternative regional organizations that exclude China, or looking to NATO to formalize a partnership program in East and South Asia to do just that.

Enhanced support for NATO operations (first humanitarian then military) and even increased demands for membership, should soft balancing fail, would constitute a natural progression. Under such conditions, NATO crisis management operations would not be UN-mandated but rather legitimized by regional organizations and NATO regional partnerships and, ultimately, their own success. NATO's Asia-Pacific regional partnership would thus become as much political instruments to legitimize operations as militarily useful. This consideration would influence the composition of partnerships, suggesting *realpolitik* interests as much as normative compatibility will shape partnership memberships. This process may have a distinctive ideological tint in that partners across the globe – particularly democratic partners that share the same values as NATO member states – are keenest to partner and then even join (with the necessary revisions to Article 10 of the NATO Charter) NATO. According to this logic, the *finalité politique* of NATO is for NATO to become the institutional core of a worldwide community of democracies, with a global geostrategic operational range, from Kinshasa to the Solomon Islands. Another expression of balancing may well be in the Global Commons, where instead of cooperative security in action, we see increasing contention and competition (building on current disagreements over the whose norms to apply to Economic Exclusion Zones and cyber space).

For the European allies, political support for the U.S. could be offered in return for U.S. economic security commitments and solidarity, more necessary in the context of China leveraging its net creditor status and 3.2 trillion US dollar reserves to directly shape the rules of the game in global trade and finance as well as seeking to influence the foreign and security policies of individual European states. For the U.S. the institutional weight and political legitimacy of NATO acting though the North Atlantic Council would be more important than the military efficiency and effectiveness of NATO allies. (In East Asia and facing China, the military efficiency and effectiveness of U.S. allies and partners in this region will be as important as the political legitimacy that such an alliance system would bring).

Cooperative multipolar system: implications for a Transatlantic Bargain?

What are the strategic effects of growing interdependence? The economy-environment-energy nexus, the rise of non-state actors – whether organized criminals or terrorists, and system collapse triggered by systemic shocks present two hard truths: all states are threatened; no single state can address these challenges alone. This suggests the emergence of a world order driven by a cooperative imperative as reciprocal cooperation and collective action constitutes a rational response to shared threats. The recognition of mutual indispensability creates incentives for peace with a global security community. A shared "market-democratic/good governance" modernity paradigm would be championed by the U.S. and China and normative convergence between these Great Powers would be in evidence – whether around the application of "Responsibility to Protect" or agreement on the definition and practice of a "responsible stakeholder." This realization finds fullest expression in the need to preserve, sustain, and secure the Global Commons. The international system is increasingly congested, contested, and interconnected. The Global Commons is territory or space with no exclusive ownership as it lies outside national jurisdiction and is understood increasingly as the fabric or connective tissue of the international system.

It is this kind of world order which NATO encourages and is designed to address. As NATO Secretary General Rasmussen notes in his "Annual Report 2011": "Today's security challenges are increasingly transnational and the most effective responses include the broadest range of partners, countries and international organizations alike."[16] The mantra of "multinational solutions to global problems" becomes the operating principle. Cooperative security makes the most sense given the nature of contemporary threats and budgetary cutbacks. Within this cooperative multipolar/partner world order, NATO would be viewed as a key element in a globalized collective security and crisis management system, a forum for allied security debates on the full range of global issues and how best to address transnational shared threats.

Such circumstances would favor a move towards a nuclear free world – as discussed by Michael Rühle (Chapter 9) and a more globally inclusive understanding of the "comprehensive approach" as outlined by Thierry Tardy (Chapter 7), allowing for much greater inter-institutional cooperation in conflict management. As noted in Chapter 6 (John Kriendler) the most favorable NATO–Russia scenario involves Russian membership of NATO. Russian membership of the Alliance would render Gustav Lindstrom's (Chapter 11) third scenario – a joint US/NATO–Russian missile defense system most likely. Within such a context, Pál Dunay (Chapter 4) envisages "accelerated enlargement with the accession of the countries of the Western Balkans followed by several countries in the post-Soviet space, with the prospect of further enlargement in the offing." Partnerships with the Global Contact Group are strengthened through joint operations, and the existing bi-annual "back-door" NATO-China strategic exchanges are translated into a dialogue and then strategic partnership. India also becomes a Strategic Partner with this enlarged institutionalized West and, according to Graeme Herd (Chapter 5), NATO would: "create additional partnership programs to facilitate UN-mandated operations to manage regional flashpoints." As Phillip Cornell (Chapter 12) suggests within the IEA "Pacific NATO" scenario: "existing cooperation in the context of anti-piracy actions in the western Indian Ocean holds significant scope for expansion." Expansion to "the Gulf waters and especially the Strait of Hormuz (through which almost 16 million barrels of oil currently pass each day)" could be envisaged, as well as the Indian Ocean and ultimately the Pacific.

The U.S.'s ability to project and sustain power in, demonstrate unfettered access to and "mastery" over all five Global Commons (high seas and sea-beds, space, Antarctica, and cyber space) has proved to be the *sine qua non* of its global leadership role within the international system. An open Global Commons has allowed for global energy and food supply chains and international trade and commerce to operate, buttressing the U.S.'s economic and military primacy. Thus, the U.S. would be a key driver to in this regard, expanding partnerships to cover the functional cyber threats, and creating bilateral partnerships to include states whose proximity to (South Africa) or increasing normative and physical role within the Global Commons (China, India, Brazil) renders their cooperation essential.

The "Transatlantic Bargain" negotiated and implied within such a construct would suggest that from a U.S. perspective the institutional weight and political legitimacy of NATO acting though the North Atlantic Council will be more important than the military efficiency and effectiveness of NATO and its members, for the simple reason that coalitions made up from an expanded partner base bring political/geo-political legitimacy for NATO-led or enabled cooperative security and crisis management operations in different partners of the globe. As Michael Rühle (Chapter 9) argues:

> if the major problems that lead nations to acquire nuclear weapons were removed, the world would be by definition largely peaceful. In such a world, NATO might no longer be needed except as an insurance policy in case the system were violated, in order to address smaller, non-existential conflicts, or to manage humanitarian relief operations.

It would be these niches which European NATO allies would seek to address. Being able to fulfill military commitments to NATO operations increases the weight and influence of such states in a highly market-competitive world; the pressure to modernize militaries will come from member state capitals determined to have a voice in global hotspots and so a seat at the multipolar table shaping the roles of the game.

A reality check: strategic pause and patience

The twin impact of increasing power-shifts and interdependence shapes a strategic environment that is uncertain and ambiguous with unclear strategic effects and has yet to constitute a catalyst for a new "Transatlantic Bargain" that would renovate and modernize NATO for the next two decades. While some strategic analysts view China in open military and ideological competition with the U.S., others view China as wanting to be in the front seat of global governance and strategic decision-making, besides the U.S. driver as a co-equal, but in reality both unable and unwilling to build a Sino-centric regional order, let alone attain global hegemony. Others still see a natural and peaceful historical shift underway, one that brings in its wake points of tension and friction in the relationship between China as an ascendant and the U.S. as a descending power: "China's rise means that it is now involved in areas of the world and on issues where previously it had little or no stake. As China becomes a global power it is bound to come into conflict with the United States on a number of subjects."[17]

If we take the Cold War as a guide then one would expect the swift and extensive militarization of rivalry, the renewal and extension of formal structure of alliances to contain China and Chinese efforts to escape such encirclement. While there is a regional arms race as evidence of an intensified "integrate but hedge" strategy, China has not sent warships to protect its oil and gas drilling and pipeline interests in Burma or submarines patrolling the Bay of Bengal, nor has China used its financial leverage to directly influence U.S. foreign policy. China has over the last 30 years managed an economy structured on export-led growth (based on cheap, low technology goods), with the result that it is integrated into world trade and the largest holder of U.S. securities. Economic interdependence provides a shock absorber for more fractious security relations. China plans to restructure its economy around a different growth model, one that is domestic consumption-led with a macro-economic environment that would encourage domestic spending. This would change the size and function of its foreign exchange reserves, allowing China to leverage these reserves for geo-political goals. As this shift is ten to fifteen years in the future, if indeed it does occur at all, for now while we can note a lack of strategic trust, suspicion and unease, strategic caution, and a lack of strategic confidence, open hostility is not in evidence.

In 2012, the year of the Dragon, elections and power transfers in Russia, the U.S. and China add a potentially combustible ingredient to the pot of global transformation. Elections are traditionally a time for blame and tough assertiveness rather than compromise and accommodation, increasing the chances of strategic misunderstanding and of uncertainty driving events. Until the new leaderships are settled in, or old leaderships confirmed, we can expect few new strategic initiatives that build strategic trust or confidence. Rather, the best that we can hope for is net-zero sum outcomes; strategic damage limitation through this electoral year is imperative. Group-think within strategic and decision-making elites on both sides of the China-U.S. divide can all too easily argue themselves down paths leading to conflict rather than cooperation and so the need to manage expectations and perceptions through 2012 is all important.

When new or re-legitimized old leaderships emerge in China and the U.S. after October/November 2012, will the U.S. and China be able to discover a common strategic purpose or joint endeavor, a strategic challenge or problems that can be addressed cooperatively? First a mechanism or framework needs to be created within which agreed strategic agendas can be implemented. The G3 has been posited as an inclusive burden sharing mechanism capable of achieving a balance of mutual benefit not power. Together the EU, China and U.S. constitute 60 percent of the world economy. The U.S. is the prime military power and consumer, China offers capital and labor, and EU rules and technology and can play the role of strategic buffer between the U.S. and China. Each of these entities is systemically relevant. Not only are they too big to fail, but their individual actions and decisions impact on the whole world.

The G3 are producers of global governance while most other states are receivers – but does this common characteristic forge common interests? Can China and the U.S. identify areas of strategic cooperation? Afghanistan might constitute one such topic for strategic dialogue. However, U.S. strategic interest in Afghanistan will diminish following drawdown of U.S. forces and transition to Afghan-led stability operations. A stagnating and gradually destabilized Russia is another possible topic for a U.S.-China strategic dialogue. However, the risk of strategic miscalculation makes Russia a difficult focus for a Sino-U.S. strategic dialogue. Managing India's rise is also a non-starter for a U.S.-Chinese strategic dialogue. The ongoing Sino-Indian border dispute and China's non-ideological strategic partnership with Pakistan mean India is already a counter-point to China. The preservation of the "Global Commons" also appears to be a non-starter as a cooperative venture, given the normative differences between China and the U.S. over rights and responsibilities within maritime Exclusive Economic Zones, as well as an undeclared war in cyberspace and inability to judge each other's intentions.

A third "Transatlantic Bargain": when "good" is "good enough"?

The Chicago Summit has called for greater unity of purpose amongst allies while stressing its natural resilience and celebrating shared values and interests, common cause, and common ground. However, rhetoric aside, a sustainable third Transatlantic Bargain will only become possible after (and if) the U.S. and China forge a trans-Pacific bargain which structures their relationship in a sustainable way. Before the allies can reach a conclusion about NATO's future relevance, they must first clarify how the West engages with the world. A viable Sino-U.S. partnership would settle the nature of a stable East Asian regional order and make possible more effective global governance. Once such a bargain is struck, the purpose and direction of NATO's future will become more apparent. Trans-Atlantic relations are now driven by trans-Pacific affairs as much as by domestic political and economic conditions among the allies; the substance and content of a trans-Pacific bargain provides the requisite clarity for transatlantic allies to commit to the type of NATO that will evolve. NATO's future lies in Asia.

However, if the future is like the past, only more so, as American philosopher and baseball catcher Yogi Berra has posited, then the preconditions for a third "Transatlantic Bargain" are not yet in place. If there is no clear change to a bipolar or multipolar world with observable cooperative or competitive strategic effects that are broadly recognized by NATO allies, we might assume that under conditions of "business and usual," it will become harder to maintain compatible (not identical) interests, and the Alliance will lose importance. Increasing inability to forge compatible views on the nature and importance of threats as well as their management will result in greater reluctance to generate appropriate capabilities to effectively combat such threats and the political will to deploy capabilities for this purpose. NATO will not measure up to the challenges of defining shared political objectives relevant for the evolving security environment or of marshaling military capabilities to support those objectives. It is likely that the U.S. would increasingly use coalitions of NATO member states and their military assets, hoping to get political consensus around a given operation it deems necessary. Coalitions within NATO partnerships will become as important for the U.S. – giving both military assets and more importantly regional political legitimacy. The U.S. would then seek to leverage such partnerships, tried and tested through operations, in its own strategic dialogue with rising powers – India and China in particular. The U.S. would recognize NATO's utility but a "Transatlantic Bargain" that brings reciprocal benefits to all allies will not have been struck – this default pathway will hollow NATO out and render a real "Transatlantic Bargain," once the strategic effects of power shifts are understood and shared, much harder to achieve. A Transatlantic Bargain consisting of three parts can be posited:

> NATO should continue to guarantee territorial defence; the EU should take the lead for external operations in Europe's neighbourhood where the U.S. has no interest; and NATO would only act beyond Europe's borders when the U.S. wished it to be involved.[18]

Such thinking is overly deterministic and prescriptive. We must acknowledge that NATO inhabits a world of both interdependence and power shifts, geo-economic convergence and geopolitical rivalry. Within this contradictory context, the sum of NATO's parts is weighed and understood differently depending on where one begins to count. The breadth and depth of the range of NATO activities from missile defense to nuclear policy to combat operations, to energy and cyber security via enlarged membership and the full spectrum of partnerships means that NATO can be, if not quite all things to all interlocutors, at least an entity that does not lend itself to simple black and white interpretations and understandings about its identity. As the Chicago Summit declaration points out, NATO is not just a military alliance held together by external threats, but is also a community of liberal democratic values and norms: "NATO supports the aspirations of the people of the region for democracy, individual liberty and the rule of law – values which underpin the Alliance."[19] Loyalty, solidarity, mutual trust, confidence and a common history, ethos, and ideology help first and foremost manage security relations amongst existing members.[20] These same characteristics present a multifaceted face to the world.

We can be certain of uncertainty – NATO will operate in a complex global order – in which something akin to Asia-Pacific regional bipolarity may arise within a broad global context of a slower evolution to multipolarity. Here a series of paradoxes may become apparent: as, for example, the U.S. reduces conventional military forces in Europe in order to increase its presence in the Asia-Pacific, a greater weight is given to the political and symbolic utility of its theater nuclear weapons (TNW) in Europe. Despite this, NATO's adaptive Missile Defense system may at best engender low to mid-level cooperation between NATO and Russia, as argued by Gustav Lindstrom in Chapter 11. As the U.S. increases conventional forces (particularly naval) in the Asia-Pacific region, the more likely Russia and China will seek to boost strategic forces to counter this trend. Russia, hitherto, has argued that its TNWs have a military utility when forward deployed in European Russia, while in reality they are bargaining chips designed to extract political concessions. These same weapons have a real military utility when deployed along the Chinese border, but until now it has been politically taboo to officially state the obvious. The location and purpose of conventional and nuclear forces cannot be viewed in isolation but rather within increasingly interlocking strategic triangles – the U.S., European allies, and Russia at the Atlantic side of the Eurasian landmass, the U.S., Asia-Pacific allies, and China at the Pacific side. To take another example, as Pal Dunay in Chapter 4 suggests, further NATO enlargement is close to an end, but as is clear from Chapter 5 which addresses partnerships, the substantive differences between partners and members is already shrinking, and this is most clearly demonstrated when we turn our focus to NATO operations (Chapter 8) and the demands of a Comprehensive Approach (Chapter 7). Indeed, when we turn to the U.S.-China relationship, another paradox is apparent: the growing realization that power shifts deepen shared strategic vulnerabilities (nuclear, cyber, and space) between the U.S. and China (and Russia to a lesser extent) will encourage mutual strategic restraint.[21]

NATO's growing heterogeneity is both a weakness and strength. From the perspective of Alliance members on a wet Wednesday afternoon in

Brussels, the notion of "dead-alliance walking" could strike several chords, but earlier that week on a cold Monday morning, strategic defense planners in Beijing and Moscow could take the view that NATO is enjoying robust and rude health and conclude that if it looks like a duck, walks like a duck, and quacks like a duck – it may well be one. The multiple roles, functions, membership and partnerships of NATO allow it chameleon-like to adapt to this age of strategic uncertainty. A stress on shared interests amongst members and the compatibility of interests among partners is key to NATO's sustainability. Attempts to boost the politico-military efficiency and effectiveness of NATO could well be counter-productive. NATO's heterogeneity would accelerate under the strain and the gap between rhetoric and reality become intolerable – the Alliance would irredeemably fracture between "activists," "defenders," and "free-riders." Externally, the Alliance would be perceived to constitute a direct effort to confront and contain former adversaries. For NATO for now, being "good" should not be made the enemy of "good enough."

Notes

1 R. de Wijk, "European Author," in M.D. Ducasse (ed.), *The Transatlantic Bargain*, NDC Forum Paper 20, p. 142.
2 These three enduring principles find their most recent expression in H. Clinton, "America's Pacific Century," *Foreign Policy*, Vol. 189, November 2011, pp. 57–63.
3 "Remarks by Secretary Panetta at the Shangri-La Dialogue in Singapore," U.S. Department of Defense, Office of the Assistant Secretary of Defense (Public Affairs), News Transcript, 2 June 2012. Online Available: www.defense.gov/transcripts/transcript.aspx?transcriptid=5049.
4 However, as Walt notes: "When Americans speak of preserving the balance of power in East Asia through their military presence, the Chinese understandably take this to mean that they intend to maintain the strategic hegemony they now enjoy in the *absence* of such a balance." K. Waltz, "Structural Realism after the Cold War," *International Security*, Vol. 25, No. 1, Summer 2000, pp. 36. Italics in the original.
5 S. Chan, "An Odd Thing Happened on the Way to Balancing: East Asian States' Reactions to China's Rise," *International Studies Review*, Vol. 12, 2010, p. 391.
6 S. Walt, "China's New Strategy," *Foreign Policy*, 26 April 2010. Online. Available: http://walt.foreignpolicy.com/posts/2010/04/25/chinas_new_strategy. For a more nuanced understanding of China's foreign policy motivations, see L. Jakobsen and D. Knox, *New Foreign Policy Actors in China*, SIPRI Policy Paper, No. 26, September 2010. Online. Available: http://books.sipri.org/product_info?c_product_id=410. See also an excellent complimentary account: D. Shambaugh, "Coping with a Conflicted China," *Washington Quarterly*, Vol. 31, 1, 2011, pp. 7–27.
7 Y. Koike, "Cold War with China not Inevitable," *The Australian*, 10 January 2011, p. 10.
8 P. Khanna, *The Second World: Empires and Influence in the New World Order*, New York: Random House, 2008, p. 257.
9 P. Kelly, "Top thinker says China may 'push the US out of Asia'," *The Australian*, 3 August 2010, p. 4.

10 H.A.S. Kissinger, *On China*, New York: The Penguin Press, 2011, p. 438.
11 R. Callick, "President's 'Sputnik moment' signals strategic shift to Asia," *Weekend Australian*, 29 January 2011, p. 2. Richard Rigby is Director of the China Institute at the Australian National University.
12 I. Clark, "Bringing Hegemony Back in: The United States and International Order," *International Affairs*, Vol. 85, No. 1, 2009, pp. 23–36.
13 J.S. Nye, Jr., "Should China be 'contained'?" *Korea Times*, 6 July 2011. Walt 1997 argues alliances are strongest when there is a clear *raison d'etre*, a common overarching threat generates unity and cohesion.
14 Choe Sang-Hun, "North Korea Profits by a turn to Cold War allies; Seoul fears its hard line has allowed China to seize economic openings," *The International Herald Tribune*, 26 October 2011, p. 1.
15 G. Rachman, *Zero-sum Future: American Power in an Age of Anxiety*, New York: Simon and Schuster, 2011, p. 175.
16 NATO, "Secretary General's Annual Report 2011," 26 January 2012. Online. Available: www.nato.int/cps/en/SID-68267CB2-C8C6573E/natolive/opinions_82646.htm.
17 M. Jacques, "Crouching Dragon, Weakened Eagle," *International Herald Tribune*, 17 February 2010, p. 6.
18 D. Keohane, "Does NATO matter for US defence policy?" *FRIDE Policy Brief*, No. 129, May 2012, p. 5.
19 NATO, "NATO Summit Declaration," Issued by the Heads of State and Government participating in the meeting of the North Atlantic Council in Chicago on 20 May 2012," Press Release (2012) 062, para. 39. See also J. Sjursen, "On the Identity of NATO," *International Affairs*, Vol. 80, No. 4, 2004, pp. 687–703.
20 A. Gheciu, "Security Institutions as Agents of Socialization? NATO and the 'New Europe'," *International Organization*, Vol. 59, No. 4, Autumn, 2005, pp. 973–1012; S. Sloan, *NATO, The European Union, and the Atlantic Community*, Maryland: Rowman & Littlefield, 2003, p. 220; G. Lundestad, *No End to Alliance*, New York: St Martins Press, 1998, pp. 251–252.
21 D.C. Gompert and P.C. Saunders, *The Paradox of Power: Sino American Strategic Restraint in an Age of Vulnerability*, Institute for National Strategic Studies, Washington, DC, December 2011.

Bibliography

Primary sources

Printed official documents

Atlantic Council, *Foreign Policy Survey: The Future of NATO*. Online. Available: www. acus.org/event/atlantic-councilforeign-policy-survey-future-nato.

"Comprehensive Approach: Trends, Challenges and Possibilities for Cooperation in Crisis Prevention and Management," Seminar Publication, Crisis Management Initiative, 2008.

"Counterinsurgency," Field Manual 3–24 (MCWP 3–33.5), Headquarters Department of the Army, United States, December 2006.

Delegation of the European Union to the USA, "International Aid," 20 September 2010.

European Defence Agency, An Initial Long-Term Vision for European Defence Capability and Capacity Needs, October 2006, pp. 10–12. Online. Available: www.eda.europa.eu/webutils/downloadfile.aspx?fileid=106.

Federal Ministry of the Interior, Germany. *Cyber Security Strategy for Germany*. Federal Ministry of the Interior, Alt-Moabt 101 D, 10559 Berlin: February 2011, pp. 11.

Final Communiqué, Meeting of the North Atlantic Council in Defence Ministers Session held in Brussels, Press Release M-NAC(DM)-3(96) 172, Issued on 18 Dec. 1996. Online. Available: www.nato.int/cps/en/natolive/official_texts_25057.htm?mode=pressrelease.

Final Communiqué, Meeting of the North Atlantic Council at the level of Foreign Ministers held in Brussels, 3 December 2008. Online. Available: www.nato.int/cps/en/natolive/official_texts_46247.htm.

Harmel, P., "The Future Tasks of the Alliance. Report of the Council," North Atlantic Council Ministerial Communiqué: Brussels, NISCA 4/10/1, C-R (66)68&69, 15 December 1967.

IEA, *Monthly Oil Market Report*, 18 January 2007, pp. 12. Online. Available: http://omrpublic.iea.org/omrarchive/18jan07full.pdf.

IEA, *Perspectives on Caspian Oil and Gas Development*, Working Paper Series: International Energy Agency, December 2008. Online. Available: www.iea.org/papers/2008/caspian_perspectives.pdf.

IEA, "Energy Transformation by Sector," *World Energy Outlook 2010*.

IEA, "Is the World Entering a Golden Age of Gas?," *World Energy Outlook 2010*, June 2011.

IEA, "Natural Gas Market Outlook," *World Energy Outlook 2010*, November 2010, pp. 179.

IEA, "Oil Market Outlook," *World Energy Outlook 2010*, November 2010, pp. 119.

IEA, *Russia Country Analysis Brief*, November 2010. Online. Available: www.eia.gov/ cabs/Russia/pdf.pdf.

IEA, *Saudi Arabia Country Analysis Brief*, June 2010. Online. Available: www.eia.gov/ countries/country-data.cfm?fips=SA.

IEA, "Energy Policies of IEA Countries: Hungary 2011," *In-Depth Review Series*, 2011, pp. 14.

IEA, *Monthly Oil Market Report*, 13 July 2011, pp. 3. Online. Available: http://omr-public.iea.org/omrarchive/13jul11full.pdf.

International Court of Justice, Application of the Interim Accord of 13 September 1995 (The Former Yugoslav Republic of Macedonia v. Greece), 5 December 2011, para. 113, pp. 38. Online. Available: www.icj-cij.org/docket/files/142/16827.pdf.

"Military Committee Position on an Effects Based Approach to Operations," NATO Military Committee, MCM 0052–2006, June 2006.

NATO, "Declaration on a transformed North Atlantic Alliance issued by the Heads of State and Government participating in the meeting of the North Atlantic Council ('The London Declaration')," 6 July 1990. Online. Available: www.nato.int/cps/en/natolive/official_texts_23693.htm (accessed 31 October 2011).

NATO, "The Alliance's Strategic Concept agreed by the Heads of State and Government participating in the meeting of the North Atlantic Council," Rome, 8 November 1991.

NATO, "Partnership for Peace: Framework Document," January 1994. Online. Available: www.nato.int/cps/en/natolive/official_texts_24469.htm (accessed 1 September 2011).

NATO, "A more Ambitious and Expanded Framework for the Mediterranean Dialogue," Istanbul Summit, 28–29 July 1994. Online. Available: www.nato.int/docu/comm/2004/06-istanbul/docu-meddial.htm (accessed 20 August 2011).

NATO, "Study on NATO Enlargement," September 1995, point 6. Online. Available: www.nato.int/docu/basictxt/enl-9502.htm (accessed 5 September 2011).

NATO, "Founding Act on Mutual Relations, Cooperation and Security between NATO and the Russian Federation," signed in Paris, France, 27 May 1997. Online. Available: www.nato.int/cps/en/natolive/official_texts_25468.htm (accessed 19 June 2011).

NATO, "The Alliance's Strategic Concept approved by the Heads of State and Government participating in the meeting of the North Atlantic Council," Washington D.C., 23–24 April 1999. Online. Available: www.nato.int/cps/en/natolive/official_texts_27433.htm (accessed 31 August 2011).

NATO, "Membership Action Plan (MAP) approved by Heads of State and Government participating in the Meeting of the North Atlantic Council," 24 April 1999. Online. Available: www.nato.int/cps/en/natolive/official_texts_27444.htm.

NATO, "NATO–Russia Relations: A New Quality," Declaration by Heads of State and Government of NATO Member States and the Russian Federation, 28 May 2002. Online. Available: www.nato.int/cps/en/SID-7FFC1EC0–7FB6DEA1/natolive/official_texts_19572.htm (accessed 19 June 2011).

NATO, *Upgrading the Mediterranean Dialogue including on inventors of possible areas of cooperation*, official document approved at the Prague Summit of NATO Heads of State and Government, November 2002. Online. Available: www.nato.int/med-dial/2003/mdwp-2003.pdf (accessed 20 August 2011).

NATO, Prague Summit Declaration issued by the Heads of State and Government participating in the meeting of the North Atlantic Council in Prague, Czech Republic. 21 November 2002. Online. Available: www.nato.int/cps/en/SID-46B57300–925B0762/natolive/official_texts_19552.htm (accessed 5 September 2011).

NATO, "STOPWATCH 2," Bridging the Mediterranean, Special Interactive Video Forum series with Jamie Shea, March 12, 2005. Online. Available: www.nato.int/docu/speech/2005/s050311a.htm (accessed 20 August 2011).

NATO, "Riga Summit Declaration," Issued by the Heads of State and Government participating in the meeting of the North Atlantic Council in Riga, 29 November 2006.

NATO, "Summit Declaration," Issued by the Heads of State and Government participating in the meeting of the North Atlantic Council in Bucharest on 3 April 2008. Online. Available: www.nato.int/cps/en/natolive/official_texts_8443.htm?mode_pressrelease (accessed 23 July 2011).

NATO, "Multiple Futures Project – Navigating Towards 2030: Findings and Recommendations," Final Report, April 2009. Online. Available: www.iris-france.org/docs/pdf/up_docs_bdd/20090511–112315.pdf.

NATO, *NATO 2020, Assured security: dynamic engagement*, Analysis and recommendations of the group of experts on a new strategic concept for NATO, May 17, 2010, pp. 22–23. Online. Available: www.nato.int/strategic-concept/expertsreport.pdf (accessed 20 August 2011).

NATO, "Active Engagement, Modern Defence," Strategic Concept for the Defense and Security of the Members of the North Atlantic Treaty Organization, November 2010. Online. Available: www.nato.int/lisbon2010/strategic-concept-2010-eng.pdf.

NATO, "Improving the Management of our Partnerships – Menu of Cooperation and Individual programmes," Annex 1, PPC-M(2011)0024, adopted 12 April 2011.

NATO, "Policy for a more efficient and flexible partnership," PO(2011)0124, adopted 12 April 2011.

NATO, "Political Military Framework for Partner Involvement in NATO-Led Operations," PO(2011)0141, adopted 13 April 2011. NATO Unclassified.

NATO, Meeting of NATO Foreign Ministers, Berlin, Germany – 14–15 April 2011. Online. Available: www.nato.int/cps/en/SID-F1453434–3403F503/natolive/news_71542.htm (accessed 20 August 2011).

NATO, "NATO Defense ministers adopt new cyber defense policy," 8 June 2011. Online. Available. www.nato.int/cps/en/SID-001632DA-6B60591F/natolive/news_75195.htm (accessed 27 July 2011).

NATO, "Istanbul Cooperation Initiative," NATO Istanbul Summit, 28–29 July 2011. Online. Available: www.nato.int/docu/comm/2004/06-istanbul/docu-cooperation.htm (accessed 20 August 2011).

NATO, *Defending the Networks: The NATO Policy on Cyber Defence*, 4 October 2011. Online. Available: www.nato.int/cps/en/natolive/search.htm.

NATO, "Lisbon Summit Declaration," Issued by the Heads of State and Government participating in the meeting of the North Atlantic Council in Lisbon, Press Release (2010) 155, 20 November 2011. Online. Available: www.nato.int/cps/

en/natolive/official_texts_68828.htm?mode=pressrelease (accessed 20 August 2011).

NATO, "The Partnership for Peace Programme." Online. Available: www.nato.int/cps/en/natolive/topics_50349.htm (accessed 1 September 2011).

NATO, "Secretary General's Annual Report 2011," 26 January 2012. Online. Available: www.nato.int/cps/en/SID-68267CB2-C8C6573E/natolive/opinions_82646.htm.

NATO, "NATO Summit Declaration," Issued by the Heads of State and Government participating in the meeting of the North Atlantic Council in Chicago on 20 May 2012, Chicago Summit, 20 May 2012. Online. Available: www.nato.int/cps/en/natolive/official_texts_87593.htm.

NATO, "Deterrence and Posture Review," Press Release (2012) 063, 20 May 2012. Online. Available: www.nato.int/cps/en/natolive/official_texts_87597.htm?mode=pressrelease.

NATO, "Defending Against Cyber Attacks." Online. Available: www.nato.int/cps/en/natolive/topics_49193.htm?selectedLocale=en (accessed 27 September 2010).

NATO, "The Euro-Atlantic Partnership Council (EAPC)." Online. Available: www.nato.int/cps/en/natolive/topics_49276.htm (accessed 29 August 2011).

NATO Parliamentary Assembly, "074 CDS 11E – Information and National Security – draft general report by Lord Jopling," 2011 Spring Season.

North Atlantic Treaty, Art. 10. Online. Available: www.nato.int/cps/en/natolive/official_texts_17120.htm?.

OCHA, "Civil-Military Relationship in Complex Emergencies. An IASC Reference Paper," 28 June 2004, pp. 9.

President Signed Law of Ukraine On the Foundations of Domestic and Foreign Policy, RISU 15 July 2010, pp. 2. Online. Available: www.risu.org.ua/en/index/all_news/state/legislation/36488/.

Russian Federation, *National Security Strategy of the Russian Federation to 2020*, May 2009, p. 9.

Sager, A., "The Gulf and NATO: Time to Revisit Relations," *NATO Review*, December 2008. Online. Available: www.nato.int/docu/review/2008/08/NATO_GULF_RELATIONS/EN/index.htm 31 December 2008.

Summit NATO–Russia Council [NRC], 28 May 2002. Online. Available: www.nato.int/docu/comm/2002/0205-rome/rome-eng.pdf.

U.S. Congressional Budget Office, *Estimated Costs and Technical Characteristics of Selected National Missile Defense Systems*, January 2002.

U.S. Congressional Budget Office, *The Long-Term Implications of Current Defense Plans and Alternatives: Detailed Update for Fiscal Year 2006*, January 2006.

U.S. Department of Defense, *Measuring Security and Stability in Iraq*, Washington, DC, March 2007, p. 20.

U.S. Department of Defense, *Ballistic Missile Defense Review Report*, February 2010.

U.S. Department of Defense, *Nuclear Posture Review Report*, April 2010. Online. Available: www.defense.gov/npr/docs/2010%20nuclear%20posture%20review%20report.pdf.

U.S. Department of Defense, *Defense Budget Priorities and Choices*, January 2012. Online. Available: www.defense.gov/news/Defense_Budget_Priorities.pdf.

U.S. Department of Defense, *Sustaining U.S. Global Leadership: Priorities for 21st Century Defense*, January 2012, p. 6.

U.S. Department of State, *Country Reports on Human Rights Practices for 2011: Russia*, 24 May 2012. Online. Available: www.state.gov/j/drl/rls/hrrpt/humanrightsre-port/index.htm?dynamic_load_id=186397 (accessed 26 May 2012).

U.S. Department of State, White House, Office of the Press Secretary, 21 May 2012.

U.S. General Accounting Office, *Missile Defense: Actions are Needed to Enhance Testing and Accountability*, Report to Congressional Committees, GAO-04-409, April 2004.

U.S. General Accounting Office, *Missile Defense: Actions Needed to Improve Planning and Cost Estimates for Long-Term Support of Ballistic Missile Defense*, Report to the Subcommittee on Strategic Forces, Committee on Armed Services, House of Representatives, GAO-08-1068, September 2008.

U.S. Government Accounting Office, *Ballistic Missile Defense*, GAO-11-220, January 2011.

U.S. National Intelligence Council, *Mapping the Global Future: Report of the National Intelligence Council's 2020 Project*, December 2004. Online. Available: www.foia.cia.gov/2020/2020.pdf.

U.S. National Intelligence Council, *Global Trends 2025: A Transformed World*, November 2008. Online. Available: www.dni.gov/nic/NIC_2025_project.html.

Voyennaya Doktrina Rossiiskoi Federatsii, 5 February 2010. Online. Available: www.scrf.gov.ru/documents/33html.

White House, *The National Security Strategy of the United States of America*, May 2010, pp. 41.

Published speeches

Birol, F., Interview with IEA Chief Economist, *Financial Times*, 29 March 2011.

Brzezinski, Z., Brookings Institution and the Atlantic Council, 7 July 2011, pp. 3–4.

Clinton, H.R., "Remarks," Town Hall at Kyiv Politechnic Institute, Ukraine, 2 July 2010. Online. Available: www.state.gov/secretary/rm/2010/07/143941.htm.

Clinton, H.R., "Remarks at the NATO Strategic Concept Seminar," 22 February 2010, Washington, D.C. Online. Available: www.state.gov/secretary/rm/2010/02/137118.htm (accessed 20 August 2011).

Council on Foreign Relations, "NATO At 60 Symposium: Session II: NATO, Russia and Eastern Europe," Transcript, 26 February 2010. Online. Available: www.cfr.org/nato/council-foreign-relations-nato-60-symposium-session-ii-nato-russia-eastern-europe/p18692 (accessed 28 June 2011).

Declaration on a Transformed North Atlantic Alliance, Issued by the Heads of State and Government participating in the meeting of the North Atlantic Council ("The London Declaration"), 6 July 1990. Online. Available: www.nato.int/cps/en/natolive/official_texts_23693.htm.

Gates, R., speech at the United States Military Academy, 25 February 2011. Online. Available: www.defense.gov/speeches/speech.aspx?speechid=1539.

Haass, R., "Charting a New Course in the Transatlantic Relationship," Remarks to Centre for European Reform, London, 10 June 2002.

Jones, J., Comments at the Brussels Forum, "Do we need a transatlantic energy policy?," 30 April 2006.

Karunakara, U., Address by International President of Médecins sans Frontières, to the NATO Deputy Permanent Representatives Committee, Brussels, 14 December 2010.

Kupchan, C., "NATO: Chicago and Beyond," Senate Committee on Foreign Relations, *United States Senate*, 2nd Session, 112th Congress, 10 May 2012. Online. Available: www.cfr.org/nato/nato-chicago-beyond/p28204 (accessed 11 May 2011).

Makarov, N., "Views of the Ministry of Defense of the Russian Federation on Missile Defence Issues," presentation at the international conference "Missile Defence Factor in Establishing New Security Environment," 3–4 May, 2012, Online. Available http: www.mil.ru/conference_of_pro/news/more.htm?id= 11108033@egNews.

Medvedev, D., "Statement in connection with the situation concerning the NATO countries' missile defence system in Europe," 23 November 2011. Online. Available: http://eng.kremlin.ru/news/3115.

NATO–Russia Council Joint Statement issued at the meeting of the NATO–Russia Council held in Lisbon, 20 November 2010. Online. Available: www.nato.int/cps/en/natolive/news_68871.htm.

Obama, B., Remarks by the President on the Way Forward in Afghanistan, 22 June 2011. Online. Available: www.whitehouse.gov/the-press-office/2011/06/22/remarks-president-way-forward-afghanistan.

Obama, B., Speech at the Ronald Reagan Building, 15 July 2008. Online. Available: www.americanrhetoric.com/speeches/barackobama/barackobamairaqwarreaganbuilding.htm.

O'Reilly, P., Deputy Director, Missile Defense Agency speech at Atlantic Council, 19 April 2007.

O'Reilly, P., "Phased Adaptive Approach to Missile Defence in Europe – Overview for the Atlantic Council," 7 October 2009. Online. Available: www.acus.org/files/OReilly%20Powerpoint%20Atlantic%20Council%20Missile%20Defense%20Conference.pdf.

Panetta, L., "Balance Military Budget and Security Needs," Senate Armed Services Committee (Budget Request) in Georgia, 14 February 2012. Online. Available:www.defense.gov/speeches/speech.aspx?speechid=1650.

Petraeus, D., U.S. Army, Commander, International Security Assistance Force, before the Senate Armed Services Committee, Washington, 15 March, 2011.

Rasmussen, A.F., "First NATO Press conference," 3 August 2009. Online. Available: www.nato.int/cps/en/natolive/opinions_56776.htm (accessed 20 August 2011).

Rasmussen, A.F., "Afghanistan and the Future of Peace Operations," University of Chicago, 8 April 2010. Online. Available: www.nato.int/cps/en/natolive/opinions_62510.htm.

Rasmussen, A.F., Monthly press briefing, 15 September 2010. Online. Available: www.nato.int/cps/en/SID-BCD82CEB-83B4AF4B/natolive/opinions_66220.htm (accessed 24 Sept. 2010).

Rasmussen, A.F., NATO Secretary General, "Speech to RUSI on how NATO can defend against ballistic missile attack," Twelfth RUSI Missile Defence Conference," Whitehall, London, 15–16 June 2011.

Rasmussen, A.F., "The Future of Peace Operations," Speech by NATO Secretary-General at University of Edinburgh, 17 November 2009.

"Remarks by Secretary Panetta at the Shangri-La Dialogue in Singapore," U.S. Department of Defense, Office of the Assistant Secretary of Defense (Public Affairs), News Transcript, 2 June 2012. Online Available: www.defense.gov/transcripts/transcript.aspx?transcriptid=5049.

Rizzo, A.M., NATO Deputy Secretary General, Keynote address at conference on "NATO's Aims and Actions for the Mediterranean Dialogue and the Broader Middle East Region," Amman, Jordan, 26 June 2006.

Scheffer, J.H., NATO Secretary General, Keynote Address at the EAPC Security Forum, 29 June 2007. Online. Available: www.nato.int/docu/speech/2007/s070629b.html (accessed 1 August 2007).

Scheffer, J.H., Press conference by NATO Secretary General following the meeting of the NATO–Russia Council, 10 February 2006. Online. Available: www.nato.int/docu/speech/2006/s060210c.htm (accessed 10 Feb 2006).

Scheffer, J., "Speech given at the 43rd Munich Conference on Security Policy," 10 February 2007. Online. Available: www.nato.int/docu/speech/2007/s070209d.html (accessed 20 August 2011).

Schröder, G., Speech on the 41st Munich Conference on Security Policy, 12 February 2005, pp. 2.

Solana, J., "Discours du Haut Représentant de l'Union européenne pour la Politique étrangère et de sécurité commune," Annual Conference of the EU Institute for Security Studies, 30 October 2008.

Toner, Mark C., Acting Deputy Spokesman Office of the Spokesman, Washington, DC, 30 April 2011.

Secondary sources

"8–9 October 2008 – Report: Seminar in the UAE," NATO Parliamentary Assembly, Mediterranean and Middle East Special Group. Online. Available: http://natopa.ibicenter.net/default.Asp?CAT2=0&CAT1=0&CAT0=578&SHORTCUT=1655 (accessed 12 November 2008).

Abbott, K.W. and D. Snidal, "Why States Act through Formal International Organizations," Chapter 1 in P.F. Diehl and B. Frederking (eds), *The Politics of Global Governance: International Organizations in an Interdependent World*, 2nd edn, Boulder, CO: Lynne Rienner, 2001.

Altman, R.C. "The Great Crash, 2008: A Geopolitical Setback for the West," *Foreign Affairs*, Vol. 88, No. 1, 2009, pp. 217–242.

Ames, P., "NATO: Russia Halts Military Cooperation," *Associated Press*, 22 August 2008.

Anderson, R.H., *Research and Development Initiatives Focused on Preventing, Detecting, and Responding to Insider Misuse of Critical Defense Information Systems: Results of a Three-Day Workshop*, RAND CF-151-OSD, 1999.

Andrey, M., "Security Implications of Neutrality: Switzerland in the Partnership for Peace Framework," *Connections: the PfP Quarterly*, Vol. 9, No. 4, 2011, pp. 83–96.

Andreychuk, R., "Resetting Relations with Russia," NATO Parliamentary Report 032 PC 09 E, May 2009.

Arne Petersen, F. and H. Binnendijk, "The Comprehensive Approach Initiative: Future Options for NATO," *Defense Horizons*, No. 58, Center for Technology and National Security Policy of the National Defense University, September 2007.

Asmus, R., "Europe's Eastern Promise: Rethinking NATO and EU Enlargement," *Foreign Affairs*, Vol. 87, No. 1, January/February 2008, pp. 95–106.

Asmus, R., *Is Enlargement Dead?* The German Marshall Fund of the United States, 10 May 2010, p. 2.

Asmus, R., *Opening NATO's Door: How the Alliance Remade Itself for a New Era*, A

Council on Foreign Relations Book, New York, Chichester, and West Sussex: Columbia University Press, 2002.

Asmus, R., S. Czmur, C. Donnelly, A. Ronis, T. Valasek and K. Wittmann, *NATO, New Allies and Reassurance*, Centre for European Reform Policy Brief, May 2010.

Asmus, R., S. Czmur, C. Donnelly, A. Ronis, T. Valasek and K. Wittmann, *NATO 2020: Assured Security; Dynamic Engagement. Analysis and Recommendations of the Group of Experts on a New Strategic concept for NATO*, Policy Brief, London: Centre for European Reform, 17 May 2010.

Asmus, R.D, R.L. Kugler and F. Stephen Larrabee, "NATO Expansion: The Next Steps," *Survival*, Vol. 37, 1995, pp. 7–33.

Aybet, G. and R.R. Moore (eds) *NATO in Search of a Vision*, Washington D.C.: Georgetown University Press, 2010.

Barry, E. and S. Kishkovsky, "Russia Warns of Missile Deployment," *New York Times*, 6 November 2008.

Benantar, A., "NATO, Maghreb and Europe," *Mediterranean Politics*, Vol. 11, No. 2, July 2006, pp. 170, 173–174.

Bennett, C., "Building Effective Partnerships," *NATO Review*, Autumn 2003.

Berlijn, D., "Continuously Transforming to Fit in Comprehensive Approached Operations," *NATO's Nations and Partners for Peace*, 2008.

Biermann, R., "NATO Enlargement: Approaching a Standstill," *Security Insights of The George C. Marshall European Center for International and Security Studies*, No. 4, December 2009, p. 1. Online. Available: www.marshallcenter.org/mcpublicweb/MCDocs/files/College/F_Publications/secInsights/SecurityInsights_04_fullsize.pdf.

Biscop, S., *From Lisbon to Lisbon: Squaring the Circle of EU and NATO Future Roles*, Security Policy Brief No. 16, Egmont, Brussels, January 2011.

Blair, D.C., "Annual Threat Assessment of the Intelligence Community for the House Permanent Select Committee on Intelligence," Washington, Director of National Intelligence, 2009. Online. Available: http://intelligence.senate.gov/090212/blair.pdf (accessed 27 September 2010).

Blank, S., *The NATO–Russia Partnership: A Marriage of Convenience or a Troubled Relationship?* Strategic Studies Institute, U.S. Army War College, Carlisle, Pennsylvania, November 2006, p. 2.

Blitz, J., "NATO Chief Warns Europe over Defence Budgets," *Financial Times*, 8 February 2011.

Borgomano-Loup, L., *Improving NATO-NGO Relations in Crisis Response Operations*, Forum Paper No. 2, NATO Defense College, March 2007.

Bracken, P., "The Second Nuclear Age," *Foreign Affairs*, Vol. 79, January/February 2000, pp. 146–156.

Brands, H., "Non-Proliferation and the Dynamics of the Middle Cold War: The Superpowers, the MLF, and the NPT," *Cold War History*, Vol. 7, 2007, pp. 389–423.

Bremmer, I., "Every Nation for Itself: Winners and Losers in a G-Zero World," *South China Morning Post*, 25 March 2012, p. 15.

Brooks, S., and W. Wohlforth, *World Out of Balance: International Relations and the Challenge of American Primacy*, Princeton: Princeton University Press, 2008.

Brunnstrom, D., "NATO Chiefs to Underline Georgia Support with Visit," Reuters, 11 September 2008.

Bryanski, G. and D. Busvine, "Putin to Dominate New Russian Government," Reuters, 21 May 2012.

Brzezinski, Z., *The Choice: Global Domination or Global Leadership*, New York: Basic Books, 2004, pp. 101–103.

Brzezinski, Z., *Second Chance: Three Presidents and the Crisis of American Superpower*, New York: Basic Books, 2007.

Brzezinski, Z., "An Agenda for NATO," *Foreign Affairs*, Vol. 88, No. 5, September/October 2009, pp. 2–20.

Brzezinski, Z., *Strategic Vision: America and the Crisis of Global Power*, New York: Basic Books, 2012.

Buckley, N., C. Clover and J. Thornhill, "Medvedev Rules out Poll Tussle with Putin," *Financial Times*, 19 June 2011. Online. Available: www.ft.com/cms/s/0/85bb3016–9a9c-11e0-bab2–00144feab49a.html#ixzz1PzVx4eaK.

Burns, R. and D. Butler, "Gates: NATO Alliance Future could be 'Dim, Dismal'," Associated Press, 10 June 2011. Online. Available: http://news.yahoo.com/s/ap/20110610/ap_on_re_eu/eu_gates_nato_doomed.

Butt, Y., "Re-examining the Conceptual Basis of Strategic Missile Defense," *Bulletin of the Atomic Scientists*, 3 December 2010. Online. Available: www.thebulletin.org/web-edition/features/re-examining-the-conceptual-basis-of-strategic-missile-defense (accessed 29 June 2011).

Butt, Y. and T. Postol, *Upsetting the Reset: The Technical Basis of Russian Concern over NATO Missile Defence*, FAS Special Report No. 1, Federation of American Scientists, September 2011.

Caldwell, W.B. "NATO and the Afghan Surge," blog posted 15 August 2011. Online. Available: www.acus.org/new_atlanticist/nato-and-afghansurge.

Callick, R., "President's 'Sputnik Moment' Signals Strategic Shift to Asia," *Weekend Australian*, 29 January 2011, p. 2.

Chalmers, M. and A. Somerville, *If the Bombs Go: European Perspectives on NATO's Nuclear Debate*, Whitehall Report 1–11, Royal United Services Institute, 2011. Online. Available: www.rusi.org/downloads/assets/IFTHEBOMBSGO.pdf.

Chan, R., "The West's Preaching to the East Must Stop," *Financial Times*, 4 January 2010, p. 11.

Chan, S. "An Odd Thing Happened on the Way to Balancing: East Asian States' Reactions to China's Rise," *International Studies Review*, Vol. 12, 2010, pp. 387–412.

Chernhoff, F., *The Power of International Theory: Reforging the Link to Foreign Policy-Making Through Scientific Enquiry*, London: Routledge, 2005.

Chernov, V.L., "The Collapse of the CFE Treaty and the Prospects for Conventional Arms Control in Europe," in W. Zellner, H-J. Schmidt, and G. Neuneck (eds), *The Future of Conventional Arms Control in Europe*, Baden-Baden: Nomos Verlag, 2009, pp. 186–187.

"China 'No. 1 economy by 2016': reports," *The Global Times*, 26 April 2011.

Choe Sang-Hun, "North Korea Profits by a Turn to Cold War Allies: Seoul Fears its Hard Line has Allowed China to Seize Economic Openings," *The International Herald Tribune*, 26 October 2011, p. 1.

Cienski, J., "The Polish Tiger," *Foreign Policy Dispatch*, 27 May 2011. Online. Available: www.foreignpolicy.com/articles/2011/05/27/the_polish_tiger.

Clark, I., "Bringing Hegemony Back in: The United States and International Order," *International Affairs*, Vol. 85, No. 1, 2009, pp. 23–36.

Clarke, R.A. and R. Knake, *Cyber War: The Next Threat to National Security and What to Do About It*, New York: Harper Collins, 2010.

Clark, W., *Waging Modern War: Bosnia, Kosovo, and the Future of Conflict*, New York: Public Affairs, 2001.

Clawson, P. and S. Henderson, "Reducing Vulnerability to Middle East Energy Shocks: A Key Element in Strengthening US Energy Security," *Policy Focus*, No. 49, November 2005, pp. ix–x.

Clinton, H., "America's Pacific Century," *Foreign Policy*, Vol. 189, November 2011, pp. 57–63.

Collina, T., "New START in Force; Missile Defense Looms," *Arms Control Today*, March 2011.

Collins, J. and M. Rojansky, "Why Russia Matters: Ten Reasons Why Washington Must Engage Moscow," *Foreign Policy*, August 2010. Online. Available: www.unc.edu/world/2011Seminars/Why_Russia_Matters.pdf (accessed 19 June 2011).

Comprehensive Approach. Trends, Challenges and Possibilities for Cooperation in Crisis Prevention and Management, Seminar Publication, Crisis Management Initiative, Helsinki, 2008.

Corder, M., *NATO, Russia Clash Again on Missile Defense Plan*, Associated Press, 8 June 2011.

Cornish, S., "No Room for Humanitarianism in 3-D Policies: Have Forcible Humanitarian Interventions and Integrated Approaches Lost their Way?" *Journal of Military and Strategic Studies*, Vol. 10, Issue 1, Fall 2007, pp. 1–48.

Council on Foreign Relations, "NATO At 60 Symposium: Session II: NATO, Russia and Eastern Europe." Online. Available: www.cfr.org/nato/council-foreign-relations-nato-60-symposium-session-ii-nato-russia-eastern-europe/p18692 (accessed 28 June 2011).

Creedon, M., "U.S. Ballistic Missile Defense," presentation at the international conference "Missile Defence Factor in Establishing New Security Environment," 3–4 May 2012. Online. Available: http://photos.state.gov/libraries/russia/231771/PDFs/ASD_Creedon_MD_Conference_Remarks.pdf.

Daalder, I.H., *The Nature and Practice of Flexible Response. NATO Strategy and Theater Nuclear Forces Since 1967*, New York: Columbia University Press, 1991.

Daalder, I.H., "A New Alliance for a New Century" (Commentary), *RUSI Journal*, Vol. 155, October-November 2010, pp. 6–10. Online. Available: http://photos.state.gov/libraries/lithuania/331079/pdf/Ivo%20Daalder%20-%20A%20New%20Alliance%20For%20A%20New%20Century.pdf.

Daalder, I.H., *Looking to Lisbon*, Ecole Militaire, Paris, 18 October 2010. Online. Available: http://nato.usmission.gov (accessed 1 November 2010).

Daalder, I.H., "Who Needs NATO? We All Do," *New York Times*, 18–19 June 2011. Online. Available: www.nytimes.com/2011/06/18/opinion/18iht-eddaalder.html (accessed 29 June 2011).

Daalder, I.H. and J. Goldgeier, "Global NATO," *Foreign Affairs*, Vol. 85, No. 5, September/October 2006, pp. 105–113.

Dahl, E., "Naval Innovation: From Coal to Oil," *Joint Force Quarterly*, Vol. 27, 2000–01, pp. 50–56.

Dahl Thruelsen, P., *Implementing the Comprehensive Approach in Helmand: Within the Context of Counterinsurgency*, Royal Danish Defence College, 2008.

de Coning, C. and K. Friis, "Coherence and Coordination: The Limits of the Comprehensive Approach," *Journal of International Peacekeeping*, Vol. 15, 2011, pp. 243–272.

de Coning, C. *et al.*, *Norway's Whole-of-Government Approach and its Engagement with Afghanistan*, NUPI Report, 2009, pp. 40–42.

de Dardel, J-J., *Whither the Euro-Atlantic Partnership? Partnership and NATO's New Strategic Concept*, Geneva Paper 10, pp. 35–36.

de Wijk, R., "European Author," in M.D. Ducasse (ed.), *The Transatlantic Bargain*, NDC Forum Paper 20.

Degnan, K., "Bulgaria Exemplifies Approaches for NATO's New Strategic Concept," Hungarian Newswire, 29 July 2010.

Dempsey, J. and D. Bilefsky, "U.S. and Czechs Sign Accord on Missile Shield," 09 July 2008.

Deutsch, K., *Political Community and the North Atlantic Area: International Organization in Light of Historical Experience*, Princeton: Princeton University Press, 1957.

DeWeese, S., *et al.*, *Capability of the People's Republic of China to Conduct Cyber Warfare and Computer Network Exploitation*, Report prepared by Northrop Grumman Corp. for the US-China Economic and Security Review Commission, Washington, 17 February 2010. Online. Available: www.uscc.gov/researchpapers/2009/Northrop-Grumman_PRC_Cyber_Paper_Final_Approved Report_16Oct2009.pdf (accessed 27 September 2010).

Dombey, D., "Obama to Recall U.S. Troops from Europe," *Financial Times*, 9 April 2011.

Donnelly, C., "Forging a NATO Partnership for the Greater Middle East," *NATO Review*, Spring 2004. Online. Available: www.nato.int/docu/review/2004/issue1/english/art3_pr.html.

Duke, S., "The Future of EU–NATO Relations: A Case of Mutual Irrelevance through Competition?" *Journal of European Integration*, Vol. 30, No. 1, 2008, pp. 27–43.

Dziedzic, M. and M. Seidl, *Provincial Reconstruction Teams: Military Relations with International and Nongovernmental Organizations in Afghanistan*, Special Report 147, USIP, Washington, DC, September 2005.

Edström, H., J. Haaland, J. Matlary and M. Petersson (eds), *NATO: The Power of Partnerships*, Basingstoke: Palgrave, 2011

Erlanger, S., "Europe Still Loves Obama, but Doubts Creep In," *New York Times*, 1 November 2009.

Fedyashin, A., "NATO Reaching out to the Black Sea," RIA Novosti, 10 July 2008.

Feickert, A., *Missile Survey: Ballistic and Cruise Missiles of Foreign Countries*, CRS Report for Congress, RL30427, March 2004.

Feller, B., "Bush Calls on Russian Leadership to Reject Independence for 2 Breakaway Regions of Georgia," Associated Press, 26 August 2008.

Fromkin, D., "Entangling Alliances," *Foreign Affairs*, Vol. 48, July 1970, pp. 688–700.

Gaddis, J.L., *Surprise, Security, and the American Experience*, Cambridge: Harvard University Press, 2004, pp. 23–24.

Garton Ash, T., *Free World: America, Europe, and the Surprising Future of the West*, New York: Random House, 2005.

Garton Ash, T., "The US has Lost its Focus on Europe," *Guardian*, 7 October 2009.

Gates, P.E., " 'Genuine interest' in Russia on missile defense," *DOD Buzz*, 9 June 2011. Online. Available: www.dodbuzz.com/2011/06/09/gates-genuine-interest-in-russia-on-missile-defense/#ixzz1QYX9lus7 (accessed 29 June 2011).

Gati, C., *Backsliding in Central and Eastern Europe*, Testimony prepared for the House Foreign Affairs Committee, 25 July 2007. Online. Available: http://foreignaffairs.house.gov/110/gat072507.htm.

Gati, C., "The Putinization of Hungary," *Washington Post*, 26 December 2010; Online. Available: www.washingtonpost.com/wp-dyn/content/article/2010/12/26/AR2010122601791.html.

Gelb, L.H., *Power Rules: How Common Sense can Rescue American Foreign Policy*, New York: Harper, 2009.

Gerasimov, V.V., "Assessment of BMD Global Capabilities," International Conference Missile Defence Factor in Establishing New Security Environment, 3–4 May 2012. Online. Available: www.mil.ru/conference_of_pro/news/more.htm?id=11108033@egNews.

Gheciu, A., "Security Institutions as Agents of Socialization? NATO and the 'New Europe'," *International Organization*, Vol. 59, No. 4, Autumn, 2005, pp. 973–1012.

Gheciu, A., "Divided Partners: The Challenges of NATO-NGO Cooperation in Peacebuilding Operations," *Global Governance*, Vol. 17, No. 1, 2011, pp. 95–113.

Gholz, E. *et al.*, "Come Home America: A Strategy of Restraint in the Face of Temptation," *International Security*, Vol. 21, No. 4, Spring 1997, pp. 5–48.

Gienger, V. and P. Donahue, "Gates Laments Delay in Missile-Defense Agreement with Russia," *Bloomberg*, 9 June 2011.

Giergerich, B., "NATO's Smart Defence: Who's Buying?" *Survival*, Vol. 54, No. 3, June-July 2012, pp. 169–177.

Giles, K., *The Military Doctrine of the Russian Federation 2010*, Research Review, Research Division, NATO Defense College, Rome, February 2010.

Goldgeier, J.M., *The Future of NATO*, Special Report No. 51, Council of Foreign Relations Press, February 2010.

Goldman Sachs, "Dreaming with BRICs: The Path to 2050," *Global Economics Paper, No. 99*, 2003.

Goldman Sachs, "The N-11: More than an Acronym," *Global Economic Paper, No. 153*, March 2007.

Goldman Sachs, "The Long Term Outlook for the BRICs and N-11 Post-Crisis," *Global Economics Paper, No. 192*, December 2009.

Gompert, D.C. and P.C. Saunders, *The Paradox of Power: Sino American Strategic Restraint in an Age of Vulnerability*, Institute for National Strategic Studies, Washington, DC, December 2011.

Gormley, D.M., *Cruise Missiles and NATO Missile Defense: Under the Radar?* Proliferation Papers No. 41, Spring 2012. Online. Available: www.ifri.org/?page=contribution-detail&id=7082.

Graham, D.E., "Cyber Threats and the Law of War," *Journal of National Security Law and Policy*, Vol. 4, No. 1, 2010, pp. 87–102.

Grevi, G., *The Interpolar World: A New Scenario*, EU-ISS Occasional Paper No. 79, Paris, 2009.

Gropp, T., "Multi-Euro Project Helios," 6 September 2011. Online. Available: www.desertec.org/en/press/press-releases/110906–01-multi-billion-euro-project-helios/.

Gutterman, S., "Russia Tests New Missile, in Warning over U.S. shield," Reuters, 23 May 2012.

Haass, R., "Regime Change and its Limits," *Foreign Affairs*, Vol. 84, No. 4, July/August 2005, pp. 66–78.

Haass, R. "The Age of Nonpolarity: What will Follow U.S. Dominance?" *Foreign Affairs*, Vol. 87, No. 3, 2008, pp. 44–56.

Haass, R., "Continental Drift," *Washington Post*, 19 June 2011.

Hamilton, D.S. (ed.), *Transatlantic Transformations: Equipping the Alliance for the 21st Century*, Washington, D.C.: Centre for Transatlantic Relations, 2004.

Harsch, M. and J. Varwick, "NATO and the UN," *Survival*, Vol. 51, No. 2, 2009, pp. 5–12.

Haugevik, K., *New Partners, New Possibilities. The Evolution of Inter-Organizational Security Cooperation in International Peace Operations*, NUPI Report, Oslo, 2007.

Heisbourg, F. *et al.*, *All Alone? What US Retrenchment Means for Europe and NATO*, London: Centre for Europe Reform, March 2012.

Hendrickson, R., "Manfred Woerner: NATO's visionary," *NATO Review*, Autumn 2004.

Hendrickson, R., *European Phased Adaptive Approach (EPAA) Ballistic Missile Defence: A Technical Overview*, Missile Defence Agency, 12-MDA-6723, 30 April 2012.

Hiatt, F., "Can Reset Push Russia toward Democracy?" *Washington Post*, 18 July 2010.

Hildreth, S.A. and C.I. Ek, "Long-Range Ballistic Missile Defense in Europe," *Current Politics and Economics of Europe*, Vol. 22, Issue 1, 2011.

Hofman, M. and S. Delaunay, *Afghanistan: A Return to Humanitarian Action*, Médecins sans Frontières, March 2010.

Horowitz, J., "Is the Donilon Doctrine the New World Order?" *Washington Post*, 21 December 2010.

Hulbert, M., "Plea for a Bold Strategic Energy Shift: Brussels Should Bet on Beijing," *European Energy Review*, 11 July 2011. Online. Available: www.europe-anenergyreview.eu/site/pagina.php?id=3124.

Hunker, J., *Cyber War and Cyber Power: Issues for NATO Doctrine*, Research Paper No. 62, Research Division, NATO Defence College, Rome, November 2010.

Hunker, J., *Creeping Failure: How We Broke the Internet and What We Can Do to Fix It*, McClelland and Stewart/Random House, 2010.

Ikenberry, G.J., "Question Two: What would a New Transatlantic Bargain Look Like?" in Mark D. Ducasse (ed.), *The Transatlantic Bargain*, NDC Forum Paper 20, January 2012.

Ikenberry, G.J., "The Rise of China and the Future of the West," *Foreign Affairs*, Vol. 87, No. 1, January/February 2008, pp. 23–37.

Iklé, F.C., "The Second Coming of the Nuclear Age," *Foreign Affairs*, Vol. 75, January/February 1996, pp. 119–128.

Ilyin, E., "Coordination in BMD Area as an Element of Military Cooperation," presentation at the international conference "Missile Defence Factor in Establishing New Security Environment," 3–4 May, 2012. Online. Available http:www.mil.ru/conference_of_pro/news/more.htm?id=11108033@egNews.

"Interview with President Dmitry Medvedev," Transcript, *Financial Times*, 19 June 2011.

"Iran's Revolutionary Guards Ready to Close Strait of Hormuz Linking Gulf to International Markets," *Al Arabiya* news agency, 4 July 2011. Online. Available: www.alarabiya.net/articles/2011/07/04/156120.html.

Jacques, M., "Crouching Dragon, Weakened Eagle," *International Herald Tribune*, 17 February 2010.

Jakobsen, L. and D. Knox, *New Foreign Policy Actors in China*, SIPRI Policy Paper No. 26, September 2010. Online. Available: http://books.sipri.org/product_info?c_product_id=410.

Jakobsen, P., *NATO's Comprehensive Approach to Crisis Response Operations. A Work in Slow Progress*, DIIS Report 2008, No. 15, Copenhagen, October 2008.

Jentleson, B.W., "The Need for Praxis: Bringing Policy Relevance back in," *International Security*, Vol. 26, No. 4, 2002, pp. 169–183.

Jervis, R., "Cooperation under the Security Dilemma," *World Politics*, Vol. 30, No. 2, January 1978, pp. 167–214.

Joffe, J., *Überpower: The Imperial Temptation of America*, New York: Norton, 2006.

Jordan, R.S. and M.W. Bloome, *Political Leadership in NATO: A Study in Multinational Diplomacy*, Boulder, CO: Westview Press, 1979.

Kaczynski, L., "NATO has a Duty to Embrace Ukraine and Georgia," *Financial Times*, 31 March 2008, p. 9.

Kagan, R., "Power and Weakness," *Policy Review*, 113, June/July 2002, pp. 3–28. Online. Available: www. policyreview.org/JUN02/kagan.html.

Kagan, R., *The Return of History and the End of Dreams*, New York: Knopf, 2008.

Kamp, K-H. and Kurt Volker, *Towards a New Transatlantic Bargain*, Carnegie Endowment for International Peace, Policy Outlook, 1 February 2012. Online. Available: http://carnegieendowment.org/files/transatlantic_bargain.pdf.

Kaplan, R., *Monsoon: The Indian Ocean and the Future of American Power*, New York: Random House, 2010.

Kaufman, R.F. (ed.), *The Full Costs of Ballistic Missile Defense*, Center for Arms Control and Non-Proliferation, January 2003.

Keating, J., "Romney's Pitch: Obama is a 'European' Leader," the Passport blog of *Foreign Policy* magazine, 2 June 2011. Online. Available: http://blog.foreignpolicy.com/posts/2011/06/02/romneys_pitch_obama_is_a_european_leader.

Kelly, P. "Top Thinker Says China may 'Push the US out of Asia'," *The Australian*, 3 August 2010, pp. 4.

Kennan, G., "A Fateful Error," *The New York Times*, 5 February 1997.

Keohane, D., *Does NATO Matter for US Defence Policy?* FRIDE Policy Brief No. 129, May 2012.

Keohane, R.O., *After Hegemony: Cooperation and Discord in the World Political Economy*, Princeton, NJ: Princeton University Press, 1984.

Khanna, P., *The Second World: Empires and Influence in the New World Order*, New York: Random House, 2008.

Kissinger, H.A., *On China*, New York: Penguin, 2011.

Kissinger, H.A., S. Lawrence and C. Kupchan, *Renewing the Transatlantic Partnership*, New York: Council on Foreign Relations, 2004.

Koike, Yuriko, "Cold War with China not Inevitable," *The Australian*, 10 January 2011, p. 10.

Korski, D., "British Civil-Military Integration: The History and Next Steps," *The RUSI Journal*, Vol. 154, No. 6, December 2009, p. 17.

Kortunov, S., "'Hard Power' Imperative: The High and Lows of the New Russian–U.S. Treaty," *Russia in Global Affairs*, July 2010. Online. Available: http://eng.globalaffairs.ru/number/Hard_Power_Imperative-14890 (accessed 12 June 2012).

Kramer, M., "The Myth of a No-NATO-Enlargement Pledge to Russia," *Washington Quarterly*, Vol. 32, No. 2, April 2009, pp. 39–61.

Krasner, S. *Structural Conflict: The Third World against Global Liberalism*, Berkeley: University of California Press, 1985.

Krasner, S., *An Orienting Principle for Foreign Policy*, Policy Review No. 163, October 2010. Online. Available: www.hoover.org/publications/policy-review/article/49786.

Krasner, S.D., J.G. Stein and R.O. Keohane, "Autobiographical Reflections on Bridging the Policy-Academy Divide," *Cambridge Review of International Affairs*, Vol. 22, No. 1, 2009, pp. 111–128.

Krauthammer, C., "The Unipolar Moment," *Foreign Affairs*, Vol. 70, No. 1, America and the World 1990/91, pp. 23–33.

Krepinevich, A.F., "The Pentagon's Wasting Assets: The Eroding Foundations of U.S. Power," *Foreign Affairs*, Vol. 88, No. 4, July/August 2009, pp. 18–33.

Kucins, A.C. and I.A. Zevelev, "Russian Foreign Policy: Continuity and Change," *Washington Quarterly*, Winter 2012, pp. 147–161.

Kugler, R.L., *Commitment to Purpose: How Alliance Partnership Won the Cold War*, Santa Monica, CA: Rand, 1993.

Kugler, R., "Deterrence of Cyber Attacks," in F.D. Kramer, S.H. Starr, and L.K. Wentz, *Cyberpower and National Security*, Washington, DC: Potomac Books, 2009.

Kupchan, C., *The End of the American Era: U.S. Foreign Policy and the Geopolitics of the Twenty-First Century*, Knopf, 2002.

Kupchan, C.A., "The Democratic Malaise," *Foreign Affairs*, 1 January 2011. Online. Available: www.foreignaffairs.com/articles/136783/charles-a-kupchan/the-democratic-malaise (accessed 4 June 2012).

Lachmann, N., "The EU-CSDP-NATO Relationship: Asymmetric Cooperation and the Search for Momentum," *Studia Diplomatica*, Vol. 63, No. 3–4, 2010, pp. 185–202.

Larson, E. *et al.*, *Interoperability of U.S. and NATO Allied Air Forces: Supporting Data and Case Studies*, Santa Monica, CA: RAND, 2003, pp. 19, 43–45.

Layne, C., "From Preponderance to Offshore Balancing: America's Future Grand Strategy, *International Security*, Vol. 22, No. 1, Summer 1997, pp. 86–124.

Layne, C., "Conclusion" in K.P. Williams, S.E. Lobell, and N.G. Jesse, *Beyond Great Powers and Hegemons: Why Secondary States Support, Follow or Challenge*, Stanford, California: Stanford University Press, 2012, p. 223.

Leonard, M., *Why Europe Will Run the 21st Century*, New York: Public Affairs, 2005.

Lepgold, J., "Is Anyone Listening? International Relations Theory and the Problem of Policy Relevance," *Political Science Quarterly*, Vol. 113, No. 1, 1998, pp. 43–62.

Libicki, M., *Conquest in Cyberspace*, New York: Cambridge University Press, 2007.

Libicki, M., *Cyber Deterrence and Cyber War*, Santa Monica, California: RAND Corporation, 2009. Online. Available: www.rand.org/pubs/monographs/MG877.

"Libyan operation starts NATO's southward enlargement-Russia's envoy," *Russia Today*, 16 June 2011.

Lin, H., "Thoughts on Threat Assessment in Cyberspace," in P. Shane and J. Hunker (eds), *Cybersecurity: Shared Risks, Shared Responsibilities*, Carolina Academic Press, forthcoming 2012.

Lindley-French, J., P. Cornish, and A. Rathmell, *Operationalizing the Comprehensive Approach*, Program Paper ISP PP 2010/01, Chatham House, March 2010.

Lizza, R., "The Consequentialist," *Atlantic Monthly*, 2011. Online. Available: www.newyorker.com/reporting/2011/05/02/110502fa_fact_lizza.

Losch, B., "Fabrications and Illusions of Emergence," in C. Jaffrelot (ed.), *Emerging States: The Wellspring of a New World Order*, New York: Columbia University Press, 2009.

Lucas, E., *The New Cold War: Putin's Russia and the Threat to the West,* New York: Palgrave MacMillan, 2008.

Lukyanov, F., "Tapping into West's Modernization Reservoir," *Moscow Times,* 16 December 2009. Online. Available: www.themoscowtimes.com/opinion/article/tapping-intowests-modernization-reservoir/396223.html (accessed 19 October 2010).

Lundestad, G., *No End to Alliance,* New York: St Martins Press, 1998.

Lynn, W., "Defending a New Domain: The Pentagon's Cyberstrategy," *Foreign Affairs,* Vol. 89, No. 5, September/October 2010, pp. 97–108.

McFaul, M., *Advancing Democracy Abroad,* Lanham, Maryland: Rowman and Littlefield, 2010.

McGregor, R., "Hawks Attack Republican Isolationism," *Financial Times,* 20 July 2010.

Malkasian, C. and G. Meyerle, *Provincial Reconstruction Teams: How do we Know they Work?* U.S. Army War College, Strategic Studies Institute, March 2009.

Markoff, J. and A.E. Kramer, "U.S. and Russia Differ on a Treaty for Cybersecurity," *New York Times,* 27 June 2009, p. A1.

Mead, W.R., "The Tea Party and American Foreign Policy," *Foreign Affairs,* Vol. 90, No. 2, March/April 2011, pp. 28–44.

Mearsheimer, J., *The Tragedy of Great Power Politics,* New York: Norton 2001.

Medvedev, D., President, "Forward, Russia!" *Gazeta,* 10 September 2009. Online. Available: www.gazeta.ru/comments/2009/09/10_a_3258568.shtml (accessed 29 June 2011).

Mesic, R., M. Hura, M.C. Libicki, A.M. Packard, and L.M. Scott, *Cyber Command (Provisional) Decision Support,* RAND Project Air Force, 2010.

Michta, A., "NATO's Last Chance," *National Interest,* Vol. VI, No. 5, May/June 2011.

Michta, M., *The Limits of Alliance: The United States, NATO, and the EU in North and Central Europe,* Lanham, MD: Rowman and Littlefield, 2006.

Middelton, D., "NATO 'Forward Defense' Draws Fire," *New York Times,* 11 January 1982.

Merriam Webster Online Dictionary. Online. Available: www.merriam-webster.com/dictionary/alliance (accessed 11 May 2011).

Monaghan, A., *What role for NATO?* NATO Defence College Research Paper No. 29, October 2006, pp. 2–7.

Monaghan, A., *The Russian* Vertikal*: the Tandem, Power and the Elections,* Russia and Eurasia Programme Paper (REP) 2011, NATO Defence College, June 2011.

"Murky Deal Ends the Russian Gas Row," *The Economist,* 4 January 2006. Online Available: www.economist.com/node/5353164.

Mushi, C., "NATO's Mediterranean Dialogue: More than Just an Empty Shell," *Mediterranean Politics,* Vol. 11, No. 3, November 2006, pp. 419–424.

NATO Defence College, "10 Things you should Know about a Comprehensive Approach," November 2008, p. 1.

"New U.S. Missile Defense Plans Less Worrying – Russian Ambassador," Interfax (Moscow), 21 June 2010.

Norris, P. and R. Inglehart, *Sacred and Secular: Religion and Politics Worldwide,* Cambridge: Cambridge University Press, 2004.

Nye, J., *Soft Power: The Means to Success in World Politics,* New York: Public Affairs, 2004.

Nye, J., "Bridging the Gap between Theory and Policy," *Political Psychology,* Vol. 29, No. 4, 2008, pp. 593–603.

Nye, J., "Should China be 'Contained'?" *Korea Times*, 6 July 2011.

O'Neil, J., and A. Stupnytska, *The Long-Term Outlook for the BRICS and N-11 Post-Crisis*, Global Economics Paper No. 192, Goldman Sachs, 4 December 2009.

Paris, R., "Understanding the 'coordination problem' in postwar statebuilding," in R. Paris and T. Sisk, *The Dilemmas of Statebuilding: Confronting the Contradictions of Postwar Peace Operations*, London, Routledge, 2009.

Paul, T.V., "Soft Balancing in the Age of U.S. Primacy," *International Security*, Vol. 30, No. 1, 2005, pp. 46–71.

"Peace under the Heavens," Editorial, *The Straits Times Singapore*, 2 July 2011.

Perkovich, G. and J.M. Acton (eds), *Abolishing Nuclear Weapons: A Debate*, Carnegie Endowment for International Peace, Washington, D.C., 2009. Online. Available: www.carnegieendowment.org/files/abolishing_nuclear_weapons_debate.pdf.

Perlo-Freeman, S. *et al.*, "Military Expenditure," *SIPRI Yearbook: 2010*, Oxford, Oxford University Press, 2010, p. 203.

Pew Research Center for the People and the Press, "Views of Middle East Unchanged by Recent Events, Public Remains Wary of Global Engagement," 10 June 2011. Online. Available: http://pewresearch.org/pubs/2020/poll-american-attitudes-foreign-poilcy-middle-east-israel-palestine-obama.

Pilkington, E., "Barack Obama Sets out Plans for Leaner Military in Historic Strategy Shift: President says armed forces will move away from large-scale ground warfare and focus more on China in wake of budget cuts," *The Guardian*, 5 January 2012. Online. Available: www.guardian.co.uk/world/2012/jan/05/barack-obama-plans-leaner-military.

Policy Options for State-building in Afghanistan: The Role of NATO PRTs in Development in Afghanistan, SAIS, May 2009.

Porter, G., "Asia's New Cold War," *The Nation*, 9 September 1978, pp. 209–212.

Posen, B., "Command of the Commons: The Military Foundations of U.S. Hegemony," *International Security*, Vol. 28, No. 1, Summer 2003, pp. 5–46.

Provincial Reconstruction Teams and Humanitarian-Military Relations in Afghanistan, Save the Children, 2004.

Pushkov, A., "Missed Connections," *The National Interest*, May/June 2007.

Quick Impact, Quick Collapse: The Dangers of Militarized Aid in Afghanistan, Paper by a coalition of NGOs, January 2010.

Rachman, G., *Zero-Sum Future: American Power in an Age of Anxiety*, New York: Simon and Schuster, 2011.

Racz, A., *Good Cop or Bad Cop: Russian Foreign Policy in the New Putin Era*, Transatlantic Academy, Analysis, January 2012.

Rasmussen, A.F., "NATO and the Arab Spring," *International Herald Tribune*, 2 June 2011, p. 6.

Rasmussen, A.F., "NATO After Libya: The Atlantic Alliance in Austere Times," *Foreign Affairs*, Vol. 90, No. 4, July/August 2011, pp. 2–6.

Ringsmose, J. and S. Rynning (eds), *NATO's New Strategic Concept: A Comprehensive Assessment*, Danish Institute for International Studies Report 2011, p. 28.

Rizzo, A.M., "NATO's Transformation and New Partnerships: The Mediterranean," *Mediterranean Quarterly*, Vol. 18, No. 3.

Rotmann, P., *Built on Shaky Ground: The Comprehensive Approach in Practice*, Research Paper No. 63, NATO Defense College, December 2010.

Rudd, K., "NATO Partners Earn Respect," *The Australian*, 23 April 2011, p. 10. Online. Available: www.foreignminister.gov.au/articles/2011/kr_ar_110423.html.

Rühe, V., "Shaping Euro-Atlantic Policies: A Grand Strategy for a New Era," *Survival*, Vol. 35, No. 2, 1993, pp. 129–137.

Rühle, M., "Re-examining the Transatlantic Bargain" (Review of S. Sloan, *NATO, the European Union and the Atlantic Community: The Transatlantic Bargain Reconsidered*, Boulder, CO: Rowman & Littlefield, 2002), *NATO Review*, 2003.

Rühle M., "NATO and Extended Deterrence in a Multinuclear World," *Comparative Strategy*, Vol. 28, January 2009, pp. 10–16.

Ruppe, D., "Pentagon Sees $20 Billion Cost Growth for National Defense System," Global Security Newswire, 16 April 2003 (quoted by Center for Defense Information).

"Russia and NATO: Rethink the Reset," *The Economist*, 19 May 2012.

"Russia Freezes Peacekeeping Operations with NATO for 6 months," RIA Novosti, 26 August 2008.

"Russia-NATO: After the Lisbon Summit," *International Affairs: A Russian Journal of World Politics, Diplomacy and International Relations* [serial online], Vol. 57, No. 2, March 2011, pp. 156–167.

"Russia Softens Stance on Missile Defence," Associated Foreign Press, 6 June 2011.

"Russia Test Fires New Ballistic Missile," RIA Novosti, 23 May 2012. Online. Available: http://en.ria.ru/mlitary_news/20120523/173620397.html.

Sarotte, M., "Perpetuating U.S. Preeminence: The 1990 Deals to Bribe the Soviets out and Move NATO in," *International Security*, Vol. 35, No. 1, Summer 2010, pp. 110–137.

Schake, K., "The Allies We Need," *The American Interest*, Vol. 6, No. 5, May/June 2011.

Schmidt, G. (ed.), *A History of NATO: The First 50 Years*, Vol. 3, Basingstoke, New York, 2001.

Schreiber, W., "The NATO Secretary-General Speaks on the Significance of the Alliance's Libya Mission and how bin Laden's Death will Affect Afghanistan," *Newsweek*, 15 May 2011.

Shambaugh, D., "Coping with a Conflicted China," *Washington Quarterly*, Vol. 31, No. 1, 2011, pp. 7–27.

Shea, J., "Energy Security: NATO's potential role?" *NATO Review*, Autumn 2006. Online. Available: www.nato.int/docu/review/2006/issue3/english/special1.html.

Shea, J., "NATO Strategy: Building the Comprehensive Approach," in *Afghanistan: Now You See Me?* IDEAS Strategic Updates, London: LSE, March 2009.

Shea, J. *Keeping NATO Relevant*, Carnegie Endowment, Policy Outlook, April 2012, p. 17. Online. Available: http://carnegieendowment.org/2012/04/19/keeping-nato-relevant/acl9 (accessed 30 May 2011).

Sheremet, I., "Russia's Assessment of NATO–Russia Theatre Missile Defence Exercise," presentation at the international conference "Missile Defence Factor in Establishing New Security Environment," 3–4 May 2012. Online. Available http: www.mil.ru/conference_of_pro/news/more.htm?id=11108033@egNews.

Simon, J., "The Future of the Alliance: Is Demography Destiny?" in G. Aybet and R. Moore (eds), *NATO in Search of a Vision*, Washington, D.C.: Georgetown University Press, 2010.

Simonyi, A., "A Case for Overhaul of NATO's Partnerships; Organization should Seek Links with Capable Nonmembers," *Washington Times*, 11 April 2012, p. 4.

"Sino-U.S. ties in multipolar era," *Chinadaily.com.cn*, 21 January 2011.

Sireci, J. and D. Coletta, "Enduring without an Enemy: NATO's Realist Foundation," *Perspectives: Central European Review of International Affairs*, Vol. 17, No. 1, Summer 2009, pp. 57–81.

Sjursen, J., "On the Identity of NATO," *International Affairs*, Vol. 80, No. 4, 2004, pp. 687–703.

Sloan, S., *NATO, The European Union, and the Atlantic Community*, Maryland: Rowman & Littlefield, 2003.

Smith-Windsor, B., *Hasten Slowly: NATO's Effects Based and Comprehensive Approach to Operations*, Research Paper No. 38, NATO Defense College, July 2008.

Solomon, G.B., *The NATO Enlargement Debate, 1990–1997: Blessings of Liberty*, Westport, Connecticut, London: Praeger, 1998.

Sperling, J. and S.V. Papacosma (eds), *NATO at 60: In a Stable Crisis*, Kent, Ohio: Kent State University Press, 2012.

Stolberg S. and D. Sanger, "Bush to Seek a Bit of Unity with Putin," *New York Times*, 5 June 2007.

Stromseth, J., *The Origins of Flexible Response: NATO's Debate over Strategy in the 1960s*, Oxford: Macmillan Press, 1988.

"Stuck in Georgia," *The New York Times*, 27 August 2008.

Talbott, S., "From Prague to Baghdad: NATO at Risk," *Foreign Affairs*, Vol. 81, No. 6, November/December 2002, pp. 46–57.

Tardy, T., *Cooperating to Build Peace: The UN-EU Inter-Institutional Complex*, Geneva Papers – Research Series No. 2, GCSP, May 2011.

Thies, W.J., *Friendly Rivals: Bargaining and Burden Shifting in NATO*, Armong, NY: M.E. Sharpe, 2003.

Thies, W.J., *Why NATO Endures*, Cambridge: Cambridge University Press, 2009.

Tiron, R., "Italy Joins Germany in Fight for Lockheed Missile System," *Bloomberg News*, 19 July 2011.

"Transcript of Defense Secretary Gates's Speech on NATO's Future," *Wall Street Journal*, 10 June 2012.

Trennin, D., "Russia Leaves the West," *Foreign Affairs*, Vol. 85, No. 4, July/August 2006.

"Ukraine Secretly Ramps up Ties with NATO," Agence France-Presse, 21 June 2011.

Valasek, T., "Central Europe and Obama: Is the Special Relationship over?" in A.W. Mitchell *et al.* (eds), *Building the New Normal: U.S.-Central European Relations 2010–2020*, Center for European Policy Analysis, May 2011.

Valasek, T., *What Libya Says about the Future of the Transatlantic Alliance*, Center for European Reform, July 2011. Online. Available: www.cer.org.uk.

Viggo Jakobsen, P., *NATO's Comprehensive Approach to Crisis Response Operations: A Work in Slow Progress*, DIIS Report 2008, No. 15, October 2008.

Wallander, C., "NATO's Price: Shape up or Ship out," *Foreign Affairs*, Vol. 81, No. 6, November/December 2002, pp. 2–8.

Walt, S.M., "The Ties that Fray," *National Interest*, No. 54, Winter 1998/99, pp. 3–11.

Walt, S.M., "International Relations: One World, Many Theories," *Foreign Policy*, No. 110, Spring 1998, pp. 29–46.

Walt, S.M., "The Relationship between Theory and Policy in International Relations," *Annual Review of Political Science*, Vol. 8, 2005, pp. 23–48.

Walt, S.M., "China's New Strategy," *Foreign Policy website*, 26 April 2010. Online.

Available: http://walt.foreignpolicy.com/posts/2010/04/25/chinas_new_strategy.

Waltz, K., *Theory of International Politics*, Reading: Addison-Wesley, 1979.

Waltz, K., "The Emerging Structure of International Politics," *International Security*, Vol. 18, No. 2, Autumn 1993, pp. 44–79.

Waltz, K., "Structural Realism after the Cold War," *International Security*, Vol. 25, No. 1, Summer 2000, p. 36.

"War in the Fifth Dimension," *The Economist*, 3 July 2010, pp. 25–28.

Warrick, J., "Cable Leak Reveals Flaws of Information Sharing Tool," *Washington Post*, 31 December 2010.

Weiner, T. and B. Crossette, "George F. Kennan Dies at 101; Leading Strategist of Cold War," *New York Times*, 18 March 2006. Online. Available: www.nytimes.com/2005/03/18/politics/18kennan.html?pagewanted=1.

Wendling, C., *The Comprehensive Approach to Civil-Military Crisis Management: A Critical Analysis and Perspective*, IRSEM, 2010.

West, J.R., "Saudi Arabia, Iraq, and the Gulf," in J.H. Kalicki and D.L. Goldwyn (eds), *Energy and Security: Toward a New Foreign Policy Strategy*, Woodrow Wilson International Center for Scholars, 2005.

Westad, O.A. and Berath Lecture, "The New International History of the Cold War: Three (Possible) Paradigms," *Diplomatic History*, Vol. 24, No. 4, Fall 2000, pp. 551–565.

Whitlock, C., "Pentagon Girds for Deeper Cuts," *Washington Post*, 21 July 2011.

Whitmore, B. "Medvedev Talks Reform in St. Petersburg," *Radio Free Europe/Radio Liberty*. Online. Available: www.rferl.org/content/medvedev_talks_reform_in_st_petersburg/24238558.html (accessed 22 June 2011).

Wigert, I., *Civil and Military Defence Planning and Scenarios Techniques*, CRN Workshop Report, 2004.

Williams, K., S. Lobell and N. Jesse (eds), *Beyond Great Powers and Hegemons: Why Secondary States Support, Follow, or Challenge*, Stanford, California: Stanford University Press, 2012.

Williams, M.J., "Empire Light Revisited: NATO, the Comprehensive Approach and State-building in Afghanistan," *International Peacekeeping*, Vol. 18, No. 1, 2011, pp. 64–78.

Williams, M.J., "(Un)Sustainable Peacebuilding: NATO's Suitability for Postconflict Reconstruction in Multiactor Environments," *Global Governance*, Vol. 17, No. 1, 2011, pp. 115–134.

Williamson, H., "Germany Blocks Ex-Soviet States," *Financial Times*, 1 April 2008, p. 4.

Wittmann, K. "The Road to NATO's New Strategic Concept," in G. Schmidt (ed.), *A History of NATO: The First 50 Years*, Vol. 3, Basingstoke, New York, 2001, pp. 219–237.

Wittmann, K., "NATO's New Strategic Concept should be More than a 'Shopping List'," in "The European Security and Defence Union," Vol. 4, 2009.

Wittman, K., *Towards a New Strategic Concept for NATO*, Forum Paper 10, NATO Defense College, Rome, September 2009.

Wittmann, K., *NATO's New Strategic Concept: An Illustrative Draft*, Berlin, 2010.

World Economic Outlook, April 2011. Online. Available: www.imf.org/external/pubs/ft/weo/2011/01/index.htm.

Yost, D.S., "The U.S. Debate on NATO Nuclear Deterrence" (unpublished manuscript).

Yost, D.S., *NATO and International Organizations*, Forum Paper 3, NATO Defense College, Rome, September 2007, pp. 155–158.

Yost, D.S., "NATO's Evolving Purposes and the Next Strategic Concept," *International Affairs*, Vol. 86, No. 2, 2010, pp. 489–522.

Young, C., "From Russia with Loathing," *The New York Times*, 21 November 2008.

Zakaria, F., *The Post-American World*, New York: W.W. Norton, 2008.

Zellner, W., H-J. Schmidt, and G. Neuneck (eds), *The Future of Conventional Arms Control in Europe*, Baden-Baden: Nomos Verlag, 2009.

Index

Page numbers in *italics* denote tables.